TEST ITEM FILE

TO ACCOMPANY

APPLIED CALCULUS, Second Edition

and BRIEF APPLIED CALCULUS, Second Edition

Geoffrey Berresford
Andrew Rockett

Jean Shutters
Harrisburg Area Community College

Christi Verity

HOUGHTON MIFFLIN COMPANY BOSTON NEW YORK

Sponsoring Editor: Paul Murphy
Associate Editor: Mary Beckwith
Editorial Assistant: Marika Hoe
Marketing Manager: Michael Busnach
Project Editor: Maria Morelli
Senior Manufacturing Coordinator: Priscilla Bailey

Printed in the U.S.A.

ISBN: 0-395-97819-X

123456789-VGI-04 03 02 01 00

Contents

Correlation Chart

Note: Chapters 1 through 5 and chapter 7 of Brief Applied Calculus and Applied Calculus are identical.

Brief Applied Calculus	Applied Calculus
Chapter 6 Section 6.1-6.4	Chapter 6 Section 6.1-6.4
Chapter 6 Section 6.5-6.6	Chapter 9 Section 9.1-9.2

Chapter 1

Functions

Section 1.1 Real Numbers, Inequalities, and Lines

MULTIPLE CHOICE 1.1

[d] 1. Rewrite $\left\{x \middle| -\frac{2}{3} \le x < \frac{5}{4}\right\}$ in interval notation.

a. $\left[-\frac{2}{3}, \frac{5}{4}\right]$ b. $\left(-\frac{2}{3}, \frac{5}{4}\right)$ c. $\left(-\frac{2}{3}, \frac{5}{4}\right]$ d. $\left[-\frac{2}{3}, \frac{5}{4}\right)$

[d] 2. Rewrite $\{x|x > 0.75\}$ in interval notation.

a. $(-\infty, 0.75]$ b. $(-\infty, 0.75)$ c. $[0.75, \infty)$ d. $(0.75, \infty)$

[a] 3. Given the equation $y = 6 - 2x$, how will y change if x decreased by 5 units?

a. increases by 10 units
b. increases by 4 units
c. decreases by 5 units
d. decreases by 10 units

[a] 4. Given the equation $y = -4x + 1$, how will y change if x increases by 3 units?

a. decreases by 12 units
b. decreases by 4 units
c. increases by 12 units
d. increases by 11 units

[b] 5. Find the slope (if it is defined) of the line through the points (–13, 12) and (–11, 34).

a. $\frac{23}{12}$ b. 11 c. $\frac{12}{23}$ d. $\frac{1}{11}$

[b] 6. Find the slope (if it is defined) of the line through the points (5, 3) and (5, 1.7).

a. 0 b. does not exist c. $\frac{3}{5}$ d. $-\frac{3}{5}$

[a] 7. Find the slope (if it is defined) of the line through the points (–6.3, 5) and (1.7, 5).

a. 0 b. does not exist c. 8 d. –8

[a] 8. A line with a slope of $\frac{2}{3}$ has which set of points on the line?

a. (4, 7) and (7, 9)
b. (3, 5) and (5, 8)
c. (–2, –3) and (–3, –2)
d. (0, 0) and (2, 3)

[c] 9. Find the slope and y-intercept (if they exist) for $6x + y = 0$.

a. $m = -6$ and y-intercept does not exist
b. $m = 6$ and y-int = 0
c. $m = -6$ and y – int = 0
d. $m = 0$ and y-int = –6

[d] 10. Find the slope and y-intercept (if they exist) for $5y = 2x - 3$.

a. $m = 2$ and y – int = 3
b. $m = 5$ and y-int = 3
c. $m = \frac{2}{5}$ and y – int = $\frac{3}{5}$
d. $m = \frac{2}{5}$ and y-int = $-\frac{3}{5}$

[c] 11. Find the slope and y-intercept (if they exist) for $y = -\frac{4}{3}(x+6)$.

a. $m = -\frac{4}{3}$ and y-int = –24
b. $m = -\frac{4}{3}$ and y-int = 8
c. $m = -\frac{4}{3}$ and y-int = –8
d. $m = \frac{4}{3}$ and y-int = 6

[a] 12. Find the slope and y-intercept (if they exist) for $y = \frac{2x+7}{6}$.

a. $m = \frac{1}{3}$ and $y - \text{int} = \frac{7}{6}$
b. $m = 2$ and $y - \text{int} = 7$
c. $m = \frac{1}{3}$ and $y - \text{int} = 7$
d. $m = 2$ and $y - \text{int} = -\frac{7}{6}$

[d] 13. Find an equation of the line that is parallel to the x-axis. If possible write your answer in the form $y = mx + b$.

a. $x = 2$
b. $y = 2x$
c. $x = -1.5$
d. $y = -1.5$

[a] 14. Find an equation of the line that is parallel to the y-axis. If possible write your answer in the form $y = mx + b$.

a. $x = \frac{5}{6}$
b. $y = -\frac{5}{6}$
c. $y = x + 11$
d. $y = 11$

[c] 15. Find an equation of the line that passes through $(7.6, 4.2)$ and $(9.7, 0)$. If possible write your answer in the form $y = mx + b$.

a. $y = 4.2x + 17.3$ b. $y = 4.2x + 21$
c. $y = -2x + 19.4$ d. $y = 2x + 2.1$

[c] 16. Find an equation of the line that passes through (2, 9) and (–1, 9). If possible write your answer in the form $y = mx + b$.

a. $x = -6$ b. $y = 0$ c. $y = 9$ d. $x = 0$

[c] 17. Write an equation of the form $y = mx + b$ for the graphed line.

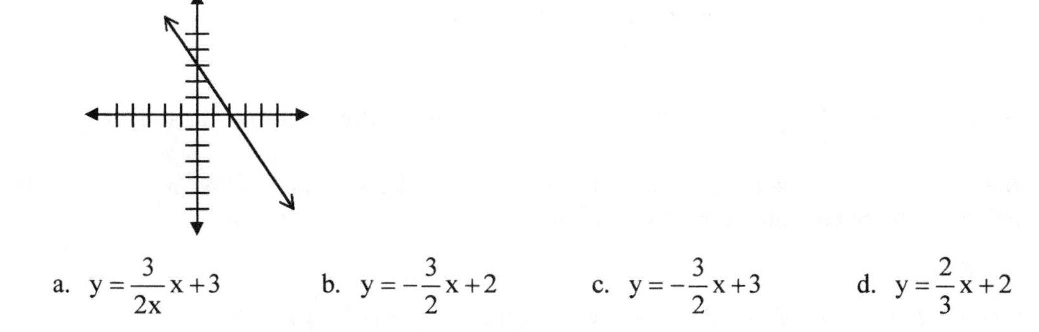

a. $y = \frac{3}{2x}x + 3$ b. $y = -\frac{3}{2}x + 2$ c. $y = -\frac{3}{2}x + 3$ d. $y = \frac{2}{3}x + 2$

[b] 18. Write an equation of the form $y = mx + b$ for the graphed line.

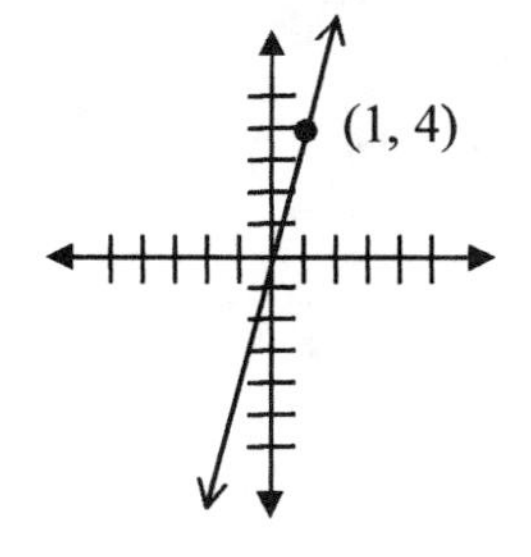

a. $y = -4x$ b. $y = 4x$ c. $y = \frac{1}{4}x$ d. $y = 4$

SHORT ANSWER 1.1

19. Write the interval (3, 7] in set notation.

Answer : $\{x|3 < x \leq 7\}$

20. Write the interval $[2, \infty)$ in set notation.

Answer : $\{x|x \geq 2\}$

21. What is wrong with the interval $(-8.5, \infty]$?

Answer : ∞ is written only with open interval notation, that is $(-8.5, \infty)$.

22. What is wrong with representing the notation $x \leq -5$ in an interval notation as $(-5, -\infty)$?

Answer : First $-\infty$ can be only a left end point. Second the interval is closed at –5 and so a bracket must be used. The correct interval notation is $(-\infty, -5]$.

23. Find the slope (if it is defined) of the line through the points (–5, 7) and (6, –3).

Answer: $m = -\frac{10}{11}$

24. Find the slope (if it is defined) of the line through the points (4, 1) and (16, –1).

Answer: $m = -\frac{1}{6}$

25. Find the slope and y-intercept (if they exist) for $y = -\frac{2}{3}x - 13.6$.

Answer: $m = -\frac{2}{3}$; $y - \text{int} = -13.6$

26. Find the slope and the y-intercept (if they exist) for $y = \frac{4}{5}x$.

Answer: $m = \frac{4}{5}$; $y - \text{int} = 0$

27. Find the slope and the y-intercept (if they exist) for $y = -1.5$.

Answer: $m = 0$; y-int $= -1.5$

28. Find the slope and the y-intercept (if they exist) for $x = \sqrt{2}$.

Answer: slope does not exist, no y-intercept

29. Find the slope and the y-intercept (if they exist) for $4x + 5y = 20$.

Answer: $m = -\frac{4}{5}$; y-int $= 4$

30. Find the slope and the y-intercept (if they exist) for $x - 3y = 21$.

Answer: $m = \frac{1}{3}$; y-int $= -7$

31. Find the slope and the y-intercept (if they exist) for $\frac{x}{5} - \frac{y}{6} = 1$.

Answer: $m = \frac{6}{5}$; y-int $= -6$

32. Find the slope and the y-intercept (if they exist) for $\frac{x}{6} + y = 5$.

Answer: $m = -\frac{1}{6}$; y-int $= 5$

33. Find an equation of the line where the slope $= \frac{5}{12}$ and the y-intercept $= -4$. If possible write your answer in the form $y = mx + b$.

Answer: $y = \frac{5}{12}x - 4$

34. Find an equation of the line where the slope $= 3.77$ and the y-intercept $= -6.32$. If possible write your answer in the form $y = mx + b$.

Answer: $y = 3.77x - 6.32$

35. Find an equation of the line where the slope $= \frac{23}{2}$ and passing through the point (–6, 5). If possible write your answer in the form $y = mx + b$.

Answer: $y = \frac{23}{2}x + 74$

36. Graph the equation $y = 5x$.

Answer:

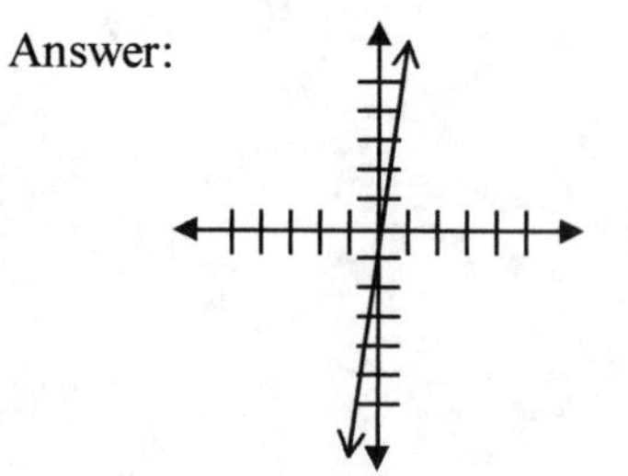

37. Graph the equation $x + 3 = 0$.

Answer:

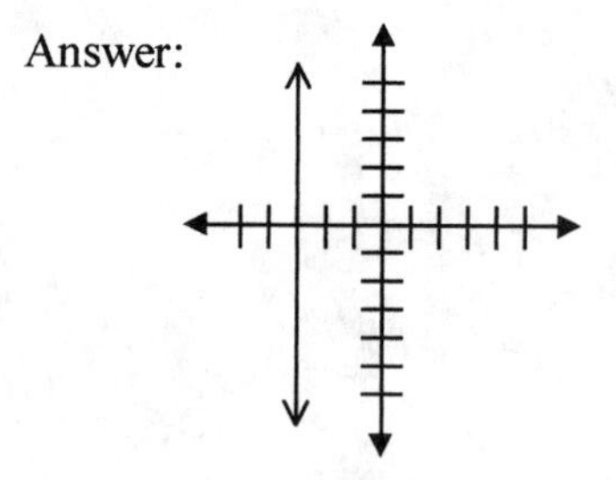

38. Graph the equation $y + 3 = 0$.

Answer:

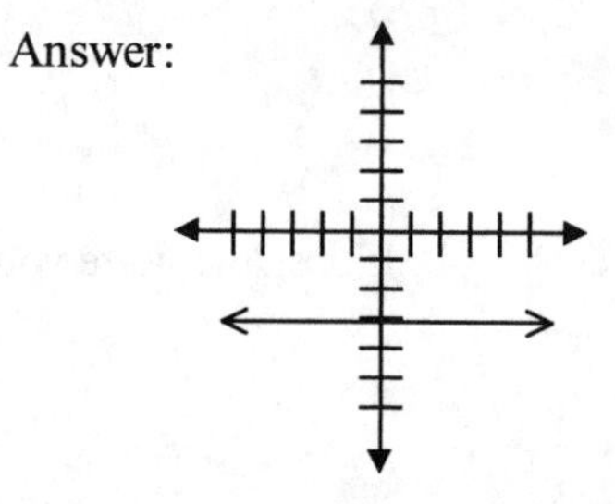

39. Graph the equation $3x - 4y = 12$.

Answer:

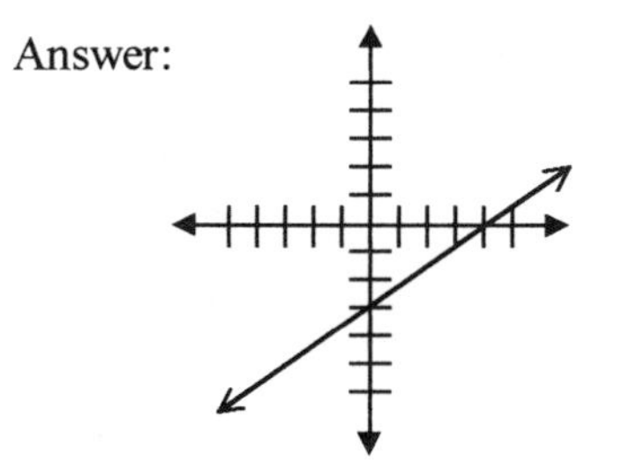

40. If a grade of 85 through 100 is an A, at least 70 but less than 85 is a B, at least 60 but less than 70 is a C, at least 50 but less than 60 is a D, and below 50 is an F, write the grade levels in interval form.

Answer: A = [85, 100], B = [70, 85), C = [60, 70), D = [50, 60), F = [0, 50)

41. A company's profit increased from $2 million at the end of year 3 to $8 million at the end of year 5.
   a. Find the linear relationship $y = mx + b$ between x = year and y = profit.
   b. Find the company's profit at the end of 8 years.

Answer: a. $y = 3x - 7$ b. $17 million

42. A company purchased a PC for $4000. After a useful life of 3 years, the scrap value is $500.
   a. Find the linear equation that relates the value V in dollars to the time t in years.
   b. Graph the equation.
   c. Find the value of the PC after one year. (Round to the nearest dollar.)

Answer: a. $V = -\frac{3500}{3}t + 4000$

b.

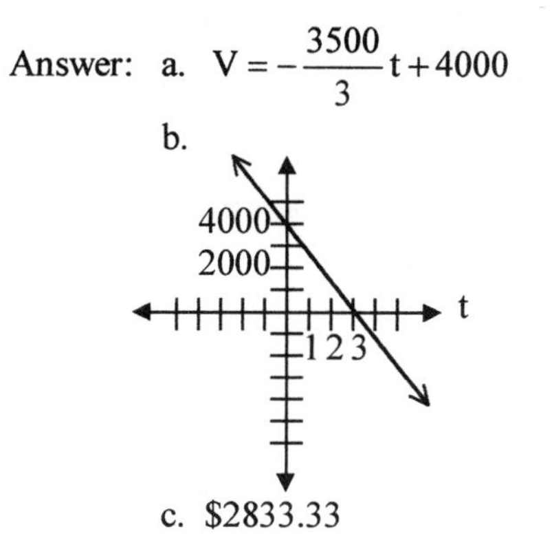

c. $2833.33

Section 1.2 Exponents

MULTIPLE CHOICE 1.2

[d] 43. Evaluate: 4^{-2}.

a. -8 b. –16 c. $\frac{1}{8}$ d. $\frac{1}{16}$

[a] 44. Evaluate: $64^{\frac{1}{2}}$.

a. 8 b. 32 c. 4 d. 16

[b] 45. Evaluate: $25^{\frac{3}{2}}$.

a. $\sqrt[3]{625}$ b. 125 c. $(\sqrt{5})^3$ d. $\frac{75}{2}$

[a] 46. Evaluate $5^{2.3}$ with a calculator. Round to four decimal places.

a. 40.5164 b. 39.1862 c. 44.0112 d. 11.5000

[b] 47. Evaluate: $\left[\left[\frac{3}{4}\right]^{-1}\right]^{-2}$

a. $-\frac{16}{9}$ b. $\frac{9}{16}$ c. $\frac{16}{9}$ d. $-\frac{9}{16}$

[b] 48. Evaluate: $(-64)^{\frac{2}{3}}$.

a. -16 b. 16 c. 4 d. -4

[c] 49. Evaluate: $16^{-\frac{1}{2}}$.

a. -8 b. -4 c. $\frac{1}{4}$ d. $-\frac{1}{4}$

[b] 50. Evaluate: $27^{-\frac{2}{3}}$.

a. -18 b. $\frac{1}{9}$ c. $\frac{1}{3}$ d. $-\frac{1}{9}$

[c] 51. Evaluate: $(-8)^{\frac{-5}{3}}$.

a. $\frac{1}{32}$ b. $\frac{40}{3}$ c. $-\frac{1}{32}$ d. $-\frac{1}{2}$

[c] 52. Evaluate: $\left[-\frac{1}{8}\right]^{-\frac{4}{3}}$.

a. $\frac{1}{6}$ b. -16 c. 16 d. $-\frac{1}{32}$

[c] 53. Simplify the expression $x^3 \cdot x^4 \cdot x$.

a. x^{12} b. x^7 c. x^8 d. x^9

[a] 54. Simplify the expression $(y^2 \cdot y^3)^2$.

a. y^{10} b. y^{12} c. y^{24} d. y^7

[c] 55. Simplify the expression $\left[\frac{x}{y^0}\right]^5$.

a. $\frac{x}{y}$ b. $\frac{x^5}{y^5}$ c. x^5 d. $\frac{x^5}{5}$

[a] 56. Simplify the expression $(5x^3y)^2$.

a. $25x^6y^2$ b. $5x^3y^2$ c. $5x^6y^2$ d. $25x^3y$

[c] 57. Simplify the expression $\frac{x^{10}}{x^{13}}$.

a. x^{23} b. $\frac{1}{x^{-3}}$ c. $\frac{1}{x^3}$ d. $\frac{x}{x^3}$

SHORT ANSWER 1.2

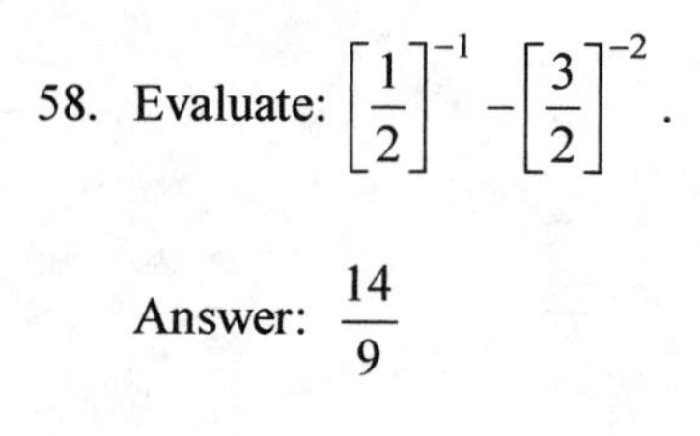

58. Evaluate: $\left[\frac{1}{2}\right]^{-1} - \left[\frac{3}{2}\right]^{-2}$.

Answer: $\frac{14}{9}$

59. Evaluate: $36^{\frac{3}{2}}$.

Answer: 216

60. Evaluate: $8^{\frac{2}{3}}$.

Answer: 4

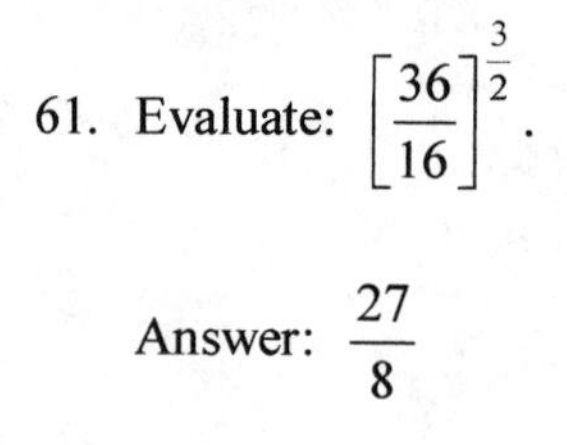

61. Evaluate: $\left[\frac{36}{16}\right]^{\frac{3}{2}}$.

Answer: $\frac{27}{8}$

62. Evaluate: $\left[\frac{9}{16}\right]^{-\frac{1}{2}}$.

Answer: $\frac{4}{3}$

63. Evaluate: $\left[\frac{9}{16}\right]^{-\frac{3}{2}}$.

Answer: $\frac{64}{27}$

64. Use a calculator to evaluate the expression $5^{0.25}$. Round answer to 4 decimal places.

Answer: 1.4953

65. Use a calculator to evaluate the expression $7^{0.04}$. Round answer to 4 decimal places.

Answer: 1.0809

66. Use a calculator to evaluate the expression $12^{-1.6}$. Round answer to 4 decimal places.

Answer: 0.0188

67. Evaluate: $\dfrac{\left[\left(z^2\right)^3\right]^2}{z \cdot z^4}$.

Answer: z^7

68. Evaluate: $\dfrac{(2x^3y)^2}{8x^2y}$.

Answer: $\dfrac{x^4y}{2}$

69. Evaluate: $\dfrac{(6x^2y^4)^2}{(3xyy^4)^3}$.

Answer: $\dfrac{4x}{3y^7}$

70. Evaluate: $\dfrac{(6u^3v^4)^2}{12(uv^2)^3}$.

Answer: $3u^3v^2$

71. Evaluate: $\left[\dfrac{2x^3y}{3x^{-4}y^3}\right]^2$.

Answer: $\dfrac{4x^{14}}{9y^4}$

72. If the learning curve for the production of the Lexus ES300 is $105x^{-0.28}$, how many man-hours did it take to build the 100th Lexus ES300?

Answer: 28.919 man-hours

73. If the learning curve for the production of the Lexus ES300 is $105x^{-0.28}$, how many man-hours did it take to build the 500th Lexus ES300?

Answer: 18.428 man-hours

74. The relationship between heart rate and weight of animals is approximately $(\text{heartrate}) = 250(\text{weight})^{-\frac{1}{4}}$, where heart rate is in beats/min and weight is in pounds. Estimate the heart rate of a 5 pound Chihuahua.

Answer: 167.2 beats/min

75. The relationship between heart rate and weight of animals is approximately $(\text{heartrate}) = 250(\text{weight})^{-\frac{1}{4}}$, where heart rate is in beats/min and weight is in pounds. Estimate the heart rate of a 300 pound tiger.

Answer: 60.1 beats/min

76. The relationship between heart rate and weight of animals is approximately $(\text{heartrate}) = 250(\text{weight})^{-\frac{1}{4}}$, where heart rate is in beats/min and weight is in pounds. Estimate the heart rate of a 95 pound great dane.

Answer: 80.1 beats/min

SECTION 1.3 Functions

MULTIPLE CHOICE 1.3

[b] 77. Which of the following graphs is *not* the graph of a function?

a.

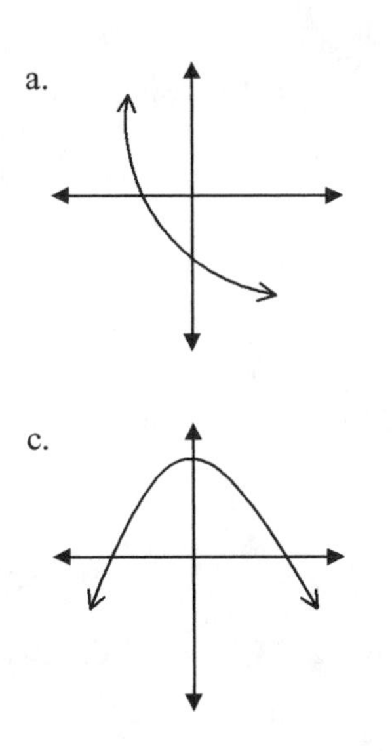

c.

b.

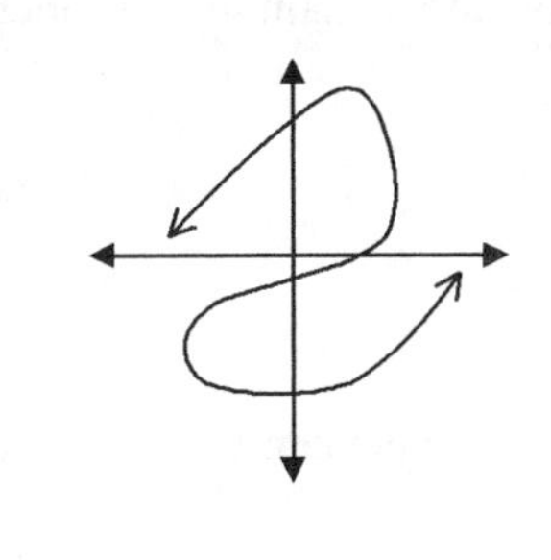

d.

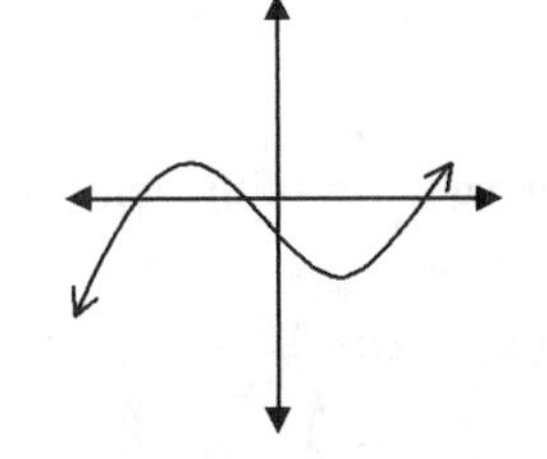

[c] 78. Which of the following graphs is the graph of a function?

a.

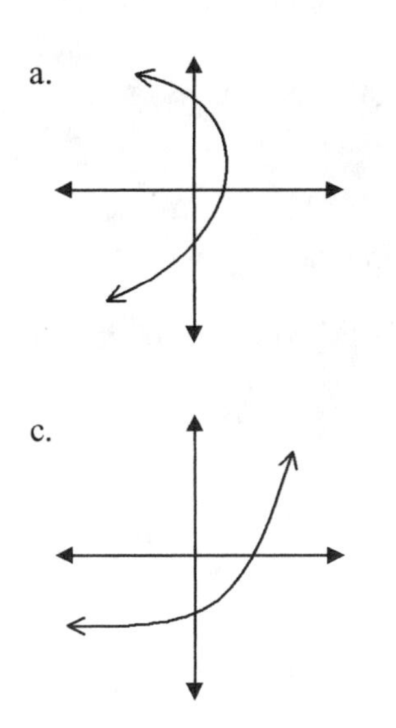

c.

b.

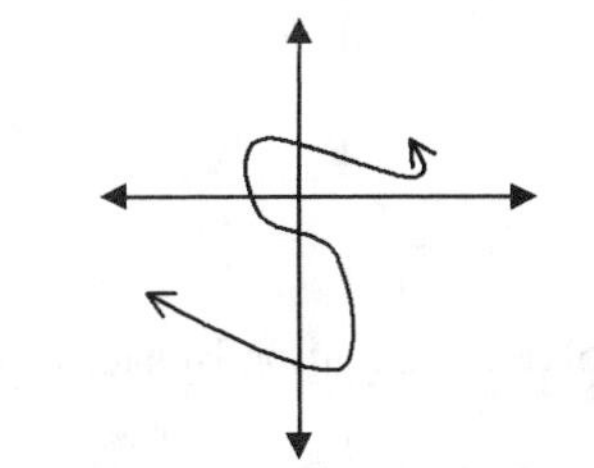

d.

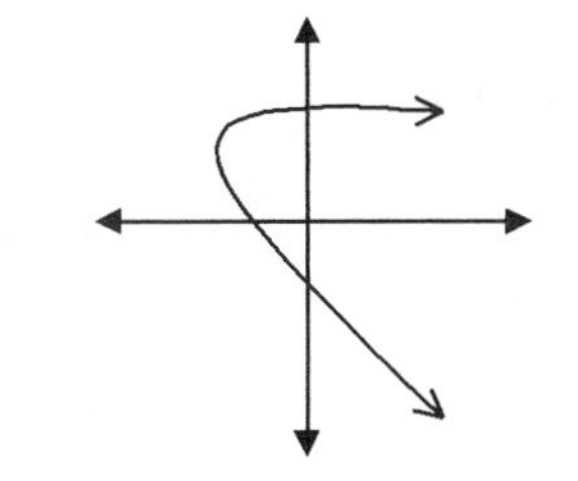

[d] 79. Give the domain for the function $f(x) = \sqrt{x+2}$.

a. $\Re$ b. $\{x|x \geq 2\}$ c. $\{x|x > -2\}$ d. $\{x|x \geq -2\}$

[b] 80. Give the domain for the function $f(x)=\frac{3}{x+5}$.

a. $\Re$ b. $\{x|x \neq -5\}$ c. $\{x|x > -5\}$ d. $\{x|x \geq 0\}$

[a] 81. Give the domain for the function $f(x)=x^{\frac{2}{3}}$.

a. $\Re$ b. $\{x|x \geq 0\}$ c. $\{x|x \leq 0\}$ d. $\left\{x \middle| x > \frac{5}{3}\right\}$

[c] 82. Give the domain for the function $f(x)=\sqrt{1-x}$.

a. $\Re$ b. $\{x|x \geq 1\}$ c. $\{x|x \leq 1\}$ d. $\{x|x \leq -1\}$

[b] 83. The equation of the following parabola is $f(x)=$

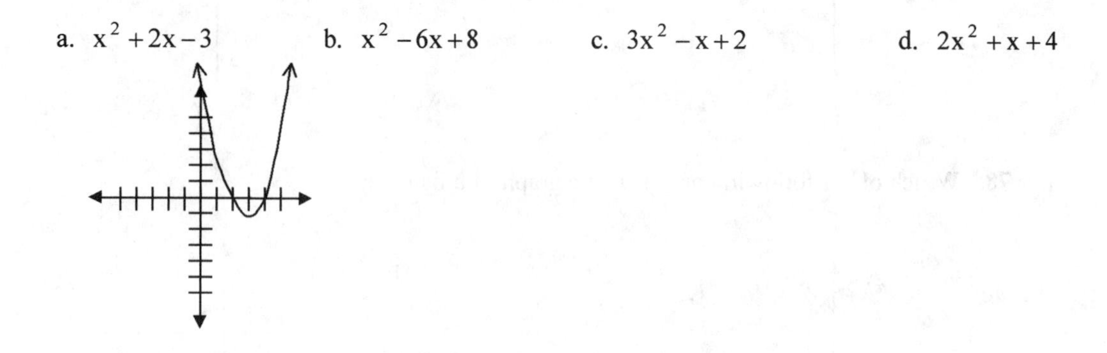

a. x^2+2x-3 b. x^2-6x+8 c. $3x^2-x+2$ d. $2x^2+x+4$

[c] 84. Solve the equation by factoring or by using the quadratic formula $x^2=-x$.

a. $x=0$ b. $x=0, 1$ c. $x=0, -1$ d. $x=-1$

[a] 85. Solve the equation by factoring or by using the quadratic formula $-2x^2-6x-4=0$.

a. $x=-1, -2$ b. $x=2, -1$ c. $x=1, 2$ d. $x=0, 1$

[b] 86. Solve the equation by factoring or by using the quadratic formula $2x^2=-16x$.

a. $x=0$ b. $x=-8, 0$ c. $x=0, 8$ d. $x=-8$

[b] 87. Solve the equation by factoring or by using the quadratic formula $x^2+64=0$.

a. $x=8$ b. no solutions c. $x=8, -8$ d. $x=0, 8$

[b] 88. The concentration K of a particular medicine in the blood stream t hours after being swallowed is $K(t)=\frac{0.02t}{1+t^3}$, $t \geq 0$. After 1 hour, what is the concentration?

a. 1 b. 0.01 c. 0.001 d. 0.1

[a] 89. The total revenue a business received from the sale of x calculators is given by the function $R(x)=11x+\frac{100}{x}$ dollars. What is the total revenue from the sale of 50 calculators?

a. $552 b. $220 c. $448 d. $650

SHORT ANSWER 1.3

90. Is the following graph a function of x?

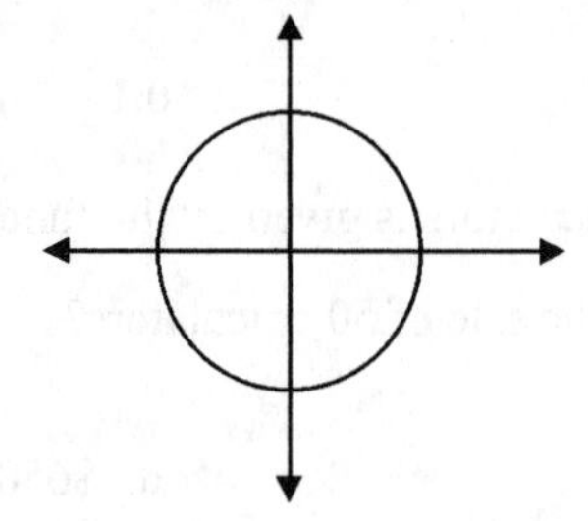

Answer: No

91. Is the following graph a function of x?

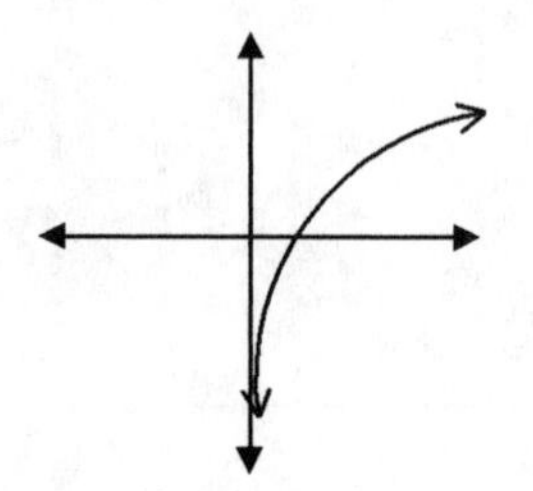

Answer: Yes

92. Is the following graph a function of x?

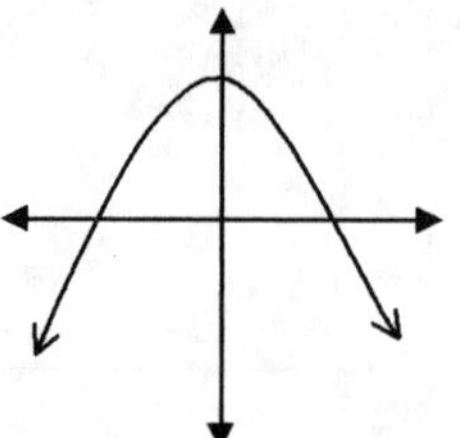

Answer: Yes

93. Is the following graph a function of x?

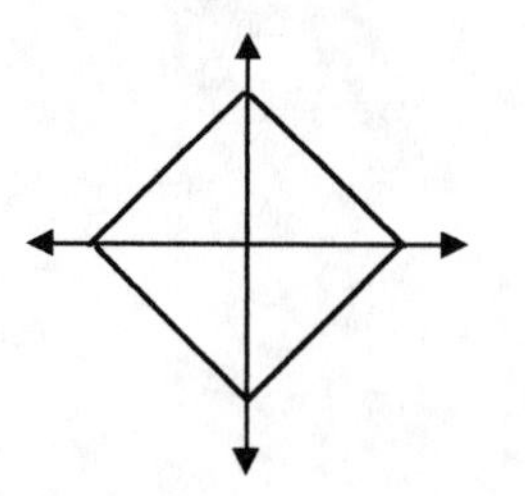

Answer: No

94. Find the domain and range of the graphed function.

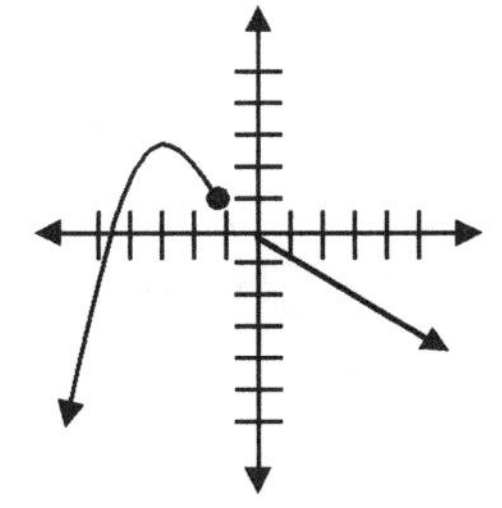

Answer: D: $\{x|x \le -1 \text{ or } x \ge 0\}$, R: $\{y|y \le 3\}$

95. Find the domain and range of the graphed function.

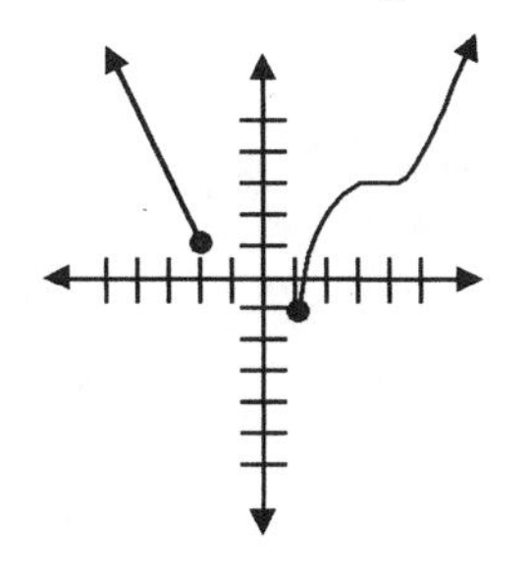

Answer: D: $\{x|x \le -2 \text{ or } x \ge 1\}$, R: $\{y|y \ge -1\}$

96. Find the domain of the function $f(x) = \sqrt{49 - x^2}$.

Answer: $\{x|-7 \le x \le 7\}$

97. Find the domain of the function $f(x) = \dfrac{1}{\sqrt{2 - x}}$.

Answer: $\{x|x < 2\}$

98. Find $f(14)$ for the function $f(x) = \sqrt{x + 2}$.

Answer: 4

99. Find $f(1)$ for the function $f(x) = \dfrac{3}{x + 5}$.

Answer: $\dfrac{1}{2}$

100. Find $f(-27)$ for the function $f(x) = x^{\frac{2}{3}}$.

Answer: 9

101. Find $f(-8)$ for the function $f(x) = \sqrt{1-x}$.

Answer: 3

102. Graph the function $f(x) = -x + 3$.

Answer:

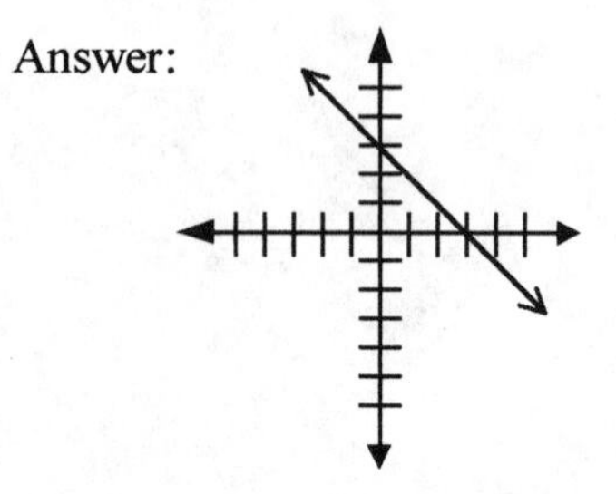

103. Graph the function $f(x) = x - 3$.

Answer:

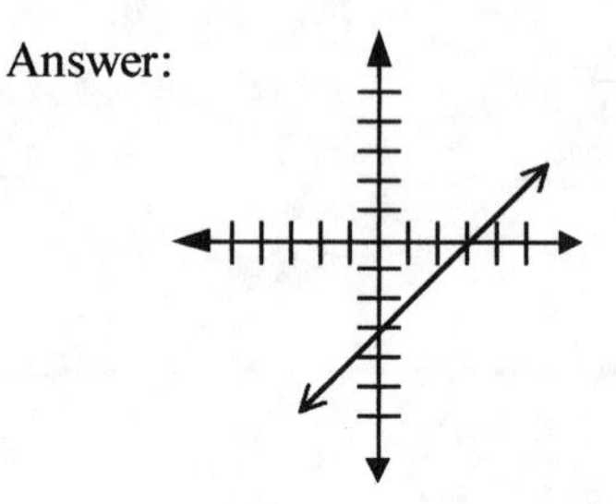

104. Graph the function $f(x) = 2x^2 - 4x - 6$.

Answer:

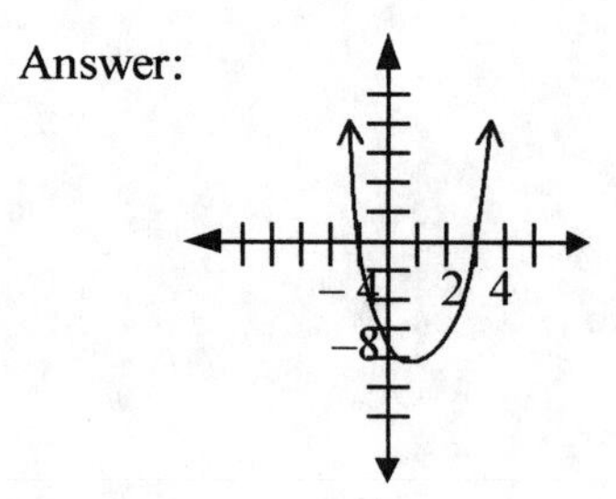

105. Solve the equation by factoring or by using the quadratic formula $50 - 15x = -x^2$.

Answer: $x = 5, 10$

106. Solve the equation by factoring or by using the quadratic formula $12x^2 + x - 6 = 0$.

Answer: $x = \frac{2}{3}, -\frac{3}{4}$

107. Solve the equation by factoring or by using the quadratic formula $21x^2 + x - 10 = 0$.

Answer: $x = \frac{2}{3}, -\frac{5}{7}$

108. Solve the equation by factoring or by using the quadratic formula $x^2 + 4x = 13$.

Answer: $x = -2 + \sqrt{17}, -2 - \sqrt{17}$

109. Solve the equation by factoring or by using the quadratic formula $3x^2 + 6x + 15 = 0$.

Answer: no real solutions

110. The function $P(d) = 1 + \frac{d}{33}$ gives the pressure, in atmospheres, at a depth d in the sea. d is measured in feet. Find the pressure at 25 feet.

Answer: 1.76 atmospheres

111. Under certain conditions, the supply of sugar is related to the price by the function $S(p) = 7p - 5.6$ where S(p) is the number of 5-lb bags (in millions) that a seller allows to be purchased at price p. Find the quantity supplied when the price is $8 per 5-lb bag.

Answer: 50.4 million

112. Under certain conditions, the demand of sugar is related to price by $D(p) = -2.1p + 14.5$, where p = price of a 5-lb bag of sugar and D(p) = quantity of bags (in millions) purchased at price p. Find the quantity purchased when the price is $4.50 per 5-lb bag.

Answer: 5.05 million

SECTION 1.4 Functions

MULTIPLE CHOICE 1.4

[c] 113. Find the domain of the function $f(x)=\frac{x^2}{2x-1}$.

a. $\{x|x \neq 0\}$ b. $\Re$ c. $\left\{x \middle| x \neq \frac{1}{2}\right\}$ d. $\left\{x \middle| x \neq -\frac{1}{2}\right\}$

[d] 114. Find the domain of the function $f(x)=\frac{5}{x(x-2)}$.

a. $\{x|x \neq 0\}$ b. $\Re$ c. $\{x|x \neq 2\}$ d. $\{x|x \neq 0, x \neq 2\}$

[a] 115. Find the domain of the function $f(x)=\left[\frac{1}{4}\right]^x$.

a. $\Re$ b. $\{x|x > 0\}$ c. $\{x|x \geq 0\}$ d. $\{x|x < 0\}$

[a] 116. Evaluate f(0) for the function $f(x)=\left[\frac{1}{4}\right]^x$.

a. 1 b. $\frac{1}{4}$ c. 0 d. 4

[c] 117. Solve the equation by factoring $x^3 - 9x = 0$.

a. $x = 0$ b. $x = 0, 3$ c. $x = 0, 3, -3$ d. $x = 3$

[a] 118. Solve the equation by factoring $x^3 = x$.

a. $x = 0, 1, -1$ b. $x = 1$ c. $x = 0, 1$ d. $x = 1, -1$

[c] 119. Identify $f(x) = 2^x$.

a. polynomial b. rational c. exponential
d. piecewise linear e. none of these

[a] 120. Identify $f(x) = 2x$.

a. polynomial b. rational c. exponential
d. piecewise linear e. none of these

[b] 121. Identify $f(x)=\frac{1}{x+5}$.

a. polynomial b. rational c. exponential
d. piecewise linear e. none of these

[a] 122. Identify $f(x)=\frac{1}{5}x+2$.

a. polynomial b. rational c. exponential
d. piecewise linear e. none of these

[d] 123. Identify $f(x)=\begin{cases}2x-1 & \text{if } x\le 1\\ x & \text{if } x>1\end{cases}$.

a. polynomial b. rational c. exponential
d. piecewise linear e. none of these

[e] 124. Identify $f(x)=x^{\frac{2}{3}}-3x+1$.

a. polynomial b. rational c. exponential
d. piecewise linear e. none of these

[a] 125. Identify $f(x)=\frac{2}{3}x^2-3x+1$.

a. polynomial b. rational c. exponential
d. piecewise linear e. none of these

[a] 126. Identify $f(x) = 12$.

a. polynomial b. rational c. exponential
d. piecewise linear e. none of these

[c] 127. Identify $f(x) = 12^x$.

a. polynomial b. rational c. exponential
d. piecewise linear e. none of these

SHORT ANSWER 1.4

128. Find the domain and range of the following function.

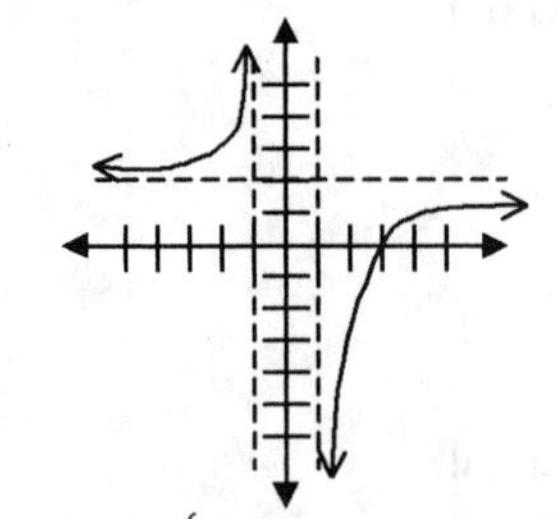

Answer: D: $\{x|x < -1 \text{ or } x > 1\}$ R: $\{y|y \neq 2\}$

129. Find the domain and range of the following function.

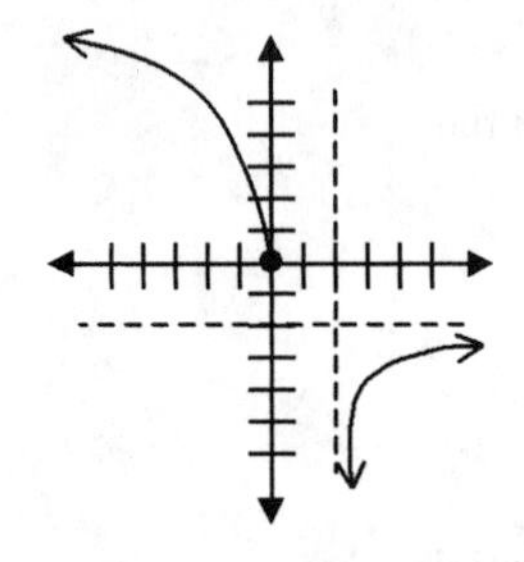

Answer: D: $\{x|x \leq 0 \text{ or } x > 2\}$ R: $\{y|y < -2 \text{ or } y \geq 0\}$

130. Evaluate f(0) for the function $f(x) = \dfrac{x^2}{2x - 1}$.

Answer: 0

131. Evaluate f(–2) for the function $f(x) = \dfrac{5}{x(x - 2)}$.

Answer: $\dfrac{5}{8}$

132. Solve the following equation by factoring $x^4 - x^3 = 6x^2$.

Answer: $x = 0, 3, -2$

133. Solve the following equation by factoring $10x^3 = 2x^4$.

Answer: $x = 0, 5$

134. Solve the following equation by factoring $4x^{\frac{5}{2}} + 16x^{\frac{3}{2}} = 48x^{\frac{1}{2}}$.

Answer: $x = 0, 2$

135. Solve the following equation by factoring $3x^{\frac{1}{2}} + 2x^{\frac{3}{2}} = x^{\frac{5}{2}}$.

Answer: $x = 0, 3$

136. Graph $f(x) = 2^{-x}$.

Answer:

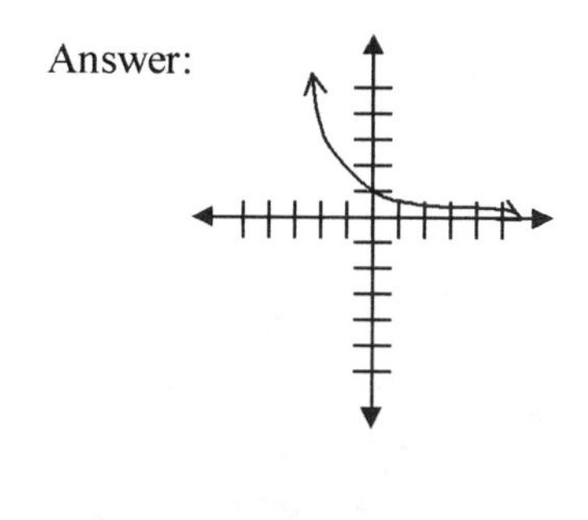

137. Graph $f(x) = \left[\frac{1}{3}\right]^{-x}$

Answer:

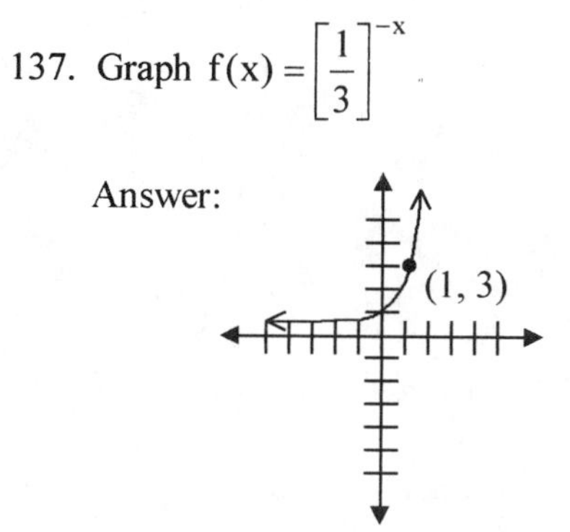

138. Graph $f(x) = \begin{cases} 4 - 2x \text{ if } x < 3 \\ x - 7 \text{ if } x \geq 3 \end{cases}$

Answer:

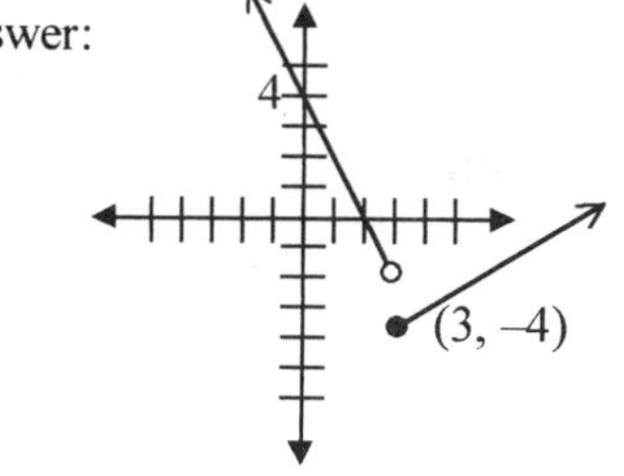

139. Graph $f(x) = \begin{cases} 7 - x \text{ if } x \le 5 \\ 2x - 8 \text{ if } x > 5 \end{cases}$

Answer:

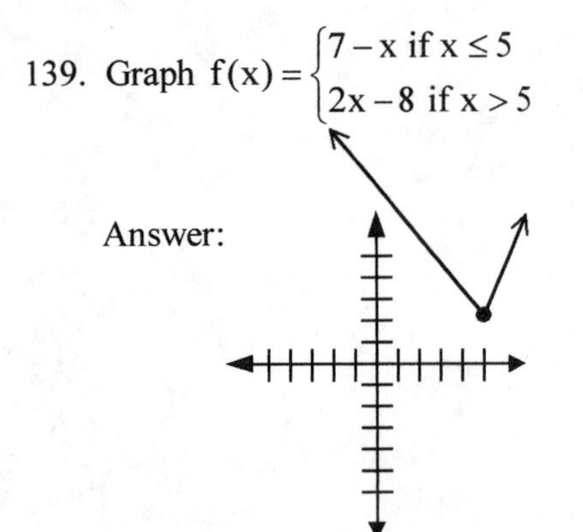

140. Graph $f(x) = \begin{cases} 11 - 2x \text{ if } x \ge 2 \\ 3 + 2x \text{ if } x < 2 \end{cases}$

Answer:

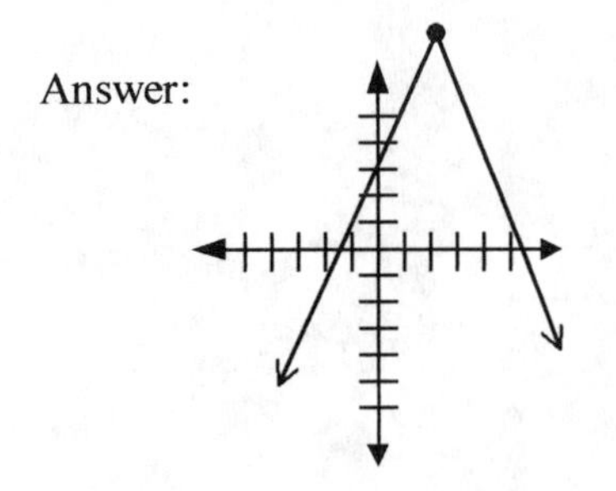

141. Graph $f(x) = \begin{cases} -x \text{ if } x \le 0 \\ -2 \text{ if } x > 0 \end{cases}$

Answer:

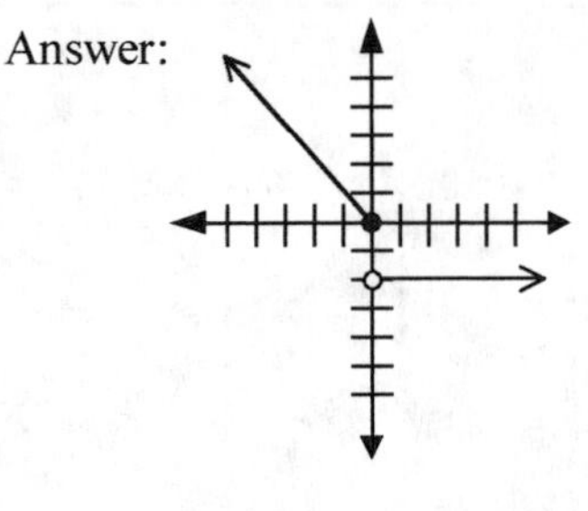

142. For the functions $f(x) = 3x - 1$ and $g(x) = x^3$, find $f(g(x))$ and $g(f(x))$.

Answer: $f(g(x)) = 3x^3 - 1$, $g(f(x)) = (3x - 1)^3$

143. For the functions $f(x) = x^2 + 3$ and $g(x) = \sqrt{x}$, find $f(g(x))$ and $g(f(x))$.

Answer: $f(g(x)) = x + 3$, $g(f(x)) = \sqrt{x^2 + 3}$

144. For the function $f(x) = \frac{2}{x}$ and $g(x) = 3x^2 + 1$, find $f(g(x))$ and $g(f(x))$.

Answer: $f(g(x)) = \frac{2}{3x^2 + 1}$, $g(f(x)) = \frac{12}{x^2} + 1$

145. For the function $f(x) = 5x^2 + 8x - 2$, find and simplify $\frac{f(x+h) - f(x)}{h}$.

Answer: $10x + 5h + 8$

146. For the function $f(x) = 3 - x^2$, find and simplify $\frac{f(x+h) - f(x)}{h}$.

Answer: $-2x - h$

147. For the function $f(x) = \frac{4}{x}$, find and simplify $\frac{f(x+h) - f(x)}{h}$.

Answer: $\frac{-4}{x^2 + xh}$

148. For the function $f(x) = \frac{2}{x^2}$, find and simplify $\frac{f(x+h) - f(x)}{h}$.

Answer: $\frac{-4x - 2h}{x^2(x+h)^2}$

149. The function below expresses a stockbroker's monthly salary with respect to the amount of sales made during the month. If the total sales are \$25,000 or less, the salary will be 20% of total sales; if sales exceed \$25,000 the salary will be \$5,000 plus 11% of total sales.

$$f(x) = \begin{cases} 0.2x \text{ if } x \le 25{,}000 \\ 5{,}000 + 0.11x \text{ if } x > 25{,}000 \end{cases}$$

a. How much will the salary be if sales are \$50,000?
b. How much will the salary be if sales are \$25,000?
c. How much will the salary be if sales are \$26,000?

Answer: a. \$10,500 b. \$5,000 c. \$7,860

150. The function below expresses the growth of a newborn infant during the first 18 months. It grows ½ inch per month for the first 8 months and then ¾ inches per month for the next 10 months.

$$f(x)=\begin{cases}\frac{1}{2}x & \text{if } 0\le x\le 8\\ 4+\frac{3}{4}(x-8) & \text{if } 8<x\le 18\end{cases}$$

a. How much has a 5-month old baby grown?
b. How long is a 1 year-old baby who was 17 inches long at birth?

Answer: a. 2 ½ inches b. 24 inches

151. The world population (in millions) since 1700 is approximately $P(x)=522(1.0053)^x$, where x is the number of years since 1700 (for $0\le x\le 200$). Estimate the world population in the year
a. 1850
b. 1900

Answer: a. about 1.154 billion b. about 1.502 billion

152. The monthly payment for purchases made with a credit card is 25% of the unpaid balance if the balance is less than $200. If the balance is $200 or more the payment is 15% of the unpaid balance.
a. Write a two-part function that describes the payment, P, as a function of the unpaid balance, B.
b. How much is the monthly payment of an unpaid balance of $150?
c. How much is the monthly payment of an unpaid balance of $200?
d. How much is the monthly payment of an unpaid balance of $199?

Answer: a. $P(B)=\begin{cases}0.25x \text{ if } B<200\\ 0.15x \text{ if } B\ge 200\end{cases}$ b. $37.50
c. $30.00 d. $49.75

153. An airport parking garage charges $4 for the first four hours or less and $2 per hour for the rest of the day, with a maximum rental time of 24 hours.
a. Write a two-part function that defines the cost, C, for the 24 hour period.
b. How much will it cost to park for three hours?
c. How much will it cost to park for eight hours?
d. How much will it cost to park for 24 hours?

Answer: a. $C=\begin{cases}4 \text{ if } x\le 4\\ 2x-4 \text{ if } x<x\le 24\end{cases}$ b. $4
c. $12 d. $44

Chapter 1 – Graphing Calculator

Functions

Section 1.1 Real Numbers, Inequalities, and Lines

1. Use a graphing calculator to graph the line, $y = -2x + 1$. Your graph will depend on the viewing window you choose. Begin with the standard window [–1, 10] by [–1, 10] and then zoom out if the line does not appear.

   Answer:

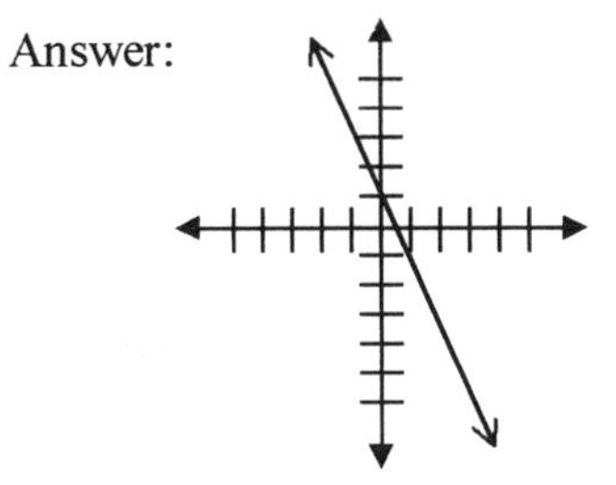

2. Use a graphing calculator to graph the line, $y = 5x - 1$. Your graph will depend on the viewing window you choose. Begin with the standard window [–1, 10] by [–1, 10] and then zoom out if the line does not appear.

   Answer:

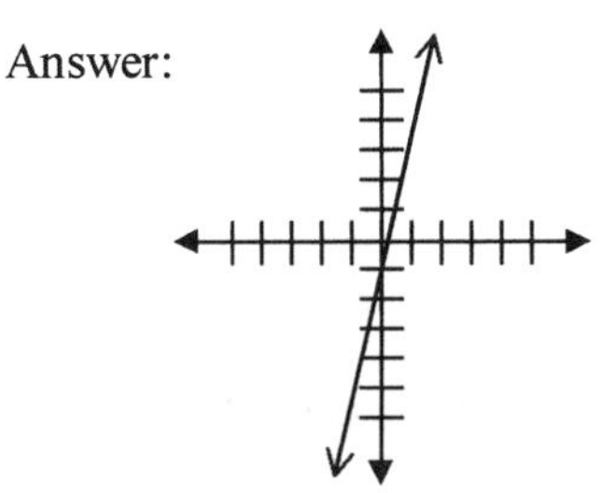

3. Use a graphing calculator to graph the line, $y = \frac{1}{4}x + 5$. Your graph will depend on the viewing window you choose. Begin with the standard window [–1, 10] by [–1, 10] and then zoom out if the line does not appear.

   Answer:

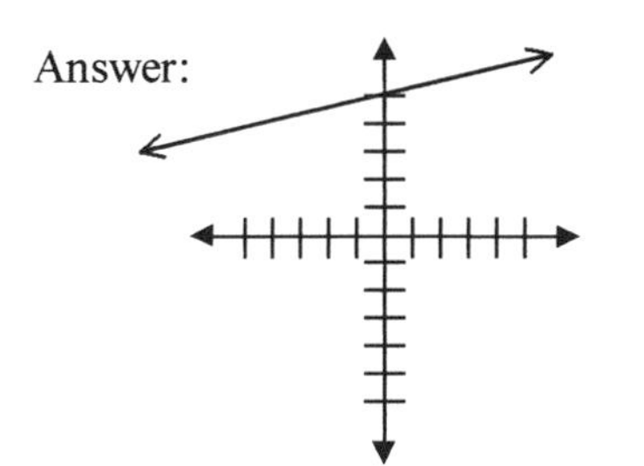

Section 1.2 Exponents

4. Use a graphing calculator to evaluate the expression, $(-216)^{7/3}$. For approximate solutions, round to two decimal places.

   Answer: –279,936

5. Use a graphing calculator to evaluate the expression, $\left[\frac{25}{49}\right]^{-0.5}$. For approximate solutions, round to two decimal places.

   Answer: 1.4

6. Use a graphing calculator to evaluate the expression, $\left[(0.6)^{0.6}\right]^{0.6}$. For approximate solutions, round to two decimal places.

   Answer: 0.83

7. Use a graphing calculator to evaluate the expression, $\left[1-\frac{1}{100}\right]^{-99}$. For approximate solutions, round to two decimal places.

   Answer: 2.70

8. Use a graphing calculator to evaluate the expression, $\left(1+10^{-4}\right)^{10^4}$. For approximate solutions, round to two decimal places.

   Answer: 2.72

SECTION 1.3 Functions

9. Use a graphing calculator to find the RANGE of the given function.

   Hint: Enter $x^{m/n}$ as $\left(x^m\right)^{1/n}$ or $\left[x^{1/n}\right]^m$

   $f(x) = \sqrt{4x-7}$

   Answer: $\{y \mid y \geq 0\}$

10. Use a graphing calculator to find the RANGE of the given function.

    Hint: Enter $x^{m/n}$ as $\left(x^m\right)^{1/n}$ or $\left[x^{1/n}\right]^m$

    $f(x) = \dfrac{3}{x-7.6}$

    Answer: $\{y \mid y \neq 0\}$

11. Use a graphing calculator to find the RANGE of the given function.

    Hint: Enter $x^{m/n}$ as $\left(x^m\right)^{1/n}$ or $\left[x^{1/n}\right]^m$

    $f(x) = x^{7/5}$

    Answer: $\Re$

12. Use a graphing calculator to find the RANGE of the given function.

    Hint: Enter $x^{m/n}$ as $\left(x^m\right)^{1/n}$ or $\left[x^{1/n}\right]^m$

    $F(x) = x^{6/5}$

    Answer: $\{y \mid y \geq 0\}$

13. Use a graphing calculator to find the RANGE of the given function.

    Hint: Enter $x^{m/n}$ as $\left(x^m\right)^{1/n}$ or $\left[x^{1/n}\right]^m$

    $F(x) = \sqrt{1.44 - x^2}$

    Answer: $\{y \mid 0 \leq y \leq 1.2\}$

14. Use a graphing calculator to find the RANGE of the given function.

    Hint: Enter $x^{m/n}$ as $\left(x^{m}\right)^{1/n}$ or $\left[x^{1/n}\right]^{m}$

    $F(x) = \sqrt{9.35 - x}$

    Answer: $\{y \mid y \geq 0\}$

15. Solve the following equation using a graphing calculator. Approximate your answer to 2 decimal places.

    $x^2 + 3.61x = 0$

    Answer: $x = -3.61$, $x = 0$

16. Solve the following equation using a graphing calculator. Approximate your answer to 2 decimal places.

    $6x^2 = 11.1x + 11.7$

    Answer: $x = 2.6$, $x = -0.75$

17. Solve the following equation using a graphing calculator. Approximate your answer to 2 decimal places.

    $6x^2 - 7x - 5 = 0$

    Answer: $x = -0.5$, $x = 1.67$

18. Solve the following equation using a graphing calculator. Approximate your answer to 2 decimal places.

    $10x^2 - 12x = 32.5$

    Answer: $x = 2.5$, $x = -1.3$

19. Solve the following equation using a graphing calculator. Approximate your answer to 2 decimal places.

    $2x^2 - 12x + 11 = 0$

    Answer: $x = 4.87$, $x = 1.13$

20. Solve the following equation using a graphing calculator. Approximate your answer to 2 decimal places.

    $0.5x^2 - 15x + 150 = 0$

    Answer: no real solutions

21. Use a graphing calculator to graph the following four equations simultaneously on viewing window [–10,10] by [–10, 10].

    $y_1 = 2.5x + 7$ $y_2 = 2.5x - 7$ $y_3 = 2.5x + 3.5$ $y_4 = 2.5x - 3.5$

    Write the equation of another line with the same slope that lies 2 units above the highest line. Check your answer by graphing it with the others.

    Answer: $y = 2.5x + 9$

22. Use a graphing calculator to graph the following four equations simultaneously on viewing window [–10,10] by [–10, 10].

    $y_1 = 5x - 1.5$ $y_2 = 10x - 1.5$ $y_3 = -x - 1.5$ $y_4 = -5x - 1.5$

    Write the equation of another line through this y-intercept with a slope of $-1/2$. Check your answer by graphing it with the others.

    Answer: $y = -1/2x - 1.5$

SECTION 1.4 Functions

23. Use a graphing calculator to find the RANGE of the following function:

$$f(x) = \frac{6x}{6x - 3.9}$$

Answer: $\{y \mid y \neq 1\}$

24. Use a graphing calculator to find the RANGE of the following function:

$$f(x) = 3.9^{x}$$

Answer: $\{y \mid y > 0\}$

25. Use a graphing calculator to find the RANGE of the following function:

$$f(x) = \left(\frac{1}{7}\right)^{x} - 7$$

Answer: $\{y \mid y > -7\}$

26. Use a graphing calculator to find the RANGE of the following function:

$$f(x) = \frac{x^2}{x + 1}$$

Answer: $\{y \mid y \leq -4 \text{ or } y \geq 0\}$

27. Use a graphing calculator to find the RANGE of the following function:

$$f(x) = \frac{17}{x(x - 3.5)}$$

Answer: $\{y \mid y > 0 \text{ or } y \leq -5.55\}$

28. Use a graphing calculator to find the RANGE of the following function:

$$f(x) = \frac{7.3}{4x - 6.7}$$

Answer: $\{y \mid y > 0\}$

29. Solve the following equation using a graphing calculator.

$$x^3 - 3x^2 = 0$$

Answer: $x = 0, x = 3$

30. Solve the following equation using a graphing calculator.

$$x^3 - 20.25x = 0$$

Answer: $x = 0$, $x = 4.5$, $x = -4.5$

31. Solve the following equation using a graphing calculator.

$$x^4 + 1.15x^3 = 3x^2$$

Answer: $x = 0$, $x = 1.25$, $x = -2.4$

32. Solve the following equation using a graphing calculator.

$$x^5 = 9.5x^4 + 23.1x^3$$

Answer: $x = 0$, $x = 11.51$, $x = -2.01$

33. Solve the following equation using a graphing calculator.

$$3x^{9/2} - 51.9x^{7/2} - 162x^{5/2} = 0$$

Answer: $x = 0$, $x = 20$

34. Solve the following equation using a graphing calculator.

$$6x^{5/2} + 25.8x^{3/2} - 144x^{½} = 0$$

Answer: $x = 0$, $x = 3.2$

35. Solve the following equation using a graphing calculator.

$$x^8 + 2x^7 - 5x^6 = 0$$

Answer: $x = 0$, $x = -3.45$, $x = 1.45$

Chapter 2

Derivatives and Their Uses

Section 2.1 Limits and Continuity

MULTIPLE CHOICE 2.1

[b] 1. Evaluate $\lim_{x \to 2}(3x^2 + 5)$.

a. 41 b. 17 c. 11 d. 0

[d] 2. Evaluate $\lim_{x \to 4}(x^3 - 2)$

a. 8 b. 14 c. 54 d. 62

[d] 3. Evaluate $\lim_{x \to -1} \frac{x^2 + 2x + 3}{x^2 + 1}$

a. undefined b. 6 c. 0 d. 1

[a] 4. Evaluate $\lim_{x \to -3}(-2x^2 + 1)$.

a. -17 b. 19 c. 37 d. $\pm\sqrt{2}$

[b] 5. Evaluate $\lim_{x \to 7} \frac{x^2 - 2x - 35}{x - 7}$

a. -10 b. 12 c. 7 d. undefined

[b] 6. Evaluate $\lim_{x \to 2} \frac{x - 2}{x^2 - 4}$

a. 0 b. ¼ c. undefined d. 1

[a] 7. Evaluate $\lim_{x \to -5} \frac{3x^2 + 13x - 10}{2x^2 + 11x + 5}$

a. $\frac{17}{9}$ b. 0 c. undefined d. -2

[a] 8. Evaluate $\lim_{x\to -4} \frac{x^3+x^2-12x}{x+4}$

a. 28
b. 44
c. undefined
d. 12

[d] 9. Evaluate $\lim_{x\to 3} \sqrt{9-x^2}$

a. undefined
b. $\sqrt{6}$
c. $3\sqrt{2}$
d. 0

[c] 10. If $f(x)=\begin{cases} x \text{ if } x\le 1 \\ 2x \text{ if } x>1 \end{cases}$, is f(x) continuous at $x = 1$?

a. Yes
b. No, since f(1) does not exist
c. No, since $\lim_{x\to 1} f(x)$ does not exist
d. No, since f(x) is a piecewise linear function.

[a] 11. If $f(x)=\begin{cases} 2x-1 \text{ if } x\le 2 \\ x+1 \text{ if } x>2 \end{cases}$, is f(x) continuous at $x = 2$?

a. Yes
b. No, since f(2) does not exist
c. No, since $\lim_{x\to 2} f(x)$ does not exist
d. No, since f(x) is a piecewise linear function.

[a] 12. Determine whether the function $f(x)=\frac{(x+1)(x-3)}{x-2}$ is continuous or discontinuous. If discontinuous, state where the function is discontinuous.

a. discontinuous at $x = 2$
b. discontinuous at $x = -1$, $x = 2$, $x = 3$
c. discontinuous at $x = -1$, $x = 3$
d. continuous

[c] 13. Determine whether the function $f(x)=\frac{4x}{x^2+1}$ is continuous or discontinuous. If discontinuous, state where the function is discontinuous.

a. discontinuous at $x = 0$
b. discontinuous at $x = 1$, $x = -1$
c. continuous
d. discontinuous at $x = 0$, $x = 1$, $x = -1$

[b] 14. The following figure is the function f(x)=

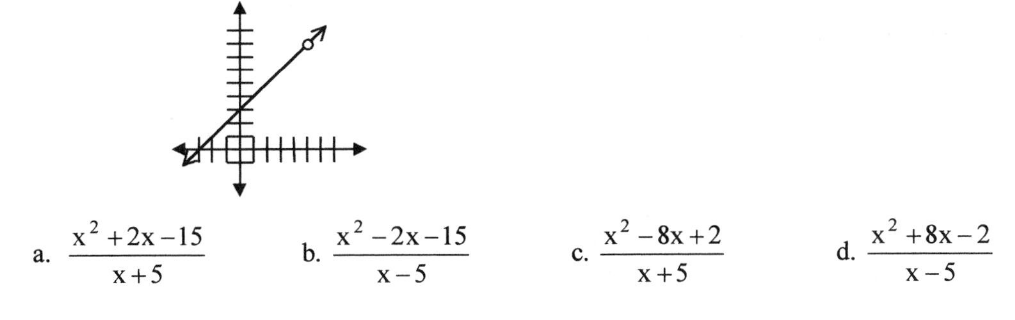

a. $\dfrac{x^2+2x-15}{x+5}$ b. $\dfrac{x^2-2x-15}{x-5}$ c. $\dfrac{x^2-8x+2}{x+5}$ d. $\dfrac{x^2+8x-2}{x-5}$

SHORT ANSWER 2.1

15. Complete the following tables and use it to find the given limit.

$\lim_{x\to 2} 3x - 2$

x	3x − 2
1.9	
1.99	
1.999	

x	3x − 2
2.1	
2.01	
2.001	

Answer: 3.7, 3.97, 3.997, 4.3, 4.03, 4.003
$\lim_{x\to 2} 3x - 2 = 4$

16. Complete the following tables and use it to find the given limit.

$\lim_{x\to -4} \frac{2x}{x+4}$

x	$\frac{2x}{x+4}$
−3.9	
−3.99	
−3.999	

x	$\frac{2x}{x+4}$
−4.1	
−4.01	
−4.001	

Answer: −78, −798, −7998, 82, 802, 8002
The limit does not exist

17. Complete the following tables and use it to find the given limit. Round calculations to 3 decimal places.

$\lim_{x\to -3} \frac{x^2-9}{x+3}$

x	$\frac{x^2-9}{x+3}$
−3.1	
−3.01	
−3.001	

x	$\frac{x^2-9}{x+3}$
−2.9	
−2.99	
−2.999	

Answer: −6.1, −6.01, −6.001, −5.9, −5.99, −5.999

$\lim_{x\to -3} \frac{x^2-9}{x+3} = -6$

18. Evaluate $\lim_{x\to 25} \frac{\sqrt{x}-5}{x-25}$

Answer: $\frac{1}{10}$

19. Evaluate $\lim_{h\to 0} 3x^2 - 2xh + h^2$

Answer: $3x^2$

20. Evaluate $\lim_{h \to 0} \frac{9x^2h - xh^2 + h^3}{h}$

Answer: $9x^2$

The temperature t(m), in degrees Fahrenheit, of a heated building after m minutes ($m \le 90$) is $t(m) = 50 + \frac{m}{2}$.

21. Evaluate $\lim_{m \to 10} t(m)$

Answer: 55

22. Interpret your result.

Answer: As the time approaches 10 minutes, the temperature of the building rises closer and closer to 55 degrees.

The temperature t(m), in degrees Fahrenheit, of a cooling oven after m minutes ($m \le 30$) is $t(m) = 650 - \frac{m^2}{3}$.

23. Evaluate $\lim_{m \to 15} t(m)$

Answer: 575

24. Interpret your result.

Answer: As the time gets closer to 15 minutes, the temperature of the oven drops closer to 575 degrees.

A rectangle has a fixed length of 6 inches and a variable width of x inches.

25. Determine the area function, A.

Answer: $A(x) = 6x$

26. Find $\lim_{x \to 0} A(x)$

Answer: 0

27. Interpret this result.

Answer: As the width gets smaller and smaller, approaching 0, the area of the rectangle also gets smaller and smaller, approaching 0.

28. The number of times a coyote howls in an hour depends on the temperature. If x is the temperature in degrees Fahrenheit and $x \geq 20$, then the number of howls per hour is $\frac{x}{2}-10$. On a night when the temperature approaches 40 degrees, how many coyote howls per hour can be expected?

    Answer: 10

29. The number of breaths a polar bear takes each minute depends on the temperature. If x is the temperature in degrees Fahrenheit, then the number of breaths per minute is $\frac{3x}{10}+9$. When the temperature approaches 20 degrees below zero, how many breaths per minute can be expected?

    Answer: 3

30. If r represents the radius of a sphere, then the volume of the sphere is $\frac{4}{3}\pi r^3$. Suppose the value of the radius approaches 0. What does the volume approach?

    Answer: 0

31. Using limit symbols, write the phrase "as t gets closer and closer to a, g(t) get closer and closer to L."

    Answer: $\lim_{t \to a} g(t) = L$

32. Using limit symbols, write the result that is implied by the following table of values.

x	2.7	2.8	2.9	2.95	2.98	2.99
f(x)	6.4	6.2	6.1	6.05	6.02	6.01

    Answer: $\lim_{x \to 3} f(x) = 6$

33. Using limit symbols, write the result that is implied by the following table of values.

x	-5.1	-5.2	-5.4	-5.45	-5.49	-5.499
g(x)	7.4	7.7	7.9	7.95	7.99	7.999

    Answer: $\lim_{x \to -5.5} g(x) = 8$

34. Using limit symbols, write the result that is implied by the following table of values.

x	2	1.5	1.1	1.01	1.001	1.0001
h(x)	8	9.5	9.9	9.99	9.999	9.9999

    Answer: $\lim_{x \to 1} h(x) = 10$

35. For the graphed function, determine whether the function is continuous or discontinuous at c.

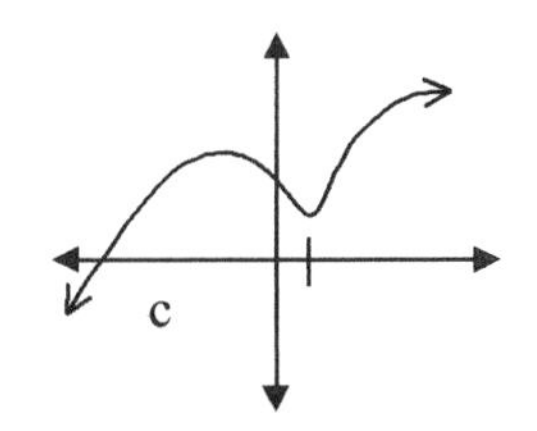

Answer: continuous at c

36. For the graphed function, determine whether the function is continuous or discontinuous at c.

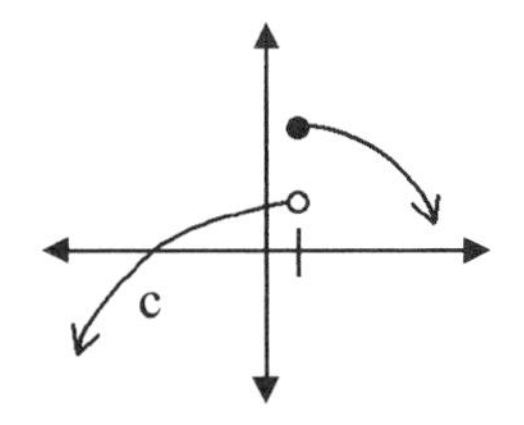

Answer: discontinuous at c

37. Determine whether the function $f(x) = 3x^3 - \frac{1}{2}x^2 + x - 7$ is continuous or discontinuous. If discontinuous, state where the function is discontinuous.

Answer: continuous

The following figure shows the selling price of a certain stock over an 8-hour period.

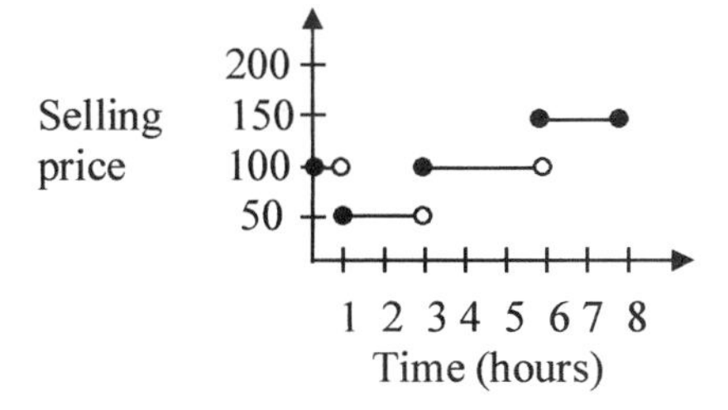

38. Where are the discontinuities?

Answer: 1, 3, 6

39. Explain what happened at the discontinuities.

Answer: The price jumped or fell.

40. The following figure shows the number of compact discs owned by a person over a 12-month period. The CD player was bought at the start of the 12-month period.

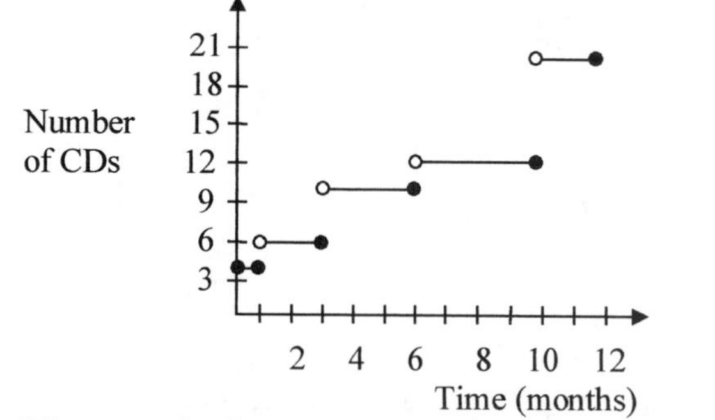

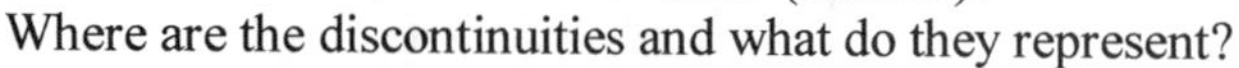

Where are the discontinuities and what do they represent?

Answer: The discontinuities are at 1, 3, 6, and 10 months. They represent times when the person bought or was given additional CDs.

An antiques appraiser charges $35 plus $20 per hour or part of an hour spent appraising.

41. Graph the function that shows the appraiser's charges for every period of time through 6 hours.

Answer:

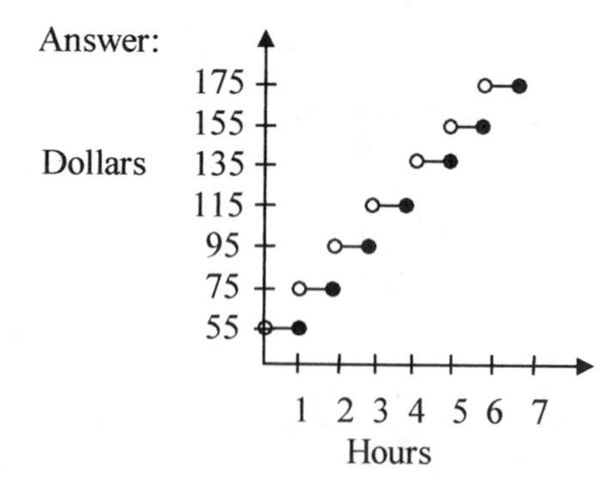

42. Where do the discontinuities occur?

Answer: At the end of each hour.

To draw up a will for a client, a lawyer charges \$50 plus \$100 per hour or part of an hour for the time spent conferring with the client and filing the will with the court.

43. Draw the graph that shows of money that must be paid to the lawyer for drawing up the will for every period of time through 6 hours.

Answer:

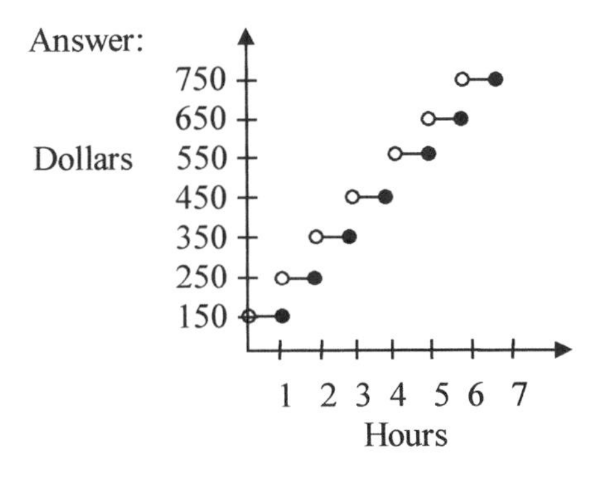

44. Indicate where the discontinuities occur.

Answer: At the end of each hour.

45. If f(3) = 8, is f necessarily continuous at x = 3? Explain.

Answer: No. $\lim_{x \to 3} f(x)$ may not exist, or if it does, the limit may not equal 8.

46. If a graph displayed the total score of both teams in a football game at any time from the start to the end of regulation time (overtime is added if the game is tied at the end of regulation time), would the graph be continuous? If the graph is not continuous, where would the discontinuities occur?

Answer: The graph would not be continuous unless the game ended in a scoreless tie. If the game were not scoreless, discontinuities would occur at the times when one of the teams scored.

47. For the function $f(x) = \dfrac{|x+1|}{x+1}$, find

a. $\lim_{x \to -1^-} f(x)$

b. $\lim_{x \to -1^+} f(x)$

c. $\lim_{x \to -1} f(x)$

Answer: a. –1 b. 1 c. does not exist

48. For the function $f(x)=\begin{cases}7-x & \text{if } x<6\\ 2x-7 & \text{if } x\geq 6\end{cases}$, find

a. $\lim\limits_{x\to 6^-} f(x)$

b. $\lim\limits_{x\to 6^+} f(x)$

c. $\lim\limits_{x\to 6} f(x)$

Answer: a. 1 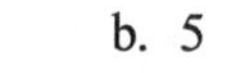 b. 5 c. does not exist

49. For the function

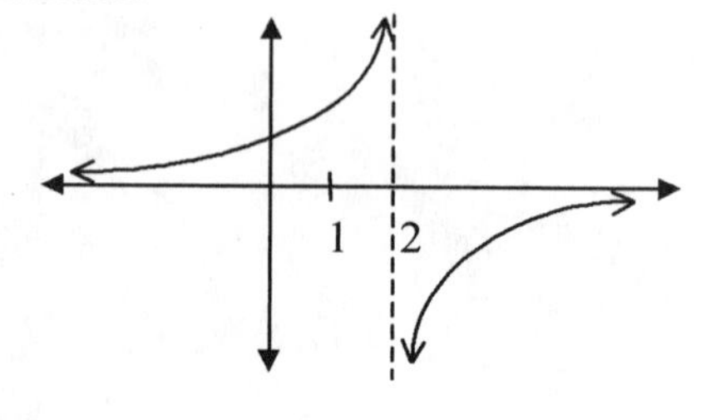

a. find $\lim\limits_{x\to 2^-} f(x)$

b. find $\lim\limits_{x\to 2^+} f(x)$

c. find $\lim\limits_{x\to 2} f(x)$

Answer: a. ∞ b. $-\infty$ c. does not exist

Section 2.2 Slopes, Rates of Change, and Derivatives

MULTIPLE CHOICE 2.2

[c] 50. Determine whether the slope(s) at the indicated point is positive, negative, or zero.

a. positive b. zero c. negative

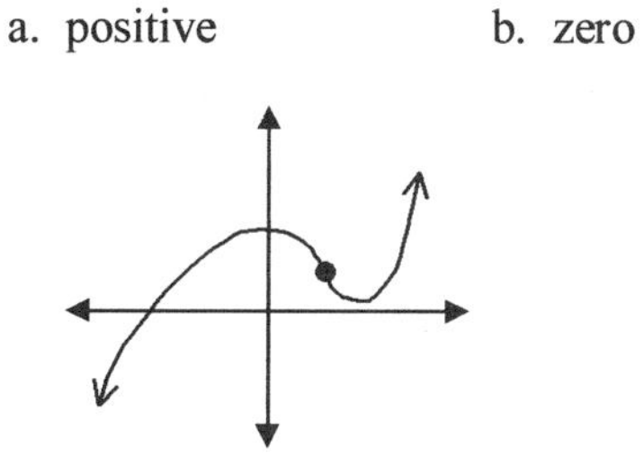

[b] 51. Determine whether the slope(s) at the indicated point is positive, negative, or zero.

a. negative b. zero c. positive

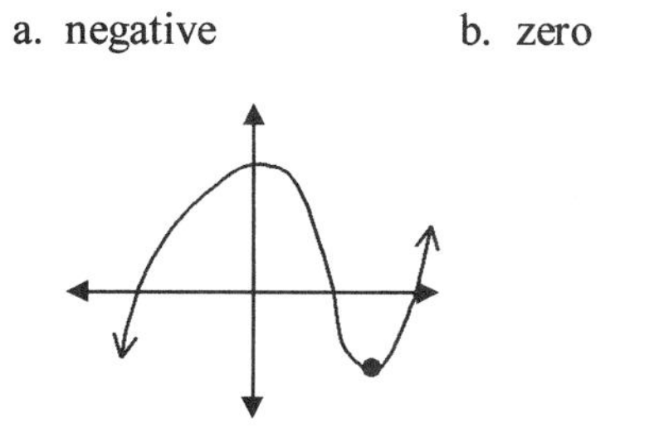

[a] 52. Determine whether the slope(s) at the indicated point is positive, negative, or zero.

a. positive b. negative c. zero

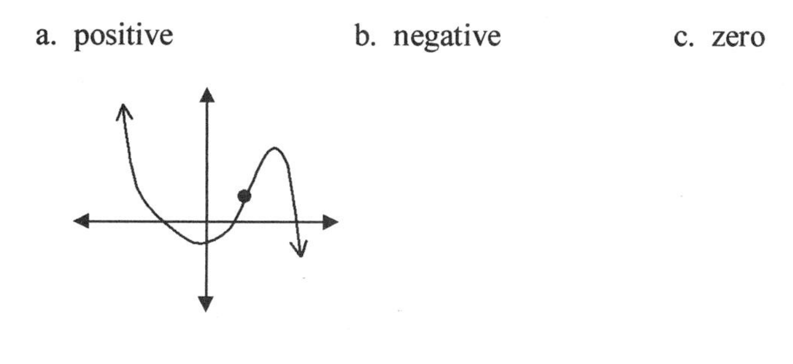

[c] 53. The derivative of $f(x)=\frac{7}{5x}$ is $f'(x)=\frac{-7}{5x^2}$. Use this result to find the equation of the line tangent to the graph of f(x) at the point $\left(-\frac{7}{10},-2\right)$.

a. $y=\frac{20}{7}\left(x+\frac{7}{10}\right)$ b. $y=-\frac{20}{7}x+2$ c. $y+2=-\frac{20}{7}\left(x+\frac{7}{10}\right)$ d. $y=\frac{20}{7}x$

[d] 54. The total cost function for the sale of backpacks is $C(x)=450+3x+0.02x^2$, where x is the number of backpacks and C(x) is in dollars. Use the definition of the derivative to find the marginal cost of 144 backpacks.

a. $1,296.72 b. $9.01 c. $5.88 d. $8.76

[b] 55. For the function $f(x) = 3.7 - 2x^2$, use the definition of the derivative to find $f(-3)$.

a. -8.3 b. 12 c. 21.7 d. -14.3

[d] 56. For the function $f(x) = 3x^2 - 2.7x - 1.1$, find $f(x + \Delta x) - f(x)$.

a. $3x^2 - 2.7x - 1.1 + \Delta x - x$
b. $6x\Delta x + 3(\Delta x)^2 - 2.7\Delta x - 5.4x - 2.2$
c. $3(\Delta x)^2 - 2.7\Delta x$
d. $6x\Delta + 3(\Delta x)^2 - 2.7\Delta x$

SHORT ANSWER 2.2

57. For the graphed function, make a rough sketch of the derivative $f'(x)$, showing where $f'(x)$ is positive, negative, and zero. (Omit scale on the y-axis.)

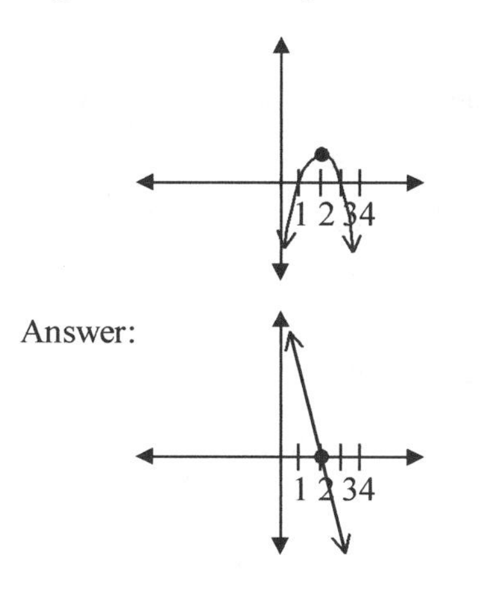

Answer:

58. For the graphed function, make a rough sketch of the derivative $f'(x)$, showing where $f'(x)$ is positive, negative, and zero. (Omit scale on the y-axis.)

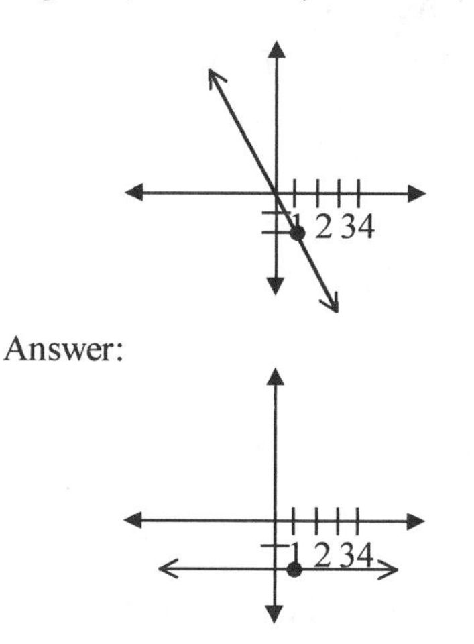

Answer:

59. For the function $f(x) = -3x + 1$, find $f'(x)$ by using the definition of the derivative.

    Answer: $f'(x) = -3$

60. For the function $f(x) = 3x^2 + 5x$, find $f'(x)$ by using the definition of the derivative.

    Answer: $f'(x) = 6x + 5$

61. For the function $f(x) = 4 - x^2$, find $f'(x)$ by using the definition of the derivative.

    Answer: $f'(x) = -2x$

62. For the function $f(x) = 0.02x - 0.15$, find $f'(x)$ by using the definition of the derivative.

Answer: $f'(x) = 0.02$

63. For the function $f(x) = 5x + \frac{1}{2}$, use the definition of the derivative to find $f'(x)$ by finding

a. $f(x + \Delta x)$

b. $f(x + \Delta x) - f(x)$

c. $\frac{f(x + \Delta x) - f(x)}{\Delta x}$

d. $\lim_{\Delta x \to 0} \frac{f(x + \Delta x) - f(x)}{\Delta x}$

Answer: a. $f(x + \Delta x) = 5(x + \Delta x) + \frac{1}{2}$

b. $f(x + \Delta x) - f(x) = 5\Delta x$

c. $\frac{f(x + \Delta x) - f(x)}{\Delta x} = 5$

d. $\lim_{\Delta x \to 0} \frac{f(x + \Delta x) - f(x)}{\Delta x} = 5$

64. For the function $f(x) = x^2 - 2x + 6$, use the definition of the derivative to find $f'(x)$ by finding

a. $f(x + \Delta x)$

b. $f(x + \Delta x) - f(x)$

c. $\frac{f(x + \Delta x) - f(x)}{\Delta x}$

d. $\lim_{\Delta x \to 0} \frac{f(x + \Delta x) - f(x)}{\Delta x}$

Answer: a. $f(x + \Delta x) = x^2 + 2x\Delta x + (\Delta x)^2 - 2x - 2\Delta x + 6$

b. $f(x + \Delta x) - f(x) = \Delta x(2x + \Delta x - 2)$

c. $\frac{f(x + \Delta x) - f(x)}{\Delta x} = 2x + \Delta x - 2$

d. $\lim_{\Delta x \to 0} \frac{f(x + \Delta x) - f(x)}{\Delta x} = 2x - 2$

65. Use the definition of the derivative to find the slope of the line tangent to the graph of $f(x) = 4x^2 - 3.1$.

Answer: m_{tan} at (x, f(x)) = 8x

66. Use the definition of the derivative to find the slope of the line tangent to the graph of $f(x) = x^2 - 2x + 5.4$ at any point (x, f(x)).

Answer: m_{tan} at (x, f(x)) = 2x – 2

67. The derivative of the function $f(x) = 5x^2 - 7.2$ is $f'(x) = 10x$. Use this result to find the equation of the line tangent to the graph of f at the point (2.4, 21.6).

Answer: $y = 24x - 36$

68. The derivative of the function $f(x) = x^2 - x + 4$ is $f'(x) = 2x - 1$. Use this result to find the equation of the line tangent to the graph of f at the point (3, 10).

Answer: $y = 5x - 5$

69. The derivative of the function $f(x) = \frac{-3}{4x}$ is $f'(x) = \frac{3}{4x^2}$. Use this result to find the equation of the line tangent to the graph of f at the point (1/4, –3).

Answer: $y = 12x - 6$

70. For the function $f(x) = 6x^2 - 3x + 7$, find $f'(x)$ by using the definition of the derivative.

Answer: $f'(x) = 12x - 3$

71. For the function $f(x) = \frac{1}{2}x^2 + 3x$, find $f'(x)$ by using the definition of the derivative.

Answer: $f'(x) = x + 3$

72. The formula $n = 5{,}000 + 10t + t^2$ gives the number of n bacteria in a colony t hours after the colony was established.
   a. Find the derivative (growth rate) function using the definition of the derivative.
   b. Find the rate at which the bacteria are increasing at the end of 5 hours.

Answer: a. $n'(t) = 10 + 2t$ b. 20 per hour

73. The number of seeds, s, dispersed by a flower each day over a 20-day period is $s(d) = -d^2 + 20d$.
   a. Find the derivative (rate of change) function for the seeds using the definition of the derivative.
   b. Find the rate of change of the number of seeds dispersed after 8 days.

Answer: a. $s'(d) = -2d + 20$ b. 4 seeds per day

Section 2.3 Some Differentiation Formulas

MULTIPLE CHOICE 2.3

[a] 74. Find the derivative of the function $f(x) = x^{100}$.

a. $100x^{99}$ b. 100 c. x^{99} d. $-100x^{99}$

[c] 75. Find the derivative of the function $f(x) = x^{\frac{1}{5}}$.

a. $\frac{1}{5}x$ b. $\frac{1}{5}x^{\frac{4}{5}}$ c. $\frac{1}{5x^{\frac{4}{5}}}$ d. $\frac{4}{x^{\frac{1}{5}}}$

[b] 76. Find the derivative of the function $f(x) = 4x^4 - 5x^3 + 2x - 3$.

a. $4x^3 - 5x^2 + 2$ b. $16x^3 - 15x^2 + 2$ c. $16x^3 - 15x^2 + 2x - 3$ d. $4x^4 - 5x^3 + 2x$

[d] 77. Find the derivative of the function $f(x) = -x - \frac{1}{x}$.

a. $-1 - x$ b. $-1 + x$ c. $\frac{x^2 - 1}{x^2}$ d. $-\frac{x^2 - 1}{x^2}$

[b] 78. Find the derivative of the function $f(x) = \sqrt[5]{x}$.

a. $\frac{1}{5x}$ b. $\frac{1}{5x^{\frac{4}{5}}}$ c. $\frac{4}{x^{\frac{4}{5}}}$ d. $\frac{x^{\frac{4}{5}}}{5}$

[a] 79. If $y = 2\pi\sqrt{x} - \pi x + \pi$, then dy/dx =

a. $\left(\frac{\pi}{\sqrt{x}}\right) - \pi$ b. $\pi - 1$ c. $2\pi x + 1$ d. $\pi\sqrt{x} - \pi$

[d] 80. If $f(x) = x - \frac{1}{x} + \frac{1}{x^2}$, then $f'(1) =$

a. 1 b. $\frac{1}{3}$ c. $\frac{1}{2}$ d. 0

[c] 81. What is the slope of the line tangent to the graph of $y = \frac{1}{3}x^3 + 7x$ at the point (6, 93)?

a. 22/3 b. 93 c. 43 d. 36

[b] 82. The point on the graph of $y = 0.2x^2 - 7x + 13$ where the slope of the tangent line is 0.4 is

a. (18.5, 0) b. (18.5, –48.05) c. (18.5, 0.4) d. (2/37, 0)

One of the acts in a circus is a human cannonball. The height of the human cannonball above the ground is $s(t) = -16t^2 + 80t$, where height is measured in feet and time in seconds.

[d] 83. How high is the human cannonball after 1 second?

a. 112 feet b. 96 feet c. 84 feet d. 64 feet.

[b] 84. How fast is the human cannonball rising at the end of 1 second?

a. 16 feet/second b. 48 feet/second c. 64 feet/second d. 72 feet/second

The formula $n = 1500 + 5t + t^3$ gives the number n of bacteria in a colony t hours after the colony was established.

[b] 85. At the very start of the observation, the number of bacteria was

a. 0
b. 1500
c. 1506
d. impossible to determine

[c] 86. The growth rate at the end of 5 hours is

a. 90 b. 1650 c. 80 d. 125

[a] 87. The number of bacteria present at the end of 5 hours is

a. 1650 b. 7500 c. 37,650 d. 1750

The number of sales of oil-burning furnaces is given by the formula $n = -x^2 + 30x + 10$, where x is the number of months the furnace distributor has been in business.

[b] 88. The number of furnaces sold in the sixth month of business was

a. 190 b. 154 c. 42 d. 18

[d] 89. The rate at which sales were changing in the sixth month was

a. 190 b. 154 c. 42 d. 18

Counted in hundreds, the number of weeks n in a lawn x weeks after a weed killer was applied is given by $n(x) = -x^2 + 2x + 3$.

[b] 90. The number of weeds in the lawn just before the weed killer was applied is

a. 0 b. 300 c. 500 d. 600

[b] 91. The number of weeds in the lawn 1 week after the weed killer was applied is

a. 300 b. 400 c. 500 d. 600

[c] 92. The rate of change of the number of weeds in the lawn at the end of the first week is
a. 100 b. 200 c. 0 d. -100

[b] 93. If the revenue function is $R(x) = 4.3x - 0.003x^2$ and the cost function is $C(x) = 3.1x + 4276$, then the number of units that makes the marginal revenue equal to the marginal cost is

a. 215 b. 200 c. 225 d. 257

The revenue from the sale of x electric pencil sharpeners is $R(x) = 23x + 0.03x^2$ dollars.

[c] 94. The revenue from the sale of 45 sharpeners is

a. $3060.00 b. $589.75 c. $1095.75 d. $1035.00

[d] 95. Use the marginal revenue function to approximate revenue from the sale of the 46th sharpener.

a. $25.73 b. $25.77 c. $25.76 d. $25.70

[d] 96. $MR(110) = R'(110) = 29.6$ means

a. The revenue from the sale of 110 sharpeners is $29.60.
b. The revenue from the sale of the 111th sharpener is $29.60.
c. The approximate revenue from the sale of the 110th sharpener is $29.60.
d. The approximate revenue from the sale of the 111th sharpener is $29.60.

A company that produces and sells cellular telephones determines that the cost of producing x telephones is $C(x) = 0.45x^2 - 15x + 250$ dollars and that the revenue from the sale of x telephones is $R(x) = 0.35x^2 - 7x$ dollars.

[d] 97. The marginal profit function is $MP(x) =$

a. $0.8x^2 - 23x + 2500$ b. $8x - 0.1x^2 - 2500$ c. $1.6x - 23$ d. $8 - 0.2x$

[a] 98. The profit from the production and sale of x cellular phones is $P(x) = 80x - 0.1x^2 - 250$ dollars. The approximate profit from the production and sale of the 101st telephone is

a. $60.00 b. $59.80 c. $59.85 d. $69.90

[d] 99. The difference between the approximate and the exact profit from producing and selling the 101st telephone is

a. $10.00 b. $0.01 c. $0.05 d. $0.10

[d] 100. $MP(75) = 65$ means

a. The exact profit from the production and sale of the 75th telephone is $65.
b. The approximate profit from the production and sale of the 75th telephone is $65.
c. The exact profit from the production and sale of the 76th telephone is $65.
d. The approximate profit from the production and sale of the 76th telephone is $65.

A hammock maker estimates that its hammocks can be priced at $p = 75 - 0.85x$ dollars each, where x is the number sold. The cost to produce x hammocks is $300 + 45x - 0.35x^2$.

[c] 101. What is the marginal profit when 5 hammocks are sold?

a. $30.50 b. $83.75 c. $25.00 d. $70.75

[d] 102. What is the marginal profit when 25 hammocks are sold?

a. $16.75 b. $3.50 c. $32.50 d. $5.00

SHORT ANSWER 2.3

103. Find the derivative of the function $f(x) = 12\sqrt{x^3} - \frac{1}{x}$.

Answer: $18x^{\frac{1}{2}} + x^{-2}$

104. Find the derivative of the function $f(x) = 6\sqrt[3]{x^5} - \frac{1}{x^2}$.

Answer: $10x^{\frac{2}{3}} + 2x^{-3}$

105. Find the derivative of the function $f(x) = 3x^{-3} - 2x^{-2} + x^{-1} + 1$.

Answer: $\frac{-9}{x^4} + \frac{4}{x^3} - \frac{1}{x^2}$

106. Find $\frac{d}{dx}\left(\frac{x^7}{7} - \frac{x^5}{5} - \frac{x^3}{3} - x\right)$

Answer: $x^6 - x^4 - x^2 - 1$

107. If $y = 2.4x^{-3} - 6.5x^{-2} + 13.7x^{-1} + 12.3$, then $D_x y =$

Answer: $\frac{-7.2}{x^4} + \frac{13}{x^3} - \frac{13.7}{x^2}$

108. If $y = \frac{5}{4x^2}$, then

a. $y' =$
b. the slope of the tangent to the graph of y at $x = -1$ is
c. the y-coordinate of the point on the graph where $x = -1$ is
d. the equation of the line tangent to the graph of y at $x = -1$ is

Answer: a. $\frac{-5}{2x^3}$ b. $\frac{5}{2}$ c. $\frac{5}{4}$ d. $10x - 4y = -15$

109. If $f(x) = 2x^4$, then $f'(-2) =$

Answer: –64

110. If $f(x) = \frac{2}{x^3}$, then $\left.\frac{df}{dx}\right|_{x=-3} =$

Answer: $-\frac{2}{27}$

111. A country's population x years from now is predicted to be $P(x) = 10{,}000{,}000 - 9{,}000x + 500x^2 + 100x^3$. Find the rate of change of the population 10 years from now and interpret your answer.

Answer: 31,000; 10 years from now, the population will be growing at the rate of 31,000 per year.

112. An automobile company's cost function is $16{,}000\sqrt{x} + 4{,}800\sqrt[3]{x} + 800$ dollars, where x is the number of cars produced each day. Find the marginal cost when 64 cars are produced each day, and interpret your answer.

Answer: \$1,100; When 64 cars are produced each day, there is approximately \$1,100 cost per additional car.

113. Records indicate that x years after 1990, the average property tax on a 3-bedroom home in a certain Texas community was $T(x) = 20x^2 + 40x + 600$ dollars. At what rate was the property tax increasing in 1995?

Answer: \$240 per year

114. One of the acts in a circus is a human cannonball. The height of the human cannonball above the ground is $s(t) = -16t^2 + 80t$, where height is measured in feet and time in seconds. The vertical velocity of the human cannonball at the end of 2 seconds is 16 feet per second, and at the end of 3 seconds it is -16 feet per second. Why are one of those velocities positive and the other negative?

Answer: The positive velocity reflects the fact that the human cannonball is rising, and the negative velocity indicates that the human cannonball is falling.

115. The formula $n = 1500 + 5t + t^3$ gives the number n of bacteria in a colony t hours after the colony was established. If r represents the rate of growth of the bacteria at any time t, then the formula for r is

Answer: $r = 5 + 3t^2$

The number of sales of oil-burning furnaces is given by the formula $n = -x^2 + 30x + 10$, where x is the number of months the furnace distributor has been in business.

116. If r represents the rate at which sales are changing for any month x, then the formula for r is

Answer: $r = -2x + 30$

117. During what month will the rate of change of sales be 20 furnaces per month?

Answer: 5

Counted in hundreds, the number of weeks n in a lawn x weeks after a weed killer was applied is given by $n(x) = -x^2 + 2x + 3$.

118. Find the function r that describes the rate at which the number of weeds is changing.

Answer: $r(x) = -2x + 2$

119. What is the rate of change after ½ week? What does this result mean?

Answer: $r(\frac{1}{2}) = 1$. After ½ week, the number of weeds is still growing at the rate of 100 weeds per week.

120. What is the rate of change after 2 weeks? What does this result mean?

Answer: $r(2) = -2$. After 2 weeks, the weeds are disappearing at the rate of 200 weeds per week.

121. How many weeds are in the lawn at the end of the third week?

Answer: 0

122. What is the marginal cost function for the cost function $C(x) = 200 + 35x - 0.4x^2$?

Answer: $MC(x) = 35 - 0.8x$

123. If $P(x) = 135x + 0.3x^2 - 0.006x^3$, what is the marginal profit function?

Answer: $MP(x) = 135 + 0.6x - 0.018x^2$

The revenue from the sale of x electric pencil sharpeners is $R(x) = 23x + 0.03x^2$ dollars.

124. What is the revenue from the sale of 75 sharpeners?

Answer: $1893.75

125. What is the approximate revenue from the sale of the 76th sharpener?

Answer: $27.50

A company that produces and sells cellular telephones determines that the cost of producing x telephones is $C(x) = 0.45x^2 - 15x + 250$ dollars and that the revenue from the sale of x telephones is $R(x) = 0.35x^2 - 7x$ dollars.

126. Determine the profit function.

Answer: $-0.1x^2 + 8x - 250$

127. What production level results in a marginal profit of zero?

Answer: 40

A hammock maker estimates that its hammocks can be priced at $p = 75 - 0.85x$ dollars each, where x is the number sold. The cost to produce x hammocks is $300 + 45x - 0.35x^2$.

128. Determine the marginal profit function.

Answer: $MP(x) = -x + 30$

129. What production level results in a marginal profit of zero?

Answer: 30

Section 2.4 The Product and Quotient Rules

MULTIPLE CHOICE 2.4

[b] 130. If $f(x) = (3 - x^3)(2 + x^2)$, then $f'(x) = ?$

a. $5x - 6x^2 + 6x^4$ b. $6x - 6x^2 - 5x^4$ c. $6x + 5x^2 - 6x^4$ d. $5x + 6x^2 + 6x^4$

[d] 131. If $y = \dfrac{8x^3}{13x - 5}$, then $\dfrac{dy}{dx} = ?$

a. $\dfrac{24x^2}{13}$ b. $\dfrac{8x^2(52x - 15)}{(13x - 5)^2}$ c. $\dfrac{24x^2}{(13x - 5)^2}$ d. $\dfrac{8x^2(26x - 15)}{(13x - 5)^2}$

[a] 132. The slope of the line tangent to the graph of $f(x) = (x^3 - 4)(1 - x)$ at the point (2, –4) is

a. –16 b. 124.8 c. 53.1 d. -108

[b] 133. The equation of the line tangent to the graph of $f(x) = (9x^3 - 1.2)(2.5 - x)$ at the point (2, 35.4) is

a. $168x - 10y + 180 = 0$ b. $168x + 10y = 690$
c. $168x + 10y + 690 = 0$ d. $168x - 10y = 180$

[c] 134. The slope of the line tangent to the graph of $f(x) = \dfrac{x^2 + 1}{2x + 1}$ at the point (2, 1) is

a. $\dfrac{6}{5}$ b. $-\dfrac{6}{5}$ c. $\dfrac{2}{5}$ d. $-\dfrac{2}{5}$

[d] 135. The equation of the line tangent to the graph of $f(x) = \dfrac{x^2 + 1}{2x + 1}$ at the point (2, 1) is

a. $2x + 5y - 9 = 0$ b. $2x - 5y - 1 = 0$ c. $2x + 5y + 9 = 0$ d. $2x - 5y + 1 = 0$

[c] 136. If $y = (8x^3 - 6.3)(3.7 - x^2)$, then the instantaneous rate of change of y with respect to x when x= –1 is

a. –38.61 b. 4.59 c. 36.2 d. 48

[b] 137. If $y = \frac{4x^2 - \frac{2}{3}}{3x - 5}$, then the instantaneous rate of change of y with respect to x when $x = 2$ is

a. $\frac{16}{3}$ b. –30 c. 30 d. 62

[c] 138. A self-propelled machine travels such that after t minutes its distance in yards from a starting point is $s = \frac{5t^2}{t+1}$, $0 \le t \le 60$. The machine's instantaneous rate of change after 9 minutes is

a. 4.5 yards/minute b. 130.5 yards/minute c. 4.95 yards/minute d. 17.5 yards/minute

[a] 139. A battery-powered toy travels such that after t minutes its distance in feet from a starting point is $s = \frac{8t^2 - 1}{t+2}$, $1 \le t \le 10$. The toy's instantaneous rate of change after 6 minutes is

a. 7.5 feet/minute b. 12.0 feet/minute c. 19.5 feet/minute d. 27.0 feet/minute

[c] 140. If $r = r(x)$ and $s = s(x)$, then $\frac{d}{dx}(r \cdot s) = ?$

a. $rs + r's'$ b. $r's - rs'$ c. $rs' + r's$ d. $rr' + ss'$

[a] 141. If $r = r(x)$ and $s = s(x)$, then $D_x\left(\frac{r}{s}\right) = ?$

a. $\frac{r's - s'r}{s^2}$ b. $\frac{rs' - sr'}{s^2}$ c. $\frac{r's - s'r}{r^2}$ d. $\frac{rs' - sr'}{r^2}$

[c] 142. If $f(3) = 7$, $g(3) = 19$, $f'(3) = 4$, and $g'(3) = -2$, then $\frac{d}{dx}(f \cdot g)(3) = ?$

a. –90 b. –8 c. 62 d. 8

[d] 143. If $f(3) = 2$, $g(3) = 9$, $f'(3) = -5$ and $g'(3) = -7$, then $\frac{d}{dx}\left(\frac{f}{g}\right)(3)$?

a. $-\frac{59}{81}$ b. $\frac{5}{7}$ c. $-\frac{31}{4}$ d. $-\frac{31}{81}$

SHORT ANSWER 2.4

144. If $y=\left(\frac{1}{4}x^2+\frac{2}{3}x-6\right)\left(\frac{1}{5}x^3-7\right)$, then y' = ?

Answer: $\frac{1}{4}x^4+\frac{8}{15}x^3-\frac{18}{5}x^2-\frac{7}{2}x-\frac{14}{3}$

145. Find $D_x\left(2x^3(1.8x^2-8.4x+135)\right)$.

Answer: $18x^4-67.2x^3+810x^2$

146. Given $y=\left(x+\sqrt{x}\right)\left(x^2-\frac{1}{x}\right)$, find y'. Do not simplify your answer. However, your answer should not show negative or fractional exponents.

Answer: $y'=\left(x+\sqrt{x}\right)\left(2x+\frac{1}{x^2}\right)+\left(x^2-\frac{1}{x}\right)\left[1+\frac{1}{2\sqrt{x}}\right]$

147. Find $f'(t)$ if $f(t)=\frac{3t^2-7t+13}{4t-1}$.

Answer: $f'(t)=\frac{3(4t^2-2t-15)}{4t-1}$

148. If $y=\frac{x^2+1}{x^3+1}$, find y'.

Answer: $y'=\frac{-x^4-3x^2+2x}{(x^3+1)^2}$

149. Find the marginal cost function that corresponds to the cost function $C(x)=\frac{7x^2-3.2x+3.5}{x-0.4}$.

Answer: $MC(x)=C'(x)=\frac{7x^2-5.6x-2.22}{(x-0.4)^2}$

A company selling laser disc players has determined that the profit, in dollars, from the sale of x players is approximately $P(x) = \frac{12x^2 - 36x}{x+2}$.

150. What is the profit from the sale of 3 players?

Answer: 0

151. What is the profit from the sale of 8 players?

Answer: $48

152. What is the marginal profit function?

Answer: $MP(x) = P'(x) = \frac{12(x^2 + 4x - 6)}{(x+2)^2}$

The amount of a drug, in milligrams, in the bloodstream t hours after the drug was injected is given by $d(t) = \frac{0.2t}{t^2 + 1}$.

153. How many milligrams are still in the blood after 1 hour?

Answer: 0.1

154. Find $d'(2)$ and explain the result.

Answer: $d'(2) = -0.024$. This is the rate at which the drug is leaving the bloodstream at the end of 2 hours.

The number of subscribers to a new magazine t months after initial publication is $n(t) = \frac{10{,}388t}{3.5t + 7}$.

155. How many subscribers are there after 2 months?

Answer: 1484

156. After 2 months, at what rate is the number of subscribers changing?

Answer: 371

157. One hour after x milligrams of a particular drug are given to a person, the change in body temperature T is given by $T(x) = \left[1 - \frac{x}{9}\right]x^2$. Find the instantaneous rate at which the temperature is changing after 1 hours when a dose of 3 milligrams of the drug is given. Interpret your answer.

Answer: 3; body temperature is increasing at a rate of 3°F/hr.

158. The number of portable CD players that a store will sell at a price of p dollars each is $N(p) = \frac{50{,}000}{p+10}$. Find the instantaneous rate of change of the number of CD players sold when the price is $40, and interpret your answer.

Answer: –20; sales are decreasing by approximately 20 CD players for each $1 price increase.

A company's profit function is $P(x) = 2x^2 + 4x - 200$ dollars.

159. Find the average profit function $AP(x) = \frac{P(x)}{x}$.

Answer: $AP(x) = 2x + 4 - \frac{200}{x}$

160. Find the marginal average profit function $MAP(x)$.

Answer: $MAP(x) = 2 + \frac{200}{x^2}$

161. Evaluate $MAP(x)$ at $x = 10$.

Answer: $MAP(10) = \$4$

Section 2.5 Higher Order Derivatives

MULTIPLE CHOICE 2.5

[a] 162. Evaluate $\frac{d^2}{dx^2}\left[\frac{3}{x}\right]\Bigg|_{x=2}$

a. $\frac{3}{4}$ b. $-\frac{9}{8}$ c. $-\frac{9}{4}$ d. $\frac{3}{8}$

[c] 163. For the cost function $C(x) = x^4 - x^3 + 14x + 15$, the rate of change of the marginal cost when 5 items are produced is

a. 585 b. 429 c. 270 d. 330

[d] 164. Find f″(x) for the function $f(x) = \frac{x+3}{x-1}$.

a. 0 b. $\frac{-8}{(x-1)^3}$ c. $\frac{-4}{(x-1)^3}$ d. $\frac{8}{(x-1)^3}$

[a] 165. Find f″(x) for the function $f(x) = \frac{-x+1}{2-x}$.

a. $\frac{-2}{(2-x)^3}$ b. 1 c. $\frac{2}{(2-x)^3}$ d. $\frac{-2}{(2-x)^2}$

[a] 166. Find f″(x) for the function $f(x) = \frac{x+2}{x-3}$.

a. $\frac{10}{(x-3)^3}$ b. 0 c. $\frac{-10}{(x-3)^3}$ d. $\frac{2}{(x-3)^3}$

[a] 167. Find f″(x) for the function $f(x) = \frac{2}{\sqrt{6x}}$.

a. $\frac{54}{(6x)^{\frac{5}{2}}}$ b. $\frac{-6}{(6x)^{\frac{3}{2}}}$ c. $\frac{12}{(6x)^{\frac{5}{2}}}$ d. $\frac{-9}{(6x)^{\frac{3}{2}}}$

[d] 168. Evaluate $\frac{d^2}{dx^2}\left[\frac{1}{x}-\frac{1}{\sqrt{x}}\right]\Bigg|_{x=1}$.

a. 1

b. 0

c. $-\frac{1}{2}$

d. $\frac{5}{4}$

SHORT ANSWER 2.5

169. For the function $f(x) = 2x^4 - 3x^3 + 2x^2 - x + 6$, find $f'(x)$, $f''(x)$, and $f'''(x)$.

Answer: $f'(x) = 8x^3 - 9x^2 + 4x - 1$, $f''(x) = 24x^2 - 18x + 4$, $f'''(x) = 48x - 18$

170. For the function $f(x) = 1 + x + \frac{1}{2}x^2 + \frac{1}{6}x^4 + \frac{1}{120}x^5 + \frac{1}{720}x^6$, find $f'(x)$, $f''(x)$, and $f'''(x)$.

Answer: $f'(x) = 1 + x + \frac{2}{3}x^3 + \frac{1}{24}x^4 + \frac{1}{120}x^5$, $f''(x) = 1 + \frac{2}{3}x^2 + \frac{1}{6}x^3 + \frac{1}{24}x^4$,
$f'''(x) = 4x + \frac{1}{2}x^2 + \frac{1}{6}x^3$

171. For the function $f(x) = \frac{2x+1}{x}$, find $f''(x)$.

Answer: $f''(x) = \frac{2}{x^3}$

172. For the function $f(x) = \frac{x-1}{2x}$, find $f''(x)$.

Answer: $f''(x) = -\frac{1}{x^3}$

173. For the function $f(x) = 5\sqrt{x} + \frac{3}{x^2} + \frac{1}{3\sqrt{x}} + \frac{1}{2}$, find $f''(x)$.

Answer: $f''(x) = \frac{-5}{4x^{\frac{3}{2}}} + \frac{18}{x^4} + \frac{1}{4x^{\frac{5}{2}}}$

174. For the function $f(x) = 3x^{-2} + 4x^{-1} - 18$, find $f''(x)$.

Answer: $f''(x) = \frac{18}{x^4} + \frac{8}{x^3}$

175. For the function $f(x) = 2x^{-2} - 8x^{\frac{3}{2}}$, find $f''(x)$.

Answer: $f''(x) = \frac{12}{x^4} - \frac{6}{x^{\frac{1}{2}}}$

176. Evaluate $\frac{d^2}{dr^2}\left[4\pi r^2\right]$.

Answer: 8π

177. Evaluate $\frac{d^2}{dr^2}\left[\frac{8}{3}\pi r^3\right]$

Answer: $16\pi r$

178. Evaluate $\left.\frac{d^2}{dx^2}\left[x^{12}\right]\right|_{x=1}$

Answer: 132

179. Find the rate of change of $f'(x)$ for the function $f(x) = x^3 - 7x^2$.

Answer: $6x - 14$

180. Find the rate of change of $f'(x)$ for the function $f(x) = 6x^{\frac{3}{2}}$ at $x = 1$.

Answer: 4.5

181. The weekly cost to produce x thousand political campaign buttons is $C(x) = 0.4x^3 + 0.02x^2 + 15x + 25$. Determine the rate of change of the marginal cost when 5 (thousand) buttons are produced.

Answer: 12.04

182. For the revenue function $R(x) = 50x + \frac{10}{x}$, determine the rate at which the marginal revenue is changing when 20 items are sold.

Answer: $\frac{1}{400}$

183. For the revenue function $R(x) = 375x - 0.25x^3$, determine the rate at which the marginal revenue is changing when 50 items are sold.

Answer: -75

184. A rocket rises to a height of $h(t) = 10t^2 + 9t^{\frac{4}{3}}$ feet in t seconds. Find the rocket's velocity and acceleration at time $t = 8$ seconds.

Answer: velocity at $t = 8$ is 184 ft/sec; acceleration at $t = 8$ is 21 ft/sec^2

185. An experimental rocket travels $\frac{8}{3}t^3 + 200t$ feet in t seconds. What is the acceleration of the rocket at the end of 5 seconds?

Answer: 80

186. A car in an amusement park ride travels according to the function $s(t) = -t^3 + 60t^2$, where t is measured in seconds $(0 \le t \le 60)$ and $s(t)$ in feet. What is the car's acceleration at the end of 15 seconds?

Answer: 30

187. A country's gross national product (GNP) t years from now is predicted to be $g(t) = 40 + 27t^{\frac{5}{3}}$ million dollars. Find $g'(8)$ and $g''(8)$ and interpret your answers.

Answer: $g'(8) = 180$; GNP is growing at the rate of \$180 million per year 8 years from now.
$g''(8) = 15$; GNP's rate of growth is increasing by \$15 million per year each year.

188. A country's defense budget t years from now is to be $D(t) = 65 + 8t^{\frac{3}{2}}$ million dollars. Find $D'(4)$ and $D''(4)$ and interpret your answers.

Answer: $D'(4) = 24$; 4 years from now, the defense budget will be growing by \$24 million per year.
$D''(4) = 3$; 4 years from now, the rate of growth of the defense budget will be increasing at a rate of \$3 million per year each year.

Section 2.6 The Chain Rule and the Generalized Power Rule

MULTIPLE CHOICE 2.6

[b] 189. Use the generalized power rule to find the derivative of the function $f(x) = (3x^2 - 2x)^{-9}$.

a. $-9(6x-2)^{-10}$
b. $-9(3x^2-2x)^{-10}(6x-2)$
c. $-9(3x^2-2x)^{-10}$
d. $-9(3x^2-2x)^{-8}(6x-2)$

[c] 190. Use the generalized power rule to find the derivative of the function $f(x) = \sqrt{x^2 - 2x + 1}$.

a. $2x-2$
b. $\frac{1}{2}(x^2-2x+1)^{-\frac{1}{2}}$
c. $\frac{1}{2}(x^2-2x+1)^{-\frac{1}{2}}(2x-2)$
d. $\frac{1}{2}(2x-2)^{-\frac{1}{2}}$

[c] 191. Use the generalized power rule to find the derivative of the function $f(x) = (2x^2+5)^7$.

a. $7(4x)^6$
b. $(4x)^7$
c. $28x(2x^2+5)^6$
d. $7(2x^2+5)^6$

[c] 192. The slope of the line tangent to $y = \sqrt{3x+1}$ at (8, 5) is

a. $\frac{1}{2}$
b. $\frac{3}{5}$
c. $\frac{3}{10}$
d. $\frac{2}{5}$

[a] 193. What is the rate of change of y with respect to x at x = 5 if $y = \dfrac{7.2}{(x-4.8)^2}$?

a. –1800
b. –360
c. 180
d. –180

[d] 194. Use the generalized power rule to find the derivative of the function $f(x) = (x^3+7)^9(6x-1)^4$.

a. $36(x^3+7)^8(6x-1)^3$
b. $18x^2(x^3+7)^8(6x-1)^3$
c. $18(x^2+2)(x^3+7)^8(6x-1)^3$
d. $3(x^3+7)^8(6x-1)^3(62x^3-9x^2+56)$

SHORT ANSWER 2.6

195. Use the generalized power rule to find the derivative of the function $f(x)=\frac{1}{\left(1-x^2\right)^4}$

Answer: $\frac{8x}{\left(1-x^2\right)^5}$

196. Use the generalized power rule to find the derivative of the function $f(x)=(x+2)^3(2x-1)^5$.

Answer: $(x+2)^2(2x-1)^4(16x+17)$

197. Use the generalized power rule to find the derivative of the function $f(x)=\left[\left(x^2-9\right)^4+x^4\right]^3$.

Answer: $3\left[\left(x^2-9\right)^4+x^4\right]^2\left[8x\left(x^2-9\right)^3+4x^3\right]$

198. Use the generalized power rule to find the derivative of the function $f(x)=\left[\frac{2x-1}{2x+1}\right]^5$.

Answer: $\frac{20(2x-1)^4}{(2x+1)^6}$

199. Use the generalized power rule to find the derivative of the function $f(x)=\frac{(x+3)^2}{x-1}$.

Answer: $\frac{(x+3)(x-5)}{(x-1)^2}$

200. Use the generalized power rule to find the derivative of the function $f(x)=\frac{x^2+4x}{(x+2)^2}$.

Answer: $\frac{8}{(x+2)^3}$

201. Use the generalized power rule to find the derivative of the function $f(x)=x^3\sqrt{2x+1}$.

Answer: $\frac{x^2(7x+3)}{\sqrt{2x+1}}$

202. Find $f''(x)$ if $f(x) = (2x-3)^5$.

Answer: $80(2x-3)^3$

203. The daily profit, in hundreds of dollars, a company earns from producing x items is given by $P(x) = \sqrt{1200x - x^3}$. What is the marginal profit when the production level is 10 units per day?

Answer: $429.06

204. If $100 is invested at an interest rate of i compounded semiannually, the amount in the account at the end of 5 years is given by $A = 100\left[1 + \frac{i}{200}\right]^{10}$. Find $\frac{dA}{di}$ at $i = 6$ and interpret your result.

Answer: $\left.\frac{dA}{di}\right|_{i=6} = 6.52$; When the interest rate is 6%, the account increases by an amount of $6.52 for each 1% increase in interest rate.

205. A small town has changed its zoning bylaws to allow more land to be developed for commercial use. It is estimated that the increase I in the town's tax base in hundreds of dollars, due to the zoning change, after t years is given by $I(t) = 5t\sqrt{2t+1}$. At the end of 12 years, what is the annual rate of change of the town's tax base?

Answer: $I'(12) = \$3700$

206. Determine the marginal cost function for $C(x) = \frac{x^2}{4.1x-1} + 13.7$.

Answer: $MC(x) = C'(x) = \frac{x(4.1x-2)}{(4.1x-1)^2}$

207. The revenue from the sale of x units is $R(x) = \sqrt{x^2 + 15x}$ hundreds of dollars.

a. What is the revenue from 5 units?
b. At what rate is the revenue changing when $x = 5$?

Answer: a. $1000 (that is, 10 hundreds) b. $125 (that is, 1.25 hundreds)

208. The depth of a weight sinking into a vat of thick syrup is $s = \sqrt{3t}$, where t is the time in seconds $(t \geq 1)$ and s is measured in inches.

a. What is the depth of the weight after 12 seconds?
b. At what rate is the weight sinking at the end of 12 seconds?

Answer: a. 6 inches. b. ¼ inch/second

209. An antibacterial agent has been introduced into a colony of bacteria. The number of bacteria n in the colony t minutes after the agent was introduced is given by $n(t) = 500(100 - 5t)^2$.

a. How many bacteria were in the colony when the agent was introduced?
b. How many bacteria are alive after 10 minutes?
c. What is the rate of change of the number of bacteria after 10 minutes?

Answer: a. 5,000,000 b. 1,250,000 c. –250,000

Section 2.7 Nondifferentiable Functions

MULTIPLE CHOICE 2.7

[c] 210. For the following graphed function, state the x-values for which the derivative $f'(x)$ does not exist.

a. $x=-1, x=0, x=2$ b. $x=-1, x=2$ c. $f'(x)$ exists for all x d. $x=0$

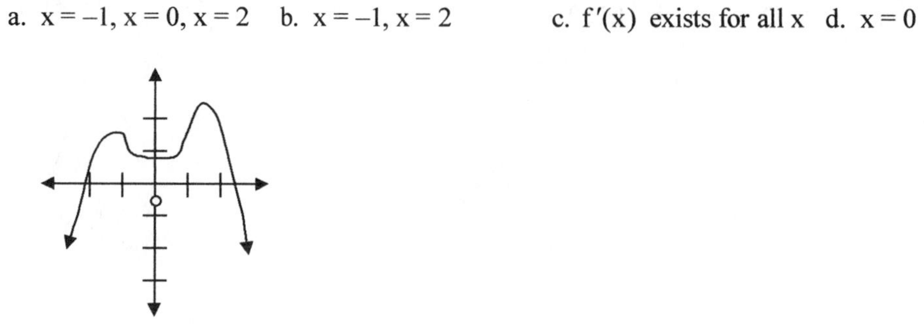

[b] 211. For the following graphed function, state the x-values for which the derivative $f'(x)$ does not exist.

a. $f'(x)$ exists for all x b. $x=-2, x=2$ c. $x=2$ only d. $x=-2$ only

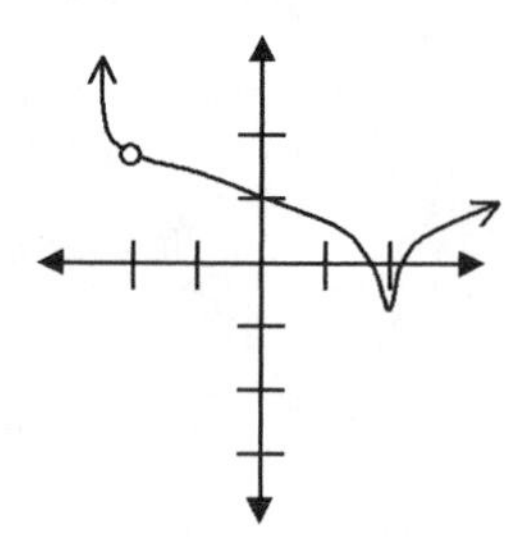

[c] 212. For the following graphed function, state the x-values for which the derivative $f'(x)$ does not exist.

a. $x=-2, x=2$ b. $f'(x)$ exists for all x c. $x=-2, x=1, x=2$ d. $x=1$

SHORT ANSWER 2.7

213. For the following graphed function, state the x-values for which the derivative $f'(x)$ does not exist.

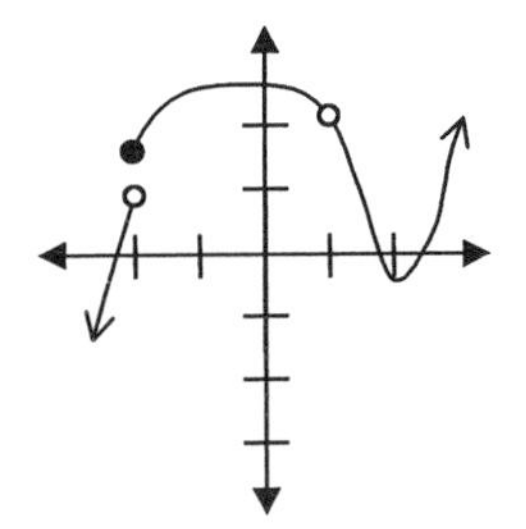

Answer: $x = -2, x = 1$

214. For the following graphed function, state the x-values for which the derivative $f'(x)$ does not exist.

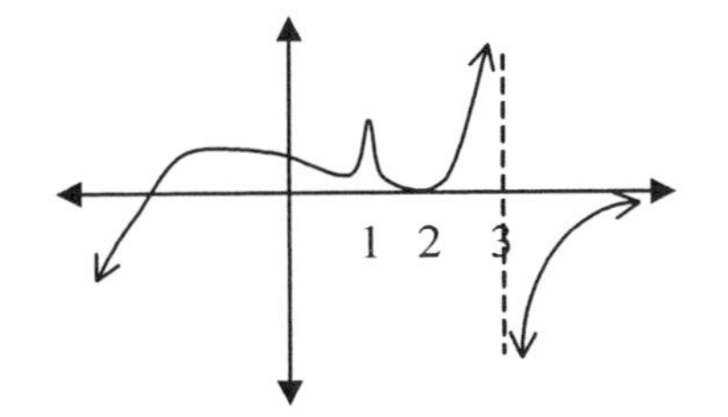

Answer: $x = 1, x = 3$

Chapter 2 – Graphing Calculator

Derivatives and Their Uses

Section 2.1 Limits and Continuity

1. Use a graphing calculator with a table feature to find the limit.

$$\lim_{x \to 3.25}\left[\frac{x^3 - 34.328125}{x - 3.25}\right]$$

Answer: 31.6875

2. Use a graphing calculator with a table feature to find the limit.

$$\lim_{x \to 36}\frac{x^{1.5} - 36x^{0.5}}{x^{1.5} - 6x}$$

Answer: $\frac{4}{3}$

3. Use a graphing calculator with a table feature to find the limit.

$$\lim_{x \to 1}\frac{x^2 + 2x + 1}{x^2 - x}$$

Answer: limit does not exist

4. Use a graphing calculator with a table feature to find the limit.

$$\lim_{x \to 1}\frac{x^2 - 2x + 1}{x^2 - x}$$

Answer: 0

5. Use a graphing calculator with a table feature to find the limit.

$$\lim_{x \to 5}\sqrt{x^2 - 9}$$

Answer: 4

6. Use a graphing calculator with a table feature to find the limit.

$$\lim_{x \to 8} \frac{\sqrt{2x+1}}{2x+1}$$

Answer: 0.295

7. Use a graphing calculator with a table feature to find the limit.

$$\lim_{x \to 2} \frac{\frac{1}{x} - \frac{1}{2}}{x-2}$$

Answer: –0.25

8. Use a graphing calculator with a table feature to find the limit.

$$\lim_{x \to -4} \frac{2x+8}{x^2+x-12}$$

Answer: –0.286

9. Use a graphing calculator with a table feature to find the limit.

$$\lim_{x \to 4} \frac{2-x}{x^2-2x-8}$$

Answer: limit does not exist

10. Use a graphing calculator with a table feature to find the limit.

$$\lim_{x \to 0} \frac{|x|}{x}$$

Answer: limit does not exist

11. If you deposit $1 into a bank paying 3% interest compounded continuously, a year later its value will be

$$\lim_{x \to 0} \left[1+\frac{x}{33}\right]^{\frac{1}{x}}$$

Use a graphing calculator to make tables to find this limit correct to 2 decimal places, thereby finding the value of the deposit in dollars/cents.

Answer: $1.03

12. Determine whether the function $f(x) = \frac{2x-1}{x+5}$ is continuous or discontinuous. If discontinuous, state where the function is discontinuous.

    Answer: discontinuous at $x = -5$

13. Determine whether the function $f(x) = -|x|$ is continuous or discontinuous. If discontinuous, state where the function is discontinuous.

    Answer: continuous

Section 2.2 Slopes, Rates of Change, and Derivatives

14. Show that the definition of the derivative applied to the function $f(x) = |x - 6.3|$ at $x = 6.3$ gives

    $$f'(6.3) = \lim_{h \to 0} \frac{|h|}{h}$$

    a. Use a calculator to evaluate the difference quotient for values of h: 0.1, 0.01, 0.001, and –0.1, –0.001, –0.001.
    b. Use the results to describe the derivative $f'(x)$ at $x = 6.3$.

    Answer: a. 1, 1, 1, –1, –1, –1
    b. The derivative does not exist.

15. Show that the definition of the derivative applied to the function $f(x) = |2x - 1.7|$ at $x = -0.85$ gives

    $$f'(-0.85) = \lim_{h \to 0} \frac{|h|}{h}$$

    a. Use a calculator to evaluate the difference quotient for values of h: 0.1, 0.01, 0.001, and –0.1, –0.001, –0.001.
    b. Use the results to describe the derivative $f'(x)$ at $x = -0.85$.

    Answer: a. 1, 1, 1, –1, –1, –1
    b. The derivative does not exist.

Section 2.4 – 2.6

16. Given the profit function $P(x) = 0.35x^{3/2} - 5762$, use a graphing calculator to find the difference $P(9{,}000{,}000) - P(8{,}999{,}999)$ and interpret the results.

    Answer: The marginal profit of the 9 millionth item is $1575.35

17. Given the cost function $C(x) = 13.92\sqrt{2.7x - 0.3} + 41.663$, use a graphing calculator to find the difference $C(3{,}000{,}000) - C(2{,}999{,}999)$ and interpret the results.

    Answer: The marginal cost of the 3 millionth item is 0.006602

18. Given the cost function $C(x) = \sqrt{3.1x^2 + 3.5}$, use a graphing calculator to find $\dfrac{C(32{,}333{,}367)}{32{,}333{,}367}$ and interpret the results.

    Answer: The average cost is $1.76 when 32,333,367 units are produced.

19. Given the profit function $P(x) = \sqrt[3]{0.7x^3 + 6.78}$, use a graphing calculator to find $\dfrac{P(4{,}766{,}666)}{4{,}766{,}666}$ and interpret the results.

    Answer: The average profit is $0.89 when 4,766,666 units are produced and sold.

20. A person's temperature after x hours of strenuous exercises is $T(x) = x^3(4 - x^2) + 98.6$ for $0 \le x \le 2$. Use the $\dfrac{dy}{dx}$ or slope feature of your graphing calculator to find the rate of change of the temperature after 1.5 hours.

    Answer: 1.69° per hour

21. A highly infectious skin rash is spreading through a school. The number x of people with the rash at a particular time t is given by $x = 40t - t^2 + 1$, where t is the number of hours since the rash began. Use the slope of $\dfrac{dy}{dx}$ feature on your graphing calculator to find the rate at which the rash is spreading after 10 hours.

    Answer: 20 people per hour

22. A battery-operated toy travels such that after t minutes its distance in feet from a starting point is $s = \dfrac{8t^2 - 1}{t + 2}$. Use the slope or $\dfrac{dy}{dx}$ feature on your calculator to find the toy's velocity (rate of change in distance) after 6 minutes.

    Answer: 7.52 ft/min

23. The position equation for the movement of a particle is given by $s = (t^3 + 1)^2$, where s is measured in feet and t is measured in seconds.
    a. Evaluate s'(1) and s"(1). (Enter the given function as y_1, define y_2 to be the derivative of y_1 using NDERIV, and define y_3 to be the derivative of y_2 then use TRACE.)
    b. Interpret the results in part a.

    Answer: a. s'(1) = 12 ft/sec
    s"(1) = 42, ft/sec^2
    b. s'(1) represents the velocity of the moving particle after 1 second, while s"(1) represent the acceleration of the particle after 1 second.

24. A projectile shot into the air travels according to the equation $s = 100 + 64t - 16t^2$, where s is vertical height in feet and t is time in seconds.
    a. Use NDERIV to find the instantaneous velocity of the projectile after 3 seconds.
    b. Is the projectile rising or falling at this instant?

    Answer: a. –32 ft/sec
    b. falling, since $s'(t) < 0$

25. Graph the cost function $y_1 = \sqrt{6x^2 + 300}$ on the viewing window [0, 10] by [0, 40]. Then use NDERIV to define y_2 as the derivative of y_1.
    a. Evaluate the marginal cost function at x = 5.
    b. Use the TRACE function on y_2 to find the number x of units at which the marginal cost is 0.85.

    Answer: a. 1.414
    b. 2.62

26. Use NDERIV to find the derivative of the function $f(x) = \sqrt{x}$ at x = 0. Is the result correct? (Graph the function given as Y_1. Use NDERIV to define Y_2 as derivative of Y_1. Graph and use TRACE.)

    Answer: The derivative does not exist.

27. The number of enrollments, in thousands, of an HMO is given by $f(x) = 4.32x^{1.4} + 0.217x^{0.83}$ for $0 \le x \le 65$, where x is given in months. Use your graphing calculator to determine f(8.94), f;(8.94), f'(8.94) and f(60), f'(60), f'(60) and interpret the results.

    Answer: After 8.94 months, the HMO has 94,096 members, the membership is increasing at a rate of 14,585 and the change of rate of increase is 648. After 60 months, the membership is 1,339,692 is increasing at a rate of 31,198 and the change of rate of increase is 207.

28. The function $f(x) = 13.7 - 4.3t^{-½}$ for $0 \le t \le 150$ represents the ice cream sales in thousands of dollars over the days of summer. Use your graphing calculator to determine f(1.32), f'(1.32), f'(1.32) and f(149), f'(149), f'(149) and interpret the results.

    Answer: After 1.32 days, sales totaled $9957, were increasing at a rate of $1418 but the rate of increase declined by $1611. After 149 days sales totaled $13,348 and increased at a rate of $1 and the change of rate is 0.

Chapter 3

Further Applications of Derivatives

Section 3.1 Graphing Using the First Derivative

MULTIPLE CHOICE 3.1

[b] 1. The function f(x) has critical values at

a. $x = -1, x = 1, x = 3$ only
b. $x = -1, x = 1, x = 2, x = 3$ only
c. $x = -1, x = 0, x = 1, x = 2, x = 3$
d. $x = 2, x = 3$ only

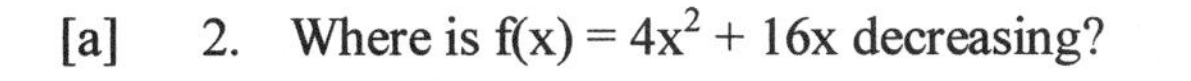

[a] 2. Where is $f(x) = 4x^2 + 16x$ decreasing?

a. $x < -2$
b. $x > 4$
c. $x < 0$
d. all real numbers

[c] 3. The critical value(s) for $f(x) = x^2 - 49$ is (are)

a. $x = 7$
b. $x = 7, x = -7$
c. $x = 0$
d. $x = -7$

[d] 4. Find the values of x that give relative extrema for $f(x) = (x + 1)^2(x - 2)$

a. relative maximum: $x = -1$; relative minimum: $x = 2$
b. relative minimum: $x = 2$
c. relative maximum: $x = 1, x = 3$; relative minimum: $x = 2$
d. relative maximum: $x = -1$; relative minimum: $x = 1$

[b] 5. The relative extrema of $f(x) = 2x^3 - 15x^2 + 36x - 20$ occur at

a. $x = -2$ and $x = -3$
b. $x = 2$ and $x = 3$
c. $x = -2$ and $x = 3$
d. $x = 2$ and $x = -2$

[b] 6. At (0, 0), $f(x) = 2x^3 - 3x^2 - 12x$ is:

a. increasing
b. decreasing
c. neither

[b] 7. At (1, –16), $f(x) = x^3 - 3x^2 - 24x + 10$ is:

a. increasing
b. decreasing
c. neither

[a] 8. At (3, 1), $f(x) = 2x^3 - 3x^2 - 12x + 10$ is:

a. increasing b. decreasing c. neither

[a] 9. Where is $f(x) = 4x^2 + 16x$ decreasing?

a. $x < -2$ b. $x > 4$ c. $x < 0$ d. all real numbers

[d] 10. A stone thrown vertically such that its distance d, in feet, from the ground at any time t is $d(t) = 480t - 16t^2$. When is the stone rising?

a. $t < 20$ b. $t < 45$ c. $t < 30$ d. $t < 15$

[b] 11. If $f(x) = 3x^5 - 5x^3$ has a relative maximum at $x = -1$, which of the following would be correct?

a. $f'(x)$ is positive on $(-1, \infty)$
b. $f'(x) < 0$ on $(-1, 0)$
c. $f'(x) > 0$ on $(-\infty, \infty)$
d. $f'(x) < 0$ on $(-\infty, -1)$

[d] 12. The graph of $f(x) = -x^3 + 3x$ has a relative maximum at

a. $x = 0$ b. $x = -2$ c. $x = 3$ d. $x = 1$

[a] 13. The graph of $f(x) = 11 - 2x^2 - 20x$ has

a. a maximum at $x = -5$
b. a maximum at $x = -20$
c. a minimum at $x = 10$
d. a minimum at $x = 0$

[d] 14. The function $f(x) = x^2(x - 4)^4$ has

a. relative minimum at $x = 0$ and relative maxima at $x = -\frac{4}{3}$ and $x = 4$

b. relative maximum at $x = -\frac{4}{3}$ and relative minima at $x = -4$ and $x = 0$

c. relative minimum at $x = 0$ and relative maxima at $x = -4$ and $x = \frac{4}{3}$

d. relative maximum at $x = \frac{4}{3}$ and relative minima at $x = 0$ and $x = 4$

SHORT ANSWER 3.1

15. Find the critical value(s) of the function $f(x) = 3x^4 - 4x^3$.

    Answer: $x = 0, x = 1$

16. Find the critical value(s) of the function $f(x) = 2x^3 + x^2 - 20x + 4$.

    Answer: $x = -2, x = \frac{5}{3}$

17. Find the critical value(s) of the function $f(x) = x^4 - 32x$.

    Answer: $x = 2$

18. Find the critical value(s) of the function $f(x) = -x + 16$.

    Answer: none

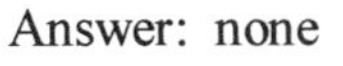

19. Find the critical value(s) of the function $f(x) = 3x^5 - 5x^3$.

    Answer: $x = -1, \ x = 0, x = 1$

20. Find the critical value(s) of the function $f(x) = x^2(x-3)^3$.

    Answer: $x = 0, x = 3, x = \frac{6}{5}$

21. Sketch the graph of the function $f(x) = x^3 - 6x^2 + 9x + 1$ "by hand" by making a sign diagram for the first derivative and plotting all critical points.

    Answer:

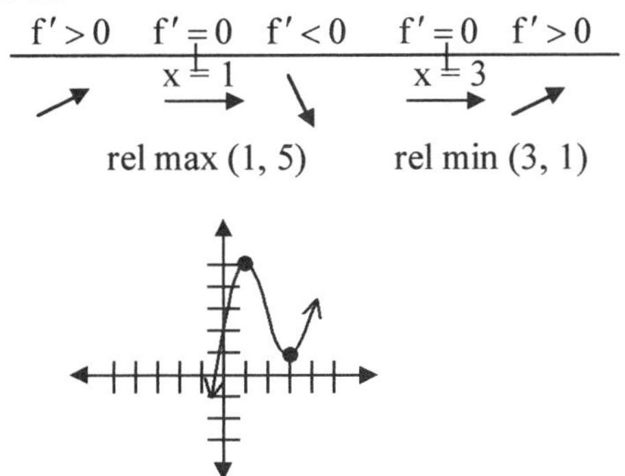

22. Sketch the graph of the function $f(x) = x^4 + 4x^3 + 4x^2 + 3$ "by hand" by making a sign diagram for the first derivative and plotting all critical points.

Answer:

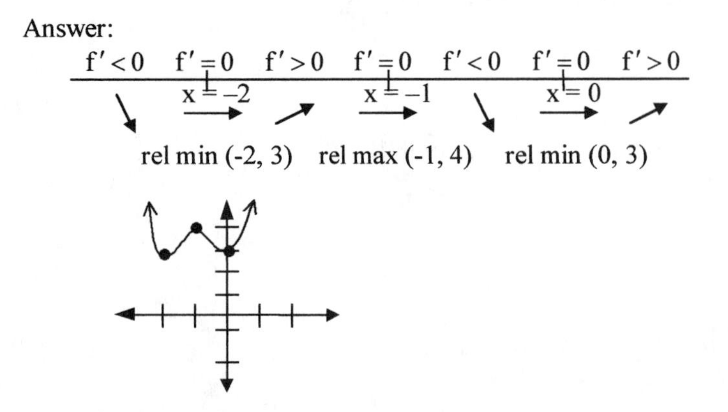

23. Sketch the graph of the function $f(x) = 3x^4 - 4x^3 + 1$ "by hand" by making a sign diagram for the first derivative and plotting all critical points.

Answer:

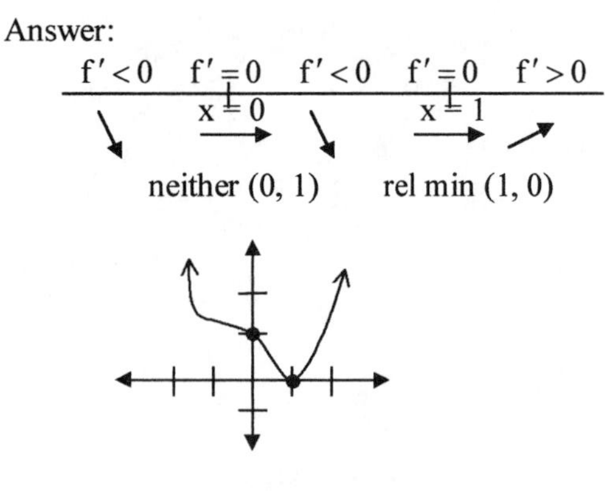

24. Sketch the graph of the function $f(x) = (x^2 - 4x + 3)^2$ "by hand" by making a sign diagram for the first derivative and plotting all critical points.

Answer:

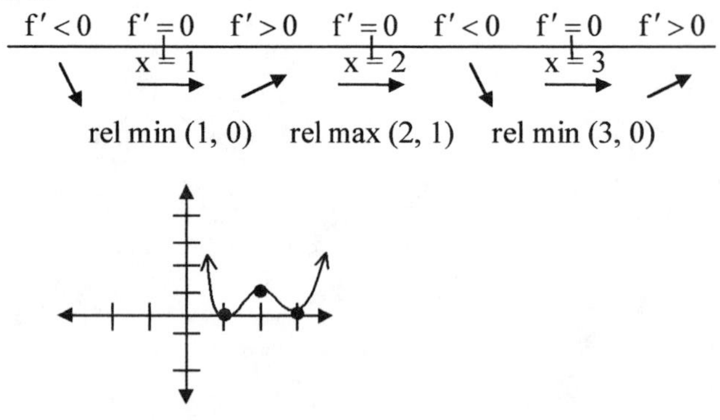

25. Sketch the graph of the function $f(x) = x^2(x-2)^2$ "by hand" by making a sign diagram for the first derivative and plotting all critical points.

Answer:

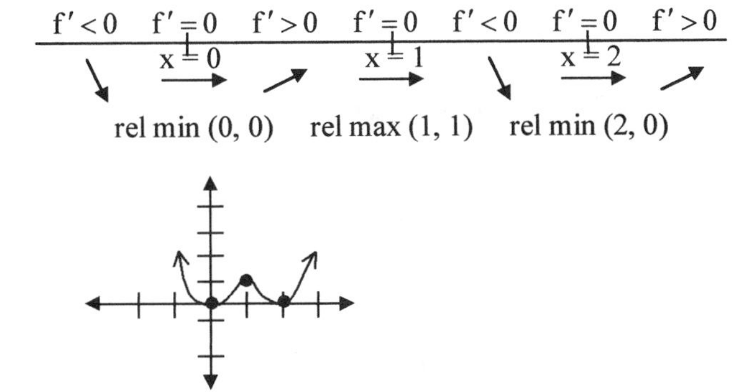

26. Sketch the graph of the function $f(x) = 10x^3(x-1)^2$ "by hand" by making a sign diagram for the first derivative and plotting all critical points.

Answer:

$f' > 0$	$f' = 0$	$f' > 0$	$f' = 0$	$f' < 0$	$f' = 0$	$f' > 0$
↗	$x = 0$	↗	$x = \frac{3}{5}$	↘	$x = 1$	↗
	→		→		→	

rel max $(\frac{3}{5}, 0.35)$ rel min $(1, 0)$

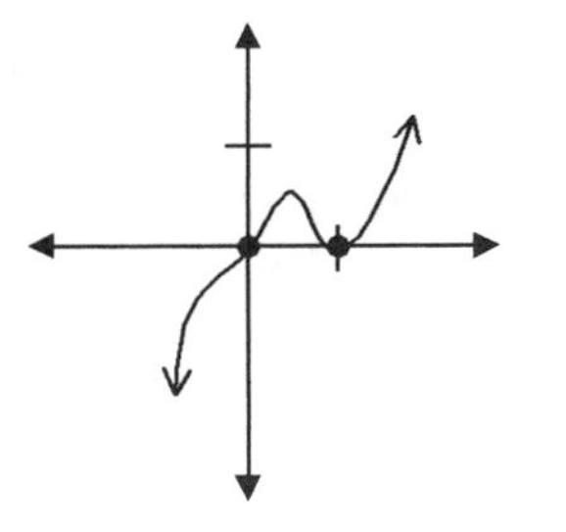

Section 3.2 Graphing Using the First and Second Derivatives

MULTIPLE CHOICE 3.2

[b] 27. Where is $f''(x) = 0$?

a. G and F b. B and D c. A, C and E d. A and E

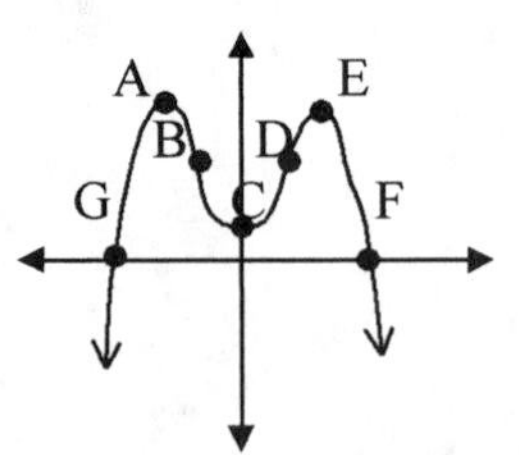

[c] 28. Where is $f'(x) = 0$?

a. A and G b. C and E c. B, D and F d. B and F only

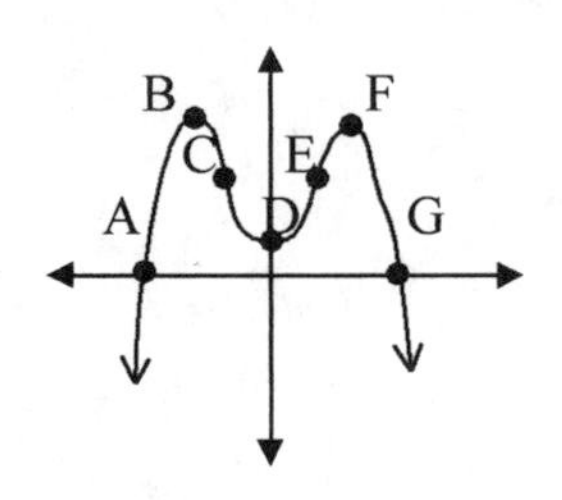

[d] 29. Given the following curve which passes through $(1, 2)$, determine the true statement.

a. $f'(2) > 0$ and $f''(x) > 0$
b. $f'(2) > 0$ and $f''(x) < 0$
c. $f'(2) < 0$ and $f''(x) > 0$
d. $f'(2) < 0$ and $f''(x) < 0$

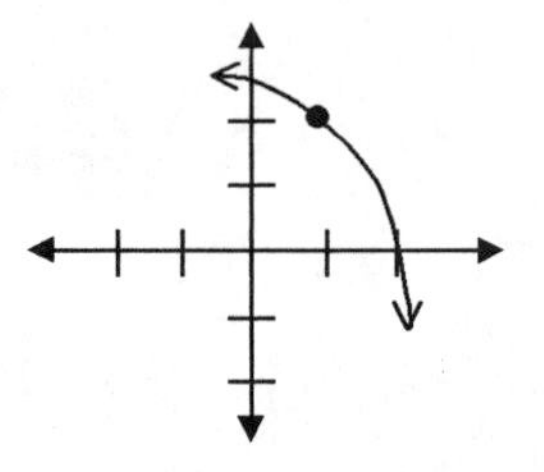

[a] 30. On what interval(s) is f(x) concave down?

a. $(-2, 0)$ and $(0, 2)$ b. $(-\infty, -2)$ and $(2, \infty)$ c. $(-\infty, 0)$ d. $(0, \infty)$

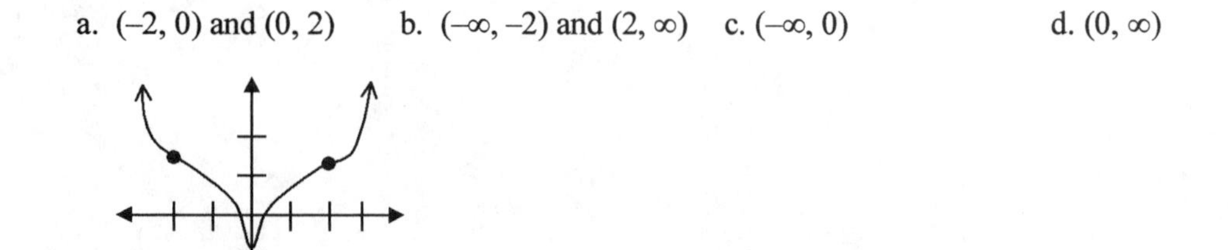

[b] 31. The graph of $f(x) = 2x^2 + 6x + 1$ is concave up

a. when $x > -\frac{3}{2}$ b. for all values of x c. for no values of x d. when $x < -\frac{3}{2}$

[d] 32. The graph of $f(x) = -x^3 - 3x^2 + 9x + 7$ is concave down when

a. $x < 1$ b. $x > -3$ c. $x < 3$ d. $x > -1$

[b] 33. The point of inflection for the graph of $f(x) = x^3 - 3x^2 + 9x + 7$ is

a. $(1, -20)$ b. $(1, 14)$ c. $(-1, 36)$ d. $(-1, 30)$

[d] 34. Find all points of inflection for $f(x) = x^4 - 6x^3$

a. $(0, 0)$ b. $(3, -81)$ c. $(0, 0)$ and $\left(\frac{9}{2}, -\frac{2187}{16}\right)$ d. $(0, 0)$ and $(3, -81)$

[a] 35. Find all points of inflection for $f(x) = x^4 + x^3$.

a. $(0, 0)$ and $\left(-\frac{1}{2}, -\frac{1}{16}\right)$ b. $(0, 0)$

c. $\left(-\frac{1}{2}, -\frac{1}{16}\right)$ d. $(0, 0)$ and $\left(-\frac{3}{4}, -\frac{27}{256}\right)$

[b] 36. Use the second derivative test to find all relative maxima/minima for the following function:
$f(x) = 3x^4 - 8x^3 - 18x^2$

a. relative maximum at $x = -1$, $x = 3$; relative minimum at $x = 0$
b. relative maximum at $x = 0$; relative minimum at $x = -1$, $x = 3$
c. relative maximum at $x = -1$, $x = 3$; no relative minimum
d. no relative maximum; relative minimum at $x = -1$, $x = 3$

[d] 37. The graph of $f(x) = -3x^2 + 4x - 1$ is concave up

a. when $x > \frac{2}{3}$ b. for all values of x c. when $x < \frac{2}{3}$ d. for no values of x

[a] 38. The graph of $f(x) = \frac{1}{3}x^3 - x^2 - 3x + 7$ is concave down

a. $x < 1$ b. $x > -1$ c. $x > 3$ d. $x < 7$

[b] 39. The point of inflection for the graph of $f(x) = x^3 - 3x^2 - 24x + 10$ is

a. $(1, -20)$ b. $(1, -16)$ c. $(-1, 36)$ d. $(-1, 30)$

[d] 40. Use the second derivative test to find all relative maxima/minima for the function $f(x) = 2x^3 - 17x^2 - 12x + 9$.

a. relative maximum at $x = 6$, relative minimum at $x = -\frac{1}{3}$

b. relative maximum at $x = \frac{1}{3}$, relative minimum at $x = -6$

c. relative maximum at $x = -6$, relative minimum at $x = \frac{1}{3}$

d. relative maximum at $x = -\frac{1}{3}$, relative minimum at $x = 6$

SHORT ANSWER 3.2

41. Find the point(s) of inflection of the function $f(x) = \frac{x^4}{6} - \frac{4x^3}{3} + 2$.

    Answer: (0, 2) and $\left(4, -\frac{122}{3}\right)$

42. Find the point(s) of inflection of the function $f(x) = (x - 2)^3$.

    Answer: (2, 0)

43. Use the second derivative test to find all relative maxima/minima for the function $f(x) = x^4 + 2x^3 - 3x^2 - 4x + 4$.

    Answer: relative maximum at $x = -\frac{1}{2}$; relative minimum at $x = -2$ and $x = 1$

44. User the second derivative test to find all relative maxima/minima for the function $f(x) = 2 + x^{2/3}$.

    Answer: relative minimum at x = 0

45. For the function $f(x) = x^3 + 3x^2 - 24x - 20$,
    a. make a sign diagram for $f'(x)$
    b. make a sign diagram for $f''(x)$
    c. sketch the graph by hand, showing all relative extreme points and inflection points.

    Answer:

    a.

$f' > 0$	$f' = 0$	$f' < 0$	$f' = 0$	$f' > 0$
↗	$x = -4$ →	↘	$x = 2$ →	↗

    rel max (-4, 60) rel min (2, -48)

    b.

$f'' < 0$	$f'' = 0$	$f'' > 0$
concave down	$x = -1$ IP(-1,6)	concave up

    c.

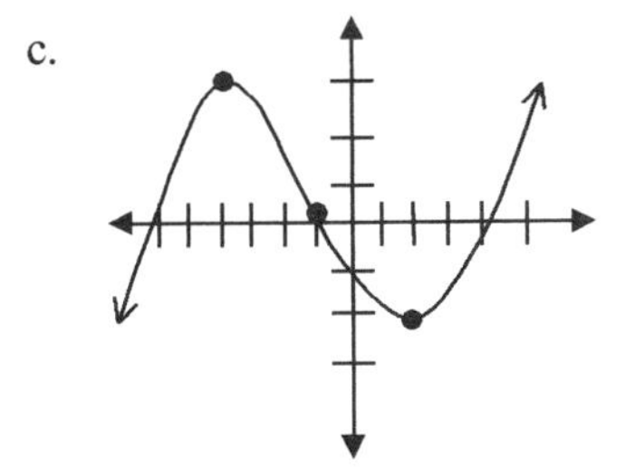

46. For the function $f(x) = x^4 - \frac{8}{3}x^3 + 3$

a. make a sign diagram for $f'(x)$

b. make a sign diagram for $f''(x)$

c. sketch the graph by hand, showing all relative extreme points and inflection points.

Answer:

a. $f' < 0$ | $f' = 0$, $x = 0$ | $f' < 0$ | $f' = 0$, $x = 2$ | $f' > 0$

↘ → ↘ → ↗

neither   rel min $(2, -\frac{7}{3})$

b. $f'' > 0$ | $f'' = 0$ | $f'' < 0$ | $f'' = 0$ | $f'' > 0$

concave up | $x = 0$ IP(0, 3) | concave down | $x = \frac{4}{3}$ IP$\left(\frac{4}{3}, -0.16\right)$ | concave up

c.

47. For the function $f(x) = x^4 + 2x^3 - 1$

a. make a sign diagram for $f'(x)$

b. make a sign diagram for $f''(x)$

c. sketch the graph by hand, showing all relative extreme points and inflection points.

Answer:

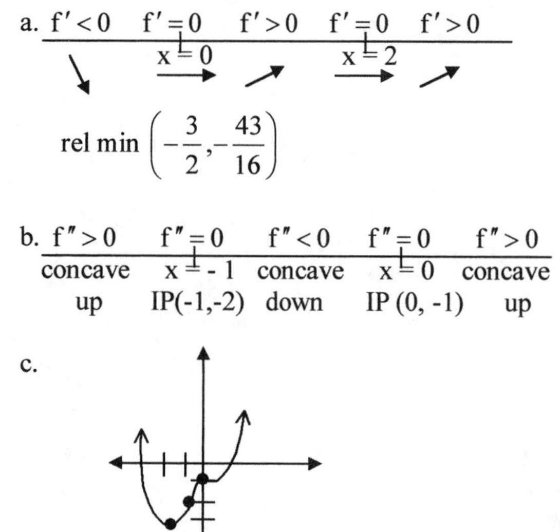

a. f' < 0 f' = 0 f' > 0 f' = 0 f' > 0
x = 0
x = 2
rel min (-3/2, -43/16)
b. f'' > 0 f'' = 0 f'' < 0 f'' = 0 f'' > 0
concave up
x = - 1 IP(-1,-2)
concave down
x = 0 IP (0, -1)
concave up
c.

48. For the function $f(x) = x(x-4)^3$
    a. make a sign diagram for $f'(x)$
    b. make a sign diagram for $f''(x)$

Answer:

a. $f'<0$ | $f'=0$, $x=1$ | $f'>0$ | $f'=0$, $x=4$ | $f'>0$

↘ → ↗ → ↗

rel min $(1, -27)$

b. $f''>0$, concave up | $f''=0$, $x=2$, IP$(2, -16)$ | $f''<0$, concave down | $f''=0$, $x=4$, IP $(4, 0)$ | $f''>0$, concave up

49. For the function $f(x) = 2x^{5/3} - 5x^{4/3}$, determine all relative extreme points and inflection points.

Answer: relative max (0, 0), relative min (8, –16), IP (1, –3)

50. For the function $f(x) = \sqrt[5]{x} - 2$, determine all relative extreme points and inflection points.

Answer: no extrema, IP (0, –2)

51. For the function $f(x) = 9\sqrt[3]{(x+1)^2}$, determine all relative extreme points and inflection points.

Answer: relative min (–1, 0), concave down everywhere

Section 3.3 Optimization

MULTIPLE CHOICE 3.3

[a] 52. Given $f(x) = x^3 - 3x^2 - 24x + 15$ on the interval $[-5, 0]$, which of the statements is true?

a. The absolute maximum is $f(x) = 43$, and it occurs at $x = -2$.
b. The absolute maximum is $f(x) = 15$, and it occurs at $x = 0$.
c. The absolute maximum is $f(x) = 75$, and it occurs at $x = -5$.
d. The absolute maximum is $f(x) = 98$, and it occurs at $x = 4$.

[b] 53. Given $f(x) = x^4 - 8x^2 + 10$ on the interval $[-1, 3]$, which of the statements is true?

a. The absolute minimum is $f(x) = -12$, and it occurs at $x = 0$.
b. The absolute minimum is $f(x) = -6$, and it occurs at $x = 2$.
c. The absolute minimum is $f(x) = -5$, and it occurs at $x = -1$.
d. The absolute minimum is $f(x) = 0$, and it occurs at $x = 3$.

[c] 54. The lowest point on the graph of $f(x) = 2x^3 + 3x^2 - 12x - 7$ when graph on the interval $[-3, 0]$ is

a. $(-1, -13)$ b. $(-2, 1)$ c. $(0, -7)$ d. $(-3, 2)$

[a] 55. The highest point on the graph of $f(x) = x^4 - 8x^2 + 10$ when graphed on the interval $[-1, 3]$ is

a. $(3, 19)$ b. $(0, 12)$ c. $(-1, 3)$ d. $(2, 14)$

[d] 56. The absolute maximum of $f(x) = \dfrac{x^3 + 16}{x}$ on $[1, 4]$ is

a. $(1, 17)$ b. $\left(3, 14\frac{1}{3}\right)$ c. $(2, 12)$ d. $(4, 20)$

[a] 57. The absolute minimum of $f(x) = \dfrac{x^2 + 1}{x}$ on $\left[\frac{1}{2}, 3\right]$ is

a. $(1, 2)$ b. $\left(3, \frac{10}{3}\right)$ c. $(-1, -2)$ d. $\left(\frac{1}{2}, \frac{5}{2}\right)$

[b] 58. The jump taken by a college high jumper follows the path described by $s(t) = (-100/3)t^2 + 100t$, where s is the high jumper's distance (in inches) above the ground at time t (in seconds), Which of the following statements is true?

a. The maximum height is 100 inches, reached at the end of 3 seconds.
b. The maximum height is 75 inches, reached at the end of 1.5 seconds.
c. The maximum height is 50 inches, reached at the end of 2.5 seconds.
d. The maximum height is 67 inches, reached at the end of 2 seconds.

[b] 59. An investment research firm has concluded that the value of a certain group of stocks over the next two years can be described by the function $v(t) = t^3 - (57/2)t^2 + 180t + 350$, where t is time (in months) and $0 \leq t \leq 24$. Because the research firm will advise a client to by at the lowest possible price and sell when the price is highest, the advice on this group of stocks will be

a. buy in month 4 and sell in month 15.
b. buy in month 15 and sell in month 24.
c. buy in month 4 and sell in month 24.
d. buy in month 4, sell in month 15, and buy again in month 24.

[c] 60. The percent of effectiveness of a medicine t hours after it is taken is given by $P(t) = (75/16)t^2 - (25/64)t^3$, $0 \leq t \leq 12$. How many hours will it take for the medicine to be 100% effective (maximum effectiveness)?

a. 2 hours b. 6 hours c. 8 hours d. 10 hours

[b] 61. The concentration K of a particular medicine t hours after it is swallowed is $K(t) = \dfrac{.2t}{(t+3)^2}$, $t \geq 0$.

After how many hours will the concentration be the highest?

a. 1 b. 3 c. 2 d. 2.5

[c] 62. The daily cost to produce x hundred smoke alarms is $C(x) = 0.02x^2 + x + 450$. For what number of smoke alarms will the daily average cost be a minimum? The average cost is $C(x) = c(x)/x$.

a. 450 b. 2500 c. 15,000 d. 150

[a] 63. A manufacturer of in-line skates can make up to 100 pairs of skates per day. The daily cost function is $C(x) = 0.03x^2 + 5x + 75$. How many pairs of skates should be made to minimize the daily average cost? The average cost is $AC(x) = C(x)/x$.

a. 50 b. 100 c. 83 d. 75

[d] 64. The profit from the manufacture and sale of x snow shovels is $P(x) = -0.4x^2 + 1600x - 300$. The number of snow shovels made and sold that will result in a maximum profit is

a. 20,000 b. 200 c. 4000 d. 2000

[b] 65. For x items, a company's cost function is $C(x) = 9x + 100$ and its revenue function is $R(x) = -0.02x^2 + 21x$. The number of items that will yield a maximum profit for the company is

a. 210 b. 300 c. 420 d. 475

[c] 66. A company's profit, in thousands of dollars, from the production of x hundred items is $P(x) = 4x^2 - x^3/3$. Currently the production level is at 700 units, resulting in a profit of $81,667 (that is $P(x) = 81.667$). Which of the following statements is true about profit and the production level?

a. The current production level is resulting in a maximum profit.
b. The production level should be decreased by 100 units in order to achieve a maximum profit.
c. The production level should be increased by 100 units in order to achieve a maximum profit.
d. The production level should be increased by 300 units in order to achieve a maximum profit.

[c] 67. The lowest point on the graph of $f(x) = 2x^3 + 3x^2 - 12x - 7$ when graphed on the interval $[-3, 0]$ is

a. $(-1, -13)$ b. $(-2, 1)$ c. $(0, -7)$ d. $(-3, 2)$

[a] 68. The absolute maximum of $f(x) = 3x^5 - 5x^3$ on $[-2, 1]$ is

a. $(-1, 2)$ b. $(0, 0)$ c. $(-2, 56)$ d. $(1, -2)$

SHORT ANSWER 3.3

69. Find the absolute extreme values of the function $f(x) = x^3 - 9x^2 + 15x$ on the interval [0, 10].

    Answer: max f is 225 (at x = 10); min f is –25 (at x = 5)

70. Find the absolute extreme values of the function $f(x) = x^3 - 75x$ on the interval [0, 10].

    Answer: max f is 250 (at x = 10); min f is –250 (at x = 5)

71. Find the absolute extreme values of the function $f(x) = \sqrt[3]{x^2}$ on the interval [–8, 8].

    Answer: max f is 4 (at $x = \pm 8$); min f is 0 (at x = 0)

72. Determine the absolute extrema of $f(x) = x^{3/5} + 1$ on [–1, 32].

    Answer: The absolute maximum is 9 and the absolute minimum is 0.

73. Find the absolute extreme values of the function $f(x) = \dfrac{1}{x^2 + 9}$ on the interval [–4, 4].

    Answer: max f is $\dfrac{1}{9}$ (at x = 0); min f is $\dfrac{1}{25}$ (at $x = \pm 4$)

74. Find the absolute extreme values of the function $f(x) = \sqrt{x} + x + 1$ on the interval [1, 9].

    Answer: max f is 13 (at x = 9); min f is 3 (at x = 1)

75. A lake is being observation for a period of 10 months, and the number of catfish, in hundreds is given by $N(t) = \dfrac{t^3}{3} - \dfrac{11}{2}t^2 + 24t + 50$, where t is the time in months ($0 \le t \le 10$). In what month is the number of catfish the greatest, and how many catfish are there? (round to the nearest hundred)

    Answer: in month 3; 8,200 catfish

76. Suppose the total cost in dollars of manufacturing x units is given by $C(x) = 3x^2 + x + 48$.
    a. Find the average cost function.
    b. For what value of x is the average cost the smallest?

    Answer: a. $AC(x) = 3x + 1 + \dfrac{48}{x}$; b. x = 4 units

77. An efficiency study of the morning shift at a factory indicates that an average worker who arrives on the job at 8:00 am will have produced $Q(t) = -t^3 + 3t^2 + 9t$ units , t hours later. At what time during the morning is the worker performing most efficiently? (When is the rate of production the largest?)

    Answer: t = 3, that is 11:00 am.

78. A retired carpenter can build model boats at a cost of $60 each. He estimates his price function to be $p = 180 - 6x$, where x is the number of boats sold in a week if the price is p dollars. Find the number of boats that he should produce and the price he should charge to maximize his profit. Also find the maximum profit.

    Answer: produce 10 units per week; sell at a price of $120 each; maximum profit is $600 per week

79. Suppose a firm has its total cost given by $C(x) = \frac{x^2}{2} + 12x + 1{,}200$ and its total revenue by

    $R(x) = 100x - \frac{x^2}{2}$. Find the quantity that will maximize the profit and find the maximum profit.

    Answer: 44 units; $736 profit.

80. The temperature in a kiln heating pieces of ceramics is $T(t) = -0.5t^2 + 30t + 75$ degrees, t minutes after the heating begins. Determine when the temperature is hottest and what that temperature is.

    Answer: the temperature, 525 degrees, occurs after 30 minutes.

The profit P in dollars from the manufacture and sale of laptop computers is given by $P = -0.03x^2 + 120x - 3000$, where x is the number of computers.

81. How many computers must be sold to make a maximum profit?

    Answer: 2000 computers

82. What is the maximum profit?

    Answer: $117,000

83. In order to sell x thousand newly released videos each week, the price per video must be $p = \sqrt{784 - 2x^2}$ dollars. Find out how many videos must be sold each week to maximize the revenue. Determine the price of the video for that sales level.

    Answer: The maximum revenue will be obtained when 14,000 videos are sold each week at a cost of $19.80 each.

84. A book publisher's profit from the production and sale of x comic books is $P(x) = -0.007x^2 + 35x - 5450$ dollars.
    a. Find the number of comic books that will result in a maximum profit.
    b. Find the maximum amount of profit.

    Answer: a. 2500 books b. $38,300

Section 3.4 Further Applications of Optimization

MULTIPLE CHOICE 3.4

[b] 85. There are two positive numbers whose sum is 60 and whose product is a maximum. The value of that maximum product is

a. 1200 b. 900 c. 3600 d. 500

[b] 86. A rectangular beam is to be cut from a log that has a 1-foot radius. The strength S of a beam is given by the formula $S = kwd^2$, where w is the width of the beam, d is the depth of the beam, and k is a constant. The dimensions of the strongest beam that can be cut from the log are

a. $\frac{2}{\sqrt{3}}$ by $\frac{\sqrt{6}}{3}$ b. $\frac{2\sqrt{3}}{3}$ by $\frac{2\sqrt{6}}{3}$ c. $\frac{\sqrt{3}}{3}$ by $\frac{\sqrt{6}}{3}$ d. $\frac{\sqrt{3}}{3}$ by $\frac{2\sqrt{6}}{3}$

[a] 87. A rectangular lot is to be bounded by a fence on 3 sides and by a wall on the fourth side. Two kinds of fencing will be used, with heavy duty selling for $4 per foot on the side opposite the wall. The 2 remaining sides will use standard fencing selling for $3 per foot. If $6,600 is available for fence, determine the maximum area of the rectangle that can be enclosed by the fence.

a. 453,750 ft^2 b. 302,500 ft^2 c. 680,625 ft^2 d. 472,656.25 ft^2

[d] 88. An apple farmer finds that if he plants 50 trees per acre, each tree will yield 24 bushels of apples. He estimates that for every decrease in the number of trees planted per acre, the yield of each tree will increase by 2 bushels. Determine the maximum harvest per acre.

a. 961 bushels b. 4624 bushels c. 361 bushels d. 2108 bushels

[c] 89. If the amount of a drug in a person's blood after t hours is given by $f(t) = \frac{t}{t^2 + 4}$, when will the drug concentration by the greatest?

a. immediately b. after 4 hours c. after 2 hours d. after $1\frac{1}{3}$ hours

[a] 90. A farmer with 800 feet of fence wants to enclose a rectangular field and then divide it into four plots with three fences parallel to one of the sides. What is the largest area that can be enclosed?

a. 16,000 ft^2 b. 6400 ft^2 c. 40,000 ft^2 d. 20,000ft^2

[d] 91. A window in the shape of a rectangle surmounted by a semicircle is called a Norman window. The width of the rectangular region is equal to the diameter of the semicircle. In order to maximize the light coming through the Norman window, the area of the window must be maximized. If the perimeter of the window is 20 feet, determine the radius of the window that will admit the most light.

a. $5+\frac{20}{\pi}$ b. $\frac{20}{4+3\pi}$ c. $\frac{5}{1+\pi}$ d. $\frac{20}{4+\pi}$

[c] 92. The owner of a car rental company has 24 sedans to rent. If he sets the day rental price at \$12, hie can rent all 24 cars. For each \$2 increase in the daily rental price, one of the cars remains unrented. What daily price will maximize the revenue?

a. \$18 b. \$15 c. \$30 d. \$9

[d] 93. The number of hundreds of trout in a lake for the first 12 months if an observation period is given by $n(t)=\frac{1}{3}t^3-\frac{11}{2}t^2+24t+50$, where t is the time in months and $0 \le t \le 12$. In what month is the number of trout the greatest, and how many trout (rounded to the nearest hundred) are there?

a. in month 3, there are 8200 trout
b. in month 8, there are 6100 trout
c. in month 15, there are 29,800 trout
d. in month 12, there are 12,200 trout

SHORT ANSWER 3.4

94. Lease-A-Lemon Incorporated finds that it can rent 40 cars if it charges $60 for a weekend. It estimates that for each $5 price increase it will rent 2 fewer cars. What price should it charge to maximize its revenue? How many cars will it rent at this price?

    Answer: price is $80 per weekend; the number of cars is 32.

95. An airline finds that if it charges $400 to fly to London, it will sell 500 tickets per day. It estimates that each $10 price reduction will result in 25 more tickets sold per day. Find the ticket price that will maximize the airline's revenue. How many tickets will be sold at this price?

    Answer: price is $300 per ticket; the quantity is 750 tickets.

96. A sporting goods store can sell 20 tennis rackets per day at a price of $80 each. The manager estimates that each $5 price reduction will result in 2 more tennis rackets being sold per day. If each tennis racket costs the store $20, and fixed costs are $200 per day, find the price that will maximize profit. Also find the number of rackets that will be sold at that price, and the maximum profit.

    Answer: price is $75 per racket; the quantity is 22 rackets; the profit is $1,010.

97. A store can sell 8 pocket calculators per day at a price of $30 each. The manager estimated that each $3 price reduction results in 2 more pocket calculators being sold per day. If each pocket calculator costs the store $12, and fixed costs are $40 per day, find the price that will maximize profit. Also find the number that will be sold at that price, and the maximum profit.

    Answer: price is $27 each; the quantity is 10; the profit is $110.

98. A peach farmer finds that if he plants 25 trees per acre, each tree will yield 15 bushels of peaches. He estimates that for every decrease in the number of trees planted per acre, the yield of each tree will increase by 3 bushels. How many trees should he plant per acre to maximize his harvest?

    Answer: 15 trees per acre

99. Suppose that the relationship between the tax rate, t on foreign automobiles and the total sales, S, is given by $S = 6 - 20\sqrt{t}$, where S is measured in millions of dollars. Find the tax rate that maximizes revenue for the government.

    Answer: tax rate of 4%.

100. Suppose that the relationship between the tax rate, t, on imported handbags and the total sales, S, is given by $S(t) = 100 - 160t^{1/4}$, where S is measured in millions of dollars. Find the tax rate t that maximizes revenue for the government.

     Answer: tax rate of 6.25%

101. If the amount of a drug in a person's blood after t hours is $f(t) = t/(t^2 + 4)$, when will the drug concentration be the greatest?

Answer: after 2 hours.

102. A case of wine appreciates in value each year, but there is also an annual storage charge. The net value of the wine after t years is $V(t) = 1{,}500 + 72\sqrt{t} - 12t$ dollars (for $t < 25$). Find the storage time that will maximize the value of the wine.

Answer: 9 years

103. A farmer needs to buy fencing to enclose 1,000 ft^2 of rectangular pasture. He wants to put more expensive fence on the side of the pasture beside the highway and cheaper fence on the other 3 sides. The expensive fence will cost $15 per foot and the cheaper fence will cost $10 per foot. What are the dimensions of the pasture to be enclosed that will minimize the cost of the fence, and what is the minimum cost of the fence?

Answer: 28.284 ft by 35.355 ft; minimum cost is $1414.21

104. A tuxedo rental shop is making a special offer to the senior class. When there are exactly 30 suits rented, the rental price per suit is $80. When there are more people, each person's fee is reduced by $2 for each person beyond the basic group of 30. Find the number of suits rented and the fee per suit for which the shop's revenue will be a maximum. What is the maximum revenue?

Answer: the maximum revenue is $2450 when 35 suits are rented at a fee of $70 per suit.

105. A shop owner wishes to set up a display in the corner of her shop. The display area is to be rectangular in shape and will use two adjacent walls for two of the sides. A heavy decorative cord that is 25 feet long will be used to form the other two sides. Determine the dimensions of the rectangle that will provide the largest display area.

Answer: The rectangle will be a square that measures 12.5 feet on each side.

106. When hamburgers were sold at $2 each at a concession stand of a sports stadium in Tokyo, 100,000 hamburgers were sold. When the price was increased by $.10, the number of hamburgers sold decreased by 400. Find the price of the hamburger that will maximize the revenue.

Answer: The price is $13.50 per hamburger.

107. An airplane hangar is to be built. It front is in the shape of a semicircle and is to include a large rectangular door. (See the figure.) The radius of the semicircle is 15 feet. Find the dimensions of the rectangle so that the area of the doors will be largest. Round your answer to the nearest foot.

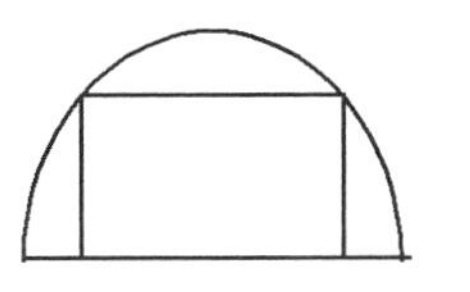

Answer: the dimensions are 21 feet by 11 feet.

A manufacturer can sell x pairs of gloves for $10 - 0.001x$ dollars per pair. It costs $5x + 1000$ dollars to produce all x pairs.

108. How many pairs should be produced in order to maximize the profit?

    Answer: 2500 pairs

109. Find the price of a pair of gloves that will maximize the profit.

    Answer: $7.50 per pair

Section 3.5 Optimizing Lot Size and Harvest Size

MULTIPLE CHOICE 3.5

[c] 110. A garage expects to sell 1,200 radial tires in a year. Each tire costs the garage $50, and there is a fixed delivery charge of $100 per order. If it costs $6 to store a tire for a year, how many tires should be ordered at a time and how many orders should be placed in a year to minimize inventory cost?

a. order size is 300; the number of orders per year is 4.
b. order size is 400; the number of orders per year is 3.
c. order size is 200; the number of orders per year is 6.
d. order size is 600; the number of orders per year is 2.

[a] 111. A record manufacturer estimates the demand for a record to be 90,000 per year. It costs $400 to set up the presses for the record, plus $8 for each record pressed. If it costs $2 to store a record for a year, how many records should be pressed at a time and how many production runs should there be to minimize costs?

a. run size is 6,000; the number of runs per year is 15.
b. run size is 15,000; the number of runs per year is 6.
c. run size is 5,000; the number of runs per year is 18.
d. run size is 9,000; the number of runs per year is 10.

[b] 112. A fisherman estimates the reproduction curve for trout in a lake to be $f(x) = 48\sqrt{x}$, where x and f(x) are in thousands. Determine the population that gives the maximum sustainable yield, and the size of the yield.

a. the population is 576 and the yield is 1,152,000
b. the population is 576,000 and the yield is 1,152,000
c. the population is 4,899 and the yield is 106,242
d. the population is 1,699 and the yield is 62,555

[a] 113. The reproduction function for the blue whale is estimated to be $f(p) = -0.0006p^2 + 1.09p$, where p and f(p) are in thousands. Find the population that gives the maximum sustainable yield, and the size of the yield.

a. the population is 75,000 and the yield is 3,375
b. the population is 7,500 and the yield is 3,375
c. the population is 908 and the yield is 495
d. the population is 1,742 and the yield is 1,820

SHORT ANSWER 3.5

114. A lumberyard expects to sell 1,600 sheets of plywood in a year. Each sheet costs the lumber yard \$20, and there is a fixed delivery charge of \$200 per order. If it costs \$4 to store a plywood sheet for a year, how many sets should be ordered at a time and how many orders should be placed in a year to minimize inventory cost?

Answer: order size is 400; the number of orders per year is 4.

115. A store expects to sell 500 microwave ovens in a year. Each oven costs the store \$300, and there is a fixed delivery charge of \$200 per order. If it costs \$20 to store an oven for a year, how many ovens should be ordered at a time and how many orders should be placed in a year to minimize inventory cost?

Answer: Order size is 100; the number of orders per year is 5.

116. A book publisher estimates the demand for a book to be 40,000 copies per year. It costs \$10,000 to set up the presses to print the book, plus \$12 for each book printed. If it costs \$2 to store a book for a year, how many books should be printed at a time and how many production runs should there be to minimize costs?

Answer: run size is 20,000; the number of runs per year is 2.

117. A paper manufacturer estimates the demand for a certain type of paper to be 15,000 rolls per year. It costs \$3,000 to set up the factory for the paper, plus \$100 for each roll produced. If it costs \$10 to store a roll for a year, how many rolls should be produced at a time and how many production runs should there be to minimize costs?

Answer: run size is 3,000; the number of runs per year is 5.

118. If the reproduction function for bay scallops is $f(p) = -0.03p^2 + 13p$, where p and f(p) are in thousands, find the population that gives the maximum sustainable yield, and the size of the yield.

Answer: population is 200,000 (from $p = 200$); the yield is 1,200,000.

119. If the reproduction function for blue fish is $f(p) = -0.005p^2 + 2p$, where p and f(p) are in hundreds, find the population that gives the maximum sustainable yield, and the size of the yield.

Answer: population is 10,000 (from $p = 100$); the yield is 5,000.

120. If the reproduction function for Abacore tuna is $f(p) = 3\sqrt[3]{p^2}$, where p and f(p) are in thousands, find the population that gives the maximum sustainable yield, and the size of the yield.

Answer: population is 8,000 (from $p = 8$); the yield is 4,000.

Section 3.6 Implicit Differentiation and Related Rates

MULTIPLE CHOICE 3.6

[c] 121. For the equation $y^3 - x^2 = 0$, use implicit differentiation to find $\frac{dy}{dx}$.

a. $\frac{2y}{3x^2}$ b. $\frac{3y}{2x^2}$ c. $\frac{2x}{3y^2}$ d. $\frac{2x}{3y}$

[a] 122. For the equation $1 = xy + y^2$, use implicit differentiation to find $\frac{dy}{dx}$.

a. $\frac{-y}{x+2y}$ b. $\frac{y+2x}{3y^2}$ c. $\frac{x-y}{2x}$ d. $\frac{1-2xy}{y}$

[c] 123. Given the equation $(y + 8.2)^3 = (x - 5.7)^4$, find $\frac{dy}{dx}$ by using implicit differentiation.

a. $\frac{(y+8.2)^2}{(x-5.7)^3}$ b. $\frac{3(y+8.2)^2}{4(x-5.7)^3}$ c. $\frac{4(x-5.7)^3}{3(y+8.2)^2}$ d. $\frac{4x(x-5.7)^3}{3y(y+8.2)^2}$

[a] 124. For the equation $\sqrt{x} + \sqrt{y} = 1$, use implicit differentiation to find $\frac{dy}{dx}$.

a. $\frac{-\sqrt{y}}{\sqrt{x}}$ b. $\frac{1-\sqrt{y}}{\sqrt{x}}$ c. $\frac{\sqrt{x}-1}{\sqrt{y}}$ d. $\sqrt{\frac{x}{y}}$

[d] 125. For the equation $5x^2 - 2xy + 7y^2 = 0$, use implicit differentiation to find $\frac{dy}{dx}$.

a. $\frac{10x+14y}{2x}$ b. $-\frac{10x+2y}{14y}$ c. $10x - 2y + 14$ d. $\frac{y-5x}{7y-x}$

[c] 126. For the equation, $y^2 - 6 = -xy$, find dy/dx at $x = 1$, $y = 2$.

a. 0 b. −1/4 c. −2/5 d. 2/5

[b] 127. For the equation, $x^2 + 2y^2 = 3$,find dy/dx at $x = 1$, $y = 1$.

a. 1/2 b. −1/2 c. 2 d. −2

[b] 128. The slope of the line tangent to the graph of $y^4 = x^5$ at the point (1, –1) is

a. –1 b. –5/4 c. 5/4 d. –4/5

[b] 129. The equation of the line tangent to the graph of $x^3 - y^2 = -1$ at the point (2, 3) is

a. $x + 2y + 1 = 0$ b. $2x - y - 1 = 0$ c. $x - 2y + 1 = 0$ d. $2x + y - 1 = 0$

[c] 130. A bottle producer is increasing its production at the rate of 250 bottles per week. The weekly revenue from the sale of all x bottles produced is $R(x) = 70x - .02x^2$ dollars. What is the rate of change of revenue with respect to time when the weekly production level is 1,500 bottles per week?

a. $4,100/week b. $3,800/week c. $2,500/week d. $1,000/week

[d] 131. As pancake batter is poured onto a hot griddle, the shape of the batter is circular and is getting larger. The radius of the pancake is increasing at the rate of 5 centimeters per second. Determine the approximate rate of change of the area of the pancake when the radius is 3 centimeters?

a. 15 cm^2/sec b. 30 cm^2/sec c. 79 cm^2/sec d. 94 cm^2/sec

[a] 132. The burned skin on a person's leg is circular in shape. The radius of the burned region is decreasing at the rate of 5 millimeters per month. Determine the approximate change of the area of the burn when the radius is 30 millimeters.

a. –942 mm^2/month b. –756 mm^2/month c. –471 mm^2/month d. –155 mm^2/month

[b] 133. Gas is being released from a balloon on a cross-country trip in order to lose altitude. The balloon is approximately spherical in shape. The radius of the balloon is decreasing at the rate of .75 yard per minute. Approximately how fast is the volume of the balloon decreasing when the radius is 25 yards? (The volume of a sphere is given by $V = (4/3)\pi r^3$).

a. 707 yd^3/min b. 5890 yd^3/min c. 1875 yd^3/min d. 1963 yd^3/min

[d] 134. An air conditioner manufacturer will be increasing production at the rate of 50 air conditioners per day. The revenue from the sale of x air conditioners is $R(x) = 100x - .001x^2$ dollars. Find the rate of change of revenue with respect to time when the daily production level is 250 air conditioners.

a. $75/day b. $525/day c. $1525/day d. $4975/day

[b] 135. A flashlight manufacturer is going to increase production at the rate of 250 flashlights per week. The weekly revenue from the sale of all x flashlights produced is $R(x) = 70x - .02x^2$ dollars. What is the rate of change of revenue with respect to time when the weekly production level is 1500 flashlights per week?

a. $1000/day b. $2500/day c. $3800/day d. $4100/day

SHORT ANSWER 3.6

136. For the equation $y^3 - x^4 = 10x$, use implicit differentiation to find $\frac{dy}{dx}$.

Answer: $\frac{dy}{dx} = \frac{10 + 4x^3}{3y^2}$

137. For the equation $(x - 1)^2 + (y - 1)^2 = 8$, use implicit differentiation to find $\frac{dy}{dx}$.

Answer: $\frac{dy}{dx} = \frac{-(x-1)}{y - 1}$

138. For the equation $x^2 - 4xy + y^2 = 1$, use implicit differentiation to find $\frac{dy}{dx}$.

Answer: $\frac{dy}{dx} = \frac{2y - x}{y - 2x}$

139. Given the equation $\frac{7.5x^2}{2y} = x^2 + y^4$, find dy/dx by using implicit differentiation.

Answer: $\frac{15x - 4xy}{2x^2 + 10y^4}$

140. Given the equation $3y^2 - 6.5xy - 2.4x^5 = 0$, find dy/dx by using implicit differentiation.

Answer: $\frac{12x^4 + 6.5y}{6y - 6.5x}$

141. Given the equation $(x^2 + 3y)^2 = 1$, find dy/dx by using implicit differentiation.

Answer: $-\frac{2x}{3}$

142. What is the slope of the line tangent to the graph of $y^2 + xy = 6$ at the point (1, 2)?

Answer: $-\frac{2}{5}$

143. Given the equation $x^3 - 2xy = 4$
   a. What is the slope of the line tangent to the graph of the equation at the point (2, 1)?
   b. What is the equation of the line tangent to the graph of the equation at the point (–2, 3)?

   Answer: a. 5/2 b. $3x + 2y = 0$

144. For the following equation, find dy/dx evaluated at the given values:
   $\sqrt{x} + 3 = \sqrt{y}$ at $x = 1, y = 16$.

   Answer: 4

145. For the following demand equation $p^2 + p + x = 40$, use implicit differentiation to find dp/dx.

   Answer: $\frac{dp}{dx} = \frac{-1}{2p+1}$

146. For the following demand equation $4p^2 + 3p + 20 = x$, use implicit differentiation to find dp/dx.

   Answer: $\frac{dp}{dx} = \frac{1}{8p+3}$

147. For the following demand equation $(p + 3)(x + 2) = 100$, use implicit differentiation to find dp/dx.

   Answer: $\frac{dp}{dx} = \frac{-3-p}{x+2}$

148. A company's demand equation is $x = \sqrt{116 - p^2}$. Find dp/dx when $p = 4$, and interpret the answer.

   Answer: dp/dx = –5/2. Interpretation: The rate of change of price with respect to quantity is –2.5, so price decreases by \$2.50 when the quantity increases by 1.

149. In the following equation $x^3 - y^2 = 10$, x and y are functions of t. Differentiate with respect to t to find a relation between $\frac{dx}{dt}$ and $\frac{dy}{dt}$.

   Answer: $3x^2 \frac{dx}{dt} - 2y \frac{dy}{dt} = 0$

150. In the following equation $x^2y^3 = 120$, x and y are functions of t. Differentiate with respect to t to find a relation between $\frac{dx}{dt}$ and $\frac{dy}{dt}$.

   Answer: $2xy^3 \frac{dx}{dt} + 3x^2y^2 \frac{dy}{dt} = 0$

151. In the following equation $x^3y^2 = 160$, x and y are functions of t. Differentiate with respect to t to find a relation between $\frac{dx}{dt}$ and $\frac{dy}{dt}$.

Answer: $3x^2y^2\frac{dx}{dt} + 2x^3y\frac{dy}{dt} = 0$

152. A company's revenue from selling x units of an item is $R(x) = 1{,}000x - 20x^2$ dollars. If sales are increasing at the rate of 60 units per day, find how rapidly revenue is growing (in dollars per day) at the time when 20 units have been sold.

Answer: $12,000 per day

153. The number of welfare cases in a city having a population p is expected to be $W = 0.002p^{3/2}$. If the population is growing by 2,000 people per year, find the rate at which welfare cases will be rising when the population is p = 1,000,000.

Answer: 6000 cases per year

154. A machine is rolling a metal cylinder under pressure. The radius of the cylinder is decreasing at a constant rate of .05 inches per second and the volume is 128π in^3. At what rate is the length h changing when the radius is 1.8 inches? (Volume of a cylinder: $v = \pi r^2 h$)

Answer: dh/dt = 2.195 in./sec

155. Given the supply function $p = 45 + \sqrt{6x+10}$ dollars, if the price is increasing at a rate of $0.45 per week, find the rate at which the supply is changing (with respect to time) when x = 15.

Answer: 1.5 per week

156. Grain is being poured on to the floor of a storage warehouse at the rate of 25 cubic feet per minute and is forming a cone-shaped pile. Suppose that the radius is always five times the height (that is, r = 5h).
   a. The volume of a cone is give by $V = (1/3)\pi r^2 h$. Use the given supposition to rewrite this equation showing V as a function of h.
   b. How fast is the height of the pile increasing when it is 4 feet high?

Answer: a. $V = \frac{25\pi h^3}{3}$ b. $\frac{1}{16\pi}$ ft / min

157. The cost of producing x pads of paper is $C(x) = 0.15x + 20$ dollars. The manufacturer decides to increase production by 1000 pads per day. Determine the rate of change of cost with respect to time.

Answer: $150 per day

158. A soda can producer is increasing its production at the rate of 1500 cans per day. The daily demand function is $p = 8 - 0.0003x$ cents, where p is the selling price per can and x is the number of cans produced and sold.
   a. Determine the daily revenue function R.
   b. Find the rate of change of revenue with respect to time when the daily production level is 9000 cans.

   Answer: a. $R = 8x - 0.0003x^2$ b. 3900 cents per day (that is $39 per day)

159. A flashlight manufacturer is going to increase production at the rate of 250 flashlights per week. The weekly revenue from the sale of all x flashlights is $C(x) = 300 + 0.75x$ dollars. What is the rate of change of cost with respect to time at any time t?

   Answer: $187.50 per week

Chapter 3 – Graphing Calculator

Further Applications of the Derivative

Section 3.1 Graphing Using the First Derivative

1. For the function, $f(x) = x^3 - 9x^2 - 48x + 52$, using a graphing calculator to find all relative extrema.

   Answer: relative maximum at (–2, 104), relative minimum at (8, –396)

2. Graph the function, $f(x) = -x^3 - 3x^2 + 9x + 7$, using a graphing calculator to find all relative extrema.

   Answer: relative minimum at (–3, –20), relative maximum at (1, 12)

3. Graph the function, $f(x) = x^4 + 4x^3$, using a graphing calculator to find all relative extrema.

   Answer: relative minimum at (–3, –27)

4. Graph the function, $f(x) = 1 + 2x^2 - \frac{1}{4}x^4$, using a graphing calculator to find all relative extrema.

   Answer: relative maximum at (–2, 5) and (2, 5), relative minimum at (0, 1)

5. Graph the function, $f(x) = \frac{x^3}{3} + \frac{x^2}{2} - 6x$, using a graphing calculator to find all relative extrema.

   Answer: relative maximum at (-3, 27/2), relative minimum at (2, –22/3)

6. Graph the function, $f(x) = \frac{x^4}{6} - \frac{4x^3}{3} + 2$, using a graphing calculator to find all relative extrema.

   Answer: relative minimum at (6, –70)

7. Graph the function, $f(x) = \frac{1}{5}x^5 - \frac{4}{3}x^3 + 1$, using a graphing calculator to find all relative extrema.

   Answer: relative maximum at (–2, 79/15), relative minimum (2, –49/15)

8. Graph the function, $f(x) = 3x^{2/3} - x^2$, using a graphing calculator to find all relative extrema.

   Answer: relative maximum at (–1, 2) and (1, 2), relative minimum at (0, 0)

9. Graph the function, $f(x) = \sqrt{x^2 - 1}$, using a graphing calculator to find all relative extrema.

   Answer: relative minimum at (–1, 0) and (1, 0)

10. Graph the function, $f(x) = \sqrt{100 - x^2}$, using a graphing calculator to find all relative extrema.

    Answer: relative maximum at (0, 10)

11. For the function $f(x) = \frac{x^2}{x^2 - 1}$, use a graphing calculator to find all the critical points.

    Answer: critical point at (0, 0)

12. For the function $f(x) = \frac{x}{1 + x^2}$, use a graphing calculator to find all the critical points.

    Answer: critical points at (–1, –½) and (1, ½)

13. For the function $f(x) = \frac{(x-1)^2}{x^2}$, use a graphing calculator to find all the critical points.

    Answer: critical point at (1, 0)

14. For the function $f(x) = \frac{3x^2 - 4x - 4}{x^2}$, use a graphing calculator to find all the critical points.

    Answer: critical point at (–2, 4)

15. For the function $f(x) = \frac{x^3 - 1}{x}$, use a graphing calculator to approximate all the critical points.

    Answer: critical point at (–0.8, 1.9)

16. For the function $f(x) = \frac{x - 1}{x - 2}$, use a graphing calculator to find all the critical points.

    Answer: no critical points

17. For the function $f(x) = \frac{(x-2)^3}{x^2}$, use a graphing calculator to find all the critical points.

    Answer: critical points at (–4, –13.5) and (2, 0)

Section 3.2 Graphing Using the First and Second Derivatives

18. For the function $f(x) = 3x^4 - 4x^3 + 6$, use a graphing calculator to find the relative extrema and points of inflection.

    Answer: relative minimum at (1, 5), points of inflection at (0, 6) and (2/3, 27/5)

19. For the function $f(x) = x^3 + 6x^2$, use a graphing calculator to find the relative extrema and points of inflection.

    Answer: relative maximum at (–4, 32), relative minimum at (0, 0), point of inflection at (–2, 16)

20. For the function $f(x) = -x^3 + 3x^2 + 9x - 2$, use a graphing calculator to find the relative extrema and points of inflection.

    Answer: relative minimum at (–1, –7), relative maximum at (3, 25), point of inflection at (1, 9)

21. For the function $f(x) = x^3 - 3x^2 + 3x - 1$, use a graphing calculator to find the relative extrema and points of inflection.

    Answer: point of inflection at (1, 0)

22. For the function $f(x) = 2x^6 - 6x^4$, use a graphing calculator to find the relative extrema and points of inflection.

    Answer: relative minimum at $\left(-\sqrt{2},-8\right)$ and $\left(\sqrt{2},-8\right)$, relative maximum at (0, 0)

    Points of inflection at $\left(-\sqrt{\frac{6}{5}},-5.18\right)$ and $\left(\sqrt{\frac{6}{5}},-5.18\right)$

23. For the function $f(x) = x^3 + \frac{3}{2}x^2 - 6x + 12$, use a graphing calculator to find the relative extrema and points of inflection.

    Answer: relative maximum at (–2, 22), relative minimum at (1, 17/2), point of inflection at (–1/2, 61/4)

24. For the function $f(x) = x^4 - 4x^3 + 16x$, use a graphing calculator to find the relative extrema and points of inflection.

    Answer: relative minimum at (–1, –11), points of inflection at (0, 0) and (2, 16)

25. For the function $f(x) = 3\sqrt[3]{x^2} - 2x$, use a graphing calculator to find the relative extrema and points of inflection.

    Answer: relative minimum at (0, 0), relative maximum at (1, 1)

26. For the function $f(x) = x\sqrt[3]{(x-3)^2}$, use a graphing calculator to find the relative extrema and points of inflection.

    Answer: relative maximum at (1.8, 2.03), relative minimum at (3, 0), point of inflection at (3.6, 2.56)

27. For the function $f(x) = 8x^{\frac{1}{3}} + \sqrt[3]{x^4}$, use a graphing calculator to find the relative extrema and points of inflection.

    Answer: relative minimum at (–2, –7.6), points of inflection at (0, 0) and (4, 19.05)

28. For the function $f(x) = x^{2/3}(x + 5)$, use a graphing calculator to find the relative extrema and points of inflection.

    Answer: relative maximum at (–2, 4.76), relative minimum at (0, 0), point of inflection at (1, 6)

29. For the function $f(x) = x^{1/3} + 1$, use a graphing calculator to find the relative extrema and points of inflection.

    Answer: point of inflection at (0, 1)

30. Use your graphing calculator to estimate the x-coordinates of the points of inflection of the function $f(x) = x^5 - x^3 + 2x + 5$, rounding your answers to 2 decimal places. (Graph f"(x) either by calculating it directly or using NDERIV twice, and see where it crosses the x-axis.)

    Answer: points of inflection at $x = -0.55$, $x = 0$, $x = 0.55$

31. Use your graphing calculator to estimate the x-coordinates of the points of inflection of the function $f(x) = x^5 - 4x^3 + 6x + 1$, rounding your answers to 2 decimal places. (Graph f"(x) either by calculating it directly or using NDERIV twice, and see where it crosses the x-axis.)

    Answer: points of inflection at $x = -1.10$, $x = 0$, $x = 1.10$

Section 3.3 – 3.5

32. Solve the optimization problem using your graphing calculator. Enter the function to be minimized/maximized as y_1. Then define y_2 to be the derivative function of y_1 using NDERIV. To find maximum/minimum values of y, simply find the x-intercept(s) of y_2 ($f'(x) = 0$). A manufacturer of telephones is $P(x) = -0.01x^3 + 60x - 500$ dollars. How many phones should be produced in order to maximize the company's profit?

    Answer: 3,000

33. Solve the optimization problem using your graphing calculator. Enter the function to be minimized/maximized as y_1. Then define y_2 to be the derivative function of y_1 using NDERIV. To find maximum/minimum values of y, simply find the x-intercept(s) of y_2 ($f'(x) = 0$). The temperature in a kiln heating pieces of ceramics is given by $T(x) = -0.25x^2 + 30x + 75$ degrees, x minutes after the heating begins. Determine when the temperature is the hottest.

    Answer: after 60 minutes

34. Solve the optimization problem using your graphing calculator. Enter the function to be minimized/maximized as y_1. Then define y_2 to be the derivative function of y_1 using NDERIV. To find maximum/minimum values of y, simply find the x-intercept(s) of y_2 ($f'(x) = 0$). The relationship between sensitivity to a drug and size of dosage is given by $S(x) = 2000x - 4x^2$, where S is sensitivity and x is dosage size. Find the dosage that maximizes sensitivity.

    Answer: 250

35. Solve the optimization problem using your graphing calculator. Enter the function to be minimized/maximized as y_1. Then define y_2 to be the derivative function of y_1 using NDERIV. To find maximum/minimum values of y, simply find the x-intercept(s) of y_2 ($f'(x) = 0$). The total cost function for producing widgets is $C(x) = 432 + 20x + 0.03x^2$. Find the minimum average cost. (average cost = $C(x)/x$)

    Answer: $120.00

36. Solve the optimization problem using your graphing calculator. Enter the function to be minimized/maximized as y_1. Then define y_2 to be the derivative function of y_1 using NDERIV. To find maximum/minimum values of y, simply find the x-intercept(s) of y_2 ($f'(x) = 0$). In order to sell x thousand newly released CD's each week, the price p must be $p(x) = \sqrt{784 - 2x^2}$ dollars. Determine how many CD's must be sold each week to maximize revenue. (Revenue = $p(x) \cdot x$)

    Answer: 14,000 CD's

37. Solve the optimization problem using your graphing calculator. Enter the function to be minimized/maximized as y_1. Then define y_2 to be the derivative function of y_1 using NDERIV. To find maximum/minimum values of y, simply find the x-intercept(s) of y_2 ($f'(x) = 0$). The total number of VCR's assembled by a machine in t hours is given by $P(t) = t^3 + 200 - 768/t$. Find the point of diminishing returns (the point where the rate of production is maximized).

    Answer: 4 hours (72 VCR's produced)

38. Solve the optimization problem using your graphing calculator. Enter the function to be minimized/maximized as y_1. Then define y_2 to be the derivative function of y_1 using NDERIV. To find maximum/minimum values of y, simply find the x-intercept(s) of y_2 ($f'(x) = 0$). The amount of material required to make an open top box with a square base that contains 108 in^3 is given by $M = x^2 + 432/x$, where x is the length of a side of the base. Find the length of a side of the base that minimizes the amount of material used.

    Answer: 6 inches

39. Solve the optimization problem using your graphing calculator. Enter the function to be minimized/maximized as y_1. Then define y_2 to be the derivative function of y_1 using NDERIV. To find maximum/minimum values of y, simply find the x-intercept(s) of y_2 ($f'(x) = 0$). It is known from past experiments that the height in feet of a given plant after t months is given by $H(t) = 4\sqrt{t} - 2t$. How long will it take a plant to reach its maximum height?

    Answer: 1 month

40. Solve the optimization problem using your graphing calculator. Enter the function to be minimized/maximized as y_1. Then define y_2 to be the derivative function of y_1 using NDERIV. To find maximum/minimum values of y, simply find the x-intercept(s) of y_2 ($f'(x) = 0$). The concentration of a drug in a person's bloodstream t hours after the drug is administered is given by $B(t) = \dfrac{t}{20(t^2 + 6)}$. At what time is the concentration of the drug the largest?

    Answer: 2.45 hours

41. Solve the optimization problem using your graphing calculator. Enter the function to be minimized/maximized as y_1. Then define y_2 to be the derivative function of y_1 using NDERIV. To find maximum/minimum values of y, simply find the x-intercept(s) of y_2 ($f'(x) = 0$). A manufacturer of light fixtures has daily production costs of $C = 800 + \frac{1}{4}x^2 - 10x$, where C is the total cost of producing x light fixtures. How many fixtures should be produced each day to minimize costs?

    Answer: 20

Chapter 4

Exponential and Logarithmic Functions

Section 4.1 Exponential Functions

MULTIPLE CHOICE 4.1

[c] 1. Which of the following is a sketch of the graph of $y = a^x$ where $a > 1$?

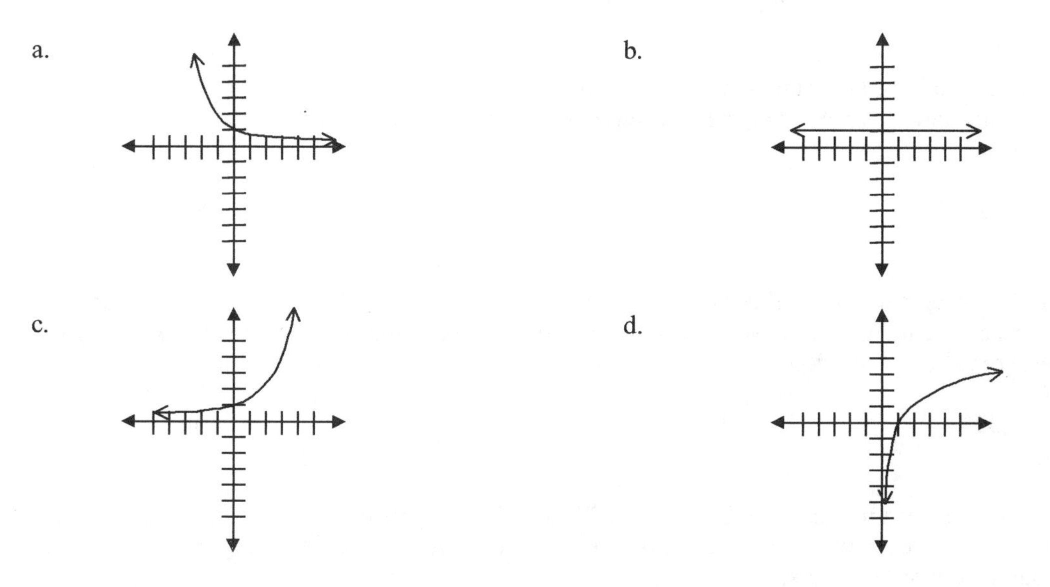

[c] 2. Which of the following is the function corresponding to the given graph?

a. $y = 4^x$ b. $y = 4x$ c. $y = 4^{-x}$ d. $y = \left[\frac{1}{4}\right]^{-x}$

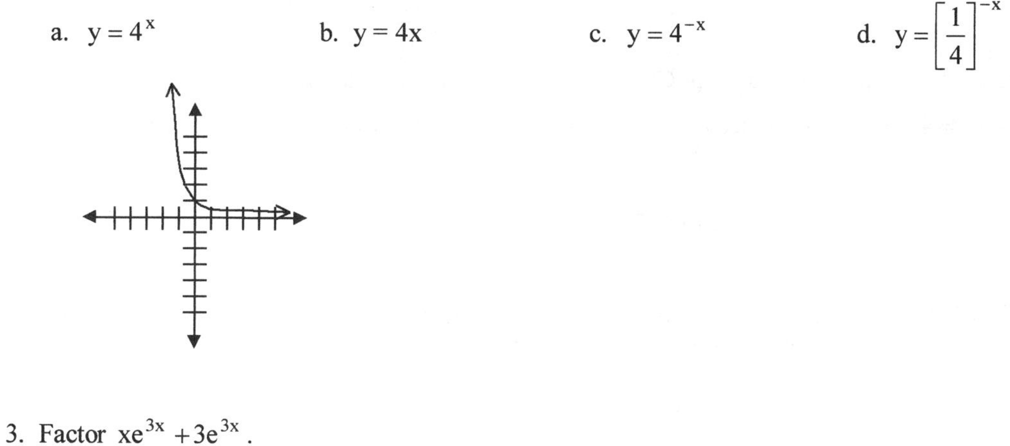

[c] 3. Factor $xe^{3x} + 3e^{3x}$.

a. $x + 3$ b. $3xe^{3x}$ c. $e^{3x}(x+3)$ d. $3^x e^{3x}$

[b] 4. If \$1,500 is invested in a savings account at 5% annual interest compounded continuously, how much will accrue in 10 years? Round your answer to the nearest dollar.

a. \$2,557 b. \$2,473 c. \$2,319 d. \$2,250

[b] 5. If $1,500 is invested in a savings account at 5% annual interest compounded continuously, how much will accrue in 10 years? Round your answer to the nearest dollar.

a. $2,557 b. $2,473 c. $2,319 d. $2,250

[b] 6. If the tuition at a certain college is determined to cost $25,000 in eight years, how large a trust fund paying 12% compounded continually must be established for a child on her tenth birthday to ensure sufficient funds at age 18?

a. $10,584 b. $9,572 c. $15,817 d. $6,409

[a] 7. The value of a certain painting in 5 years is determined to be $15,000. How much should be deposited now at 10.5% compounded continuously so that there would be sufficient funds to pay for the painting in 5 years?

a. $8,873.33 b. $10,194.13 c. $25,147.06 d. $9,847.10

[b] 8. A certificate of deposit will be worth $12,000 when it matures in 10 years. If the annual interest rate is 6% compounded continuously, what should be the price of the certificate today? Round your answer to the nearest dollar.

a. $4318 b. $6586 c. $7112 d. $5024

[d] 9. In order to buy a new car, you borrow $18,500 at 9.5% per year compounded continuously. If your loan is for 4 years, what will be the total amount you pay for the car, including financing? Round your answer to the nearest dollar.

a. $19,641 b. $37,000 c. $25,530 d. 27,052

[b] 10. The cost of producing x units is $C(x) = 41xe^{-0.03x}$ dollars, and the revenue from the sale of x units is $R(x) = 41xe^{0.02x}$. Rounded to the nearest dollar, the profit from the production and sale of 75 units is

a. $32,943 b. $13,457 c. $26,058 d. $28,330

[c] 11. If $1753 is invested at 4.5% annual interest compounded continuously, how much will accrue in 7 years? Round your answer to the nearest dollar.

a. $2398 b. $2386 c. $2402 d. $2403

[c] 12. A bank is offering home improvement loans at an annual rate of 11.5% compounded continuously. For a loan of $18,500 taken for 6 years, what is the total amount that will have to be repaid? Round your answer to the nearest dollar.

a. $36,527 b. $36,763 c. $36,884 d. $37,000

In a wildlife sanctuary, the rabbit population is growing monthly according to the logistic growth function

$$y = \frac{4575}{(1+25e^{-0.6t})}.$$

[a] 13. The number of rabbits in the sanctuary after 10 months is approximately

a. 4308 b. 4325 c. 2500 d. 4380

[b] 14. The maximum number of rabbits that can survive in the sanctuary is approximately

a. 176 b. 4575 c. 45,750 d. 118,950

[d] 15. The logistic growth function $n(t) = 5/(1 + 15e^{-0.3t})$ gives the number of thousands of people, n, who have been stricken with the flu t weeks after its outbreak. At the end of 4 weeks, the approximate number of people who have had the flu is

a. 1157 b. 1384 c. 1291 d. 906

[b] 16. A drug taken intravenously is removed from the blood at a rate that declines exponentially. The concentration of a drug is 25 units per volume when administered, and the decay constant is known to be –0.03. What is the approximate concentration, in units per volume, after 10 minutes?

a. 15 b. 19 c. 62 d. 18

SHORT ANSWER 4.1

17. Use the graphs $y = x^3$ and $y = e^x$ to solve the inequality $x^3 > e^x$ on the interval [0, 6]. Round to one decimal place.

    Answer: [0, 4.5]

18. Graph $y = 5^x$ and $y = \left[\frac{1}{5}\right]^x$ on the same set of axes.

    Answer:

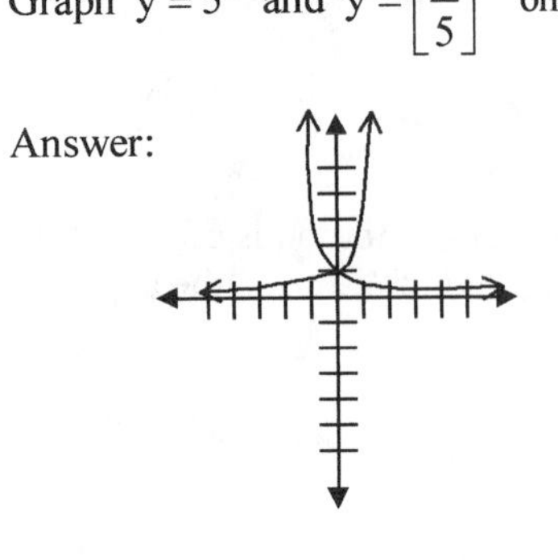

19. If $f(x) = e^{0.5x}$, find f(3). Round your answer to one decimal place.

    Answer: 4.5

20. If $f(x) = 12e^{1.5x}$, find f(0.5). Round your answer to one decimal place.

    Answer: 25.4

21. If x units of a product can be supplied at a cost of $75xe^{-0.04x}$ dollars each, determine the cost function C(x) and the cost to produce 50 units. Round your answer to the nearest dollar.

    Answer: The cost function is $C(x) = 75xe^{-0.04x}$. The cost of 50 units is C(50)=$508.

22. A $40,000 Lexus depreciates by 30% per year. Find its value after 3 years.

    Answer: $13,720

23. A tractor, originally worth $250,000 depreciates by 25% per year. Find its value after 6 months.

    Answer: $216,506.35

24. The population density t miles from the center of a certain city is $D(t) = 12e^{-0.07t}$ thousand people per square mile.
    a. What is the population density at the center of the city?
    b. What is the population density 10 miles from the center of the city?

    Answer: a. 12,000 people/mi^2 b. 5,959 people/mi^2

25. When a certain industrial machine is x years old, its resale value will be $v(x) = 4800e^{-\frac{x}{5}} + 400$ dollars.
   a. How much was the machine worth new?
   b. How much will the machine be worth in 10 years?

   Answer: a. \$5,200 b. \$1,049.61

26. It is estimated that t years from now, the population of a certain country will be $P(t) = \frac{30}{2+3e^{-0.05t}}$ million.
   a. What is the current population?
   b. What will be the population 50 years from now?

   Answer: a. 6 million b. 13.36 million

Section 4.2 Logarithmic Functions

MULTIPLE CHOICE 4.2

[c] 27. Simplify: 7(ln e) =

a. e^7 b. 7e c. 7 d. 1

[d] 28. Simplify: $\frac{5}{2}(\ln e^4) =$

a. $e^{\frac{8}{5}}$ b. $e^{\frac{5}{8}}$ c. e^{10} d. 10

[d] 29. Simplify: 2 ln e + log 10 =

a. 2e + 10 b. log (2e + 10) c. 12 d. 3

[a] 30. If $e^x = 7$, then x =

a. ln 7 b. log 7 c. 7 d. e^7

[b] 31. The logistic growth function $n(t) = 5/(1 + 15e^{-0.3t})$ gives the number of thousands of people, n, who have been stricken with the flu t weeks after its outbreak. The maximum number of people who will get the flu is approximately

a. 7500 b. 5000 c. 9000 d. 4500

[d] 32. A drug taken intravenously is removed from the blood at a rate that declines exponentially. The concentration of a drug is 25 units per volume when administered, and the decay constant is known to be –0.03. Find the time it takes for 75% of the drug to be eliminated from the bloodstream.

a. 9 minutes b. 57 minutes c. 62 minutes d. 46 minutes

[c] 33. Find $\log_3 \frac{1}{27}$ without using a calculator or tables.

a. 2 b. ½ c. –3 d. –½

[c] 34. Find 7 ln e without using a calculator or tables.

a. e^7 b. 7e c. 7 d. 1

[d] 35. Find $\frac{5}{2}(\ln e^4)$ without using a calculator or tables.

a. $e^{\frac{8}{5}}$ b. $e^{\frac{5}{8}}$ c. e^{10} d. 10

[b] 36. If $(0.001)^x = 10{,}000$, then x = ?

a. 3 b. $-\frac{4}{3}$ c. -3 d. -1

[c] 37. Find $\ln\left[\sqrt{e^3}\right]$ without using a calculator or tables.

a. $\sqrt{e^3}$ b. $\frac{2}{3}$ c. $\frac{3}{2}$ d. $\frac{3}{2}\ln e^3$

[b] 38. Find $\ln\left(\frac{5}{e}\right)$ without using a calculator or tables.

a. $5 - e$ b. $\ln 5 - 1$ c. $\frac{\ln 5}{\ln e}$ d. $\frac{\ln 5}{e}$

[a] 39. If $3 \ln x = 21$, then x = ?

a. e^7 b. 63 c. 7 d. e^{63}

[c] 40. Find $\ln(\ln e^2)$ without using a calculator or tables.

a. $\ln^2 e^2$ b. $3 \ln e$ c. $\ln 2$ d. $\ln 2 \ln e^2$

[a] 41. Approximately what annual interest rate is needed to triple an investment of $3450 in 7 years if compounding is continuous?

a. 16% b. 7% c. 21% d. 11.5%

[d] 42. If the population of the earth grows at a rate of 1.5% each year compounded continuously, approximately how long will it take for the population to double?

a. 73 years b. 51 years c. 30 years d. 46 years

[b] 43. A small piece of an ancient rope, recently discovered by an anthropologist, was found to contain 60% of the carbon-14 that would be contained in a similar piece of modern rope. Using the decay constant for carbon-14 ($k = -0.00012$), find the approximate age of the piece of rope, rounded to the nearest 100 years.

a. 3500 b. 4300 c. 2800 d. 5500

[c] 44. Twenty thousand bacteria are placed in a bactericide. Two hours later, only 5000 bacteria remain. If the decrease in the number of bacteria is exponential, approximately how many bacteria will remain 7 hours after they were placed in the bactericide?

a. 1221 b. 3779 c. 156 d. 4844

[c] 45. An entomologist has concluded that in a certain swampy area, the mosquito population is growing exponentially. Further, over a 5-day period, the approximate number of mosquitoes has brown from 40,000 to 65,000. After 30 days, approximately how many mosquitoes will there be? Round your answer to the nearest thousand.

a. 190,000 b. 581,000 c. 737,000 d. 902,000

[a] 46. A company's total revenue has declined over the last 3 years from $427,000 to $358,000. If the revenue is declining exponentially, what will the company's revenue be next year? Round your answer to the nearest thousand.

a. $338,000 b. $358,000 c. $301,000 d. $289,000

SHORT ANSWER 4.2

47. Simplify: log 1 – ln e.

    Answer: –1

48. If 3 ln x = 21, then determine the value of x.

    Answer: e^7

49. If $(0.001)^x = 10{,}000$, then determine the value of x.

    Answer: –4/3

50. The half-life of plutonium-230 is approximately 24,000 years. Determine the decay constant k, rounded to five decimal places.

    Answer: k = –0.00003

51. A small piece of an ancient rope, recently discovered by an anthropologist, was found to contain 60% of the carbon-14 that would be contained in a similar piece of modern rope. Using the decay constant for carbon-14 (k = –0.00012), find the approximate age of the piece of rope, rounded to the nearest 100 years.

    Answer: 4300 years

52. Approximately what annual interest rate is needed to triple an investment of $3450 in 7 years if compounding is continuous?

    Answer: 16%

53. An entomologist has concluded that in a certain swampy area, the mosquito population is growing exponentially. Further, over a 5-day period, the approximate number of mosquitoes has grown from 40,000 to 65,000. After 30 days, approximately how many mosquitoes will there be? Round your answer to the nearest thousand.

    Answer: 737,000

54. Use the properties of natural logarithms to simplify the function $f(x) = \ln(e^{4x}) - 3x + \ln e$.

    Answer: x + 1

55. Use the properties of natural logarithms to simplify the function $f(x) = \ln \pi + 2 \ln r$.

    Answer: $\ln \pi r^2$

56. Use the properties of natural logarithms to simplify the function $f(x) = \ln(e^{-\frac{x}{2}}) + e^{\ln\frac{x}{2}} + \ln 1$.

Answer: 0

57. Use the properties of natural logarithms to simplify the function $f(x) = 2x - e^{\ln x} + \ln(e^{2x})$.

Answer: 3x

58. A bacterial population grows by an amount given by $N(t) = 150e^{\frac{t}{110}}$ where N is the number of bacteria present and t is the time in minutes. In how many minutes will the original number of bacteria triple?

Answer: 120.8 minutes

59. After t days of advertising a new movie, the proportion of people in a town who have seen the movie advertisement is estimated to be $A(t) = 1 - e^{-0.02t}$. How long must the ad run to reach 95% of the people?

Answer: 150 days

60. If the demand function for a CD player is $p = 1000e^{-\frac{q}{20}}$, where q is the number of units demanded, how many units will be demanded if the price of the CD player is \$135.00?

Answer: 40 units

61. The decay in sales of a product after the end of an advertising campaign is given by $S(x) = 40{,}000e^{-0.5x}$, where x is the number of months after the end and S is the number of sales. After how many months will sales be below 750?

Answer: 7.95 months

62. The number of people infected by a disease in t days is given by $N(t) = \dfrac{30{,}000}{1+100e^{-0.5t}}$. How many days would it take for 20,000 people to be infected?

Answer: 10.6 days

63. The mastery of learning the art of painting is approximated by $M(t) = 100(1 - e^{-0.04t})$, where t is the number of hours of instruction and M is the percentage of master. How many hours of instruction would be necessary in order to achieve 75% master of painting? (Hint: M = 75)

Answer: 35 hours

64. If an automobile depreciates by 15% per year, how soon will it be worth only 40% of its original value?

Answer: 5.6 years.

Section 4.3 Differentiation of Logarithmic and Exponential Functions

MULTIPLE CHOICE 4.3

[c] 65. Find the derivative of the function $y = \ln \sqrt{x^2+4}$.

a. $\frac{x}{\sqrt{x^2+4}}$ b. $\frac{2x}{\sqrt{x^2+4}}$ c. $\frac{x}{x^2+4}$ d. $\frac{1}{x}$

[b] 66. Find the derivative of the function $y = \ln (5-x)^6$.

a. $\frac{1}{(5-x)^6}$ b. $\frac{6}{x-5}$ c. $-6(5-x)^5$ d. $6(5-x)^5$

[d] 67. Find the derivative of the function $y = \ln [\ln (2x)]$.

a. $\frac{1}{\ln(2x)}$ b. $\frac{2}{x \ln(2x)}$ c. $\frac{1}{2\ln(2x)}$ d. $\frac{1}{x\ln(2x)}$

[d] 68. Find the derivative of the function $y = x^2 \ln x$.

a. $2x \ln x$ b. $2x$ c. $x + 2 \ln x$ d. $x(1 + 2 \ln x)$

[a] 69. Find the derivative of the function $y = \sqrt{3+e^x}$.

a. $\frac{e^x}{2\sqrt{3+e^x}}$ b. $\frac{1}{2\sqrt{3+e^x}}$ c. $\frac{xe^{2x-1}}{\sqrt{3+e^x}}$ d. e^x

[a] 70. Find the derivative of the function $y = \ln (e^x - x)$.

a. $\frac{e^x-1}{e^x-x}$ b. $1-\frac{1}{x}$ c. $e^x - 1$ d. $\frac{e^x-x}{e^x-1}$

[c] 71. Find the derivative of the function $y = 2^{4-x^2}$.

a. $-2x\left(2^{4-x^2}\right)$ b. $-4x\left(2^{4-x^2}\right)\ln 2$ c. $-2x\left(2^{4-x^2}\right)\ln 2$ d. $-4x\left(2^{4-x^2}\right)$

[d] 72. Find the derivative of the function $y = x \cdot 2^x$.

a. $x^2 \cdot 2^{x-1} + 2x$ b. $2^x \ln 2$ c. $x \cdot 2^{x-1} + 1$ d. $2^x(x \ln 2 + 1)$

[c] 73. Find the derivative of the function $y = \dfrac{x}{\ln x}$.

a. $\dfrac{1}{(\ln x)^2}$ b. $\dfrac{x-1}{x(\ln x)^2}$ c. $\dfrac{\ln x - 1}{(\ln x)^2}$ d. $\dfrac{x \ln x + 1}{(\ln x)^2}$

[d] 74. Find the derivative of the function $y = 3xe^{2x}$.

a. $6xe^{2x}$ b. $6e^{2x}(x + 1)$ c. $6x^2e^{2x}$ d. $3e^{2x}(2x + 1)$

[c] 75. Find the derivative of the function $y = e^x + x^e$.

a. e^x b. $2e^{x-1}$ c. $e^x + ex^{e-1}$ d. $\dfrac{e-1}{x}$

[d] 76. Find the derivative of the function $y = 4^{2x}$.

a. $32e^{2x}$ b. $8(4^{2x})$ c. $(\ln 4)(8e^{2x})$ d. $2(\ln 4)(4^{2x})$

[a] 77. Find the derivative of the function $y = 3^{\ln x}$.

a. $\dfrac{3^{\ln x} \ln 3}{x}$ b. $3^{\ln x}$ c. $3^{\ln x} \ln 3$ d. $\dfrac{3^{\ln x}}{x}$

[c] 78. Find the derivative of the function $y = \log_3(x^2 - 4)$.

a. $\dfrac{2x}{x^2 - 4}$ b. $\dfrac{1}{(\ln 3)(x^2 - 4)}$ c. $\dfrac{2x}{(x^2 - 4)(\ln 3)}$ d. $\dfrac{x^2 - 4}{2x \ln 3}$

[c] 79. For the function $f(x) = \ln(x e^x)$, find $f'(3)$.

a. $\ln 3 + 3$ b. $e^3 + \ln 3$ c. $\dfrac{4}{3}$ d. $\dfrac{1}{3}$

[c] 80. For the function $f(x) = e^x + x^e$, find $f'(2)$.

a. e^2 b. $2e$ c. $e^2 + \dfrac{e}{2}(2^e)$ d. $\dfrac{e-1}{2}$

[c] 81. Which of the following statements about the graph of the function $f(x) = x e^{-x}$ is false?

a. There is a relative maximum at $x = 1$. b. There is a point of inflection at $x = 2$.
c. The graph is concave up at $x = 0$. d. The graph is rising at $x = 0$.

[a] 82. The critical number(s) for $f(x) = x\,e^{5x}$ is (are)

a. $x = -\frac{1}{5}$ b. $x = \frac{1}{5}$ c. $x = 0, \frac{1}{5}$ d. $x = 0, -\frac{1}{5}$

[c] 83. If $y = x^{e} + e^{x} + e^{e}$, then $y' =$

a. $e^{x} + x^{e}$ b. $e(x + e)^{e-1}$ c. $e^{x} + ex^{e-1}$ d. $e\,x^{e-1} + e^{x} + e(e^{e-1})$

[c] 84. Which of the following points is a relative minimum for the graph $f(x) = e^{x+1} - x - 1$?

a. $(-1, e)$ b. $(1, e)$ c. $(-1, 1)$ d, $(-1, -\frac{1}{e})$

[c] 85. If $f(x) = \frac{1}{e^{x}}$, find $f''(x)$.

a. e^{x} b. $\frac{1}{e^{2x}}$ c. $\frac{1}{e^{x}}$ d. $-\frac{2}{e^{x}}$

[a] 86. An automobile depreciates as if gets older. The value of the automobile after t years is estimated to be $V(t) = 25{,}000e^{-.2t}$ where $V(t)$ is the value in dollars. How fast is the car's value changing at the end of 5 years?

a. –$1,839.40/yr b. –$5,133.81/yr c. –$3,024.67/yr d. –$9,196.99/yr

SHORT ANSWER 4.3

87. Find the derivative of the function $y = x^3 \ln(x+1)$.

Answer: $3x^2 \ln(x+1) + \frac{x^3}{x+1}$

88. Find the derivative of the function $y = \frac{\ln x}{x^4}$.

Answer: $\frac{1-4\ln x}{x^5}$

89. Find the derivative of the function $y = \ln(x^3 + 2x)^3$.

Answer: $\frac{3(3x^2+2)}{x(x^2+2)}$

90. Find the derivative of the function $y = \ln\sqrt{3-x^2}$.

Answer: $\frac{x}{x^2-3}$

91. Find the derivative of the function $y = (e^x + 1)^4$.

Answer: $4e^x(e^x + 1)^3$

92. Find the derivative of the function $y = x^e \cdot e^x$.

Answer: $e^x x^{e-1}(e + x)$

93. Find the derivative of the function $y = e^{x^2-1}$.

Answer: $2xe^{x^2-1}$

94. Find the derivative of the function $y = \log_5 x$.

Answer: $\frac{1}{x\ln 5}$

95. Find the derivative of the function $y = \log_{10}(5x^4 - x)$.

Answer: $\dfrac{20x^3 - 1}{(5x^4 - x)\ln 10}$

96. Find the derivative of the function $y = \ln e^{x^3}$.

Answer: $3x^2$

97. Find the derivative of the function $y = e^{-x} + x \ln x - x^2 + 5$.

Answer: $-e^{-x} + 1 + \ln x - 2x$

98. For the function $f(x) = \ln(e^{-x} + e^{x})$, find $f'(0)$.

Answer: 0

99. For the function $f(x) = \dfrac{x^4}{\ln x}$, find $f'(e)$.

Answer: $3e^3$

100. For the function $f(x) = e^{x^4+1}$, find $f''(x)$.

Answer: $4x^2(4x^4 + 3)\, e^{x^4+1}$

101. The value of a home t years after its purchase is estimated to be $V(t) = 100{,}000e^{.06t}$ dollars. Find the rate of change of its value at
a. the time of purchase
b. $t = 5$

Answer: a. increasing by $6,000 per year
b. increasing by $8,099 per year

102. After t weeks of training, a typist can type at a speed of $S(t) = 100 - 100e^{-.25t}$ words per minute (wpm). Find the rate of change of the typist's speed at
a. $t = 0$
b. $t = 4$

Answer: a. increasing by 25 wpm per week
b. increasing by 9.2 wpm per week

103. A political activist is staging a protest by beginning a starvation diet. The person's weight t days after the starvation begins is given by $W(t) = 180e^{-.01t}$. Determine the rate of weight loss 10 days after the protest began.

Answer: The rate of loss is approximately 1.6 pounds per day.

104. The consumer expenditure for a product is $E(p) = 40{,}000pe^{-.01p}$, where p is the selling price in dollars. Find the price that maximizes consumer expenditure E(p).

Answer: p = $100

105. Ten milliliters of a drug are injected into a person's body. The amount of the drug remaining in the body t hours after the injection is given by $D(t) = 10e^{-.04t}$. Determine how much of the drug is still in the body at the end of 3 hours. How fast is the amount of the drug in the body increasing?

Answer: At the end of 3 hours, there are 8.87 milliliters of the drug left in the body and the drug is decreasing at the rate of .355 milliliters per hour.

106. The sales of a new product can be approximated for its first few years on the market by the function $S(t) = \dfrac{100{,}000}{1+100e^{-.3t}}$ where t is time in years since the introduction of the product. Determine the rate of change in sales after the product has been on the market for 2 years.

Answer: sales increase by 527 units per year

107. The total revenue received from the sale of x items is estimated to be $R(x) = 30 \ln(2x + 1)$ while the total cost to product x items is given by $C(x) = x/2$. Deter the number of items that should be manufactured so that profit is a maximum.

Answer: 59.5 items

108. The temperature of a casserole t minutes after it was removed from an oven is given by $T(t) = 285e^{-.02t} + 65$.
a. Determine the temperature of the casserole immediately after it was taken from the oven.
b. Determine the temperature of the casserole 10 minutes later.
c. Find the rate at which the temperature is dropping at the end of 10 minutes.

Answer: a. 350 degrees
b. Approximately 298 degrees
c. Approximately 4.7 degrees per minute

109. The cost of x items of a certain commodity can be supplied at $85e^{-.04x}$ each. Determine the marginal cost when 20 items are supplied.

Answer: $7.64

110. If the price p at which x units ($x > 1$) can be sold is given by the demand equation $p = 13.50 - 3\ln x$, determine the marginal revenue function MR(x).

Answer: $MR(x) = 10.50 - 3 \ln x$

111. In an experiment dealing with memory retention, a group of people memorized 30 "nonsense" words. The approximate number of words remembered t minutes ($t \geq 1$) after the memorization stopped is described by the function $w(t) = 29 - 11 \ln t$. One of the results of this experiment stated, "People continue to to forget." Tell where this conclusion came from.

Answer: Because $w'(t) = -11/t$, then $w'(t) < 0$ for all $t \geq 1$. Thus w is a decreasing function; that is, memory decreases, or people continue to forget.

Section 4.4 Two Applications to Economics: Relative Rates and Elasticity of Demand

MULTIPLE CHOICE 4.4

[a] 112. For the demand equation $D(p) = 50 - \frac{1}{4}p$, the elasticity of demand at price p = 25 is approximately

a. 0.14 b. 0.33 c. 1.67 d. 1.88

[a] 113. For the demand equation $D(p) = 16 - 8p^2$, the elasticity of demand at price p = .5 is approximately

a. $\frac{2}{7}$ b. $\frac{8}{7}$ c. $\frac{7}{2}$ d. $\frac{3}{7}$

[c] 114. For the demand equation $D(p) = \frac{10}{p} - p$, the elasticity of demand at price p = 1 is

a. $\frac{9}{11}$ b. $\frac{4}{9}$ c. $\frac{11}{9}$ d. $\frac{1}{2}$

[c] 115. For the demand equation $D(p) = 30 - 10\sqrt{p}$, the elasticity of demand at price p = 4 is

a. 10 b. $\frac{1}{10}$ c. 1 d. $\frac{1}{3}$

[b] 116. The demand for the Sunday newspaper is given by D(p) = 5,000- 1,250p where the price p is in dollars. Determine the elasticity of demand when the price of a Sunday newspaper is $2.25.

a. $\frac{5}{8}$ b. $\frac{9}{7}$ c. $\frac{3}{8}$ d. $\frac{7}{5}$

[c] 117. The demand for a TI graphing calculator is give by $D(p) = 100\sqrt{225 - p}$ where p is the price in dollars. Determine the elasticity of demand if the graphing calculator price is set at $100.

a. 0.25 b. 1.6 c. 0.4 d. 1.0

At a shop, the weekly demand for souvenir tee shirts is $x = 300 - 10p$, $7.50 \leq p \leq 25$, where x is the number of shirts and p is the price for a single shirt.

[c] 118. The shop owner is currently selling the shirts for $16.50 each. What advice would you give him in order to maximize the weekly revenue?

a. Raise the price of a shirt to $20.00.
b. Raise the price of a shirt to $17.50.
c. Lower the price of a shirt to $15.00.
d. Lower the price of a shirt to $12.50.

[a] 119. The elasticity of demand when the price of a shirt is $10.00 is

a. .5 b. 2 c. .75 d. 5

[c] 120. If the price of a shirt is set to produce maximum revenue, how much will that revenue be?

a. $1500 b. $1850 c. $2250 d. $2700

The demand for tickets to a theme park is given by $x = 1000\sqrt{36 - p}$, $0 \le p \le 36$, where x is the number of tickets and p is the price for a single ticket.

[b] 121. How should the ticket be priced in order to maximize the revenue?

a. $20.00 b. $24.00 c. $30.00 d. $36.00

[d] 122. Find the range of prices for which demand is elastic.

a. $0 \le p \le 24$ b. $30 \le p \le 36$ c. $0 \le p \le 20$ d. $24 \le p \le 36$

[c] 123. Determine the elasticity of demand if the price of a ticket is wet at $18.

a. .25 b. .3 c. .5 d. 1.0

[b] 124. Determine the price of a ticket that results in an elasticity of 0.75.

a. $17.00 b. $21.60 c. $23.00 d. $22.50

SHORT ANSWER 4.4

125. For the function $f(t) = 50\,e^{.4t}$, find the RELATIVE rate of change at $t = 9$.

Answer: 0.4

126. For the function $f(t) = e^{t^4}$, find the RELATIVE rate of change at $t = \frac{1}{2}$.

Answer: $\frac{1}{2}$

127. For the function $f(t) = e^{t^5}$, find the RELATIVE rate of change at $t = 1$.

Answer: 5

128. For the function $f(t) = 40\sqrt{t+1}$, find the RELATIVE rate of change at $t = 3$.

Answer: $\frac{1}{8}$

129. For the demand function $D(p) = 500 - 4p$, find the elasticity of demand, E(p) and determine whether the demand is elastic, inelastic or unitary elastic at the given price $p = 25$.

Answer: $E(p) = \dfrac{4p}{500-4p}$; $\frac{1}{4}$; inelastic

130. For the demand function $D(p) = 32 - 2p^2$, find the elasticity of demand, E(p) and determine whether the demand is elastic, inelastic or unitary elastic at the given price $p = 2$.

Answer: $E(p) = \dfrac{4p^2}{32-2p^2}$; $\frac{2}{3}$; inelastic

131. For the demand function $D(p) = 50e^{-.02p}$, find the elasticity of demand, E(p) and determine whether the demand is elastic, inelastic or unitary elastic at the given price $p = 100$.

Answer: $E(p) = \dfrac{p}{50}$; 2; elastic

132. A movie theatre estimates its ticket demand function to be $D(p) = \frac{27}{p^2 + 1}$ where p is the price of a ticket in dollars. If the theatre is currently charging $5 per ticket, determine the elasticity of demand to decide whether they should raise the price or lower the price in order to increase revenue?

Answer: $E(p) = \frac{2p^2}{p^2 + 1}$; E(5) = 1.9; lower the price to increase revenue

133. A toy dealer estimates its demand function for a particular toy to be $D(p) = 9{,}000 - 30p^2$, where p is the price of the toy in dollars. If the toy dealer raises the price of the toy from the current price of $7, use the elasticity of demand to determine if it will increase revenue.

Answer: E(7) = 0.39; yes, raising the price will increase revenue

134. A car wash company estimates its demand function to be $D(p) = 500\,e^{-0.2p}$ where p is the price of a car wash in dollars. If the current price of a car wash is $5, use the elasticity of demand to determine how a price increase will affect the total revenue.

Answer: E(5) = 1; unitary elasticity; there will be no change in revenue as a result of a price increase.

135. At an electronics store, the weekly demand for compact discs is D(p) = 300 – 10p, where p is the price of a CD in dollars. If CDs are currently selling for $16.50 each, use the elasticity of demand th determine whether the price should be raised or lowered to increase revenue.

Answer: E(16.50) = 1.22; lower the price to increase revenue

Chapter 4 – Graphing Calculator

Exponential and Logarithmic Functions

Section 4.1 Exponential Functions

1. Graph $y_1 = ex$ and $y_2 = e^x$ on the same window, which curve is higher for large values of x?

   Answer: $y_2 = e^x$ is higher

2. Graph $y_1 = x^e$ and $y_2 = e^x$ on the same window, which curve is higher for large values of x?

   Answer: $y_2 = e^x$ is higher

3. Graph the two functions $y_1 = 16.09e^{0.071x}$ and $y_2 = 21.29e^{0.039(x-4)}$ on the same window, which curve is higher for large values of x?

   Answer: $y_1 = 16.09e^{0.071x}$ is higher

4. Graph the two functions $y_1 = 76.1\,e^{0.031x}$ and $y_2 = 50 - 6.02e^{0.091x}$ on the same window, which curve is higher for large values of x?

   Answer: $y_1 = 76.1\,e^{0.031x}$ is higher

Section 4.2 Logarithmic Functions

5. Use a graphing calculator to find the domain of the following function.

$f(x) = \ln(1.96 - x^2)$

Answer: $\{x \mid -1.4 < x < 1.4\}$

6. Use a graphing calculator to find the domain of the following function.

$g(x) = \ln(5.3 + \ln x)$

Answer: $\{x \mid x > 0\}$

7. Solve the following problem on a graphing calculator by graphing the appropriate exponential function together with the appropriate constant function, and using INTERSECT to find where they meet. Choose an appropriate window. Answers may vary slightly due to the size of the viewing screen. A beanie baby collection is predicted to grow in value by 4% compounded annually. How soon will the value be double? Round your answer to one decimal place.

Answer: The functions are $y_1 = (1.04)^x$ and $y_2 = 2$, and the doubling time is 17.7 years

8. Solve the following problem on a graphing calculator by graphing the appropriate exponential function together with the appropriate constant function, and using INTERSECT to find where they meet. Choose an appropriate window. Answers may vary slightly due to the size of the viewing screen. A money market grows at 7% compounded quarterly. How soon will the account triple? Round your answer to one decimal place.

Answer: The functions are $y_1 = \left[1 + \frac{0.07}{4}\right]^{4x}$ and $y_2 = 3$, and the tripling time is 15.83 years.

9. Solve the following problem on a graphing calculator by graphing the appropriate exponential function together with the appropriate constant function, and using INTERSECT to find where they meet. Choose an appropriate window. Answers may vary slightly due to the size of the viewing screen. A bank account grows at 9.5% compounded continuously. How soon will the account increase by 50%? Round your answer to one decimal place.

Answer: The functions are $y_1 = e^{0.095x}$ and $y_2 = 1.5$, the time is 4.3 years.

Section 4.3 Differentiation of Logarithmic and Exponential Functions

10. Using a graphing calculator, graph the following function, including all extreme points and inflection points. Indicate the coordinates of all relative extreme points and inflection points.

$$f(x) = \frac{e^{-\frac{x^2}{2}}}{\sqrt{2\pi}}$$

Answer: rel max at (0, 0.4), points of inflection at (–1, 0.24) and (1, 0.24)

11. Using a graphing calculator, graph the following function, including all extreme points and inflection points. Indicate the coordinates of all relative extreme points and inflection points.

$$f(x) = \frac{x^2}{e^x}$$

Answer: rel min at (0, 0), rel max at (2, 0.54), points of inflection (3.4, 0.38) and (0.58, 0.19)

12. Using a graphing calculator, graph the following function, including all extreme points and inflection points. Indicate the coordinates of all relative extreme points and inflection points.
$f(x) = x \ln x$

Answer: rel min at (0.37, – 0.37), no rel max, no inflection points

13. Graph the following function on the indicated interval using the graphing calculator. Indicate the coordinates of the absolute maximum and absolute minimum.

$$y = \frac{\ln x}{x} \text{ on } [2, 10]$$

Answer: absolute max at (e, 1/e) or (2,7, 0.37), absolute min at (10, 0.23)

14. Graph the following function on the indicated interval using the graphing calculator. Indicate the coordinates of the absolute maximum and absolute minimum.
$y = x^2e^{-2x}$ on [0, 3]

Answer: absolute max at (1, 0.14), absolute min at (0, 0)

15. The consumer expenditure for a product is given by $E(p) = 10{,}000pe^{-0.02p}$, where p is the selling price in dollars. Find the price that maximizes consumer expenditure. [Find the critical value of E(p) by hand, and then graph it using your graphing calculator to verify that it is a maximum at this critical value.]

Answer: p = $50

16. If a company is growing so that its value t years from now will be 5,000t dollars, then its present value (at 10% interest compounded continuously) is $V(t) = 5{,}000te^{-0.10t}$. Find the number of years that maximizes the present value V(t). [Find the critical value of V(t) by hand, then graph it using your graphing calculator to verify that it does take on the maximum value at its critical point.]

Answer: 10 years

Section 4.4 Two Applications to Economics: Relative Rates and Elasticity of Demand

17. Sketch the revenue function using the demand function $x = 1490e^{-0.5p}$ using a window of [0, 15] by [0, 1200] and determine the values of p for which the demand is elastic.

    Answer: $p > 2$

18. Sketch revenue function using the demand function of $x = \sqrt{2.25 - p^2}$ with the window [0, 1.5] by [0, 2] and determine the values of p for which the demand is elastic.

    Answer: $p > 1.06$

19. Sketch the revenue function using the demand function $x = p^2e^{-(p+3)}$ using a window of [0, 10] by [0, 0.1] and determine the values of p for which the demand is elastic.

    Answer: $p > 3$

Chapter 5

Integration and Its Applications

Section 5.1 Antiderivatives and Indefinite Integrals

MULTIPLE CHOICE 5.1

[b] 1. Antidifferentiate. $\int \frac{3}{2} dx$

a. $\frac{9x}{2} + C$ b. $\frac{3x}{2} + C$ c. $\frac{3x}{4} + C$ d. $\frac{3}{2} + C$

[a] 2. Antidifferentiate $\int 6.4x dx$.

a. $3.2x^2 + C$ b. $12.8 + C$ c. $12.8x^2 + C$ d. $3.2x + C$

[d] 3. The value of the indefinite integral $\int 2\pi dx$ is

a. $\pi^2 + C$ b. $2\pi + C$ c. C d. $2\pi x + C$

[a] 4. The value of the indefinite integral $\int t^{\frac{-1}{10}} dt$ is

a. $\frac{10}{9} t^{0.9} + C$ b. $\frac{9}{10} t^{0.9} + C$ c. $\frac{10}{9} t^{1.1} + C$ d. $1.1t^{1.1} + C$

[c] 5. The value of the indefinite integral $\int \left(\frac{3}{4}x^2 - \frac{5}{7}x \right) dx$ is

a. $\frac{3x}{2} - \frac{5}{7} + C$ b. $\frac{1}{4}x^2 - \frac{5x}{14} + C$ c. $\frac{1}{4}x^3 - \frac{5x^2}{14} + C$ d. $\frac{1}{4}x^3 - \frac{10x^2}{7} + C$

[c] 6. Find the integral $\int (3x^3 - 2x^2 + 5) dx$.

a. $\frac{3}{4}x^4 - \frac{2}{3}x^3 + C$ b. $9x^2 - 4x + C$ c. $\frac{3}{4}x^4 - \frac{2}{3}x^3 + 5x + C$ d. $9x^3 - 8x^2 + 60x + C$

[a] 7. Find the integral. $\int \sqrt[3]{x}dx$

a. $\frac{3}{4}x^{4/3}+C$ b. $\frac{3}{2}x^{2/3}+C$ c. $\frac{1}{3x^{2/3}}+C$ d. $\sqrt[3]{\frac{x^2}{2}}+C$

[b] 8. The value of the indefinite integral $\int \frac{4}{\sqrt{3x}}dx$ is

a. $-\frac{4}{\sqrt{3x}}+C$ b. $\frac{8\sqrt{x}}{\sqrt{3}}+C$ c. $-2\sqrt{3x}+C$ d. $-\frac{2}{\sqrt{3x}}\ C$

[d] 9. The value of the indefinite integral $\int \frac{5}{2\sqrt[3]{y}}dy$ is

a. $-\frac{5}{2}y^{1/3}+C$ b. $\frac{5}{3}y^{2/3}+C$ c. $-5y^{2/3}+C$ d. $\frac{15}{4}y^{2/3}+C$

[b] 10. Find the integral. $\int -\frac{1}{x^2}dx$

a. $-\frac{1}{6x^6}+C$ b. $\frac{1}{x}+C$ c. $\frac{1}{3x^3}+C$ d. $-\frac{1}{x}+C$

[a] 11. Evaluate $\int \frac{x-\sqrt[3]{x}}{x}dx$

a. $x-3\sqrt[3]{x}+C$ b. $\frac{x-\sqrt[3]{x}}{3x}+C$

c. $\frac{x^2}{2}-\frac{3}{4}x^{4/3}+\ln|x|+C$ d. $x+x^{3/2}+C$

[d] 12. Evaluate $\int \frac{x-\sqrt{x}}{x}dx$

a. $\frac{3x-2\sqrt{x}}{3x}+C$ b. $x+2\sqrt{x}+C$ c. $\frac{2x-\sqrt{x}}{x}+C$ d. $x-2\sqrt{x}+C$

[b] 13. Given the marginal cost function $MC(x)=\frac{2.5}{\sqrt{x}}$ and the fact that the fixed cost if \$37.50. The cost for 25 items is

a. \$187.50 b. \$62.50 c. \$50.00 d. \$162.50

[a] 14. A company's marginal revenue function is $MR(x) = 17.50 - 0.06x$. Assuming that there is no revenue when no units are sold, find the revenue from the sale of 100 items.

a. $1450 b. $1750 c. $2050 d. $2350

[b] 15. The marginal profit function for a personal computer company is $MP(x) = 1200 - 4x$. If the company loses $1000 when no computers are sold, then the profit from the manufacture and sale of 200 computers is

a. $99,000 b. $159,000 c. $138,000 d. $39,000

[d] 16. Given the marginal revenue function $MR(x) = 45 - 0.3x^2$. Assuming that there is no revenue when no units are sold, the revenue from the sale of 10 items is

a. $150 b. $449 c. $390 d. $350

[c] 17. Given the marginal profit function $MP(x) = 50 + 0.2x - 0.03x^2$ and that $P(0) = -\$100$. The profit from the sale of 20 units is

a. $420 b. $940 c. $860 d. $780

[d] 18. The daily marginal cost of a cycle helmet manufacturer is $MC(x) = 43 + 0.04x$. The daily fixed cost is $253. Determine the cost to produce 50 helmets.

a. $2200 b. $2403 c. $1997 d. $2453

[b] 19. The marginal profit function for a cash register manufacturer is $MP(x) = 1375 - 1.5x$. If the company loses $2425 when no cash registers are sold, then the profit from the manufacture and sale of 50 cash registers is

a. $65,000 b. $64,450 c. $72,500 d. $66,875

SHORT ANSWER 5.1

20. Evaluate $\int \frac{1}{x^2} - 3\sqrt{x}dx$

    Answer: $-\frac{1}{x} - 2x^{3/2} + C$

21. Evaluate $\int x(x+6)^2 dx$

    Answer: $\frac{x^4}{4} + 4x^3 + 18x^2 + C$

22. Evaluate $\int \sqrt{x}\left(x^2 - 1\right)dx$

    Answer: $\frac{2}{7}x^{\frac{7}{2}} - \frac{2}{3}x^{\frac{3}{2}} + C$

23. Evaluate $\int \frac{x^2 + 4x + 3}{x+1} dx$

    Answer: $\frac{x^2}{2} + 3x + C$

24. What is the value of the integral $\int 0.3x^{-0.7}dx$?

    Answer: $x^{0.3} + C$

25. A company's marginal revenue function is MR(x) = 17.50 – 0.06x. Assume that there is no revenue when no units are sold. Find the revenue function R(x).

    Answer: $R(x) = 17.50x - 0.03x^2$

26. If a person can memorize words at the rate of $r(t) = 2t^{-2/3}$ words per minute, find a formula for the total number of words that can be memorized in t minutes and use the formula to find the total number of words that can be memorized in 27 minutes.

    Answer: $6t^{1/3}$; 18 words

27. A home, initially worth $100,000 is increasing in value at the rate of $r(t) = 600\sqrt{t}$ dollars per year after t years. Find a formula for its value after t years, and use the formula to find its value after 16 years.

    Answer: $400t^{3/2} + 100{,}000$; $125,600

28. An office duplicating machine is depreciating at a rate given by the formula $dV/dt = -275e^{-.4t}$, Where V is the value of the machine in dollars and t is time in years. When the machine was purchased (that is, at t = 0), its value was $3500. Find the function V(t) that gives the value of the duplicating machine at any time.

    Answer: $V(t) = 687.5e^{-.4t} + 2812.5$

29. It is estimated that t months from now the population of a certain town will be changing at the rate of $p(t) = 4 + 5t^{\frac{2}{3}}$ people per month. If the current population is 10,000, determine the population 8 months from now.

    Answer: 10,128

30. The resale value of a certain machine decreases at a rate that changes with time. When the machine is t years old, the rate at which its value is changing is 300(t – 10) dollars per year. If the machine was bought new for $15,000, how much will it be worth 5 years later?

    Answer: $3750

31. The daily marginal cost of a cycle helmet manufacturer is MC(x) = 43 + 0.43x. The daily fixed cost is $253. Determine the daily cost function.

    Answer: $C(x) = 43x\ 0.02x^2 + 253$

32. The marginal profit function for a cash register manufacturer is MP(x) = 1375 – 1.5x. Determine the profit function P(x) if P(0) = –$2425.

    Answer: $P(x) = 1375x - 0.75x^2 - 2425$

33. The equation dn/dt = 40 – 2t describes the rate at which people are being infected by a virus, where n is the number of people, and t is time measured in days. It is known that the spread of the virus began with 1 person. Find the function that describes the number of people who get the virus at any time t.

    Answer: $n(t) = 40t - t^2 + 1$

34. The rate at which a kiln heats is given by dT/dx = –0.6x + 23. The variable T represents temperature, and x represents time in minutes. Prior to heating, the temperature in the room in which the kiln is located was 68 degrees. Find the function that describes the heat in the kiln at any time x.

    Answer: $T(x) = -0.3x^2 + 23x + 68$

35. The velocity of a model rocket shot vertically upward from the ground is v(t) = –32t + 475.5 feet per second. Determine the formula for the rocket's distance, s, above the ground at any time t.

    Answer: $s(t) = -16t^2 + 475.5t$

36. A model rocket shot vertically upward from the ground has a constant acceleration (due to gravity) of –32 feet per second. The rocket's initial velocity is 225 feet per second. Find the rocket's velocity at the end of 2 seconds and how high the rocket is then.

    Answer: The veloctiy is 161 feet per second. The height is 386 feet.

Section 5.2 Integration Using Logarithmic and Exponential Functions

MULTIPLE CHOICE 5.2

For the following demand function(s) d(x) and demand level x, find the consumer's surplus.

[d] 37. $\int e^{5x}\,dx$

a. $e^{5x} + C$ b. $e^{5x+1} + C$ c. $5e^{5x} + C$ d. $\frac{e^{5x}}{5} + C$

[b] 38. $\int e^{0.02x}\,dx$

a. $\frac{1}{50}e^{0.02x} + C$ b. $50\,e^{0.02x} + C$ c. $\frac{e^{0.02x}}{0.02} + C$ d. $0.02x\,e^{0.02x} + C$

[c] 39. $\int 4e^{(5/3)x}\,dx$

a. $4\,e^{(5/3)x} + C$ b. $\frac{20}{3}e^{(5/3)x} + C$ c. $\frac{12}{5}e^{(5/3)x} + C$ d. $\frac{20}{3}xe^{(5/3)x} + C$

[d] 40. $\int 3x^{-1}\,dx$

a. $\frac{3x^{-2}}{-2} + C$ b. $-3x^{-2} + C$ c. $-3\ln|x| + C$ d. $3\ln|x| + C$

[a] 41. $\int \left(e^{5x} - \frac{3}{x} \right) dx$

a. $\frac{1}{5}e^{5x} - 3\ln|x| + C$ b. $e^{5x} - 3\ln|x| + C$

c. $5e^{5x} - \frac{3}{x^2} + C$ d. $5xe^{5x} - 3\ln|x| + C$

SHORT ANSWER 5.2

42. Evaluate the integral $\int(e^{.01x}+\frac{4}{x})dx$

Answer: $100e^{.01x}+4\ln|x|+C$

43. Evaluate the integral $\int(2x^{-3}+4x^{-2}+6x^{-1}+8)dx$

Answer: $-\frac{1}{x^2}-\frac{4}{x}+6\ln|x|+8x+C$

44. Evaluate the integral $\int(2e^{.01t}-5e^{-.05t})dt$

Answer: $200e^{.01t}+100e^{-.05t}+C$

45. What is the value of the integral $\int(e^e+e^x+x^e)dx$

Answer: $e^e x+e^x+\frac{x^{e+1}}{e+1}+C$

46. Evaluate the integral $\int\frac{(x-5)(x-2)}{x^2}dx$

Answer: $x-7\ln|x|-\frac{10}{x}+C$

47. Evaluate the integral $\int\frac{(x-5)^2}{x^2}dx$

Answer: $x-10\ln|x|-\frac{25}{x}+C$

48. Evaluate the integral $\int\frac{(x+3)(3x-1)}{x}dx$

Answer: $\frac{3x^2}{2}+8x-3\ln|x|+C$

49. Evaluate the integral $\int \frac{18x^3 - 14x^2 + 8x - 26}{2x} dx$.

Answer: $3x^3 - \frac{7x^2}{2} + 4x - 13\ln|x| + C$

50. Find the particular antiderivative f(x) if $f'(x) = 2.7 - \frac{4}{x}$, given that f(1) = 5.

Answer: $f(x) = 2.7x - 4 \ln |x| + 2.3$

51. Find the particular antiderivative f(t) if $f'(t) = 9e^{-3t} + 9$, given that f(0) = 7.

Answer: $f(t) = -3e^{-3t} + 9t + 10$

52. The rate at which a drug is being absorbed by the body after t hours is given by the formula $dD/dt = 0.4e^{-0.02t}$, where D is the amount of drug in milliliters. Find the function D(t) that describes how much drug is in the body at any time t. (At time t = 0, there is no drug in the body.)

Answer: $D(t) = -20e^{-0.02t} + 20$

53. A country expects to consume its reserves of oil at the rate of $r(t) = 25e^{.05t}$ million barrels per year, where t is the number of years from now. Find a formula for the total amount of oil that will be consumed during the next t years, if 500 million barrels are consumed this year (t = 0).

Answer: $500e^{.05t}$

54. The rate at which a disease spreads is given by $r(t) = e^{-.02t}$ where r(t) is the percentage of the general population that has contracted the disease in t years. If none has the disease at t = 0, what percent of the population will have the disease, in 3 years?

Answer: 2.91%

55. If consumption is $11 billion when disposable income is x = 0 and the marginal consumption is $M(x) = 0.6 - e^{-3x}$ billion dollars, find the consumption when disposable income is $5 billion.

Answer: $13.7 billion

56. Given the marginal revenue function $MR(x) = 8e^{-0.2x} + 5$ and assuming there is no revenue when no units are sold, find the revenue from the sale of 10 items.

Answer: $84.59

57. An office machine is depreciating at a rate of $V(t) = -300e^{-.2t}$ where V is the value of the machine in dollars and t is time in years of the machine cost $2000 originally, find the function that gives the value of the machine at time t.

Answer: $1500e^{-.2t} + 500$

58. A fax dealer decides to sell her machines at a discount. She predicts the sales rate during month t to be $r(t) = \frac{150}{t}$. Use t = 1 as the beginning of the discount period. Determine a formula for the number of fax machines that will be sold up to month t, and use it to find the total fax machines sold during the first 3 months of the sale.

Answer: 150 ln t; 164 machines

59. If the world consumption of silver is estimated to be $r(t) = 12e^{.025t}$ thousand metric tons per year where t is measured in years, determine a formula for the total amount of silver that will be consumed with in t years. Use this formula to find the total consumption during the first 5 years, if 480 thousand metric tons are consumer this year (t = 0).

Answer: $480e^{.025t}$; 63,911 metric tons

60. A culture of bacteria is growing at a rate of $r(t) = 15e^{.7t}$ cells per day where t is the number of days since the culture was started. If the culture began with 50 cells, how long will it take for the population to reach 500 cells?

Answer: 4.42 years

Section 5.3 Definite Integrals and Areas

MULTIPLE CHOICE 5.3

Find the exact value of the area under the following curve(s) between the given x-values.

[d] 61. $f(x) = x^2 - x + 5$ from $x = 1$ to $x = 2$

a. $\frac{10}{3}$ b. $\frac{101}{15}$ c. 6 d. $\frac{35}{6}$

[c] 62. $f(x) = x^3 + 2x^2 - 3x$ from $x = -3$ to $x = 1$

a. $\frac{7}{6}$ b. $\frac{45}{2}$ c. $\frac{32}{3}$ d. $\frac{71}{6}$

[a] 63. $f(x) = 3e^x + 1$ from $x = 0$ to $x = 1$

a. $3e - 2$ b. $2e + 3$ c. $3e + 2$ d. $2e - 3$

[b] 64. $f(x) = 4x - 1 + 3/x$ from $x = 1$ to $x = e$

a. $e^2 + e + 5$ b. $2e^2 - e + 2$ c. $e^2 - e - 1$ d. $2e^2 + e - 3$

[d] 65. $f(x) = 2x + 2/x$ from $x = 1$ to $x = e$

a. $2e - 1$ b. $e + 2$ c. $e^2 - 2$ d. $e^2 + 1$

[a] 66. $\int_1^2 (5x^4 + 1)dx$

a. 32 b. 75 c. 64 d. 47

Find the exact value of the area under the following curve(s) between the given x-values.

[c] 67. $\int_0^{10} e^{.2t}dt$

a. $5e + 5$ b. $5e$ c. $5e^2 - 5$ d. $5e^2 - 1$

[d] 68. $\int_1^4 x^{3/2}dx$

a. $\frac{31}{5}$ b. $\frac{57}{2}$ c. $\frac{31}{2}$ d. $\frac{62}{5}$

[a] 69. $\int_{e}^{e^2} \frac{1}{x} dx$

a. 1 b. e c. $e^2 - e$ d. 2

[d] 70. $\int_{0}^{1} e^{2x} dx$

a. e b. e^2 c. $2e + 2$ d. $\frac{1}{2}(e^2 - 1)$

[b] 71. $\int_{0}^{10} \frac{5}{e^{.4x}} dx$

a. 10.9 b. 12.3 c. 15.1 d. 12.7

[a] 72. $\int_{1}^{5} 2.5x^4 dx$

a. 1562 b. 512 c. 7810 d. 1562.5

[b] 73. $\int_{5}^{7} (5t - 7) dt$

a. 0 b. 46 c. 106 d. 10

[d] 74. $\int_{2}^{3} (1.5t^2 - 0.5t - 3.25) dt$

a. 7 b. 22.5 c. 21 d. 11.5

[c] 75. $\int_{1.5}^{2.5} \frac{60}{x^2} dx$

a. −17.07 b. −60 c. 16 d. 15

[a] 76. $\int_{0}^{1} (1 - 1.5e^{2t}) dt$

a. $1.75 - 0.75e^2$ b. $2.5 - 1.5e^2$ c. $1 = 0.75e^2$ d. $1.5 - 0.5e^3$

[a] 77. $\int_1^e \left(\frac{4}{5}x + \frac{4}{x}\right)dx$

a. $3.6 + 0.4e^2$ b. $4 + 0.4e^2$ c. $(4 - 4.8e + 0.8e^2)/e$ d. $3.2 + 0.8e^2$

[b] 78. $\int_3^6 (2x-5)^2\,dx$

a. 114 b. 57 c. 78 d. 57.17

[c] 79. $\int_0^{100} e^{0.02t}\,dt$

a. $50e^{-2} + 1$ b. $50e^{-2} + 50$ c. $50 - 50e^{-2}$ d. $1 - 50e^{-2}$

[d] 80. $\int_1^4 \frac{5.75x + 3.25}{x}\,dx$

a. –2.4375 b. 52.875 + ln 4 c. 28.75 + 2.75ln 4 d. 17.25 + 6.5 ln 2

[c] 81. $\int_0^1 \frac{e^x + e^{-x}}{2}\,dx$

a. $e - e^{-1}$ b. $\frac{e^{-1} - e}{2}$ c. $\frac{e - e^{-1}}{2}$ d. $\frac{e + e^{-1}}{2}$

[b] 82. $\int_1^e \frac{5.4x^2 - 2.6x + 4}{x}\,dx$

a. $5.4e^2 - 2.6e - 1.8$ b. $2.7e^2 - 2.6e + 3.9$ c. $1.4e^2 + 2.6$ d. $2.7e^2 - 2.6e + 3.9$

[a] 83. The area bounded by the graph of $y = 0.5x^2 + 2.75$, the x-axis, and the vertical lines x = 1 and x = 3 is

a. 14.3 b. 9.83 c. 18.5 d. 4

[d] 84. The area bounded by the graph of $y = \sqrt[3]{x}$, the x-axis, and the vertical lines x = 1 and x = 8 is

a. 0.25 b. 0.75 c. 12 d. 11.25

[a] 85. The area bounded by the graph of y = 2.5/x, the x-axis, and the vertical lines x = 1 and x = e^2 is

a. 5 b. 2.5 c. 7.5 d. 6.25

[b] 86. The marginal cost for producing x units is MC = 500 – 0.2x dollars. The cost of increasing the number of units from 10 to 20 is

a. $14,950 b. $4,970 c. $5,050 d. $15,000

[c] 87. The rate at which a child gains weight is $R(t) = 3.5\sqrt{t}$ pounds per year where t is the time in years for the first 12 years. The total weight gained from age 4 through age 9 is approximately

a. 23 pounds b. 27 pounds c. 44 pounds d. 40 pounds

[b] 88. A high school student can memorize words and their definitions at the rate of $6e^{-.3t}$ words per minute. Approximately how many words can the student memorize in the first 8 minutes?

a. 20 b. 18 c. 15 d. 19

[b] 89. Suppose you wish to approximate the area bounded by the function $f(x) = 6x^2 + 7$, the x-axis, and the vertical lines x = –2 and x = 4. If you wish to use four subintervals, the length of each subinterval is

a. 1 b. 1.5 c. 0.75 d. 2

SHORT ANSWER 5.3

Find the exact value of the area under the following curve(s) between the given x-values.

90. $f(x) = 1 + x^{-1} + x^{-2}$ from $x = 1$ to $x = 3$

    Answer: $\frac{8}{3} + \ln 3$

Find the exact value of the area under the following curve(s) between the given x-values.

91. $f(x) = \sqrt{x} - \frac{1}{\sqrt{x}}$ from $x = 1$ to $x = 9$

    Answer: 40/3

92. $f(x) = 6x^2 + 4e^{2x}$ from $x = 0$ to $x = 3$

    Answer: $52 + 2e^6$

93. $f(x) = 9x^2 + 3/x$ from $x = 1$ to $x = 2$

    Answer: $21 + 3 \ln 2$

94. $f(x) = 1 + x\sqrt{x} - \frac{1}{x^2}$ from $x = 1$ to $x = 4$

    Answer: $\frac{293}{20}$

95. $f(x) = (x^7 + 1)(3x^2 + 1)$ from $x = -1$ to $x = 1$

    Answer: 4

96. $f(x) = 2/x + e^x$ from $x = 1$ to $x = 4$

    Answer $2 \ln 4 + e^4 - e$

97. Evaluate the integral $\int_1^3 (6x^2 - 4x + 1)dx$

    Answer: 38

98. Evaluate the integral $\int_0^1 (e^{-x} + 4)dx$

Answer: $5 - e^{-1}$

99. Evaluate the integral $\int_{-3}^{-1} \frac{x+1}{x^3} dx$

Answer: 2/9

100. Evaluate the integral $\int_{\ln 3}^{\ln 5} e^x dx$

Answer: 2

101. Evaluate the integral $\int_1^{e^4} \frac{5}{x} dx$

Answer: 20

102. Evaluate the integral $\int_1^e \frac{(x+2)^2}{x} dx$

Answer: $e^2/2 + 4e - ½$

103. Approximate the area bounded by the graph of $f(x) = 2x^2$, the x-axis, and the vertical lines $x = 1$ and $x = 5$. Use four subintervals.

Answer: 108

104. Approximate the area bounded by the graph of $f(x) = -x^2 + 4x - 1$, the x-axis, and the vertical lines $x = 1$ and $x = 3$. Use four subintervals.

Answer: 5.25

105. Approximate the area bounded by the graph of $f(x) = \sqrt{2x-1} + 2$, the x-axis, and the vertical lines $x = 1$ and $x = 5$. Use four subintervals.

Answer: 17.61

106. Approximate the area bounded by the graph of $f(x) = -x^2 + 10$, the x-axis, and the vertical lines $x = -1$ and $x = 3$. Use four subintervals.

Answer: 26

107. Approximate the area bounded by the graph of $f(x) = \frac{4}{x^2}$, the x-axis, and the vertical lines x = 5 and x = 5. Use four subintervals.

Answer: 1669/900 (approximately 1.854)

108. A function gives the growth rate of a colony of bacteria from the time the colony was introduced into a growth medium until 12 hours later. Interpret the area under the graph of this function.

Answer: The total number of bacteria present during this time period.

109. A company is considering a new manufacturing process. It is known that the rate of savings from this process is given by S(t) = 1000/t where t is in years. Determine the total savings from the third year through the sixth year.

Answer: $693.15

110. The depreciation rate for an all-terrain vehicle is d(t) = 225(t – 9) dollars, where t is time in years and $0 \leq t \leq 9$. The cost of the vehicle, when new, was $8000.
a. How much was the depreciation of the vehicle in the first year (that is, from t = 0 to t = 1)?
b. How much was the depreciation in the ninth year?

Answer: a. $1912.50; b. $112.50

111. Unemployment in a city is increasing at the rate of 3.5t + 235 people per month. Determine the number of people who will be unemployed 1 year from now. (Use t = 0 to represent this month.)

Answer: 3072 people

112. A worker can assemble calculators at the rate of $-4.5t^2 + 26t + 4.2$ calculators per hour. Approximately how many calculators can the worker assemble in the first half of a 7-hour shift? (Use t = 0 through t = 3.5.)

Answer: 110 calculators

113. World consumption of copper is running at the rate of $r(t) = 10e^{.05t}$ billion tons per year, where t is the number of years since 1990. Determine the total consumption of copper from the year 1995 to the year 2000.

Answer: 72.9 billion tons

114. Divorces in America are estimated to be increasing at a rate of $r(t) = 1.2e^{.01t}$ million divorces per year, where t is the number of years since 1990. Assuming this rate continues, determine the total number of divorces from the year 1990 to the year 2000.

Answer: 12.62 million divorces

115. A city's rate of water consumption is $r(t) = -3t^2 + 12t + 6$ thousand gallons per hour, where t is the number of hours after noon. Determine the total water consumption between the hours 1pm and 4 pm.

Answer: 45,000 gallons

116. An average child of age t years grows at the rate of $r(t) = 4.4t^{-1/3}$ inches per year. Determine the total growth from age one to age eight.

Answer: 19.8 inches

117. An epidemic is spreading at the rate of $r(t) = 12e^{.04t}$ new cases per day, where t is the number of days since the epidemic began. Find the total number of new cases in the first 10 days of the epidemic.

Answer: $30e^4 - 30 \approx 1608$ cases

118. A certain function gives the rate of depreciation of a piece of machinery from the first through the third year. Interpret the area under the graph of this function.

Answer: The total amount of depreciation of the machinery over the 3-year period.

119. A certain function describes the rate, in words per minute, at which words from a previously memorized list are forgotten. Interpret the area under the graph of this function between the first and third minutes.

Answer: The number of words forgotten in those minutes.

120. A certain function describes the rate at which a drug, intravenously administered, is being absorbed by the body over a 6 hour period. Interpret the area under the graph of this function.

Answer: The total amount of the drug absorbed in those 6 hours.

Section 5.4 Further Applications of Definite Integrals: Average Value and Area Between Curves

MULTIPLE CHOICE 5.4

Find the average value of the following function(s) over the given interval.

[c] 121. $f(x) = x^2 - 1$ on [0, 3]

a. 4 b. 8 c. 2 d. 6

[b] 122. $f(x) = 2x^2 + 3$ on [0, 2]

a. 4 b. 17/3 c. 22/3 d. 27

[a] 123. $f(x) = \frac{2}{x}$ on [1, 3]

a. ln 3 b. 2 ln 3 c. 2 ln 2 d. $\frac{\ln 3}{2}$

[c] 124. $f(x) = e^{-3x}$ on [0, 2]

a. $-\frac{1}{3e^6}+\frac{1}{3}$ b. $-3e^{-6} + 3$ c. $-\frac{1}{6e^6}+\frac{1}{6}$ d. $-\frac{3}{2}e^{-6}+6$

[d] 125. $f(x) = 1.8x + 7$ on [5, 9]

a. 28.8 b. 78.4 c. 23.2 d. 19.6

[d] 126. $f(x) = 7.5x^2 - 0.3$ on [2, 5]

a. 291.6 b. 7 c. 8 d. 97.2

[a] 127. A stone is dropped off a building and falls with velocity $v(t) = 32t$ feet per second. What is the average velocity of the stone during the first 5 seconds?

a. 80 ft/sec b. 400 ft/sec c. 160 ft/sec d. 200ft/sec

[b] 128. Find the area of the region bounded by $y = x^2 - 4x$ and $y = x - 4$.

a. 23/6 b. 9/2 c. 8/3 d. –9/2

[d] 129. Find the area of the region bounded by $f(x) = 6x - x^2$ and $g(x) = x^2 - 2x$.

a. 20/3 b. 32 c. 128 d. 64/3

[c] 130. Find the area of the region bounded by $y = -x^2 + 2x + 3$ and $y = 3$.

a. 22/3 b. 9/2 c. 4/3 d. –4/3

[b] 131. Which of the following expressions gives the area of the region enclosed by the x-axis and the graph of $y = x^3 - x^2 - 6x$?

a. $\int_{-3}^{0} -(x^3 - x^2 - 6x)dx - \int_{0}^{2}(x^3 - x^2 - 6x)dx$

b. $\int_{-2}^{0}(x^3 - x^2 - 6x)dx + \int_{0}^{3} -(x^3 - x^2 - 6x)dx$

c. $\int_{-2}^{0} -(x^3 - x^2 - 6x)dx + \int_{0}^{3}(x^3 - x^2 - 6x)dx$

d. $\int_{-3}^{0} -(x^3 - x^2 - 6x)dx + \int_{0}^{2} -(x^3 - x^2 - 6x)dx$

[b] 132. The marginal cost for producing x units is 452.50 + 28x dollars. The cost of increasing the number of units from 15 to 25 is

a. $11,487.50 b. $10,125 c. $4553 d. $11,400

[a] 133. The marginal revenue from the sale of x thousand units is $3x^2 + 4x$ thousand dollars. If 5000 units are now sold, what will be the additional revenue if sales increase to 8000 units?

a. $465,000 b. $815,000 c. $129,000 d. $763,000

[a] 134. At the top of a hill that is 135 feet high, an objet is launched directly upward with a velocity $v = 145 - 32t$ feet per second. How high above the ground is the object at the end of 3 seconds?

a. 426 feet b. 579 feet c. 280 feet d. 184 feet

[c] 135. A stone is dropped from a cliff that is 484 feet high and falls with a velocity of 32t feet per second. How many seconds will it take for the stone to hit the ground?

a. 16 seconds b. 6 seconds c. 5.5 seconds d. 8 seconds

[a] 136. A vehicle's velocity (in feet per second) is $v = 7.5\sqrt{t}$ for $0 \le t \le 65$. The distance the vehicle travels between $t = 4$ and $t = 25$ is

a. 585 feet b. 91 feet c. 457.5 feet d. 625 feet

[d] 137. The rate at which water is pumped into a town's water supply is $dw/dt = 675 + 46t$ gallons per hour for $0 \le t \le 5$. The total pumped in 5 hours is

a. 3900 gallons b. 4525 gallons c. 2263 gallons d. 3950 gallons

[a] 138. A city's population is increasing at the rage of $2275e^{-0.05t}$ people per year. If this growth continues, what will be the increase in population over the next 5 years?

a. 12,923 b. 2921 c. 45,500 d. 6501

[b] 139. The area enclosed by the curves $y = 2x + 1$ and $y = x^2 + 1$ is

a. 2/3 b. 4/3 c. 15/3 d. 20/3

[c] 140. The area enclosed by the curves $y = 4 - x$ and $y = 4x - x^2$ is

a. 9 b. 11/2 c. 9/2 d. 32/2

[d] 141. The area enclosed by the curves $y = \sqrt{x}$ and $y = x/2$ is

a. 1/3 b. 3/2 c. ½ d. 4/3

[c] 142. The area enclosed by the curves $y = x^2 - 4x + 2$ and $y = -x + 6$ is

a. 115/6 b. 119/6 c. 125/6 d. 56/3

[c] 143. The area enclosed by the curves $y = \sqrt{x}$ and $y = x^2$ is

a. 2/3 b. 1/3 c. 3/2 d. 3

[d] 144. The area enclosed by the curves $y = -x - 4$ and $y = x^2 + 5x - 4$ is

a. 44 b. 6 c. 10 d. 36

[a] 145. The area enclosed by the curves $y = 6x - 7$ and $y = 5 + 2x - x^2$ is

a. 256/3 b. 88 c. 34 2/3 d. 118 1/3

[d] 146. The area enclosed by the curves $y = 2.5/x$ and $y = 2.5x$ from $x = 1$ to $x = e$ is

a. 2.5e b. e + 2.25 c. $1.25e^2 - 1$ d. $1.25e^2 - 3.75$

[c] 147. Find the area of the region bounded by the graph of $y = 2x - 2$, the x-axis, and the vertical lines $x = -1$ and $x = 2$. (HINT: Find the x-intercept of the graph.)

a. 3 b. 8 c. 5 d. 9

[b] 148. Determine the area of the region between the x-axis and the graph of the curve $y = \sqrt{x} - 1.2$ from $x = 0$ to $x = 9$. (HINT: Find the x-intercept of the graph.)

a. 7.2 b. 8.352 c. 7.776 d. 3

SHORT ANSWER 5.4

Find the average value of the following function(s) over the given interval.

149. $f(x) = 3x^2 - 5$ on [2, 5]

Answer: 34

150. $f(x) = e^{x/3}$ on [0, 6]

Answer: $\frac{1}{2}e^2 - \frac{1}{2}$

151. $f(x) = e^{-x}$ on [0, 4]

Answer: $\frac{1}{4} - \frac{1}{4}e^{-4}$

152. $f(x) = x^3 + 1$ on [0, 2]

Answer: 3

153. If the temperature at time t hours is $T(t) = -0.3t^2 + 6t + 70$ degrees, determine the average temperature between t = 0 hours and t = 10 hours.

Answer: 90 degrees

154. The amount of pollution in a river t years after the closing of a chemical plant is $P(t) = 100/t$ tons $(t \geq 1)$. Determine the average amount of pollution between 1 and 5 hours after the closing.

Answer: 40.2 tons

155. The world population is predicted to be $P(t) = 5.7e^{.01t}$ billion, where t is the number of years after the year 2000. Approximate the average population between the years 2000 and 2050.

Answer: 7.4 billion people

156. Find the area of the region bounded by $y = x^2 - 3x - 4$ and $y = x + 1$.

Answer: 36 square units

157. Suppose that t years from now, one investment plan will be generating profit at a rate of $R_1(t) = 50 + t^2$ dollars per year, while a second plan will be generating profit at a rate of $R_2(t) = 200 + 5t$ dollars per year. For the first 15 years the second plan will be more profitable than the first plan. Find the net excess profit if you invest in the second plan instead of the first plan for the first 15 years.

Answer: $1687.50

158. An industrial machine generates revenue at the rate of $R(t) = 5000\text{-}20t^2$ dollars per year and results in costs that accumulate at the rate of $C(t) = 2500 + 5t^2$ dollars per year. Find the net earnings generated by the machine during the first 5 years.

Answer: \$11,458.33

159. What expression involving definite integrals is used to find the area between the graphs of $y = x^2 - 4x + 5$ and $y = 7 - 3x$ from $x = 0$ to $x = 4$?

Answer: $\int_0^2 (2 + x - x^2)dx + \int_2^4 (x^2 - x - 2)dx$

160. The weekly marginal profit function for color laser printer manufacturer is $78 - 0.06x$ dollars, where x is the number of laser printers produced. The current production level is 250. If production is increased to 350 printers, what will be the increase in profits?

Answer: \$6000

161. If \$4300 is deposited in an account that pays 6.3% per year, compounded continuously for 7 years, what is the average amount of money in the account during the 7-year period? Round your answer to the nearest dollar.

Answer: \$5404

162. A medicine causes a person's temperature to change at the rate of $-0.0275t^4 + 0.015t^2$ degrees (Celsius) per hour. Determine the change in temperature from $t = 1$ to $t = 3$ hours.

Answer: The temperature decreases by 1.2 degrees.

163. The graph of $y = 5x - x^2$ is above the graph of $y = x - 5$ between $x = 1$ and $x = 4$. Find the area of the region between the two graphs from $x = 1$ and $x = 4$.

Answer: 24

164. The graph of $y = 3 + 2x - x^2$ is above the graph of $y = x + 1$ between $x = -1$ and $x = 2$. Find the area of the region between the two graphs from $x = -1$ to $x = 2$.

Answer: 4.5

165. The graph of $y = x^3 + 2.5$ is below the graph of $y = x + 4.25$ between $x = 0$ and $x = 1$. Find the area of the region between the two graphs from $x = 0$ to $x = 1$.

Answer: 2

166. The graph of $y = \sqrt{x} + 3.5$ is below the graph of $y = x^2 + 10.25$ between $x = 4$ and $x = 9$. Find the area of the region between the two graphs from $x = 4$ to $x = 9$.

Answer: 242.75

167. The area enclosed by the x-axis and the graph of $y = 2x + x^2 - x^3$ is

Answer: 37/12

168. Find the area enclosed by the curves $y = 11 - x - x^2$ and $y = -1$.

Answer: 57 1/16

169. Find the area of the region bounded by the graph of $y = x^2 - 3x$, the x-axis, and the vertical lines $x = 1$ and $x = 2$. (HINT: Find the x-intercept of the graph.)

Answer: 5 1/6

170. Find the area of the region between the x-axis and the graph of the curve $y = 2 - x - x^2$ from $x = -5$ to $x = -1$. (HINT: Find the x-intercepts of the graph.)

Answer: 71/3

171. Find the area of the region bounded by the graph of $y = 4.5x^2$ and the graph of $y = -4.5x^2$ from $x = 0$ to $x = 3$.

Answer: 81

172. Find the area of the region between the graphs of $y = x^2 - 2$ and $y = x$. (HINT: Find the points of intersection of the two curves.)

Answer: 4 ½

Section 5.5 Two Applications to Economics: Consumers' Surplus and Income Distribution

MULTIPLE CHOICE 5.5

[a] 173. For the following demand function d(x) and demand level x, determine the consumer's surplus: $d(x) = 200 - 0.8x$, $x = 40$

a. $640 b. $7360 c. $520 d. $750

For the supply function(s) s(x) and demand level x, determine the producer's surplus.

[d] 174. $s(x) = 1 + 0.25x$, $x = 28$

a. $100 b. $50 c. $150 d. $98

[b] 175. $s(x) = 0.1x^2 + 1$, $x = 5$

a. $9.50 b. $8.33 c. $7.67 d. $10.00

[c] 176. For supply function $s(x) = x^2 + 1$ and demand function $d(x) = 9 - 2x$, the producer's surplus is

a. $16.33 b. $6.67 c. $5.33 d. $15.67

[d] 177. For supply function $s(x) = 3\sqrt{x} + 2$, and demand function $d(x) = 17 - 2\sqrt{x}$, the consumer's surplus at the market demand level is

a. $41 b. $25 c. $11 d. $18

[d] 178. For the supply function $s(x) = 3\sqrt{x} + 2$, and demand function $d(x) = 17 - 2\sqrt{x}$, the producer's surplus at the market demand level is

a. $59 b. $17 c. $99 d. $27

[a] 179. For the supply function $S(x) = 10x - 50$ and the demand function $D(x) = 150 - x^2$, the consumer's surplus is

a. 666.67 b. 193.33 c. 233.33 d. 286.67

[d] 180. For the supply function $S(x) = 10x - 50$ and the demand function $D(x) = 150 - x^2$, the producer's surplus is

a. 150 b. 250 c. 400 d. 500

[b] 181. For the supply function $S(x) = x^2 + x + 10$ and the demand function $D(x) = x^2 - 12x + 36$, the consumer's surplus is

a. 14.93 b. 18.67 c. 15.43 d. 16.67

[a] 182. For the supply function $S(x) = x^2 + x + 10$ and the demand function $D(x) = x^2 - 12x + 36$, the producer's surplus is

a. 7.33 b. 9.47 c. 6.67 d. 8.93

[c] 183. For the supply function $S(x) = x^2$ and the demand function $D(x) = x^2 - 8x + 16$, the consumer's surplus is

a. 9.83 b. 8.87 c. 10.67 d. 11.53

[d] 184. For the supply function $S(x) = x^2$ and the demand function $D(x) = x^2 - 8x + 16$, the producer's surplus is

a. 4.67 b. 5.67 c. 6.33 d. 5.33

SHORT ANSWER 5.5

185. For the following demand function d(x) and demand level x, determine the consumer's surplus.
$d(x) = 35 - 0.03x^2$, $x = 30$

Answer: $540

For the following demand function d(x) and supply function s(x), determine
a. the market demand
b. consumer's surplus at this demand level
c. producer's surplus at this demand level

186. $d(x) = 60 - 0.2x$, $s(x) = 0.4x$

Answer: a. 100 b. $1000 c. $2000

187. $d(x) = 120 - 0.4x$, $s(x) = 0.2x$

Answer: a. 200 b. $8000 c. $4000

Find the Gini index for the following Lorenz curve(s).

188. $L(x) = x^{1.5}$

Answer: 0.2

189. $L(x) = x^4$

Answer: 0.6

190. $L(x) = 0.4x + 0.6x^3$

Answer: 0.3

191. For the supply function $S(x) = 3.5x + 7.6$ and the demand function $D(x) = -1.5x + 37.6$, determine the equilibrium point and the consumer's surplus.

Answer: The equilibrium point is (6, 28.60) and the consumer's surplus is 27.

192. For the supply function $S(x) = 3.5x + 7.6$ and the demand function $D(x) = -1.5x + 37.6$, determine the equilibrium point and the producer's surplus.

Answer: The equilibrium point is (6, 28.60) and the producer's surplus is 63.

193. For the supply function $S(x) = 4x/5 + 5/4$ and the demand function $D(x) = -11x/5 + 41/4$, determine the equilibrium point and the consumer's surplus.

Answer: The equilibrium point is (3, 3.65) and the consumer's surplus is 9.9.

194. For the supply function $S(x) = 4x/5 + 5/4$ and the demand function $D(x) = -11x/5 + 41/4$, determine the equilibrium point and the producer's surplus.

Answer: The equilibrium point is (3, 3.65) and the producer's surplus is 3.6.

195. For the supply function $S(x) = 0.23x + 4.7$ and the demand function $D(x) = -0.27x + 15.2$, determine the equilibrium point and the consumer's surplus.

Answer: The equilibrium point is (21, 9.53) and the consumer's surplus is 59.535.

196. For the supply function $S(x) = 0.23x + 4.7$ and the demand function $D(x) = -0.27x + 15.2$, determine the equilibrium point and the producer's surplus.

Answer: The equilibrium point is (21, 9.53) and the producer's surplus is 50.715.

197. For the supply function $S(x) = 0.5x^2$ and the demand function $D(x) = 225 = 0.5x^2$, determine the equilibrium point and the consumer's surplus.

Answer: The equilibrium point is (15, 112.50) and the consumer's surplus is 1125.

198. For the supply function $S(x) = 0.5x^2$ and the demand function $D(x) = 225 = 0.5x^2$, determine the equilibrium point and the producer's surplus.

Answer: The equilibrium point is (15, 112.50) and the producer's surplus is 1125.

199. For the supply function $S(x) = \sqrt{x} + 2$ and the demand function $D(x) = -3x + 32$, determine the equilibrium point and the consumer's surplus.

Answer: The equilibrium point is (9, 5) and the consumer's surplus is 121.50.

200. For the supply function $S(x) = \sqrt{x} + 2$ and the demand function $D(x) = -3x + 32$, determine the equilibrium point and the producer's surplus.

Answer: The equilibrium point is (9, 5) and the producer's surplus is 9.

201. For the supply function $S(x) = 10x - 100$ and the demand function $D(x) = 1100 = x^2$, determine the equilibrium point and the consumer's surplus.

Answer: The equilibrium point is (30, 200) and the consumer's surplus is 18,000.

202. For the supply function $S(x) = 10x - 100$ and the demand function $D(x) = 1100 = x^2$, determine the equilibrium point and the producer's surplus.

Answer: The equilibrium point is (30, 200) and the producer's surplus is 4500.

Section 5.6 Integration by Substitution

MULTIPLE CHOICE 5.6

Find the following integral(s) by the substitution method.

[a] 203. $\int x^2(x^3+5)^6 dx$

a. $\frac{1}{21}(x^3+5)^7+C$
b. $\frac{(x^3+5)^7}{7}+C$
c. $\frac{x^3}{3}\cdot\frac{(x^3+5)^7}{7}+C$
d. $\frac{x^2(x^3+5)^7}{21}+C$

[b] 204. $\int\sqrt{3x}\,dx$

a. $\frac{3}{2}\sqrt{3x}+C$
b. $\frac{2x\sqrt{3x}}{3}+C$
c. $\frac{x\sqrt{3x}}{4}+C$
d. $x\sqrt{3x}+C$

[c] 205. $\int x\sqrt{4-9x^2dx}$

a. $-\frac{1}{18}(4-9x^2)^{3/2}+C$
b. $-\frac{4}{27}(4-9x^2)^{3/2}+C$
c. $-\frac{1}{27}(4-9x^2)^{3/2}+C$
d. $\frac{2}{3}(4-9x^2)^{3/2}+C$

[c] 206. $\int\frac{3-x}{(6x-x^2)^2}dx$

a. $\frac{3-x}{2(6x-x^2)}+C$
b. $\frac{3(3-x)^2}{2(6x-x^2)^3}+C$
c. $\frac{-1}{2(6x-x^2)}+C$
d. $\frac{-2}{(6x-x^2)^3}+C$

[a] 207. $\int e^{1-x}dx$

a. $-e^{1-x}+C$
b. $e^{1-x}+C$
c. $e^{x-1}+C$
d. $-e^{x-1}+C$

[b] 208. $\int\frac{(\ln x)^5}{x}dx$

a. $\frac{(\ln x)^6}{6x}+C$
b. $\frac{(\ln x)^6}{6}+C$
c. $\frac{5(\ln x)^4}{x}+C$
d. $\frac{(\ln x)^6}{6x^2}+C$

[a] 209. $\int \frac{x}{2x^2-1}dx$

a. $\frac{1}{4}\ln\left|2x^2-1\right|+C$ b. $\ln\left|2x^2-1\right|+C$ c. $4\ln\left|2x^2-1\right|+C$ d. $\frac{1}{4(2x^2-1)^2}+C$

[d] 210. $\int e^{3x^2-4x}(3x-2)dx$

a. $e^{3x^2-4x}+C$ b. $(6x-4)e^{3x^2-4x}+C$ c. $2e^{3x^2-4x}+C$ d. $\frac{1}{2}e^{3x^2-4x}+C$

[a] 211. $\int \frac{e^{4x}}{1-e^{4x}}dx$

a. $-\frac{1}{4}\ln\left|1-e^{4x}\right|+C$ b. $\ln\left|1-e^{4x}\right|+C$ c. $-4\ln\left|1-e^{4x}\right|+C$ d. $\frac{1}{4}\ln\left|1-e^{4x}\right|+C$

[a] 212. $\int \frac{e^{3/x}}{x^2}dx$

a. $-\frac{1}{3}e^{3/x}+C$ b. $-3e^{3/x}+C$ c. $-\frac{e^{3/x}}{3x^2}+C$ d. $\frac{1}{3}e^{3/x}+C$

Evaluate the following definite integral(s).

[c] 213. $\int_5^8 \frac{3}{\sqrt{3x+1}}dx$

a. 1 b. 9 c. 2 d. 18

[b] 214. $\int_2^3 \frac{2x+5}{x^2+5x-8}dx$

a. $\ln\left[\frac{2}{5}\right]$ b. $\ln\left[\frac{8}{3}\right]$ c. $\ln\left[\frac{3}{5}\right]$ d. $\ln\left[\frac{5}{8}\right]$

[a] 215. The area under the curve $y=\sqrt{2x+3}$ from $x=3$ to $x=11$ is

a. $\frac{98}{3}$ b. $\frac{47}{2}$ c. $\frac{152}{3}$ d. $\frac{115}{2}$

[c] 216. The average value of $f(x) = \sqrt{5x+1}$ over the interval [3, 7] is

a. 304/15 b. 36/5 c. 76/15 d. 28/3

[b] 217. A company's marginal revenue function is $MR(x) = \dfrac{x}{\sqrt{x^2+1.44}}$ thousand dollars, where x is in hundreds of units. Zero units produce zero revenue dollars. The revenue from the sale of 350 units (x = 3.5) is

a. $2000 b. $2500 c. $1000 d. $4000

[c] 218. $\int (7x-8)^6\,dx =$

a. $42(7x-8)^5 + C$ b. $\dfrac{(7x-8)^7}{7} + C$ c. $\dfrac{(7x-8)^7}{49} + C$ d. $6(7x-8)^7 + C$

[b] 219. $\int \sqrt{\dfrac{x}{2}}\,dx =$

a. $3x\sqrt{2x} + C$ b. $\dfrac{x\sqrt{2x}}{3} + C$ c. $\dfrac{\sqrt{6x}}{3} + C$ d. $\dfrac{x\sqrt{6x}}{3} + C$

[a] 220. $\int \dfrac{4.1-4.6x}{(4.1x-2.3x^2)^3}\,dx =$

a. $\dfrac{-1}{2(4.1x-2.3x^2)^2} + C$ b. $\dfrac{3(4.1-4.6x)^2}{2(4.1-2.3x^2)^3} + C$

c. $\dfrac{-2}{(4.1x-2.3x^2)^2} + C$ d. $\dfrac{4.1-4.6x}{3(4.1x-2.3x^2)} + C$

[d] 221. $\int \dfrac{5(\ln x)^{\frac{3}{2}}}{x}\,dx =$

a. $\dfrac{2(\ln x)^{\frac{5}{2}}}{x} + C$ b. $\dfrac{15(\ln x)^{\frac{1}{2}}}{2x^2} + C$ c. $\dfrac{2(\ln x)^{\frac{5}{2}}}{5x^2} + C$ d. $2(\ln x)^{\frac{5}{2}} + C$

[b] 222. $\int_2^4 (1.5x-4)^5\,dx =$

a. 64/9 b. 7 65/9 d. 21/2

[c] 223. $\int_4^8 \frac{2.75}{(2.75x-3)^2} dx =$

a. –3/152 b. 3/152 c. 11/152 d. –11/152

[d] 224. $\int_2^4 \frac{6x}{\sqrt{1.5x^2+3}} dx =$

a. 12 b. $12\sqrt{3}$ c. $\frac{8\sqrt{3}-12}{3}$ d. $12(\sqrt{3}-1)$

[b] 225. $\int e^{4-0.75x} dx =$

a. $e^{4-0.75x} + C$ b. $-\frac{4}{3}e^{4-0.75x} + C$ c. $e^{0.75-1} + C$ d. $-\frac{4}{3}e^{0.75x-1} + C$

[a] 226. $\int 5e^{-1.25x} dx =$

a. $-4e^{-1.25x} + C$ b. $4e^{-1.25x} + C$ c. $5e^{-1.25x} + C$ d. $-\frac{25}{4}e^{-1.25x} + C$

[d] 227. $\int \frac{5}{e^{5x}} dx =$

a. $5e^{5x} + C$ b. $-\frac{5x}{e^{5x}} + C$ c. $-\frac{x}{e^{5x}} + C$ d. $-\frac{1}{e^{5x}} + C$

[a] 228. $\int_0^1 e^{3x} dx =$

a. $\frac{e^3-1}{3}$ b. $\frac{e^3+1}{3}$ c. $3-\frac{1}{e^3}$ d. $e^3-\frac{1}{3}$

[b] 229. $\int_4^{10} \frac{2x-1.24}{x^2-1.24x-0.04} dx =$

a. ln(98,56) b. ln(7.96) c. ln(87.56) d. ln(76.56)

[c] 230. $\int_{4}^{14} \frac{4.6}{\sqrt{2.3x - 0.2}}\,dx =$

a. $3 - 4\sqrt{2}$ b. $4\sqrt{2} - 3$ c. $16\sqrt{2} - 12$ d. $16\sqrt{2}$

[d] 231. $\int_{e}^{e^4} \frac{(\ln x)^{\frac{3}{2}}}{2x}\,dx =$

a. $e^{10} + 1$ b. $e^{10} - e$ c. 6.6 d. 6.2

[c] 232. The equation of the curve that passes through the point (2, 4) and has slope $\frac{x}{\sqrt{x^2 + 5}}$ is y =

a. $x\sqrt{x^2 + 5} + \frac{2}{3}$ b. $\frac{4}{\sqrt{x^2 + 5}} + 3$ c. $\sqrt{x^2 + 5} + 1$ d. $\frac{2\sqrt{x^2 + 5}}{x^2} + \frac{3}{2}$

SHORT ANSWER 5.6

Find the following integral(s) by the substitution method.

233. $\int \sqrt[3]{x^3 - 3x}(x^2 - 1)dx$

Answer: $\frac{1}{4}(x^3 - 3x)^{4/3} + C$

234. $\int \frac{x^3}{x^4 - 1}dx$

Answer: $\frac{1}{4}\ln|x^4 - 1| + C$

235. $\int x^2 e^{x^3 - 1}dx$

Answer: $\frac{1}{3}e^{x^3 - 1} + C$

236. $\int \frac{x^2 - 1}{(x^3 - 3x + 2)^2}dx$

Answer: $-\frac{1}{3}(x^3 - 3x + 2)^{-1} + C$

237. $\int \frac{x}{x^2 + 9}dx$

Answer: $\frac{1}{2}\ln|x^2 + 9| + C$

238. $\int \frac{x^5}{\sqrt{x^6 + 1}}dx$

Answer: $\frac{1}{3}\sqrt{x^6 + 1} + C$

239. $\int (\frac{1}{2}x - 7)^8 \, dx$

Answer: $\frac{2}{9}(\frac{1}{2}x - 7)^9 + C$

240. $\int \frac{2x^5}{\sqrt[4]{2x^6 - 4}} \, dx$

Answer: $\frac{2}{9}(2x^6 - 4)^{3/4} + C$

241. $\int \frac{2e^{4x}}{e^{4x} + 10} \, dx$

Answer: $\frac{1}{2}\ln\left|e^{4x} + 10\right| + C$

Evaluate the following definite integral(s).

242. $\int_{-1}^{e-2} \frac{1}{x+2} \, dx$

Answer: 1

243. $\int_0^1 \sqrt{x^4 + 2x^2 + 1}(x^3 + x) \, dx$

Answer: $\frac{7}{6}$

244. $\int_1^{e^2} \frac{(\ln x)^2}{x} \, dx$

Answer: $\frac{8}{3}$

245. The marginal revenue from the sale of x units of a product is $MR = 2x(x^2 + 1)^3$. Assuming there is no revenue when $x = 0$, find the total revenue when 10 units are sold.

Answer: $26,015,100

246. The rate of maintenance costs for an office machine is given by $R(t) = \sqrt{t^2 + 12t}(2t + 12)$ where t is time measured in years. Determine the total maintenance costs for the first 5 years of the machine's life.

Answer: $522.44

247. The rate of growth of profit (in millions of dollars) from a new video game technology is estimated to be $G(t) = t\,e^{-t^2}$ where t represents time in years. Find the total profit during the first 3 years that the new technology is in operation.

Answer: $499,938

248. Determine the area under the curve $y = 15\sqrt{4 + 2.5x}$ from $x = 0$ to $x = 2$.

Answer: 76

249. Determine the average value of $f(x) = \sqrt[3]{5x - 8}$ over the interval [0, 7].

Answer: 39/28

250. A company's marginal revenue function is $MR(x) = \dfrac{x}{\sqrt{x^2 + 1.44}}$ thousand dollars, where x is in hundreds of units. Zero units produce zero revenue dollars. Determine the revenue function R(x).

Answer: $R(x) = \sqrt{x^2 + 1.44} - 1.2$

251. The marginal cost function for a company is $MC(x) = 3x\sqrt{x^2 + 1.44}$. Determine the cost fruction C(x) if the fixed cost is $677.728.

Answer: $C(x) = (x^2 + 1.44)^{3/2} + 676$

252. The present number of fish in a pond is estimated to be 2550. The number of fish is increasing at the rate of $\dfrac{5t}{2.5t^2 + 1}$ fish per year (t). Determine a function n(t) that will give the number of fish in the pond at any future time t.

Answer: $n(t) = \ln(2.5t^2 + 1) + 2550$

253. Evaluate the indefinite integral: $\int 8(1.25x - 2.4)^7 \cdot \dfrac{1}{1.25} dx$.

Answer: $(1.25x - 2.4)^8 + C$

254. Evaluate the indefinite integral: $\int 7(5x^2 - 13)^6 \cdot 10x dx$.

Answer: $(5x^2 - 13)^7 + C$

255. Evaluate the indefinite integral: $\int 5(5x^3 - 7x + 6)^4 (15x - 7) dx$.

Answer: $(5x^3 - 7x + 6)^5 + C$

256. Evaluate the indefinite integral: $\int \frac{5}{2.5x - 1.5} dx$.

Answer: $2 \ln |2.5x - 1.5| + C$

257. Evaluate the indefinite integral: $\int e^{0.2x} dx$.

Answer: $5e^{0.2x} + C$

258. Determine the equation of the curve that passes through the point (1, –30) and has slope $24x(4x^2 - 7)^2$.

Answer: $y = (4x^2 - 7)^3 - 3$

259. Determine the equation of the curve that passes through the point (1, 7) and has slope $\frac{3x^2 + 4x}{x^3 + 2x^2 - 2}$.

Answer: $y = \ln | x^3 + 2x^2 - 2| + 7$

260. Determine the area under the curve $y = 5\sqrt{4 + 2.5x}$ from $x = 0$ to $x = 2$.

Answer: 76

Chapter 5 – Graphing Calculator

Integration and Its Applications

Section 5.1 Antiderivatives

1. Use a graphing calculator to graph f(x) and the antiderivative of f(x), call it F(x). Find all values of x, where F(x) has a relative extremum and all intervals where F(x) is increasing or decreasing. Verify, using the graph of f(x) on the window [–4, 11] by [–14, 7].
   $f(x) = 0.11x^3 - 0.91x^2 + 0.51x + 3.1$

   Answer: minimum at $x = -1.48$ and $x = 7.05$
   maximum at $x = 2.70$
   increasing $-1.48 < x < 2.70$ and $x > 7.05$
   decreasing $x < -1.48$ and $2.70 < x < 7.05$

Section 5.2 Integration using Logarithmic and Exponential Functions

2. Use a graphing calculator to graph f(x) and the antiderivative of f(x), call it F(x). Find all values of x, where F(x) has a relative extremum and all intervals where F(x) is increasing or decreasing. Verify, using the graph of f(x) on the window [–10, 10] by [–20, 150].
$f(x) = 2.1x - e^{-0.021x}$

   Answer: minimum at $x = 0$
   increasing $x > 0$
   decreasing $x < 0$

3. Use a graphing calculator to graph f(x) and the antiderivative of f(x), call it F(x). Find all values of x, where F(x) has a relative extremum and all intervals where F(x) is increasing or decreasing. Verify, using the graph of f(x) on the window [–3, 2] by [–4, 7].
$f(x) = 1.2x^3 + 7.2x^2 - 2.5e^{-x}$

   Answer: minimum at $x = -2.31$ and $x = 0.45$
   maximum at $x = -1.11$
   increasing $-2.31 < x < -1.11$ and $x > 0.45$
   decreasing $x < -2.31$ and $-1.11 < x < 0.45$

Section 5.3 Definite Integrals and Areas

4. Use a graphing calculator to sketch the graph of each function. Approximate the x-coordinates of intercepts for a region with $f(x) > 0$. Approximate the area of that region.
   $f(x) = 9.9 - 0.9x - 1.8/x$

   Answer: $\int_{0.18}^{10.8} f(x)dx = 45.3$

5. Use a graphing calculator to sketch the graph of each function. Approximate the x-coordinates of intercepts for a region with $f(x) > 0$. Approximate the area of that region.
   $f(x) = (4.9 - 0.9x - 0.9x^2)\ln x$

   Answer: $\int_{1}^{2.9} f(x)dx = 2.7$

Section 5.4 Further Applications of Definite Integrals: Average Value and Area Between Two Curves

6. Use a graphing calculator to approximate the average value of each function over the given interval.
   $f(x) = e^{-x^3}$ on $[-1, 1]$

   Answer: 1.07

7. Use a graphing calculator to approximate the average value of each function over the given interval.
   $f(x) = \sqrt{1+x^3}$ on $[-1, 1]$

   Answer: 0.98

8. Use a graphing calculator to approximate the average value of each function over the given interval.
   $f(x) = \ln(x + 0.1)$ on $[1, 1.5]$

   Answer: 0.29

Section 5.5 Two Applications to Economics: Consumers' Surplus and Income Distribution

9. Use a graphing calculator to find the consumers' surplus for the following demand curve at the given sales level x.

   $d(x) = 20.01\sqrt[3]{\frac{1}{x+1}}$, where $x = 124$

   Answer: 224.11

10. Use a graphing calculator to find the consumers' surplus for the following demand curve at the given sales level x.

    $d(x) = 0.21\ln\left(\frac{301}{x+1.1}\right)$, where $x = 65.9$

    Answer: 12.89

11. Use a graphing calculator to find the producers' surplus for the following supply curve at the given sales level x.
    $S(x) = 0.09x^2 + 3.7$, where $x = 10$

    Answer: 60

12. Use a graphing calculator to find the producers' surplus for the following supply curve at the given sales level x.

    $S(x) = 1 + 0.51\sqrt{x+1}$, where $x = 35$

    Answer: 33.33

13. Use a graphing calculator to determine the point of intersection, then find the consumers' surplus and the producers' surplus.
    $d(x) = \sqrt{25 - 0.2x}$ and $S(x) = \sqrt{0.2x + 9} - 1$

    Answer: $x = 45$, $p = 4$
    Consumers' surplus = 23.33, producers' surplus = 21.67

Section 5.6 Integration by Substitution

14. Use a graphing calculator to graph f(x) and the antiderivative of f(x), call it F(x). Find all values of x, where F(x) has relative extremum and all intervals where F(x) is increasing or decreasing. Verify, using the graph of f(x) on the window [–4, 4] by [–1, 2].
$$f(x) = \frac{39.7 - 79.4x}{(x^2 - x + 5.2)^3}$$

Answer: max at $x = 0.5$
increasing $x < 0.5$
decreasing $x > 0.5$

15. Use a graphing calculator to graph f(x) and the antiderivative of f(x), call it F(x). Find all values of x, where F(x) has relative extremum and all intervals where F(x) is increasing or decreasing. Verify, using the graph of f(x) on the window [–7, 2] by [–100, 100].
$f(x) = x(x + 5.1)^3$

Answer: max at $x = -5.1$, min at $x = 0$
increasing $x < -5.1, x > 0$
decreasing $-5.1 < x < 0$

16. Use a graphing calculator to graph f(x) and the antiderivative of f(x), call it F(x). Find all values of x, where F(x) has relative extremum and all intervals where F(x) is increasing or decreasing. Verify, using the graph of f(x) on the window [–2, 7] by [–2100, 2100].
$f(x) = (2.7 - x)(x^2 - 5.4x)^4$

Answer: max at $x = 2.7$
increasing $x < 2.7$
decreasing $x > 2.7$

Chapter 6

Integration Techniques

Section 6.1 Integration by Parts

MULTIPLE CHOICE 6.1

[c] 1. Find the integral $\int x(x-3)^4 dx$, by using integration by parts.

a. $\frac{x^2}{2}\frac{(x-3)^5}{5}+C$

b. $\frac{x(x-3)^4}{4}-\frac{(x-3)^5}{12}+C$

c. $\frac{x(x-3)^5}{5}-\frac{(x-3)^6}{30}+C$

d. $\frac{x^2(x-3)^5}{4}-\frac{(x-3)^5}{25}+C$

[d] 2. Find the integral $\int x\sqrt{3x+4}dx$, by using integration by parts.

a. $\frac{2}{9}x(3x+4)^{\frac{3}{2}}-\frac{4}{45}(3x+4)^{\frac{5}{2}}+C$

b. $\frac{2}{3}x(3x+4)^{\frac{3}{2}}-\frac{4}{45}(3x+4)^{\frac{5}{2}}+C$

c. $\frac{2}{9}x(3x+4)^{\frac{3}{2}}-\frac{2}{27}(3x+4)^{\frac{5}{2}}+C$

d. $\frac{2}{9}x(3x+4)^{\frac{3}{2}}-\frac{4}{135}(3x+4)^{\frac{5}{2}}+C$

[c] 3. Find the integral $\int e^x(x+2)dx$, by using integration by parts.

a. $(x+2)^2-2e^x+C$

b. $(x+2)e^{2x}-e^x+C$

c. $(x+2)e^x-e^x+C$

d. $(x+2)e^x-2e^x+C$

[a] 4. Evaluate the integral $\int x\ln(2x)dx$ using integration by parts.

a. $\frac{x^2\ln(2x)}{2}-\frac{x^2}{4}+C$

b. $2x\ln(2x)-x^2+C$

c. $\frac{x^2\ln(2x)}{4}-x^2+C$

d. $\frac{x\ln(2x)^2}{4}-\frac{x^2}{2}+C$

[d] 5. Find the integral $\int(\ln x)^3dx$, by using integration by parts.

a. $x(\ln x)^3-3(\ln x)^2+C$

b. $\frac{1}{3}(\ln x)^4+C$

c. $x\ln(2x)-x+C$

d. $x(\ln x)^3-3x(\ln x)^2+6x(\ln x)-6x+C$

[d] 6. Find the integral $\int xe^{3x}dx$ by whatever means are necessary (parts or substitution).

a. $\frac{1}{3}e^{3x}+C$ b. $3e^{3x}+C$ c. $\frac{x^2}{2}\frac{e^{3x}}{3}+C$ d. $\frac{x}{3}e^{3x}-\frac{1}{9}e^{3x}+C$

[d] 7. Evaluate the integral $\int_2^4 \frac{5x}{(x-3)^2}dx$ using integration by parts.

a. 10 b. 20 c. –20 d. –30

[a] 8. Evaluate the integral $\int_0^1 2xe^{2x}dx$ using integration by parts.

a. $\frac{e^2+1}{2}$ b. $\frac{3e^2-1}{2}$ c. $\frac{e^2-1}{2}$ d. $\frac{3e^2+1}{2}$

[c] 9. Find the integral $\int x^2e^{4x}dx$ by integration by parts using repetition.

a. $4x^2e^{4x}-32xe^{4x}+64e^{4x}+C$
b. $4x^2e^{4x}+32xe^{4x}+64e^{4x}+C$
c. $\frac{1}{4}x^2e^{4x}-\frac{1}{8}xe^{4x}+\frac{1}{32}e^{4x}+C$
d. $\frac{1}{4}x^2e^{4x}+\frac{1}{8}xe^{4x}+\frac{1}{32}e^{4x}+C$

[b] 10. Evaluate the integral $\int 24x(x-5)^2dx$ using integration by parts.

a. $16x^2(x-5)^3+C$
b. $8x(x-5)^3-2(x-5)^4+C$
c. $8x(x-5)^3-4(x-5)^4+C$
d. $16x(x-5)^3-4(x-5)^4+C$

[d] 11. Evaluate the integral $\int \frac{24x}{(x-7)^3}dx$ using integration by parts.

a. $\frac{(12x^2)(x-7)^4}{4}+C$
b. $12(x-7)^{-4}-4(x-7)^{-1}+C$
c. $-4(x-7)^{-4}-12(x-7)^{-1}+C$
d. $-12[x(x-7)^{-2}+(x-7)^{-1}]+C$

[b] 12. Evaluate the integral $\int x^3 \ln x dx$ using integration by parts.

a. $\frac{x^4}{4}-x^4\cdot\ln x+C$ b. $\frac{x^4\cdot\ln x}{4}-\frac{x^4}{16}+C$ c. $\frac{x^4}{16}-x^4\cdot\ln x+C$ d. $\frac{x^4\cdot\ln x}{4}-x^4+C$

[a] 13. Evaluate the integral $\int x \ln(2x)dx$ using integration by parts.

a. $\frac{x^2 \ln(2x)}{2} - \frac{x^2}{4} + C$ b. $2x \ln(2x) - x^2 + C$ c. $\frac{x^2 \ln(2x)}{4} - x^2 + C$ d. $\frac{x \ln(2x)^2}{4} - \frac{x^2}{2} + C$

[b] 14. $\int_2^3 (x-2)e^x dx =$

a. e b. e^2 c. e^3 d. 1

[c] 15. $\int_0^1 (x-4)e^x dx =$

a. $5e + 4$ b. $4e - 5$ c. $5 - 4e$ d. $5e - 4$

[d] 16. $\int_0^5 \frac{x}{(x+1)^2} dx =$

a. $-\frac{1}{6} + \ln 6$ b. $\ln 6$ c. $-\frac{5}{6}$ d. $-\frac{5}{6} + \ln 6$

[a] 17. $\int_e^{e^2} \frac{\ln x}{x^2} dx =$

a. $\frac{2}{e} - \frac{3}{e^2}$ b. $e^2 - 2e$ c. $\frac{3}{e} + \frac{2}{e^2}$ d. $2e^2 + 3e$

[a] 18. A company assumes that income will be produced at a rate of 1200t dollar per year for the next 10 years. Using an annual interest rate of 9%, find the present value of the income stream, rounded to the nearest thousand dollars.

a. 34,000 b. 100,000 c. 83,000 d. 79,000

[b] 19. The velocity of an object at time t is $v(t) = 2te^{2t}$ feet per second. How far does the object travel in the first 2 seconds? Round your answer to one decimal place.

a. 71.7 b. 82.4 c. 140.7 d. 228.4

[d] 20. A town's population is 7000 and is growing at the rate of $p(t) = te^{0.1t}$ people per year where t is the number of years from now. What will be the town's population in 20 years? Round your answer to the nearest whole number.

a. 10,553 b. 9,716 c. 9,470 d. 7,839

[c] 21. The average value of the function $f(x) = \frac{x}{\sqrt{x+2}}$ over the interval [2, 7] is

a. $\frac{17}{30}$ b. $\frac{19}{10}$ c. $\frac{26}{15}$ d. $\frac{23}{25}$

[d] 22. The average value of the function $f(x) = x(3x+4)^2$ over the interval [2, 4] is

a. 1084 b. 656 c. 814 d. 542

[b] 23. Determine the area under the curve $y = xe^{-0.2x}$ from $x = 0$ to $x = 5$.

a. $25+50e^{-1}$ b. $25-50e^{-1}$ c. $25-50e$ d. $25+50e$

[d] 24. Determine the equation of the curve that passes through the point (e/2, 1) and has slope ln(2x).

a. $y = \ln(2x) - x + 1$ b. $y = x \ln x + 1$ c. $y = x \ln x + x + 1$ d. $y = x \ln(2x) - x + 1$

[d] 25. A company plans to buy an industrial robot to use in its factory. The company estimates that using the robot will contribute to the company income at the rate of $f(t) = 10{,}000t$ dollars per year. Determine the present value of the income stream over the first 4 years if the prevailing interest rate is 5%. Round your answer to the nearest thousand dollars.

a. $29,000 b. $47,000 c. $51,000 d. $70,000

[c] 26. Determine the area under the curve $y = xe^{0.25x}$ from $x = 0$ to $x = 4$.

a. 0 b. 16e + 16 c. 16 d. –16

[c] 27. The velocity of an object at time t is $2te^{2t}$ feet per second. How far does the object travel in the first 2 seconds (that is, from $t = 0$ to $t = 2$)? Round your answer to one decimal place.

a. 218.4 feet b. 138.5 feet c. 82.4 feet d. 81.9 feet

[a] 28. A town's population is 7000 and is growing at the rate of $te^{0.1t}$ people per year. What will the town's population be in 20 years? Round your answer to the nearest whole number (person).

a. 8478 b. 10,037 c. 9716 d. 10,553

SHORT ANSWER 6.1

29. Use integration by parts to evaluate $\int x\sqrt{x+1.7}dx$.

Answer: $\frac{2x(x+1.7)^{\frac{3}{2}}}{3}-\frac{4}{15}(x+1.7)^{\frac{5}{2}}+C$

30. Use integration by parts to evaluate $\int xe^{-0.5x}dx$.

Answer: $-2xe^{-0.5x}-4e^{-0.5x}+C$

31. Use integration by parts to evaluate $\int\frac{3x}{\sqrt{x+10}}dx$.

Answer: $6x\sqrt{x+10}-4(x+10)^{\frac{3}{2}}+C$

32. Use integration by parts to evaluate $\int x^8 \ln xdx$.

Answer: $\frac{1}{9}x^9 \ln x-\frac{1}{81}x^9+C$

33. Use integration by parts to evaluate $\int(x+1)\ln(x+1)dx$.

Answer: $\frac{1}{2}(x+1)^2 \ln(x+1)-\frac{1}{4}(x+1)^2+C$

34. Use integration by parts to evaluate $\int(x-4)(x+3)^3dx$.

Answer: $\frac{1}{4}(x-4)(x+3)^4-\frac{1}{20}(x+3)^5+C$

35. Use integration by parts to evaluate $\int\sqrt{x}\ln xdx$.

Answer: $\frac{2}{3}x^{\frac{3}{2}}\ln x-\frac{4}{9}x^{\frac{3}{2}}+C$

36. Find the integral $\int x^{10} \ln(2x)dx$ by whatever means necessary (parts or substitution).

Answer: $\frac{x^{11} \ln 2x}{11} - \frac{x^{11}}{121} + C$

37. Evaluate the integral $\int_0^1 xe^{-5x} dx$ using integration by parts.

Answer: $\frac{1}{25}\left[1 - \frac{6}{e^5}\right]$

38. Evaluate the integral $\int_1^e x^2 \ln x dx$ using integration by parts.

Answer: $\frac{1}{9}\left[2e^3 + 1\right]$

39. Evaluate the integral $\int_1^2 x^3 \ln x dx$ using integration by parts.

Answer: $4 \ln 2 - \frac{15}{16}$

40. Find the integral $\int x^2 e^{2x} dx$ by integration by parts using a table.

Answer: $\frac{x^2}{2}e^{2x} - \frac{x}{2}e^{2x} + \frac{1}{4}e^{2x} + C$

41. Find the integral $\int x^4 e^{-x} dx$ by integration by parts using a table.

Answer: $-x^4e^{-x} - 4x^3e^{-x} - 12x^2e^{-x} - 24xe^{-x} - 24e^{-x} + C$

42. Find the integral $\int x^2 (x-2)^{\frac{3}{2}} dx$ by integration by parts using a table.

Answer: $\frac{2}{5}x^2(x-2)^{\frac{5}{2}} - \frac{8}{35}x(x-2)^{\frac{7}{2}} + \frac{16}{315}(x-2)^{\frac{9}{2}} + C$

43. Find the integral $\int \frac{2.7x}{\sqrt{x-6.1}}dx$ by using integration by parts.

Answer: $5.4x(x-6.1)^{\frac{1}{2}} - 3.6(x-6.1)^{\frac{3}{2}} + C$

44. Find the integral $\int \frac{8.7x}{(x-2.3)^2}dx$ by using integration by parts.

Answer: $-\frac{8.7x}{x-2.3} + 8.7\ln|x-2.3| + C$

45. Find the integral $\int \ln(x^{\frac{5}{2}})dx$ by using integration by parts.

Answer: $x\ln x^{\frac{5}{2}} - \frac{5}{2}x + C$

46. Find the integral $\int x^2 e^{-0.25x}dx$ by using integration by parts.

Answer: $-4x^2e^{-0.25x} - 32xe^{-0.25x} - 128e^{-0.25x} + C$

47. Find the integral $\int x^3 e^x dx$ by using integration by parts.

Answer: $x^3e^x - 3x^2e^x + 6xe^x - 6e^x + C$

48. A company's marginal profit function is $P'(x) = 2x - xe^{-2x}$. Find the profit function P(x) subject to the condition that P(0) = 0.

Answer: $P(x) = x^2 + \frac{x}{2}e^{-2x} + \frac{1}{4}e^{-2x} - \frac{1}{4}$

49. A company begins advertising a new product and finds that after t months the product is gaining customer recognition at a rate of $r(t) = t^3 \ln t$ thousand customers per week. Find the total gain in recognition between the first week and sixth week.

Answer: 499,593 customers

50. A fundraiser is generating funds at the rate of $f(t) = 25te^{-0.3t}$ thousand dollars per week during the first t weeks of a campaign. Find the total amount raised during the first 3 weeks.

Answer: $63,199

51. A company's marginal profit function is $P'(x) = 6x - xe^{-1.5x}$. Find the profit function P(x) subject to the condition that P(0) = 0.

Answer: $P(x) = 3x^2 + \frac{2}{3}xe^{-1.5x} + \frac{4}{9}e^{-1.5x} - \frac{4}{9}$

52. Determine the equation of the curve that passes through the point (0, 5) and has slope ln(5x + 1).

Answer: $y = \left(x + \frac{1}{5}\right)\ln(5x + 1) - x + 5$

Section 6.2 Integration Using Tables

MULTIPLE CHOICE 6.2

[c] 53. To evaluate the integral $\int \frac{6dx}{\sqrt{36x^2+49}}$, which of the following integral forms (from a table of integrals) would you use?

a. $\int \frac{du}{\sqrt{u^2-a^2}}$ b. $\int \frac{du}{u\sqrt{u^2+a^2}}$ c. $\int \frac{du}{\sqrt{u^2+a^2}}$ d. $\int \frac{du}{u\sqrt{a^2-u^2}}$

[b] 54. To evaluate the integral $\int \frac{3dx}{3x\sqrt{9x^2+25}}$, which of the following integral forms (from a table of integrals) would you use?

a. $\int \frac{du}{\sqrt{u^2-a^2}}$ b. $\int \frac{du}{u\sqrt{u^2+a^2}}$ c. $\int \frac{du}{\sqrt{u^2+a^2}}$ d. $\int \frac{du}{u\sqrt{a^2-u^2}}$

[d] 55. To evaluate the integral $\int \frac{10xdx}{5x^2\sqrt{16-25x^4}}$, which of the following integral forms (from a table of integrals) would you use?

a. $\int \frac{du}{\sqrt{u^2-a^2}}$ b. $\int \frac{du}{u\sqrt{u^2+a^2}}$ c. $\int \frac{du}{\sqrt{u^2+a^2}}$ d. $\int \frac{du}{u\sqrt{a^2-u^2}}$

[c] 56. To evaluate the integral $\int \frac{7dx}{49x^2\sqrt{49x^2+81}}$, which of the following integral forms (from a table of integrals) would you use?

a. $\int \frac{du}{u\sqrt{u^2+a^2}}$ b. $\int \frac{du}{u\sqrt{a^2-u^2}}$ c. $\int \frac{du}{u^2\sqrt{u^2+a^2}}$ d. $\int \frac{du}{u^2\sqrt{a^2-u^2}}$

[b] 57. Use the integral table to find the integral $\int \frac{dx}{(2x+3)(2x-3)}$.

a. $\frac{1}{6}\ln\left|\frac{2x-3}{2x+3}\right|+C$ b. $-\frac{1}{12}\ln\left|\frac{2x+3}{2x-3}\right|+C$ c. $\frac{1}{12}\ln\left|\frac{2x+3}{2x-3}\right|+C$ d. $\frac{1}{6}\ln\left|\frac{2x+3}{2x-3}\right|+C$

[d] 58. Use the integral table to find the integral $\int \frac{dx}{x^2(1-3x)}$.

a. $-\frac{1}{x}-3\ln\left|\frac{x}{1-3x}\right|+C$

b. $\frac{1}{x}-3\ln\left|\frac{x}{1-3x}\right|+C$

c. $\frac{1}{3x}-\frac{1}{9}\ln\left|\frac{x}{1-3x}\right|+C$

d. $-\frac{1}{x}+3\ln\left|\frac{x}{1-3x}\right|+C$

[a] 59. Use the integral table to find the integral $\int \sqrt{2x^2+16}dx$.

a. $\frac{x}{2}\sqrt{2x^2+16}+4\sqrt{2}\ln\left|x\sqrt{2}+\sqrt{2x^2+16}\right|+C$

b. $\frac{x}{2}\sqrt{2x^2+16}+8\ln\left|x+\sqrt{2x^2+16}\right|+C$

c. $x\sqrt{2x^2+16}+8\ln\left|x+\sqrt{2x^2+16}\right|+C$

d. $\frac{\sqrt{2x}}{2}\sqrt{2x^2+16}+512\ln\left|x\sqrt{2}+\sqrt{2x^2+16}\right|+C$

[c] 60. Use the integral table to find the integral $\int \frac{dx}{x\sqrt{1-25x^2}}$.

a. $-\ln\left|\frac{1+\sqrt{1-25x^2}}{x}\right|+C$

b. $\ln\left|\frac{-1+\sqrt{1-25x^2}}{x}\right|+C$

c. $-\ln\left|\frac{1+\sqrt{1-25x^2}}{5x}\right|+C$

d. $\ln\left|\frac{-1+\sqrt{1-25x^2}}{5x}\right|+C$

[d] 61. Use the integral table to find the integral $\int \frac{e^x dx}{9-e^{2x}}$.

a. $e^x\left[\frac{1}{6}\ln\left|\frac{3+e^x}{3-e^x}\right|\right]+C$

b. $\frac{1}{18}\ln\left|\frac{3+e^x}{3-e^x}\right|+C$

c. $\frac{1}{6}\ln\left|\frac{e^x-3}{e^x+3}\right|+C$

d. $\frac{1}{6}\ln\left|\frac{3+e^x}{3-e^x}\right|+C$

[b] 62. Use the integral table to find the integral $\int \frac{x\,dx}{3-\frac{1}{2}x}$.

a. $\frac{x}{3}+\frac{1}{18}\ln\left|3-\frac{1}{2}x\right|+C$

b. $-2x-12\ln\left|3-\frac{1}{2}x\right|+C$

c. $2x-12\ln\left|3-\frac{1}{2}x\right|+C$

d. $-x-6\ln\left|3-\frac{1}{2}x\right|+C$

[d] 63. Use the integral table to find the integral $\int \frac{5\,dx}{\sqrt{25x^2+4}}$.

a. $\ln\left|x+\sqrt{25x^2-4}\right|+C$

b. $5\ln\left|x+\sqrt{25x^2+4}\right|+C$

c. $\frac{1}{5}\ln\left|5x+\sqrt{25x^2+4}\right|+C$

d. $\ln\left|5x+\sqrt{25x^2+4}\right|+C$

[d] 64. Use a table of integrals to find the definite integral $\int_0^1 \frac{x}{\sqrt{9x^4+16}}dx$.

a. $\frac{\ln 12}{6}$

b. $\ln 9$

c. $\ln 8$

d. $\frac{\ln 2}{6}$

[d] 65. Use a table of integrals to find the definite integral $\int_1^e x^2 \ln x\,dx$.

a. $\frac{e^3+9}{2}$

b. $\frac{9e^3-1}{2}$

c. $\frac{e^3-2}{9}$

d. $\frac{2e^3+1}{9}$

[b] 66. A company's marginal cost function is $MC(x)=\frac{5.76x}{5+2.4x}$. The change in cost as the number of units produced changes from 20 to 25 is

a. $12+5\ln 65-5\ln 53$

b. $12-5\ln 65+5\ln 53$

c. $60-5\ln 65+5\ln 53$

d. $48+5\ln 65-5\ln 53$

[c] 67. Use a table of integrals to determine the area under the curve $y=\frac{1}{x^2+4x}$ from $x=5$ to $x=9$. Round your answer to three decimal places.

a. 0.239

b. 0.164

c. 0.055

d. 0.287

[a] 68. To evaluate the integral $\int \frac{x}{4\sqrt{9x^4-8}}dx$, which of the following integral forms (from a table of integrals) would you use?

a. $\int \frac{du}{\sqrt{u^2-a^2}}$ b. $\int \frac{du}{u\sqrt{u^2+a^2}}$ c. $\int \frac{du}{\sqrt{u^2+a^2}}$ d. $\int \frac{du}{u\sqrt{a^2-u^2}}$

[a] 69. To evaluate the integral $\int \frac{3x^2}{\sqrt{x^6-1}}dx$, which of the following integral forms (from a table of integrals) would you use?

a. $\int \frac{du}{\sqrt{u^2-a^2}}$ b. $\int \frac{du}{u\sqrt{u^2+a^2}}$ c. $\int \frac{du}{\sqrt{u^2+a^2}}$ d. $\int \frac{du}{u\sqrt{a^2-u^2}}$

[b] 70. To evaluate the integral $\int \frac{6x}{3x^2\sqrt{5-9x^4}}dx$, which of the following integral forms (from a table of integrals) would you use?

a. $\int \frac{du}{u\sqrt{u^2+a^2}}$ b. $\int \frac{du}{u\sqrt{a^2-u^2}}$ c. $\int \frac{du}{u^2\sqrt{u^2+a^2}}$ d. $\int \frac{du}{u^2\sqrt{a^2-u^2}}$

[d] 71. To evaluate the integral $\int \frac{dx}{x^2\sqrt{1-x^2}}$, which of the following integral forms (from a table of integrals) would you use?

a. $\int \frac{du}{u\sqrt{u^2+a^2}}$ b. $\int \frac{du}{u\sqrt{a^2-u^2}}$ c. $\int \frac{du}{u^2\sqrt{u^2+a^2}}$ d. $\int \frac{du}{u^2\sqrt{a^2-u^2}}$

[c] 72. Use a table of integrals to find the average value of $f(x)=\frac{x}{\sqrt{1+3x}}$ over the interval [5, 8].

a. 61/6 b. 348/27 c. 116/81 d. 93/15

[c] 73. Use a table of integrals to determine the area under the curve $y=\frac{1}{\sqrt{x^2-3}}$ from $x=2$ to $x=3$. Round your answer to one decimal place.

a. 0.4 b. 0.5 c. 0.6 d. 0.7

SHORT ANSWER 6.2

74. Use a table of integration to evaluate the integral $\int 414(13.8x)^5 \ln(13.8x)dx$

Answer: $5(13.8x)^6 \ln(138x) - \frac{5}{6}(13.8x)^5 + C$

75. Use a table of integration to evaluate the integral $\int \frac{dx}{x^2(x-1)}$.

Answer: $\frac{1}{x} - \ln\left|\frac{x}{x-1}\right| + C$

76. Use a table of integration to evaluate the integral $\int \frac{x}{x-1} dx$.

Answer: $x + \ln|x-1| + C$

77. Use a table of integration to evaluate the integral $\int \frac{dx}{x\sqrt{1-x}}$.

Answer: $\ln\left|\frac{\sqrt{1-x}-1}{\sqrt{1-x}+1}\right| + C$

78. Use a table of integration to evaluate the integral $\int \frac{4.5dx}{4.5x(7+9x)}$.

Answer: $\frac{1}{7}\ln\left|\frac{x}{7+9x}\right| + C$

79. Use a table of integration to evaluate the integral $\int \frac{dx}{x\sqrt{2.25-4x^2}}$.

Answer: $-\frac{2}{3}\ln\left|\frac{1.5+\sqrt{2.25-4x^2}}{2x}\right| + C$

80. Use a table of integration to evaluate the integral $\int x^3 e^x dx$.

Answer: $x^3e^x - 3x^2e^x + 6xe^x - 6e^x + C$

81. Use a table of integration to evaluate the integral $\int \frac{x}{(x-2)(x-1)}dx$.

Answer: $-\ln|x-1|+2\ln|x-2|+C=\ln\left|\frac{(x-2)^2}{x-1}\right|+C$

82. Use a table of integration to evaluate the integral $\int \frac{y}{y^4-100}dy$.

Answer: $\frac{1}{40}\ln\left|\frac{y^2-10}{y^2+10}\right|+C$

83. Use a table of integration to evaluate the integral $\int \frac{dt}{\sqrt{100t^2+1}}$.

Answer: $\frac{1}{10}\ln\left|10t+\sqrt{100t^2+1}\right|+C$

84. Use a table of integration to evaluate the integral $\int \frac{e^y}{\sqrt{e^{2y}+1}}dy$.

Answer: $\ln\left|e^y+\sqrt{e^{2y}+1}\right|+C$

85. Use a table of integration to evaluate the integral $\int \frac{\sqrt{36-x^8}}{x}dx$.

Answer: $\frac{1}{4}\sqrt{36-x^8}-\frac{3}{2}\ln\left|\frac{6+\sqrt{36-x^8}}{x^4}\right|+C$

86. Use a table of integrals to find the definite integral $\int_0^4 \frac{x}{\sqrt{2x+1}}dx$.

Answer: $\frac{10}{3}$

87. Use a table of integrals to find the definite integral $\int_0^4 \frac{x}{(2x+1)(x+3)}dx$.

Answer: $\frac{3}{5}\ln 7 - \frac{1}{10}\ln 9 - \frac{3}{5}\ln 3$

88. Use a table of integrals to find the integral $\int \frac{dx}{(1.2x-5.1)(1.2x+5.1)}$.

Answer: $\frac{1}{(2.4)(5.1)}\ln\left|\frac{1.2x-5.1}{1.2x+5.1}\right|+C$

89. Use a table of integrals to find the integral $\int 1.3\sqrt{1.69x^2+25}dx$.

Answer: $0.65\sqrt{1.69x^2+25}+\frac{25}{2}\ln\left|1.3x+\sqrt{1.69x^2+25}\right|+C$

90. Use a table of integrals to find the integral $\int \frac{7x}{\sqrt{5+7x}}dx$.

Answer: $\frac{2(7x-10)\sqrt{5+7x}}{21}+C$

91. Use a table of integrals to find the integral $\int \frac{dx}{1+e^{-0.1x}}$.

Answer: $x + 10\ln(1 + e^{-0.1x}) + C$

92. Use a table of integrals to find the average value of $f(x)=\frac{1}{x^2-19.6}$ over the interval [10,15].

Answer: 0.0068

93. Use a table of integrals to find the average value of $f(x)=\frac{1.6}{2.56x^2\sqrt{2.56x^2+25}}$ over the interval [1, 4].

Round your answer to two decimal places.

Answer: 0.03

94. Use a table of integrals to determine the area under the curve $y = \dfrac{0.2}{1+e^{0.2x}}$ from $x = 0$ to $x = 5$.

Answer: $1+\ln\left(\dfrac{2}{1+e}\right)$

95. A company's marginal cost function is $MC(x) = \dfrac{5.76x}{5+2.4x}$. Determine the cost function $C(x)$.

Answer: $C(x) = 2.4x - 5\ln|5+2.4x| + C$

96. The population of a city is expected to grow at a rate of $r(t) = \sqrt{x^2+1}$ thousand people per year after x years. Find the total change in population from year 0 to year 10.

Answer: 51,748 people

97. A welfare office estimates that the number of social security recipients t years from now will be $\dfrac{x}{\sqrt{1+3x}}$ million people. Find the average number of social security recipients during years $x = 5$ to $x = 8$.

Answer: 1.432 million people

98. During an outbreak of the flu virus at an elementary school, it is estimated that the number of children x (in hundreds) who have the flu after t days is estimated to be $x = \dfrac{1}{\sqrt{t^2-25}}$. Find the average number of children who have the flu during the tenth through the fifteenth day of the outbreak.

Answer: 89 children

99. Use a table of integrals to determine the area under the curve $y = \dfrac{0.2}{1+e^{0.2x}}$ from $x = 0$ to $x = 5$.

Answer: $1+\ln\left[\dfrac{2}{1+e}\right]$

Section 6.3 Improper Integrals

MULTIPLE CHOICE 6.3

[c] 100. Evaluate the limit $\lim_{a\to\infty} 2a^{-\frac{1}{2}} - 5$ or state that it does not exist.

a. does not exist b. 0 c. –5 d. –3

[b] 101. Evaluate the limit $\lim_{b\to\infty} 3 - 5e^{-2b}$ or state that it does not exist.

a. does not exact b. 3 c. 0 d. –2

[c] 102. Evaluate the limit $\lim_{b\to\infty} e^{5^b} - 0.2$ or state that it does not exist.

a. –1 b. –2 c. does not exist d. 0

[d] 103. Evaluate the limit $\lim_{b\to\infty} 1 - \ln b^3$ or state that it does not exist.

a. 1 b. 0 c. –2 d. does not exist

[a] 104. Evaluate the limit $\lim_{b\to\infty} \frac{1}{7\sqrt[3]{b}}$.

a. 0 b. 1/7 c. 1 d. ∞

[c] 105. Evaluate the limit $\lim_{a\to-\infty} -\frac{1.7}{a^{\frac{3}{2}}}$.

a. 1.7 b. –1.7 c. 0 d. ∞

[d] 106. Evaluate the limit $\lim_{b\to\infty} (5 + \sqrt{b})$.

a. 5 b. 0 c. –5 d. ∞

[d] 107. Evaluate the limit $\lim_{a\to\infty} a^6 e^{6a}$.

a. a^5 b. a^6e^6 c. 0 d. ∞

[d] 108. Evaluate the improper integral $\int_1^\infty \frac{dx}{x^5}$ or state that it is divergent.

a. divergent b. 0 c. -¼ d. ¼

[c] 109. Evaluate the improper integral $\int_1^\infty e^{-3t}\,dt$ or state that it is divergent.

a. $\frac{3}{e^3}$ b. divergent c. $\frac{1}{3e^3}$ d. $-\frac{1}{3e^3}$

[a] 110. Evaluate the improper integral $\int_1^\infty \frac{1}{x^{0.999}}\,dx$ or state that it is divergent.

a. divergent b. –1,000 c. 1,000 d. 0

[b] 111. Evaluate the improper integral $\int_1^\infty \frac{1}{x^{1.001}}\,dx$ or state that it is divergent.

a. divergent b. 1,000 c. –1,000 d. 0

[b] 112. Evaluate the improper integral $\int_0^\infty xe^{-x^2}\,dx$ or state that it is divergent.

a. 0 b. ½ c. divergent d. –½

[a] 113. Evaluate the improper integral $\int_0^\infty \frac{1}{\sqrt{x+1}}\,dx$ or state that it is divergent.

a. divergent b. –2 c. 2 d. 2/3

[a] 114. A college alumna wishes to endow her alma mater with an amount of money that will yield $1,000 per year, forever, for scholarships. Assuming an annual interest rate of 8%, how much should the endowment be?

a. $12,500 b. $15,000 c. $10,000 d. $8,500

[c] 115. A harborside processing plant dumps waste into the harbor at the rate of $r(t) = 20e^{-0.04t}$ pounds per week. If this continues indefinitely, what is the total amount of waste that will be dumped into the harbor by the plant?

a. 80 pounds b. 375 pounds c. 500 pounds d. 225 pounds

[b] 116. The area under the curve $y = e^{-2x}$ for $x \geq 0$ is

a. 1 b. ½ c. 3/2 d. 2

[c] 117. The area under the curve $y = \frac{1}{(1-x)^2}$ for $x \leq -2$ is

a. 1/6 b. ¼ c. 1/3 d. ½

[b] 118. Determine the capital value of a rental property if the annual rent is $6375 and the annual interest rate is 7.5%.

a. $110,000 b. $85,000 c. $97,500 d. $102,000

[c] 119. Determine the capital value of a rental property if the annual rent is $12,900 and the annual interest rate is 4.3%.

a. $554,700 b. $129,000 c. $300,000 d. $258,000

[d] 120. A real estate investment pays the investor at the rate of $\$3750e^{-0.05t}$ per year, t years from now. The total amount received by the investor will be

a. $45,000 b. $57,000 c. $72,500 d. $75,000

[b] 121. A real estate investment pays the investor at the rate of $\$5525e^{-0.065t}$ per year, t years from now. The total amount received by the investor will be

a. $72,000 b. $85,000 c. $97,000 d. $105,000

[d] 122. Pollution from internal combustion engines enters the air at the rate of $20e^{-0.04t}$ tons per year, and this continues indefinitely. What will be the total amount of pollutants from these engines?

a. 80 tons b. 225 tons c. 375 tons d. 500 tons

SHORT ANSWER 6.3

123. Evaluate the improper integral $\int_1^{\infty} \frac{1}{\sqrt[4]{x^5}} dx$ or state that it is divergent.

Answer: 4

124. Evaluate the improper integral $\int_2^{\infty} \frac{2}{x^3} dx$ or state that it is divergent.

Answer: ¼

125. Evaluate the improper integral $\int_2^{\infty} \frac{x}{\left(x^2 - 3\right)^{10}} dx$ or state that it is divergent.

Answer: $\frac{1}{18}$

126. Evaluate the improper integral $\int_{-\infty}^{0} e^{2x} dx$ or state that it is divergent.

Answer: ½

127. Evaluate the improper integral $\int_{-\infty}^{-2} \sqrt{-5x - 1} dx$ or state that it is divergent.

Answer: divergent

128. Evaluate the improper integral $\int_{-\infty}^{\infty} \frac{e^x}{\left(1 + e^x\right)^3} dx$ or state that it is divergent.

Answer: ½

129. Evaluate the improper integral $\int_1^{\infty} \frac{(\ln x)^2}{x} dx$ or state that it is divergent.

Answer: divergent

130. Evaluate the improper integral $\int_{1}^{\infty}(1-x)e^{-x}dx$ (use parts) or state that it is divergent.

Answer: $-\frac{1}{e}$

131. Evaluate the improper integral $\int_{-\infty}^{\infty}\frac{e^{-2x}}{1+e^{-2x}}dx$ or state that it is divergent.

Answer: divergent

132. Evaluate the improper integral $\int_{0}^{\infty}\frac{e^{-2x}}{1+e^{-2x}}dx$ or state that it is divergent.

Answer: $\frac{1}{2}\ln 2$

133. Evaluate the improper integral $\int_{0.16}^{\infty}\frac{1}{x^{\frac{5}{2}}}dx$ or state that it is divergent.

Answer: –125/12

134. Evaluate the improper integral $\int_{-\infty}^{0.1}\frac{1}{x^{2}}dx$ or state that it is divergent.

Answer: –10

135. Evaluate the improper integral $\int_{0}^{\infty}e^{-0.2x}dx$ or state that it is divergent.

Answer: 5

136. Evaluate the improper integral $\int_{-\infty}^{-0.1}e^{4.5x}dx$ or state that it is divergent.

Answer: 0.14

137. Evaluate the improper integral $\int_{7.35}^{\infty}\frac{6.54}{x}dx$ or state that it is divergent.

Answer: The integral diverges.

138. Evaluate the improper integral $\int_{2.7}^{\infty} x^{-\frac{1}{4}} dx$ or state that it is divergent.

Answer: The integral diverges.

139. Evaluate the improper integral $\int_{5}^{\infty} e^{-0.4x} dx$ or state that it is divergent.

Answer: $2.5e^{-2}$

140. Evaluate the improper integral $\int_{1}^{\infty} 7.4x^{-3} dx$ or state that it is divergent.

Answer: 3.7

141. Evaluate the improper integral $\int_{7.7}^{\infty} \frac{dx}{(8.3+x)^{\frac{3}{2}}}$ or state that it is divergent.

Answer: ½

142. Evaluate the improper integral $\int_{-\infty}^{6.5} \sqrt{-2x+14} dx$ or state that it is divergent.

Answer: The integral diverges.

143. Evaluate the improper integral $\int_{6.4}^{\infty} \frac{\ln(3.2x)^2}{x} dx$ or state that it is divergent.

Answer: The integral diverges.

144. Evaluate the improper integral $\int_{2e}^{\infty} \frac{dx}{x(\ln x/2)^2}$ or state that it is divergent.

Answer: 1

145. Evaluate the improper integral $\int_{-\infty}^{\pi} \pi e^{\pi x} dx$ or state that it is divergent.

Answer: e^{π^2}

146. Evaluate the improper integral $\int_0^{\infty} 10xe^{-5x^2}\,dx$ or state that it is divergent.

Answer: 1

147. Find the size of the permanent endowment needed to generate an annual $40,000 forever at a continuous interest rate of 8%.

Answer: $500,000

148. Find the size of the permanent endowment needed to generate an annual $10,000 forever at a continuous interest rate of 5%.

Answer: $200,000

149. An oil well is expected to produce oil at the rate of $r(t) = 40e^{-0.04t}$ thousand barrels per month indefinitely where t is the number of months from now. Find the total output of the oil well from now infinitely far into the future.

Answer: 1,000,000 barrels

150. If the rate of consumption of a certain mineral is $r(t) = 2e^{-0.02t}$ million tons per year, where t is the number of years from now, find the total amount of the mineral that will be consumed from now infinitely far into the future.

Answer: 100 million tons.

151. Find the area between the curve $y = \frac{1}{3x+1}$ and the x-axis from $x = 1$ to $x = \infty$.

Answer: diverges

152. Find the area between the curve $y = \frac{24}{x^3}$ and the x-axis from $x = 2$ to $x = \infty$.

Answer: 3

153. A philanthropist wishes to establish a fund that will result in a contribution of $5,000 each year to a local charity for an indefinite amount of time. Assuming an annual interest rate of 6%, find the amount he must give to establish the fund.

Answer: $83,333

Section 6.4 Numerical Integration

MULTIPLE CHOICE 6.4

[a] 154. Approximate the integral $\int_2^3 \frac{1}{(x-1)^2}dx$ by hand using trapezoidal approximation with n = 4. Round all calculations to 3 decimal places.

a. 0.509 b. 0.525 c. 2.507 d. 1.793

[d] 155. A definite integral is to be approximated by a numerical method such as the trapezoidal rule. If the interval of evaluation is [0.25, 6.75] and the number of subintervals to be used is 50, then the length of a typical subinterval (Δx) is

a. 0.135 b. 0.14 c. 0.26 d. 0.13

[b] 156. The integral $\int_{13}^{17} f(x)dx$ is to be approximated by using the trapezoidal rule. If the value of Δx is 0.25, the number of trapezoids that will be used is

a. 56 b. 16 c. 68 d. 120

[c] 157. The integral $\int_{14}^{35} f(x)dx$ is to be approximated by using the trapezoidal rule with n = 7. The first two x values to be used are

a. $x_0 = 14, x_1 = 21$ b. $x_0 = 14, x_1 = 18.5$ c. $x_0 = 14, x_1 = 17$ d. . $x_0 = 14, x_1 = 15.5$

[b] 158. The integral $\int_{1.4}^{11.2} f(x)dx$ is to be approximated by using Simpson's rule with n = 20. The first three x values to be used are

a. $x_0 = 1.4, x_1 = 2.03, x_2 = 2.66$ b. $x_0 = 1.4, x_1 = 1.89, x_2 = 2.38$
c. $x_0 = 1.4, x_1 = 1.9, x_2 = 2.4$ d. $x_0 = 1.4, x_1 = 2.9, x_2 = 4.4$

[b] 159. The following table shows a collection of x values from the interval [2, 6] and the corresponding f(x) values. Use these values and the trapezoidal rule to approximate $\int_2^6 f(x)dx$.

x	2	3	4	5	6
f(x)	5	8	9	7	5

a. 34 b. 29 c. 17 d. 58

[d] 160. The following table shows a collection of x values from the interval [1.5, 3.5] and the corresponding f(x) values. Use these values and the trapezoidal rule to approximate $\int_{1.5}^{3.5} f(x)dx$.

x	1.5	2	2.5	3	3.5
f(x)	4	5	7	6	4

a. 13 b. 4.3 c. 7.5 d. 11

[a] 161. A definite integral is to be approximated by a numeral method such as the trapezoidal rule. If the interval of evaluation is [2.5, 7.5] and the number of subintervals to be used is 10, then the length of a typical subinterval (Δx) is

a. 0.5 b. 2 c. 1 d. 0.25

[d] 162. A definite integral is to be approximated by a numerical method such as the trapezoidal rule. If the interval of evaluation is [4.4, 29.4] and the number of subintervals to be used is 100, then the length of a typical subinterval (Δx) is

a. 0.338 b. 0.294 c. 0.44 d. 0.25

[b] 163. The integral $\int_{10}^{36} f(x)dx$ is to be approximated by the trapezoidal rule. If the value of Δx is 0.4, the number of trapezoids that will be used is

a. 24 b. 65 c. 90 d. 115

[d] 164. The integral $\int_{1.25}^{38.75} f(x)dx$ is to be approximated by the trapezoidal rule. If the value of Δx is 0.375, the number of trapezoids that will be used is

a. 15 b. 75 c. 50 d. 100

[a] 165. The integral $\int_{5.6}^{11.9} f(x)dx$ is to be approximated by Simpson's rule with n = 30. The first three x values to be used are

a. $x_0 = 5.6, x_1 = 5.81, x_2 = 6.02$
b. $x_0 = 5.6, x_1 = 5.9, x_2 = 6.2$
c. $x_0 = 5.6, x_1 = 5.81, x_2 = 6.07$
d. $x_0 = 5.6, x_1 = 5.9, x_2 = 6.3$

[b] 166. Approximate $\int_{2}^{6} \frac{dx}{x}$ by the trapezoidal rule, using x = 4. Round your answer to two decimal places.

a. 0.91 b. 1.12 c. 1.35 d. 1.76

[c] 167. If the integral $\int_{1}^{3} f(x)dx$ is approximated by Simpson's rule with $n = 4$, and if the largest value $f^{(4)}(x)$ on $[1, 3]$ is 60, then the maximum error in the approximation process is

a. 0.014 b. 0.008 c. 0.0625 d. 0.0771

[b] 168. If the integral $\int_{3}^{7} f(x)dx$ is approximated by Simpson's rule with $n = 8$, and if the largest value $f^{(4)}(x)$ on $[3, 7]$ is 3, then the maximum error in the approximation process is

a. 0.000417 b. 0.00417 c. 0.0417 d. 0.417

[b] 169. If the integral $\int_{1}^{3} f(x)dx$ is approximated by trapezoidal rule with $n = 5$, and if the largest value $f''(x)$ on $[1, 3]$ is 4, then the maximum error in the approximation process is

a. 3/50 b. 8/75 c. 2/25 d. 9/125

[a] 170. If the integral $\int_{1}^{5} f(x)dx$ is approximated by trapezoidal rule with $n = 10$, and if the largest value $f''(x)$ on $[1, 3]$ is 3, then the maximum error in the approximation process is

a. 0.16 b. 0.03 c. 0.64 d. 0.41

[c] 171. If $\int_{1}^{2} (x \ln x)dx$ is approximated by the trapezoidal rule, with $n = 4$, the maximum approximate error is

a. 0.0094 b. 0.0103 c. 0.0052 d. 0.0911

[a] 172. If $\int_{1}^{5} (x \ln x)dx$ is approximated by Simpson's rule, with $n = 8$, the maximum approximate error is

a. 0.0028 b. 0.0015 c. 0.0067 d. 0.0084

SHORT ANSWER 6.4

173. For the definite integral, $\int_0^2 x^2 dx$,

   a. Approximate the value of the definite integral "by hand" using trapezoidal approximation with n = 4. Round calculations to 3 decimal places.
   b. Evaluate the integral exactly using antiderivatives.
   c. Find the actual error (difference between actual and approximation).
   d. Find the relative error (actual error ÷ actual value expressed as a percent).

   Answer: a. 2.750 b. 2.667 c. 0.083 d. 3.11%

174. For the definite integral, $\int_1^2 \frac{1}{(x+1)^2} dx$,

   a. Approximate the value of the definite integral "by hand" using trapezoidal approximation with n = 4. Round calculations to 3 decimal places.
   b. Evaluate the integral exactly using antiderivatives.
   c. Find the actual error (difference between actual and approximation).
   d. Find the relative error (actual error ÷ actual value expressed as a percent).

   Answer: a. 0.167 b. 0.168 c. 0.001 d. 0.6%

175. Approximate the integral $\int_{2.3}^{4.3} \ln x dx$ by hand using trapezoidal approximation with n = 4. Round all calculations to 3 decimal places.

   Answer: 2.352

176. Approximate the integral $\int_0^1 \sqrt{1-x^2} dx$ by hand using trapezoidal approximation with n = 4. Round all calculations to 3 decimal places.

   Answer: 0.749

177. Approximate the integral $\int_0^1 e^{-x^3} dx$ by hand using trapezoidal approximation with n = 4. Round all calculations to 3 decimal places.

   Answer: 0.802

178. Approximate the integral $\int_1^3 \sqrt{1+\ln x} dx$ by hand using trapezoidal approximation with n = 4. Round all calculations to 3 decimal places.

   Answer: 2.548

179. Approximate the integral $\int_{1.5}^{5.5} x^2 dx$ by hand using Simpson's Rule with n = 4. Round all calculations to 3 decimal places.

Answer: 54.333

180. Approximate the integral $\int_{1}^{2} \frac{1}{(x+1)^2} dx$ by hand using Simpson's Rule with n = 4. Round all calculations to 3 decimal places.

Answer: 0.167

181. Approximate the integral $\int_{5.7}^{7.7} \frac{1}{x} dx$ by hand using Simpson's Rule with n = 4. Round all calculations to 3 decimal places.

Answer: 0.301

182. Approximate the integral $\int_{0}^{1} \sqrt{1-x^3} dx$ by hand using Simpson's Rule with n = 4. Round all calculations to 3 decimal places.

Answer: 0.823

183. Approximate the integral $\int_{0}^{1} e^{-x^3} dx$ by hand using Simpson's Rule with n = 4. Round all calculations to 3 decimal places.

Answer: 0.808

184. Approximate the integral $\int_{1}^{2} \sqrt{2-\ln x} dx$ by hand using Simpson's Rule with n = 4. Round all calculations to 3 decimal places.

Answer: 1.268

185. Approximate the integral $\int_{1.5}^{5.5} x^2 dx$ by the trapezoidal rule, using n = 4.

Answer: 55

186. Approximate the integral $\int_2^8 \frac{dx}{(x+1)^2}$ by the trapezoidal rule, using n = 6. Round your answer to two decimal places.

Answer: 0.23

187. Approximate the integral $\int_{4.4}^{7.4} x^3 dx$ by Simpson's rule, using n = 6.

Answer: 655.96

188. Approximate the integral $\int_{0.25}^{1} \sqrt{x} dx$ by Simpson's rule, using n = 6. Round your answer to two decimal places.

Answer: 0.58

189. Approximate the integral $\int_{-0.49}^{0.49} \frac{dx}{1+x^2}$ by Simpson's rule, using n = 4. Round your answer to two decimal places.

Answer: 0.91

190. Determine the maximum error in approximating $\int_1^2 \frac{1}{x^2} dx$, with n = 4, by the trapezoidal rule.

Answer: 0.0313

191. Determine the maximum error in approximating $\int_1^2 \frac{1}{x^2} dx$, with n = 4, by Simpson's rule.

Answer: 0.0026

192. If the trapezoidal rule approximation of $\int_1^2 (x \ln x) dx$ is to have an error that does not exceed 0.0001, what must the value of n be?

Answer: $x \geq 29$

193. If Simpson's rule approximation of $\int_1^2 (x \ln x)dx$ is to have an error that does not exceed 0.0001, what must the value of n be?

Answer: $x \geq 10$

Chapter 6 – Graphing Calculator

Integration Techniques and Differential Equations

Section 6.1 Integration by Parts

1. Using your graphing calculator, evaluate the definite integral $\int_{-1}^{2} \ln(x+2)dx$. Round to 3 decimal places.

   Answer: 2.545

2. Using your graphing calculator, evaluate the definite integral $\int_{0}^{4} xe^{x} dx$. Round to 3 decimal places.

   Answer: 164.794

Section 6.2 Integration using Tables

3. Using your graphing calculator, evaluate the definite integral $\int_0^4 \frac{x}{x+1}\,dx$. Round to 3 decimal places.

   Answer: 2.391

4. Using your graphing calculator, evaluate the definite integral $\int_0^4 \frac{x}{\sqrt{2x+1}}\,dx$. Round to 3 decimal places.

   Answer: 3.333

5. Using your graphing calculator, evaluate the definite integral $\int_1^5 \frac{dx}{x^2\sqrt{49-x^2}}$. Round to 3 decimal places.

   Answer: 0.121

Section 6.3 Improper Integrals

6. Use a graphing calculator to find the improper integral $\int_1^{\infty} \frac{x}{1+x^2}dx$ as follows:

   a. Define y_1 to be the definite integral (using FnInt) the given lower limit to x.
   b. Make a table of values of y_1 for x values 1, 10, 100, 1000.
   c. Determine whether the integral converges or diverges. If it converges, determine what it converges to. (Round to nearest thousandth).

   Answer: diverges

7. Use a graphing calculator to find the improper integral $\int_1^{\infty} \frac{\ln x}{x}dx$ as follows:

   a. Define y_1 to be the definite integral (using FnInt) the given lower limit to x.
   b. Make a table of values of y_1 for x values 1, 10, 100, 1000.
   c. Determine whether the integral converges or diverges. If it converges, determine what it converges to. (Round to nearest thousandth).

   Answer: diverges

8. Use a graphing calculator to find the improper integral $\int_1^{\infty} \frac{dx}{(x+2)^2}$ as follows:

   a. Define y_1 to be the definite integral (using FnInt) the given lower limit to x.
   b. Make a table of values of y_1 for x values 1, 10, 100, 1000.
   c. Determine whether the integral converges or diverges. If it converges, determine what it converges to. (Round to nearest thousandth).

   Answer: 0.333

9. Use a graphing calculator to find the improper integral $\int_0^{\infty} \frac{1}{e^x+e^{-x}}dx$ as follows:

   a. Define y_1 to be the definite integral (using FnInt) the given lower limit to x.
   b. Make a table of values of y_1 for x values 1, 10, 100, 1000.
   c. Determine whether the integral converges or diverges. If it converges, determine what it converges to. (Round to nearest thousandth).

   Answer: 0.785

10. The capitalized cost of an asset is given by $C = C_0 + \int_0^n 25{,}000e^{-0.12t}\,dt$ for an asset whose annual cost of maintenance is $25,000, with an interest rate of 12% compounded continuously. C_0 represents the original investment, and t is time in years. Find the capitalized cost of an asset worth $650,000 originally for
    a. $n = 5$ years
    b. $n = 10$ years
    c. forever ($n = \infty$)
    Use your graphing calculator with Fn Int and make a table of values.

    Answer: a. $743, 997.58
    b. $795, 584.54
    c. $858, 333.33

Section 6.4 Numerical Integration

11. Using a trapezoidal approximation program, approximate the integral $\int_0^1 \sqrt{1+x^2}\,dx$ for n = 10, n = 100, and n = 500, rounding calculations to 4 decimal places. Give an estimate for the value of the integral, stating your answer to as many decimal places as the last two approximations agree.

Answer:

n	approximation
10	1.1484
100	1.1478
500	1.1478

$\int_0^1 \sqrt{1+x^2}\,dx \approx 1.478$

12. Using a trapezoidal approximation program, approximate the integral $\int_0^1 e^{x^3}\,dx$ for n = 10, n = 100, and n = 500, rounding calculations to 4 decimal places. Give an estimate for the value of the integral, stating your answer to as many decimal places as the last two approximations agree.

Answer:

n	approximation
10	1.3487
100	1.3420
500	1.3420

$\int_0^1 e^{x^3}\,dx \approx 1.3420$

13. Using a trapezoidal approximation program, approximate the integral $\int_1^3 \sqrt{1+\ln x}\,dx$ for n = 10, n = 100, and n = 500, rounding calculations to 4 decimal places. Give an estimate for the value of the integral, stating your answer to as many decimal places as the last two approximations agree.

Answer:

n	approximation
10	2.5543
100	2.5555
500	2.5555

$\int_1^3 \sqrt{1+\ln x}\,dx \approx 2.5555$

14. Using a trapezoidal approximation program, approximate the integral $\int_0^{0.5} \frac{dx}{1+x^2}$ for n = 10, n = 100, and n = 500, rounding calculations to 4 decimal places. Give an estimate for the value of the integral, stating your answer to as many decimal places as the last two approximations agree.

Answer:

n	approximation
10	0.4635
100	0.4636
500	0.4636

$$\int_0^{0.5} \frac{dx}{1+x^2} \approx 0.4636$$

15. Use the formula shown below and the trapezoidal approximation program to find the proportion of Americans with IQs between 100 and 120. Use successively higher values of n until answers agree to 4 decimal places.

$$\frac{1}{\sqrt{2\pi}} \int_{\frac{A-100}{15}}^{\frac{B-100}{15}} e^{-\frac{x^2}{2}}\,dx$$

Answer:

n	approximation
4	0.40621
8	0.40769
12	0.40797
16	0.40807
20	0.40812
24	0.40814

40.81%

16. Use Simpson's Rule program with n = 4 to approximate the following integral $\int_0^1 e^{-x^2}\,dx$. Give an estimate for the value of the integral, stating your answer to 3 decimal places.

Answer: 0.747

17. Use Simpson's Rule program with n = 4 to approximate the following integral $\int_1^5 \sqrt{35+x}\,dx$. Give an estimate for the value of the integral, stating your answer to 3 decimal places.

Answer: 24.655

18. Use Simpson's Rule program with n = 4 to approximate the following integral $\int_0^1 \sqrt{1+x^3}\,dx$. Give an estimate for the value of the integral, stating your answer to 3 decimal places.

    Answer: 1.111

19. Use Simpson's Rule program with n = 4 to approximate the following integral $\int_1^3 \sqrt{2-\ln x}\,dx$. Give an estimate for the value of the integral, stating your answer to 3 decimal places.

    Answer: 2.311

20. Use Simpson's Rule program with n = 4 to approximate the following integral $\int_0^1 \sqrt{1-x^2}\,dx$. Give an estimate for the value of the integral, stating your answer to 3 decimal places.

    Answer: 0.771

Chapter 7

Calculus of Several Variables

Section 7.1 Functions of Several Variables

MULTIPLE CHOICE 7.1

[c] 1. For the function $f(x,y)=\frac{5}{y-x^2}$, find the domain.

a. $\{(x,y)\mid y=x^2\}$
b. $\{(x,y)\mid y\neq x\}$
c. $\{(x,y)\mid y\neq x^2\}$
d. $\{(x,y)\mid x\neq 0, y\neq 0\}$

[a] 2. For the function $f(x,y)=\frac{e^{\frac{1}{x}}}{y-2}$, find the domain.

a. $\{(x,y)\mid x\neq 0, y\neq 2\}$
b. $\{(x,y)\mid y\neq 2\}$
c. $\{(x,y)\mid x\neq 0\}$
d. $\{(x,y)\mid x \text{ and } y \text{ are Real}\}$

[d] 3. For the function $f(x,y)=\frac{\sqrt{y}}{2\sqrt[3]{x}}$, find the domain.

a. $\{(x,y)\mid x>0, y\geq 0\}$
b. $\{(x,y)\mid y\geq 0\}$
c. $\{(x,y)\mid x\neq 0\}$
d. $\{(x,y)\mid y\geq 0, x\neq 0\}$

[c] 4. For the function $f(x,y)=\frac{\ln(x+2)}{y^2}$, find the domain.

a. $\{(x,y)\mid x>0, y\neq 0\}$
b. $\{(x,y)\mid x>-2, y>0\}$
c. $\{(x,y)\mid x>-2, y\neq 0\}$
d. $\{(x,y)\mid y\geq -2, y\neq 0\}$

[a] 5. For the function $f(x,y)=x^3+y^3-3x^2y+5$, find f(–1, 2).

a. 6
b. 18
c. 8
d. 24

[b] 6. For the function $f(x,y)=\sqrt{6-x^2+y^2}$, find f(–2, 5).

a. $\sqrt{35}$
b. $\sqrt{27}$
c. 3
d. $\sqrt{32}$

[d] 7. For the function $g(x, y) = \dfrac{5x - 3y}{2 - x^2}$, find $g(-1, -3)$.

a. $-\dfrac{14}{3}$ b. -14
c. $\dfrac{4}{3}$ d. 4

[a] 8. Use the Cobb-Douglas production function $f(x, y) = 23.5x^{0.35}y^{0.65}$ to determine the number of units produced with 2450 units of labor (x) and 3450 units of capital (y).

a. 71,921 b. 37,916
c. 69,412 d. 29,196

[c] 9. Use the Cobb-Douglas production function $f(x, y) = 16.7x^{0.55}y^{0.45}$ to determine the number of units produced with 1550 units of labor (x) and 2150 units of capital (y).

a. 27,905 b. 28,301
c. 29,991 d. 29,196

A bolt manufacturer makes two sizes of bolts. The larger bolts cost $0.05 each to produce, and the smaller cost $0.04 each.

[b] 10. Determine the profit function if the manufacturer sells x small bolts for $0.05 each and y large bolts for $0.07 each.

a. $P(x, y) = 0.02x + 0.03y$ b. $P(x, y) = 0.01x + 0.02y$
c. $P(x, y) = 0.07x + 0.05y$ d. $P(x, y) = 0.05x + 0.07y$

[b] 11. Suppose $f(p, r, t) = pe^{0.01rt}$ represents the amount in an account where p dollars are invested at r% (compounded continuously) for t years. How much money will be in the account if $4375 is invested at 6 ½% for 7.5 years?

a. $7027.09 b. $7123.55 c. $6698.81 d. $6901.04

[a] 12. Use the Cobb-Douglas production function $f(x, y) = 23.4x^{0.35}y^{0.65}$ to determine the number of units produced with 2450 units of labor (x) and 3450 units of capital (y).

a. 71,921 b. 37,916 c. 69,412 d. 29,196

[c] 13. Use the Cobb-Douglas production function $f(x, y) = 16.7x^{0.55}y^{0.45}$ to determine the number of units produced with 1550 units of labor (x) and 2150 units of capital (y).

a. 27,905 b. 28,301 c. 29,991 d. 29,196

[b] 14. Squares of length b are to be cut from the corners of a rectangular piece of cardboard. The length is a and the width is c. The cardboard will then be bent up to form an open0topped box. (See the following figure.) What is the volume of this box in terms of a, b, and c?

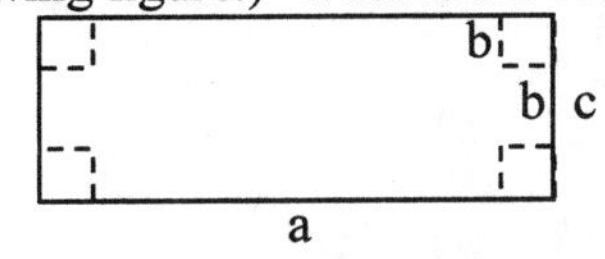

a. $V(a, b, c) = abc$
b. $V(a, b, c) = (a - 2b)(c - 2b)b$
c. $V(a, b, c) = ab^2c$
d. $V(a, b, c) = (a - b)(c - b)b$

SHORT ANSWER 7.1

15. For the function $f(x, y, z) = \frac{z \ln x}{\sqrt{y}}$, find the domain.

Answer: $\{(x, y, z) \mid x > 0, y > 0\}$

16. Evaluate $P(s, t) = 0.4s^2e^{-0.1} \ln(0.25t)$ where $s = 1$ and $t = 4$.

Answer: 0

17. For the function $f(u, v) = \ln(u^4 - v)$, find f(e, 0).

Answer: 4

18. For the function $f(x, y) = xe^{y-x} + e^{x^2+xy}$ find f(1, –1).

Answer: $\frac{1}{e^2} + 1$

19. For the function $f(x, y) = \frac{8.5y}{1.7x + 3.4y}$, find f(–3, 4).

Answer: 4

20. For the function $f(x, y) = \sqrt{3 - x^2 + y^2}$, find f(6, 7).

Answer: 4

21. For the function $g(x, y) = 0.4(x - y)^2 + y$, find g(9, 5).

Answer: 13

22. For the function $f(x, y) = 0.25x^2 - 6.5y$, find f(4, –2).

Answer: 17

23. For the function $g(x, y) = y^{\frac{5}{2}} \ln x^{\frac{5}{2}}$, find g(e, 1).

Answer: $\frac{5}{2}$

24. Suppose $f(p, r, t) = pe^{0.01rt}$ represents the amount in an account where p dollars are invested at r% (compounded continuously) for t years. Determine f(5675, 6.5, 2.75).

    Answer: $6785.72

25. Compute $P(u, v, w) = e^{0.2v} - \ln 2\sqrt{u} + 40w^2$ at the point (0.25, 0, 0.25).

    Answer: 3.5

26. Compute F(–0.1, 2, –0.3) for $F(x, y, z) = 2x + \sqrt{xyz - 0.02}$.

    Answer: 0

27. For the function $f(x, y, z) = \ln e^y - e^x + z^2$, find f(ln 2.3, –1).

    Answer: 2

28. The price-earnings ratio of a stock is defined as $R(P, E) = \frac{P}{E}$ where P is the price of a share of stock and E is its earnings. Find the price-earnings ratio of a stock that is selling for $56 with earnings of $0.85.

    Answer: 65.9

29. A paint store carries 2 brands of latex paint. Sales figures indicate that if brand A is sold for x_1 dollars per gallon and Brand B is sold for x_2 dollars per gallon, the demand for Brand A will be $D_1(x_1, x_2) = 250 - 15x_1 + 20x_2$ gallons per month and the demand for Brand B will be $D_2(x_1, x_2) = 200 + 5x_1 - 20x_2$ gallons per month.
    a. Express the store's total monthly revenue from the sale of the paint as a function of prices x_1 and x_2.
    b. Compute the total revenue if Brand A is sold for $15/gallon and Brand B is sold for $12/gallon.

    Answer: a. $250x_1 - 15x_1^2 + 25x_1x_2 + 200x_2 - 20x_2^2$ b. $4,395

A bolt manufacturer makes two sizes of bolts. The larger bolts cost $0.05 each to produce, and the smaller cost $0.04 each.

30. Determine the cost function to manufacture x small bolts and y large ones.

    Answer: $C(x, y) = 0.04x + 0.05y$

31. A sailboat manufacturer produces x day-sailors at a cost of $1675 each and y sloops at a cost of $3125 each. Her fixed costs per month are $15,725. State the monthly cost function.

    Answer: $C(x, y) = 15{,}725 + 1675x + 3125y$

32. Determine the domain of the function $f(x, y) = \frac{\sqrt{2.5 - x}}{4.7 - y}$.

Answer: $\{(x, y): x \le 2.5 \text{ and } y \ne 4.7\}$

33. Determine the domain of the function $g(x, y) = \frac{\ln(y - 6)}{x + 6}$.

Answer: $\{(x, y): x \ne -6 \text{ and } y > 6\}$

34. Determine the domain of the function $f(x, y) = 5.7xe^{0.1x-0.2y}$.

Answer: All real numbers

35. $V(r, h) = (1/3)\pi r^2 h$ represents the volume of a cone with height h and radius of the base r. Compute V(5.3, 7.4) and explain in words its meaning.

Answer: V(5.3, 7.4) = 217.7 is the volume of a cone with radius 5.3 and height 7.4.

36. $V(r, h) = (1/3)\pi r^2 h$ represents the volume of a cone with height h and radius of the base r. If the radius is four and a half times as large as the height, express the volume as a function of the height only.

Answer: $V(h) = \frac{27\pi}{4} h^3$

37. A sailboat manufacturer produces x day-sailors at a cost of $1675 each and y sloops at a cost of $3125 each. Her fixed costs per month are $15,725. State the monthly cost function.

Answer: C(x, y) = 15,725 + 1675x + 3125y

Section 7.2 Partial Derivatives

MULTIPLE CHOICE 7.2

[c] 38. For $f(x, y) = 6xy + 2x^3 + 8y^3 + 6x + 6y + 2$, find $f_y(x, y)$.

a. $6x + 6y^2 + 6$
b. $6y + 24y^2 + 6$
c. $6x + 24y^2 + 6$
d. $6y + 6x^2 + 6$

[b] 39. For $f(x, y) = x\sqrt{y}$, find $f_x(x, y)$.

a. $\dfrac{1}{2\sqrt{y}}$
b. $\sqrt{y}$
c. $\dfrac{x}{2\sqrt{y}} + \sqrt{y}$
d. $2\sqrt{y}$

[c] 40. For $f(x, y) = xe^{x^2y}$, find $f_x(x, y)$.

a. e^{x^2y}
b. $2xye^{x^2y}$
c. $e^{x^2y}(2x^2y + 1)$
d. $2xe^{x^2y}$

[d] 41. Determine $f_y(x, y)$ for $f(x, y) = \sqrt{1 - x^2y}$.

a. $\sqrt{1 - x^2}$
b. $\dfrac{1}{2\sqrt{1 - x^2y}}$
c. $\dfrac{1 - 2x}{\sqrt{1 - x^2y}}$
d. $\dfrac{-x^2}{\sqrt{1 - x^2y}}$

[c] 42. Evaluate $f_x(1,2)$ for $f(x, y) = \dfrac{0.2x - 0.1y}{0.2x + 0.1y}$.

a. 0
b. 0.02
c. 0.5
d. 0.4

[d] 43. Evaluate $g_x(-1,2)$ for $g(x, y) = \sqrt{2x^2y}$.

a. –½
b. ½
c. 2
d. –2

[a] 44. Evaluate $f_y(e,5)$ for $f(x,y) = \ln xy + xe^{0.2y}$.

a. $\frac{1+e^2}{5}$ b. $\frac{\frac{1}{e}+e^3}{5}$ c. $\frac{\frac{1}{3}e+e^4}{5}$ d. $\frac{e^{-1}+e}{5}$

[a] 45. For $f(x,y,z) = \sqrt{x^2+y^2+z^2}$, find $f_z(3,\sqrt{11},-4)$.

a. $-\frac{2}{3}$ b. $-\frac{1}{9}$ c. $\frac{1}{2}$ d. $\frac{1}{12}$

[a] 46. Evaluate $f_{xy}(1,-1,0)$ for $f(x,y,z) = x^2ye^{2z}$.

a. 2 b. 0 c. 4 d. 2e

[c] 47. Evaluate $f_y(3, 10)$ for $f(x, y) = \ln(xy) + e^{0.2y}$.

a. $\frac{1}{2}+\frac{e^2}{10}$ b. $\frac{2+e}{10}$ c. $\frac{1+2e^2}{10}$ d. $\frac{1}{2}+\frac{e}{10}$

[d] 48. Evaluate $f_x(3, -1)$ for $f(x, y) = 2x^2y - 3xy^3$.

a. –15 b. 0 c. 15 d. –9

[b] 49. Evaluate $f_y(3, 2)$ for $f(x, y) = x^3 + 2x^2y^3$.

a. 243 b. 216 c. 163 d. 147

[d] 50. Evaluate $f_{xy}(5, -10)$ for $f(x, y) = y^2e^{0.2x}$.

a. –2e b. 0.4e c. 0 d. –4e

[b] 51. Evaluate $f_{yx}(1, 0)$ for $f(x, y) = e^{-0.1y}\ln 2x$.

a. 0 b. –0.1 c. 0.1 d. –0.1e

[b] 52. Evaluate $g_z(-1, 2, -1)$ for $g(x,y,z) = \frac{1}{\sqrt{xyz-1}}$.

a. –1 b. 1 c. $-\frac{1}{2}$ d. 0

[a] 53. Consider the Cobb-Douglas production function $f(x, y) = 17.8x^{0.74}y^{0.26}$, where x is units of labor and y is units of capital. Determine the marginal productivity of capital if the current production level uses 81 units of labor and 128 units of capital.

a. 3.30 b. 2.95 c. 3.47 d. 3.91

[b] 54. Consider the Cobb-Douglas production function $f(x, y) = 14.1x^{0.25}y^{0.75}$. Determine the marginal productivity of labor $f_x(x, y)$ and evaluate it at ($x = 7$, $y = 5$).

a. 2.347 b. 2.739 c. 4.472 d. 4.408

[c] 55. The productivity of a company is given by the function $f(x, y) = 9.6x^{\frac{4}{5}}y^{\frac{1}{5}}$ with the utilization of x units of labor and y units of capital. The company is now using 625 units of labor and 81 units of capital. Determine the marginal productivity of labor.

a. 5.57 b. 5.34 c. 5.10 d. 0.46

[d] 56. Determine the instantaneous rate of change of the volume of a cylinder with respect to its radius when $r = 5.6$ and $h = 7.9$. (Note: $V = \pi r^2 h$.)

a. 31.36π b. 175.616π c. 247.744π c. 88.48π

SHORT ANSWER 7.2

57. Find $f_x(x,y)$ for $f(x,y) = 0.5x^4e^{0.2y} + 0.5\ln y$.

Answer: $f_x(x,y) = 2x^3e^{0.2y}$

58. For $g(x,y) = 2xy^5 + 3x^2y + x^2$, find $g_y(x,y)$.

Answer: $g_y(x,y) = 10xy^4 + 3x^2$

59. For $f(x,y) = \dfrac{2x+3y}{y-x}$, find $f_x(x,y)$.

Answer: $f_x(x,y) = \dfrac{5y}{(y-x)^2}$

60. For $f(x,y) = \ln(xy^3 - x^2y)$, find $f_y(x,y)$.

Answer: $f_y(x,y) = \dfrac{3xy^2 - x^2}{xy^3 - x^2y}$

61. For $f(x,y) = \dfrac{x}{y} - \dfrac{y}{x}$, find $f_x(x,y)$.

Answer: $f_x(x,y) = \dfrac{1}{y} + \dfrac{y}{x^2}$

62. For $f(x, y) = \ln(0.3x^6 + 4y)$, find $f_x(x, y)$.

Answer: $f_x(x,y) = \dfrac{1.8x^5}{0.3x^6 + 4y}$

63. For $f(x, y) = 0.25x^4e^{0.2y}$, find $f_{xx}(x, y)$.

Answer: $f_{xx}(x, y) = 3x^2e^{0.2y}$

64. For $f(x,y) = 36x^{\frac{1}{3}}y^{\frac{2}{3}}$, find f_{xx}, f_{yy}, f_{xy}, f_{yx}.

Answer: $f_{xx} = \dfrac{-8y^{\frac{2}{3}}}{x^{\frac{5}{3}}}$; $f_{yy} = \dfrac{-8x^{\frac{1}{3}}}{y^{\frac{4}{3}}}$; $f_{xy} = \dfrac{8}{x^{\frac{2}{3}}y^{\frac{1}{3}}}$; $f_{yx} = \dfrac{8}{x^{\frac{2}{3}}y^{\frac{1}{3}}}$

65. For $f(x,y) = 4y^3e^{-2x}$, find f_{xx}, f_{yy}, f_{xy}, f_{yx}.

Answer: $f_{xx} = \dfrac{16y^3}{e^{2x}}$; $f_{yy} = \dfrac{24y}{e^{2x}}$, $f_{xy} = \dfrac{-24y^2}{e^{2x}}$, $f_{yx} = \dfrac{-24y^2}{e^{2x}}$

66. For $f(x,y,z) = (x + yz + x^2z)^4$, find f_x, f_y, f_z.

Answer: $f_x = 4(x + yz + x^2z)^3(1 + 2xz)$; $f_y = 4(x + yz + x^2z)^3(z)$, $f_z = 4(x + yz + x^2z)^3(y + x^2)$

67. A company's production P is given by the Cobb-Douglas function $P(L,K) = 216L^{\frac{1}{4}}K^{\frac{3}{4}}$, where L is the number of units of labor and K is the number of units of capital.
   a. Find $P_L(81,16)$ and interpret this number.
   b. Find $P_K(81,16)$ and interpret this number.

   Answer: a. 16 (production increases by about 16 for each additional unit of labor)
   b. 243 (production increases by about 243 for each additional unit of capital)

68. A company's annual sales S depend upon its research expenditures x and its advertising budget y (both in thousands of dollars) according to the function $S(x,y) = 200x^2 + 1000y^2 - 100xy + 4000$.
   a. Find $S_x(2,4)$ and interpret this number.
   b. Find $S_y(2,4)$ and interpret this number.

   Answer: a. 400 (sales increase by about 400 for each additional \$1000 research)
   b. 7800 (sales increase by about 7800 for each additional \$1000 of advertising)

69. A company that produces x calculators and y computers per month has a cost function of $C(x) = 20{,}000 + 15x + 250y - \sqrt{xy}$. If the present production level is 100 calculators and 4 computers per month, find the approximate cost to produce one more computer per month.

   Answer: \$247.50

70. A metal plate is being heated by a torch, and the temperature T at any point (x, y) on the plate is given by $T(x, y) = 325 - 0.5x^2 - 0.6y^2$. Determine the rate of change of temperature with respect to distance at the point (2, 5), assuming x is held constant and y is allowed to vary.

Answer: –6

71. A company that produces x calculators and y computers per month has a cost function of $C(x) = 21.455 + 14.7x + 244y - 3.2\sqrt{xy}$. Find the approximate cost to produce one more computer per month if the present production level is 132 calculators and 5 computers per month.

Answer: $235.78

Section 7.3 Optimizing Functions of Several Variables

MULTIPLE CHOICE 7.3

[b] 72. Find the critical points of $f(x, y) = 0.1x^3 + 0.1y^3 - 0.06xy$.

a. (0, 0) and (0.1, 0.1)
b. (0, 0) and (0.2, 0.2)
c. (0.1, 0.1) and (0.2, –0.2)
d. (0, 0) and (0.2, –0.2)

[d] 73. Find the critical points of $f(x, y) = xe^{0.1xy}$.

a. (0, 0)
b. (0, 0.1)
c. (0.1, 0)
d. no critical points

[a] 74. Find the critical points of $f(x, y) = 2x^4 + y^2 - 12xy$.

a. (0, 0), (3, 18), (–3, –18)
b. (0, 0), (3, –18), (–3, 18)
c. (0, 0), (–3, 18)
d. (0, 0), (3, 18)

[d] 75. Find the critical points of $h(x, y) = x^3 + y^3 - 3xy$.

a. (0, 1), (1, 1), (1, –1)
b. (0, 0), (1, 1), and (–1, 1)
c. (1, 1), (–1, 1), (1, –1)
d. (0, 0), (1, 1)

[a] 76. For $f(x, y) = 4x^2 + xy + y^2 + 25x + 5y - 7$ a critical point can be found to be (–3, –1). Using the D-Test, (–3, –1) is

a. a relative minimum
b. a relative maximum
c. a saddle point
d. test is inconclusive

[c] 77. For $f(x, y) = -x^2 - 6x - y^2 + 2y - 4$, a critical point is (–3, 1). Using the D-Test, (–3, 1) is

a. a relative minimum
b. a saddle point
c. a relative maximum
d. test is inconclusive

[d] 78. Given $f(x, y) = e^{xy}$, which of the following is true?

a. $f(1,1) = e$ is a relative minimum
b. $f(0,0) = 1$ is a relative minimum
c. $f(0,0) = 1$ is a relative maximum
d. $f(0,0) = 1$ is a saddle point

[a] 79. Given $f(x, y) = 2x^2 - 2xy + 3y^2 - 4x - 8y + 20$, which of the following is true?

a. f(2, 2) = 8 is a relative minimum
b. f(1, 1) = 11 is a relative maximum
c. f(0, 0) = 20 is a relative maximum
d. f(2, 2) = 8 is a relative maximum

[c] 80. If there are any, find the relative maximum and minimum values of the function $f(x, y) = 0.6 - 0.2x^2 - 0.4x - 0.1y^2$.

a. $f(0, 0) = 0.6$ is a relative minimum
b. $f(0, -1) = 0.5$ is a relative maximum
c. $f(-1, 0) = 0.8$ is a relative maximum
d. none

[c] 81. If there are any, find the relative maximum and minimum values of the function $f(x, y) = 2x^4 + y^2 - 12xy$.

a. $f(0, 0) = 0$ is a relative maximum, and $f(3, 18) = -162$ is a relative minimum.
b. $f(0, 0) = 0$ is a relative maximum, and $f(-3, -18) = -162$ is a relative minimum.
c. Both $f(3, 18)$ and $f(-3, -18)$ are relative minima.
d. $f(3, 18)$ is the only relative minimum, and there are no relative maxima.

[b] 82. If there are any, find the relative maximum and minimum values of the function $f(x, y) = x^2 + y^2 + 2x - 6y + 14$.

a. $f(1, 3) = 44$ is a relative maximum.
b. $f(-1, 3) = 4$ is a relative minimum.
c. $f(0, 0) = 14$ is a relative maximum.
d. none

[d] 83. If there are any, find the relative maximum and minimum values of the function $f(x, y) = xy + 2y^2 - 3y - 2$.

a. $f(3, -2) = 4$ is a relative minimum.
b. $f(3, -2) = 4$ is a relative maximum.
c. $f(-3, 2) = -20$ is a relative minimum.
d. none

[c] 84. If there are any, find the relative maximum and minimum values of the function $f(x, y) = x^2 + y^2 - 10x - 2y + 36$

a. $f(0, 0) = 36$ is a relative maximum.
b. $f(1, 0) = 27$ is a relative minimum.
c. $f(5, 1) = 10$ is a relative minimum.
d. none

[d] 85. If there are any, find the relative maximum and minimum values of the function $f(x, y) = e^{0.1xy}$.
a. $f(0, 0) = 1$ is a relative maximum.
b. $f(0, 0) = 1$ is a relative minimum.
c. $f(1, 1) = e^{0.1}$ is a relative maximum.
d. none

[b] 86. If there are any, find the relative maximum and minimum values of the function $f(x, y) = 2x^2 - 2xy + 3y^2 - 4x - 8y + 20$.

a. $f(1, 1) = 11$ is a relative maximum.
b. $f(2, 2) = 8$ is a relative minimum.
c. $f(0, 0) = 20$ is a relative maximum.
d. none

[a] 87. A calculator manufacturer has developed the monthly profit equation $P(x, y) = -0.2x^2 + 0.4xy - 0.3y^2 + 0.4x - 0.2y + 7.7$, where x is the number (in hundreds) of standard calculators and y is the number (in hundreds) of graphics calculators. If $P(x, y)$ is in thousands of dollars, find the maximum monthly profit.

a. \$8000   b. \$8800   c. \$9200   d. \$9500

[b] 88. A pen manufacturer has developed the yearly profit equation $P(x, y) = -0.2x^2 + 0.2xy - 0.1y^2 + x - 0.4y + 10.7$, where x is the number (in thousands) of standard pens produced, y is the number (in thousands) of gold pens produced, and $P(x, y)$ is in thousands of dollars. What is the maximum profit?

a. \$38,000   b. \$12,000   c. \$9600   d. \$22,400

[a] 89. A company makes two types of stereos; x of type A and y of type B. The revenue function is $R(x, y) = 21.5x + 27.5y$, and the production cost function is $C(x, y) = 0.1x^2 + 0.1y^2 - 0.1xy$. (Both are in thousands of dollars.) Determine the maximum profit.

a. \$60,325,000   b. \$97,000,000   c. \$206,000,000   d. \$111,000,000

[c] 90. A company produces x thousand rugs of type A and y thousand of type B per year and has the profit equation $P(x, y) = -4x + 12y - x^2 + 2xy - 2y^2 - 5$. How many of each type of rug should be produced to maximize the profit?

a. 1000 of type A and 3000 of type B
b. 3000 of type A and 1000 of type B
c. 2000 of type A and 4000 of type B
d. 4000 of type A and 2000 of type B

[d] 91. A company wishes to design a rectangular box with no top and a volume of 32 cubic inches (see the following figure). Find the dimensions that will minimize the amount of material used.

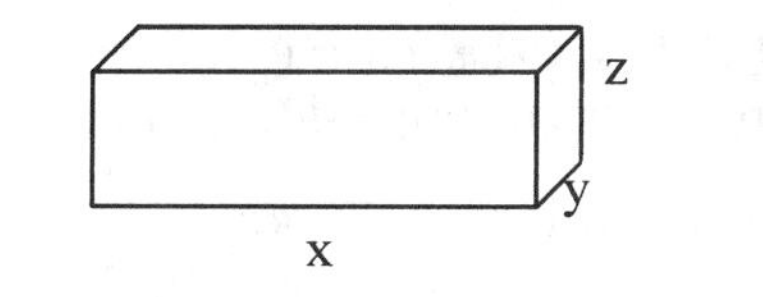

a. $x = y = z = 3.175$ b. $x = y = 2, z = 8$ c. $x = y = 2.5, z = 5$ d. $x = y = 4, z = 2$

SHORT ANSWER 7.3

92. Find the relative extrema of the function $f(x, y) = -2x^2 - y^2 + 2xy + 2x + 4y - 5$.

Answer: relative maximum value f(3, 5) = 8

93. Find the relative extrema of the function $f(x, y) = x^2 + 3y^2 + 2xy - 2x + 2y + 6$.

Answer: relative minimum value f(2, –1) = 3

94. Find the relative extrema of the function $f(x, y) = e^{2x^2 + y^2}$.

Answer: relative minimum value f(0, 0) = 1

95. Find the relative extrema of the function $f(x, y) = \ln(x^2 + 2y^2 + 1)$.

Answer: relative minimum value f(0, 0) = 0

96. Find the relative extrema of the function $f(x, y) = x^3 + y^2 - 3x - 6y + 16$.

Answer: relative minimum value f(1, 3) = 5, saddle point at x = –1, y = 3

97. Find the critical points of the function $f(x, y) = 0.2x^2 + 0.3y^2 + 7.3$.

Answer: (0, 0)

98. Find the critical points of the function $g(x, y) = -0.4x^2 - 0.4y^2 + 2.4x + 3.2y - 1.9$.

Answer: (3, 4)

99. Find the critical points of the function $f(x, y) = 7.4 - 0.1x^2 - 0.4x - 0.1y^2$.

Answer: (–2, 0)

100. A rectangular box with no top and having a volume of 12 ft^3 is to be constructed. The cost per square foot of the material to be used is \$4 for the bottom, \$3 for two of the opposite sides and \$2 for the remaining pair of opposite sides. If the cost function for building the box is $C(x, y) = 4xy + \frac{72}{y} + \frac{48}{x}$, where x and y are dimensions of the base, find the dimensions of the box that will minimize cost.

Answer: base 2 ft. × 3 ft.; height 2 ft.

101. A company sells electrical generating equipment in America and Europe, charging different prices in the two markets. The price function for generators sold in America is $p = 30 - 0.2x$, and the price function for generators sold in Europe is $q = 22 - 0.1y$ (both in thousands of dollars), where x and y are, respectively, the number of generators sold in America and Europe. The company's cost function is $C = 25 + 6(x + y)$ thousand dollars. Find how many generators should be sold in each market to maximize profit.

Answer: Maximum profit will occur when 60 generators are sold in America for $18,000 and 80 generators are sold in Europe for $14,000.

Section 7.4 Least Squares

MULTIPLE CHOICE 7.4

[c] 102. Find the least squares line for the following points.

x	1	0	–1	–2
y	2	1	1	0

a. $y = 0.8x + 1.3$
b. $y = 0.8x + 1.2$
c. $y = 0.6x + 1.3$
d. $y = 1.3x + 0.8$

[a] 103. Find the least squares line for the following points.

x	1	2	3	4	5	6
y	88	80	74	71	66	65

a. $y = -4.57x + 90.00$
b. $y = -4.41x + 90.89$
c. $y = -4.71x + 91.37$
d. $y = 4.57x + 91.78$

[c] 104. Find the least squares line for the following points.

x	2	4	6	8	10
y	–2	0	–1	0	1

a. $y = 0.7x + 1.9$ b. $y = 0.3x + 2.2$ c. $y = 0.3x - 2.2$ d. $y = 0.7x - 1.9$

[a] 105. Find the least squares line for the following points.

x	2	5	6	9
y	4	6	7	8

a. $y = 0.58x + 3.06$ b. $y = 0.73x + 2.45$ c. $y = -0.17x + 3.19$ d. $y = 0.41x + 2.86$

[a] 106. Find the least squares line for the following points.

x	0.5	1.0	1.5	2.0	2.5	3.0
y	95	88	95	90	87	74

a. $y = -6.46x + 99.47$ b. $y = -5.71x + 98.17$ c. $y = -6.91x + 100.39$ d. $y = -4.29x + 98.63$

[c] 107. Find the least squares line for the following points.

x	5	10	15	20	25
y	22	32	38	59	67

a. $y = 4.10x + 6.93$ b. $y = 3.51x + 8.96$ c. $y = 2.34x + 8.50$ d. $4.62x + 7.74$

[a] 108. Find the least squares line for the following points.

x	30	40	50	60	70	80
y	43	35	54	53	56	63

a. $y = 0.38x + 31.59$ b. $y = 0.38x + 30.17$ c. $y = 0.49x + 31.59$ d. $y = 0.49x + 30.17$

[d] 109. Find the equation of the least-squares line if n = 12, $\sum x_i = 38$, $\sum y_i = 92$, $\sum x_i^2 = 764$, and $\sum x_i y_i = 174$.

a. y = 0.32x + 7.36 b. y = –0.24x + 6.91 c. y = 0.16x + 8.99 d. y = –0.18x + 8.24

[b] 110. Find the equation of the least-squares line if n = 40, $\sum x_i = 293$, $\sum y_i = 357$, $\sum x_i^2 = 2685$, and $\sum x_i y = 3667$.

a. y = 2.31x – 5.38 b. y = 1.95x – 5.38 c. y = 2.31x – 5.91 d. y = 1.95x – 5.91

[a] 111. Determine the equation of the least-squares line for these data points:

x	2.5	3.5	4.5	6.0	8.0	10.0	12.5
y	–7	–9	–31	–52	–59	–64	–96

a. y = –8.53x + 11.83 b. y = –7.98x + 11.83 c. y = –8.53x + 11.27 d. y = –7.98x + 11.27

[c] 112. Determine the equation of the least-squares line for these data points:

x	–3	–2	0	2	3
y	–1	1	3	2	5

a. y = 0.86x + 2.00 b. y = 0.86x + 2.20 c. y = 0.77x + 2.00 d. y = 0.77x + 2.20

[d] 113. Determine the equation of the least-squares line for these data points:

x	1.6	2.3	3.0	3.9	5.1
y	–5	–4	–4	–2	–1

a. y = 0.67x – 7.01 b. y = 0.67x – 6.76 c. y = 1.35x – 7.19 d. y = 1.17x – 6.92

[b] 114. Determine the equation of the least-squares line for these data points:

x	1	2	3	4	5	6
y	88	80	74	71	66	65

a. y = –4.41x + 91.37 b. y = –4.57x + 90.00 c. y = –4.71x + 90.89 d. y = 4.20x + 91.78

[a] 115. Use the following data to estimate y for x = 8 by using the least-squares line.

x	0	3	6	11
y	9	13	19	26

a. 21.48 b. 21.11 c. 21.81 d. 21.03

[a] 116. The following data show the monthly sales of personal computers of a certain brand for various prices:

Price	$900	$980	$1030	$1065	$1090
Sales	80	70	59	56	46

Which of the following prices is most likely to generate monthly sales of 65 computers?

a. $997 b. $1009 c. $1012 d. $1018

[c] 117. Use the following data to estimate y for x = 1710 using the least-squares line

x	1600	1850	2000	2270
y	30	19	9	5

a. 23.66 b. 23.90 c. 24.23 d. 24.59

[c] 118. Use the following data to estimate y for x = 15 using the least-squares line

x	11	14	18	22
y	11	2	–6	–19

a. 1.6 b. 1.4 c. 0.3 d. –0.6

[d] 119. Use the following data to estimate x for y = –2 using the least-squares line

x	1	3	6	10
y	–9	–4	–2	5

a. 6.00 b. 6.11 c. 5.81 d. 5.34

[c] 120. Assume a college has the following data on Scholastic Aptitude Tests (SATs) and grade point averages (GPAs).

SAT	1210	1020	910	950	870	1130	1060
GPA	2.7	2.1	1.8	2.0	1.7	3.1	2.3

Use the least-squares line to determine what SAT score corresponds to a GPA of 2.0.

a. 950 b. 944 c. 969 d. 939

[b] 121. A company is trying to determine the relationship between the amount of money spent on advertising (x) and the weekly volume of sales (y). The following data were collected (both x and y are in units of thousands of dollars).

Spent on advertising (x)	1.00	1.25	1.50	2.00	2.50	3.00
Weekly sales	10.2	11.5	16.1	20.3	25.6	28.0

Determine the equation of the least-squares line.

a. y = 11.62x + 0.09 b. y = 9.39x + 1.00 c. y = 8.67x + 0.98 d. y = 10.19x + 1.08

[a] 122. Given the following data on hours spent studying for a mathematics exam (x) and the student's corresponding grade on the exam (y), determine the equation of the least-squares line.

Hours (x)	0.50	0.75	1.00	1.25	1.50	1.75	2.00	2.50	2.75
Grade (y)	54	61	59	80	73	81	89	97	86

a. y = 17.41x + 48.47 b. y = 18.29x + 46.03 c. y = 16.80x + 51.17 d. 15.31x + 50.61

[b] 123. For a brand of peanut butter, the following data on price (p) and monthly demand (x) were noted. Use the method of least squares to determine the linear price-demand equation, p = f(x).

price (p)	$1.89	$2.12	$1.98	$1.79	$1.92	$2.09	$1.69
demand (x)	87	81	86	90	86	80	93

a. y = –0.025x + 5.131 b. y = –0.033x + 4.768 c. y = –0.039x + 4.232 d. y = –0.041x + 4.983

SHORT ANSWER 7.4

124. Find the least squares line for the following points.

x	1	3	6
y	10	7	5

Answer: $y = -0.97x + 10.58$

125. A company is trying to determine the relationship between the amount of money spent on advertising (x) and the weekly volume of sales (y). The following data were collected. (Both x and y are in units of thousands of dollars).

x	0	2	3	6
y	1	4	8	11

a. Determine the equation of the least squares line.
b. Predict the weekly volume of sales if $5,000 was spent on advertising.

Answer: a. $y = 1.71x + 1.30$ b. $9,850

126. Given the following data on hours of missed lecture time (x) and the student's corresponding grade on the exam (y).
a. Determine the equation of the least square line.

x	0.5	1.0	1.5	2.0	2.5	3.0
y	95	88	95	90	87	74

b. Predict the student's grade on the exam if he/she missed 5 hours of lecture time.

Answer: a. $y = -6.46x + 99.47$ b. 67

127. A company's annual sales are shown in the following table.

Year	1	2	3	4
Sales (millions)	2	3	4	6

a. Find the least squares line.
b. Predict the sales in year 5.

Answer: a. $y = 1.3x + 0.5$ b. $7.00 million

128. On election day, the polls in a certain county open at 8AM. Every 2 hours after that, an election official determines what percentage of registered voters have already cast their ballots. The data are shown as follows:

Times	x	% turnout
10:00	2	12
12:00	4	19
2:00	6	24
4:00	8	30
6:00	10	37

Note that x represents hours since 8:00AM.
a. Find the least-squares line.
b. Predict what percentage of the registered voters will have cast their vote by closing time at 8:00PM, using the least-squares equation.

Answer: a. $y = 3.05x + 6.10$ b. 42.7%

129. Use least squares to find the exponential curve $y = Be^{Ax}$ for the following points. (Keep 2 decimal places in your calculations.

x	1	2	4
y	2	3	10

Answer: $y = 1.08e^{0.55x}$

130. Use least squares to find the exponential curve $y = Be^{Ax}$ for the following points. (Keep 2 decimal places in your calculations.

x	1	3	6
y	10	4	2

Answer: $y = 12.30e^{-0.032x}$

131. Use least squares to find the exponential curve $y = Be^{Ax}$ for the following points. (Keep 2 decimal places in your calculations.

x	1	2	3
y	4.4	3.52	2.82

Answer: $y = 5.5e^{-0.22x}$

132. The number of rabbits (Y) at time (X) in months is given in the following table:

x	0	1	2	3	4	5
y	25	43	75	130	226	391

a. Fit an exponential curve to this data.
b. Use the exponential curve to predict the rabbit population after the sixth month.

Answer: a. $y = 25e^{0.54x}$ b. 638

133. For a certain brand of automobile, the following data on fuel consumption (y, in miles per gallon) and speed (x, in miles per hour) were noted. Explain why a least-squares line would not be useful in the analysis of these data.

x (mph)	20	30	40	50	60	70	80	90
y (mpg)	21	23	26	30	30	35	25	19

Answer: The relationship between x and y is not linear because y increases as x increases from 20 to 50 but then decreases as x increases from 60 to 90.

Section 7.5 Lagrange Multipliers and Constrained Optimization

MULTIPLE CHOICE 7.5

[d] 134. Use Lagrange multipliers to find the minimum value of $f(x, y) = x^2 + y^2$ subject to the constraint $3x + 4y = 25$.

a. 18.25
b. 41
c. 50
d. 25

[c] 135. Use Lagrange multipliers to find the maximum value of $f(x, y) = 3xy$ subject to the constraint $x + 27 = 7$.

a. –56.25
b. –60.25
c. –72.25
d. –52.25

[b] 136. Use Lagrange multipliers to find the maximum and minimum values of $f(x, y) = 2xy$ subject to the constraint $x^2 + y^2 = 18$.

a. max at 24, min at –20
b. max at 18, min at –18
c. max at 20, min at –20
d. max at 24, min at –24

[b] 137. Use Lagrange multipliers to find the maximum and minimum values of $f(x, y) = 5xy$ subject to $x^2 + y^2 = 2$.

a. max at 2, min at –2
b. max at 5, min at –5
c. max at 12, min at –12
d. max at 18, min at –18

[b] 138. Use Lagrange multipliers to find the maximum and minimum values of $f(x, y) = x - y$ subject to $x^2 + y^2 = 72$.

a. max at 3, min at –3
b. max at 12, min at –12
c. max at 18, min at –18
d. max at 1, min at –1

[c] 139. Let $N(x, y) = 50x^{0.8}y^{0.2}$ be the Cobb-Douglas production function for a product, where x is the units of labor and y is the units of capital. If $400,000 is budgeted for the production of this product, with each unit of labor costing $40 and each unit of capital costing $80, determine x and y so as to maximize production.

a. $x = 5000$; $y = 5000$
b. $x = 6000$; $y = 2000$
c. $x = 8000$; $y = 1000$
d. $x = 10,000$; $y = 0$

[a] 140. The Cobb-Douglas production function for a product is $N(x, y) = 10x^{0.6}y^{0.4}$, where x is units of labor and y is units of capital. If $300,000 is budgeted for product production, with each unit of labor costing $30 and each unit of capital costing $60, determine the maximum production, $N(x, y)$.

a. 38,664 units
b. 39,107 units
c. 39,725 units
d. 40,293 units

[b] 141. A TV manufacturer produces two models of TV sets, x units of model A and y units of model B, at a cost of $C(x, y) = 0.6x^2 + 1.2y^2$. If the total number of models A and B manufactured is 97, how many of each type should be produced so as to minimize cost?

a. 52 of A and 45 of B
b. 65 of A and 32 of B
c. 67 of A and 30 of B
d. 74 of A and 23 of B

[d] 142. A large manufacturer's weekly budget is $60,000, with x thousand dollars spent on labor and y thousand on raw materials. If the weekly unit output is given by $N(x, y) = 0.4xy - 0.8x$, how should the $60,000 be allocated to labor and raw material so as to maximize output?

a. $25,000 to labor and $35,000 to materials
b. $27,000 to labor and $33,000 to materials
c. $28,000 to labor and $32,000 to materials
d. $29,000 to labor and $31,000 to materials

[b] 143. A coffee company needs to make cylindrical tin containers that hold 300 cubic centimeters. What should the radius of the can be if the company wishes to use the least amount of tin to make it? ($V = \pi r^2 h$ and $S = 2\pi rh + 2\pi r^2$)

a. r = 4.79 cm
b. r = 3.63 cm
c. r = 5.29 cm
d. r = 4.11 cm

[d] 144. Minimize $f(x, y, z) = x^2 + y^2 + z^2$ subject to the constraint $2x - y + 3z = -28$.

a. 28
b. 0
c. 82
d. 56

[c] 145. Use Lagrange multipliers to find the minimum value of the function $f(x, y) = x^2 + y^2$ subject to the constraint $x + y = 10$.

a. 52.0 b. 58.0 c. 50.0 d. 46.5

[a] 146. Use Lagrange multipliers to find the minimum value of the function $f(x, y) = 2xy$ subject to the constraint $x + y = 6$.

a. 18.0 b. 20.0 c. 24.0 d. 28.0

[b] 147. Use Lagrange multipliers to find the minimum value of the function $f(x, y) = x^2 + 2y$ subject to the constraint $x - 2y = 7$.

a. $-\frac{23}{4}$ b. $-\frac{29}{4}$ c. $-\frac{33}{4}$ d. $-\frac{15}{2}$

[d] 148. Use Lagrange multipliers to minimize the product of two numbers if their difference must be 15. Which of the following is the minimum product?

a. –52.25 b. –72.25 c. –60.25 d. –56.25

[a] 149. Use Lagrange multipliers to find the maximum value of the function $f(x, y) = 3xy$ subject to the constraint $x + 2y = 7$.

a. 18.375 b. 21.375 c. 12.375 d. 15.375

[b] 150. Use Lagrange multipliers to find the maximum value of the function $f(x, y) = x + 3y$ subject to the constraint $y = x^2 = 0$.

a. 4 b. $\frac{1}{12}$ c. $\frac{3}{2}$ d. $\frac{7}{8}$

[b] 151. Use Lagrange multipliers to find the maximum value of the function $f(x, y) = 2x + 3y$ subject to the constraint $x = y^2 = 0$. State the point (x, y), where the maximum occurs.

a. (–4, 2) b. $\left(-\frac{9}{16}, \frac{3}{4}\right)$ c. (–9, 3) d. $\left(-\frac{25}{64}, \frac{5}{8}\right)$

[a] 152. Use Lagrange multipliers to find the maximum and minimum values of the function $f(x, y, z) = 0.2x + 0.4y + 0.4z$ subject to the constraint $0.1x^2 + 0.1y^2 + 0.1z^2 = 90$.

a. 18 and –18 b. 20 and –20 c. 24 and –24 d. 28 and –28

[d] 153. Use Lagrange multipliers to find the maximum and minimum values of the function $f(x, y, z) = x + y + z$ subject to the constraint $x^2 + y^2 + z^2 = 12$.

a. 9 and –9 b. 12 and –12 c. 4 and –4 d. 6 and –6

[b] 154. Use Lagrange multipliers to find the maximum vlue of the function $f(x, y, z) = x + 2y + 3z$ subject to the constraint $x^2 + y^2 + z^2 = 10$.

a. 12 b. 11.83 c. 11.667 d. 11.875

[b] 155. A farmer's goats require 25,600 calories per week. The two available foods produce 200xy calories for a mixture of x pounds of type A food and y pounds of type B food. If type A costs $1 per pound and type B costs $2 per pound, what is the minimum weekly cost for goat food?

a. $36 b. $32 c. $60 d. $72

SHORT ANSWER 7.5

156. Use Lagrange multipliers to find the minimum value of $f(x, y) = x^2 + 2y^2 - xy$ subject to $x + y = 24$.

Answer: min f is 252 at $x = 15$, $y = 9$

157. Use Lagrange multipliers to find the minimum value of $f(x, y) = \sqrt{x^2 + y^2 + 1}$ subject to $x + 2y = 20$.

Answer: min f is 9 at $x = 4$, $y = 8$

158. Use Lagrange multipliers to find the minimum value of $f(x, y) = e^{x^2+y^2}$ subject to $2x + y = 5$.

Answer: min f is e^5 at $x = 2$, $y = 1$

159. Use Lagrange multipliers to find the maximum value of $f(x, y) = 16xy - 4x^2 - y^2$ subject to $x + y = 7$.

Answer: max f is 140 at $x = 3$, $y = 4$

160. Use Lagrange multipliers to find the maximum and minimum values of $f(x, y) = xy$ subject to $9x^2 + y^2 = 18$.

Answer: max f is 3 at $x = 1$, $y = 3$ and $x = -1$, $y = -3$
min f at -3 at $x = -1$, $y = 3$ and $x = 1$, $y = -3$

161. Use Lagrange multipliers to find the maximum and minimum values of $f(x, y) = 6x + y$ subject to $3x^2 + y^2 = 52$.

Answer: max f is 26 at $x = 4$, $y = 2$
min f is -26 at $x = -4$, $y = -2$

162. Maximize $f(x, y, z) = x + y + z$ subject to the constraint $x^2 + y^2 + z^2 = 9$.

Answer: max f is $3\sqrt{3}$ at $x = \sqrt{3}$, $y = \sqrt{3}$, $z = \sqrt{3}$

163. Use Lagrange multipliers to find the minimum value of the function $f(x, y) = 0.5xy$ subject to the constraint $y - x = 3$.

Answer: $f\left(-\frac{3}{2}, \frac{3}{2}\right) = -\frac{9}{8}$

164. Use Lagrange multipliers to find the maximum value of the function $f(x, y) = 25.4 - 0.25x^2 - 0.25y^2$ subject to the constraint $0.2x + 0.1y = 1.7$

Answer: $f(6.8, 3.4) = 10.95$

Section 7.6 Total Differentials and Approximate Changes

MULTIPLE CHOICE 7.6

[c] 165. Find the total differential of the function $f(x,y)=\frac{y}{x}$.

a. $ydx-\frac{1}{x}dy$
b. $\frac{1}{x}dy+ydx$
c. $\frac{xdy-ydx}{x^2}$
d. $\frac{1}{x}dy+\frac{y}{x^2}dx$

[a] 166. Find the total differential of the function $f(x,y)=3x^2y^3$.

a. $6xy^3dx+9x^2y^2dy$
b. $6xy^3dy+9x^2y^2dx$
c. $6x^2y^2dx+9x^2y^2dy$
d. $6xy^3dx+3x^2y^2dy$

[b] 167. Find the total differential of the function $f(x,y)=\ln(x^2-3y^3)$.

a. $\frac{2x-9y^2}{x^2-3y^3}$
b. $\frac{2xdx-9y^2dy}{x^2-3y^3}$
c. $2xdx-9y^2dy$
d. $\frac{-9y^2dx+2xdx}{x-3y^3}$

[c] 168. Find the total differential of the function $f(x,y,z)=5x^3y^2z$.

a. $15x^2dx+2ydy+dz$
b. $15x^2y^2z+10x^3yz+5x^3y^2$
c. $15x^2y^2zdx+10x^3yzdy+5x^3y^2dz$
d. $15x^2y^2dx+10x^3ydy+5x^3y^2dz$

[b] 169. Given the function $f(x,y)=\sqrt{x^2+y^2}$, and values $x=3$, $\Delta x=dx=0.04$ and $y=4$, $\Delta y=dy=-0.02$, find df using differentials.

a. 0.08
b. 0.008
c. 0.4
d. 0.04

[a] 170. Given the function $f(x,y)=ye^{-x}+2x$, and values $x=0$, $\Delta x=dx=0.1$ and $y=1$, $\Delta y=dy=0.05$, find df using differentials.

a. 0.15
b. 0.05
c. 0.25
d. 0.10

[b] 171. Use the total differential to approximate the change in f if $z = f(x, y) = 2\ln(xy) + x^2$ and x changes from 1 to 1.08 and y from 5 to 5.05.

a. 0.32
b. 0.34
c. 0.36
d. 0.38

[a] 172. Use the total differential to approximate the change in f if $z = f(x, y) = 2xe^{y^2}$ and x changes from 3 to 3.04 and y from 2 to 2.01.

a. 17.47
b. 13.16
c. 8.92
d. 3.85

[c] 173. The cost to produce x units of product A and y units of product B is given by $C(x, y) = 1000 + 0.6x - 0.01x^2 + 0.9y - 0.02y^2$. Use the total differential to determine the approximate cost to raise production from 25 to 26 for product A and from 20 to 21 for product B.

a. 0.10
b. 0.30
c. 0.20
d. 0.25

[d] 174. Use the Cobb-Douglass production function $f(x, y) = 100x^{0.7}y^{0.3}$ to determine the approximate increase in production if the units of labor (x) increase from 50 to 51 and the units of capital (y) increase from 30 to 32.

a. 147.6
b. 146.2
c. 144.3
d. 145.8

[a] 175. The cost to produce x standard light bulbs and y long-life light bulbs is given by $C(x, y) = 1000 + 0.6x + 0.9y - 0.01x^2 - 0.02y^2$. Use differentials to determine the approximate cost to raise production of the standard bulbs from 25 to 26 and production of the long-life bulbs from 20 to 21.

a. 0.20
b. 0.10
c. 0.30
d. 0.15

[d] 176. Use differentials to approximate the change in volume of a cylinder ($V = \pi r^2 h$) if the radius increases from 15 to 15.05 and the height increases from 20 to 20.03.

a. 110.3
b. 111.5
c. 112.9
d. 115.5

[d] 177. Determine the total differential dz for $z = f(x, y) = x\sqrt{2x + y}$.

a. $\frac{dx}{\sqrt{2x+y}} + x\frac{dx}{2\sqrt{2x+y}}$

b. $\left[\sqrt{2x+y} + \frac{x}{2\sqrt{2x+y}}\right]dx + x\frac{dy}{\sqrt{2x+y}}$

c. $\sqrt{2x+y}dx + x\frac{dy}{\sqrt{2x+y}}$

d. $\left[\sqrt{2x+y} + \frac{x}{\sqrt{2x+y}}\right]dx + x\frac{dy}{2\sqrt{2x+y}}$

[b] 178. Determine dz, the total differential, for $z = f(x, y) = x^2 + xy^2 + 2$ if $x = 1$, $dx = 0.01$, $y = 2$ and $dy = 0.01$.

a. 0.11 b. 0.1 c. 0.07 d. 0.09

[c] 179. Determine dz, the total differential, for $z = f(x, y) = y \ln x - xy^2$ if $x = 2$, $dx = 0.02$, $y = 6$, and $dy = 0.01$.

a. 1.162 b. 0.237 c. –0.893 d. –0.549

[a] 180. Determine dz, the total differential, for $z = 3y - 2x^2y$ if $x = 3$, $dx = 0.015$, $y = 2$ and $dy = 0.02$.

a. –0.66 b. –0.82 c. –0.52 d. –0.46

[c] 181. Determine dz, the total differential, for $z = \sqrt{xy} + e^x$ if $x = 2$, $dx = 0.05$, $y = 1$, and $dy = 0.02$.

a. 0.259 b. 0.319 c. 0.401 d. 0.506

[d] 182. The cost to produce x units of product M and y units of product N is given by $C(x, y) = 400 + 11x + 25y - 0.2x^2 - 0.1y^2$. Use the total differential to determine the approximate cost to raise production 1 unit each: from 50 to 51 for product M and from 70 to 71 for product N.

a. 0.5 b. 1.0 c. 1.5 d. 2.0

[c] 183. Consider the Cobb-Douglas production function $f(x, y) = 50x^{\frac{1}{5}}y^{\frac{4}{5}}$, where x is the units of labor, y is the units of capital, and f(x, y) is the number of units produced. Estimate the change in production (with differentials) if x increases from 30 to 31 and y increases from 60 to 62.

a. 51.9 b. 73.8 c. 87.1 d. 96.4

[c] 184. Use differentials to approximate the increase in area (dA) of a triangle if the base (b) is increased from 12 to 12.02 and the height (h) is increased from 10 to 10.01. ($A = \frac{1}{2}bh$). Also find ΔA, the exact change in area.

a. $dA = 0.19$, $\Delta A = 0.1701$
b. $dA = 0.14$, $\Delta A = 0.1401$
c. $dA = 0.16$, $\Delta A = 0.1601$
d. $dA = 0.17$, $\Delta A = 0.1601$

SHORT ANSWER 7.6

185. Determine the total differential dz for $z = f(x, y) = 6.5e^{0.2xy} + y$.

Answer: $dz = 1.3ye^{0.2xy}dx + (1.3xe^{0.2xy} + 1)dy$

186. Find the total differential of the function $f(x, y, z) = 5x^2 + 4y - 3xy^3$.

Answer: $(10x - 3y^3)dx + (4 - 9xy^2)dy$

187. Find the total differential of the function $f(x, y) = \frac{x}{y} + \ln y$.

Answer: $\frac{1}{y}dx + \left[-\frac{x}{y^2} + \frac{1}{y}\right]dy$

188. Find the total differential of the function $f(x, y, z) = x^2yz - y^2z + z^2$.

Answer: $(2xyz)dx + (x^2z - 2yz)dy + (x^2y - y^2 + 2z)dz$

189. Find the total differential of the function $f(x, y, z) = x^2 \ln(y^2 + z^2)$.

Answer: $[2x \ln(y^2 + z^2)]dx + \left[\frac{2x^2y}{y^2 + z^2}\right]dy + \left[\frac{2x^2z}{y^2 + z^2}\right]dz$

190. For the function $f(x, y) = 9 - x^2 - y^2$, and values $x = 1$, $\Delta x = dx = 0.05$ and $y = 2$, $\Delta y = dy = 0.1$, find

a. Δf
b. df

Answer: a. Δf = -0.5125   b. df = -0.500

191. Let q = h(r, t) be a function of two variables. State the equation that defines the total differential (dq) of q.

Answer: $dq = h_r(r, t)\,dr + h_t(r, t)\,dt$

192. Determine the total differential dz for $z = x^{0.2}y + e^{0.1x}$.

Answer: $(0.2x^{-0.8y} + 0.1e^{0.2x})dx + x^{0.2}dy$

193. Determine the total differential dz for $z = f(x, y) = \sqrt{x}\ \ln y + e^{0.2y}$.

Answer: $dz = \left(\frac{1}{2\sqrt{x}}\right)(\ln y)dx + \left(\frac{\sqrt{x}}{y} + 0.2e^{0.2y}\right)dy$

194. Determine the total differential dz for $z = f(x, y) = (2.8x^2 + 7.3y)^4$.

Answer: $dz = 22.4x(2.8x^2 + 7.3y)^3dx + 29.2(2.8x^2 + 7.3y)^3dy$

Section 7.7 Multiple Integrals

MULTIPLE CHOICE 7.7

[c] 195. Evaluate the following single integral $\int_0^y y\sqrt{x+1}\,dx$.

a. $(y+1)^{\frac{3}{2}} - y$
b. $\frac{2}{3}(y+1)^{\frac{3}{2}}$
c. $\frac{2y}{3}(y+1)^{\frac{3}{2}} - \frac{2}{3}y$
d. $\frac{2y}{3}(y+1)^{\frac{3}{2}}$

[b] 196. Evaluate the following iterated integral $\int_0^1\int_0^1 (2 - x^2 - y^2)\,dydx$.

a. $\frac{5}{3}$
b. $\frac{4}{3}$
c. $\frac{7}{3}$
d. 1

[d] 197. Evaluate the following iterated integral $\int_0^1\int_0^3 (4xy + 12x^2y^3)\,dxdy$.

a. 49
b. $\frac{55}{2}$
c. $\frac{83}{2}$
d. 36

[a] 198. Evaluate the following iterated integral $\int_0^3\int_{-1}^0 (x^2y^2 - xy)\,dydx$.

a. $\frac{21}{4}$
b. $\frac{25}{4}$
c. $\frac{17}{4}$
d. $\frac{31}{4}$

[b] 199. Evaluate the following iterated integral $\int_1^2\int_x^{3x} \frac{\ln x}{y^2}\,dydx$.

a. 0.36
b. 0.16
c. 0.25
d. 0.05

[a] 200. Evaluate the following iterated integral $\int_0^2 \int_{x^2}^{2x} (x^2 + 4y)\,dy\,dx$.

a. $\frac{152}{15}$ b. $-\frac{152}{15}$ c. $\frac{16}{3}$ d. $\frac{79}{30}$

[d] 201. Use integration to find the volume under the surface $f(x, y) = 4y + 3x^2$ above the region $R = \{(x, y) \mid 1 \le x \le 2, 0 \le y \le 3\}$

a. $\frac{56}{3}$ b. 47 c. $\frac{65}{3}$ d. 39

[b] 202. Use integration to find the volume under the surface $f(x, y) = 12x^2y^3$ above the region $R = \{(x, y) \mid -1 \le x \le 2, 0 \le y \le 1\}$

a. 10 b. 9 c. 8 d. 7

[c] 203. Find the average value of $f(x, y) = (x + y)^2$ over the region $R = \{(x, y) \mid 1 \le x \le 5, -1 \le y \le 1\}$.

a. $\frac{16}{3}$ b. $\frac{43}{4}$ c. $\frac{32}{3}$ d. 13

[c] 204. If a company invests x thousand labor-hours, $10 \le x \le 20$, and y million dollars, $1 \le y \le 2$, in the production of N thousand units of an item, then N is given by the Cobb-Douglas production function $N(x, y) = x^{\frac{3}{4}} y^{\frac{1}{4}}$. Find the average number of units produced for these given ranges of x and y.

a. 8125 b. 8250 c. 8375 d. 8500

[a] 205. Assume that the length in feet of skid marks left when the brakes are applied on a car is given by $L = 0.0000133xy^2$, where x is the weight of the car in pounds and y is the car's speed in miles per hour. Set up a double integral and evaluate the average skid mark length for cars weighing between 2000 and 3000 lb and traveling between 40 and 50 mph.

a. 68 feet b. 90 feet c. 58 feet d. 65 feet

[d] 206. A person's IQ is given by $Q(x, y) = 100\left(\frac{x}{y}\right)$, where x is the mental age and y is the chronological age. In a class of elementary students, the mental age ranges from 8 to 20 and the chronological age from 10 to 12. Find the average IQ for this group.

a. 119.1 b. 122.3 c. 125.1 d. 127.6

[c] 207. Which of the following is the partial integral $\int_a^b x^4 e^y dy$?

a. $\frac{x^5(e^b - e^a)}{5}$ b. $\frac{e^y(b^5 - a^5)}{5}$ c. $x^4(e^b - e^a)$ d. $4x^3(e^b - e^a)$

[a] 208. Evaluate $\int_0^3 \int_1^2 (3x^2 + 4y)dxdy$.

a. 39 b. $\frac{64}{3}$ c. 47 d. $\frac{56}{3}$

[b] 209. Evaluate $\int_0^1 \int_0^2 (6xy^2 + 3x^2)dydx$.

a. $\frac{21}{2}$ b. 10 c. $\frac{31}{3}$ d. 11

[b] 210. Evaluate $\int_{-1}^2 \int_0^1 12x^2y^3dydx$.

a. 8 b. 9 c. 10 d. 11

[c] 211. Determine the limits of integration and then evaluate the double integral $\int_R \int (xy)dxdy$, where $R = \{(x, y): 0 \le x \le 2.74, 0 \le y \le 20\}$.

a. 563.07 b. 375.38 c. 750.76 d. 548

[c] 212. Determine the limits of integration and then evaluate the double integral $\int_R \int (0.1x + 0.2y)^5 dydx$, where $R = \{(x, y): -1 \le x \le 1, 1 \le y \le 2\}$.

a. 0.0039 b. 0.0044 c. 0.000878 d. 0.0054

[a] 213. Determine the limits of integration and then evaluate the double integral $\int_R \int \sqrt{xy}dxdy$, where $R = \{(x, y): 1 \le x \le 4, 1 \le y \le 9\}$.

a. $\frac{728}{9}$ b. $\frac{28}{3}$ c. $\frac{14}{3}$ d. $\frac{28}{9}$

[d] 214. Determine the volume between the given surface $z = f(x, y)$ and the region R, where $f(x, y) = 1 + x^2 + y^2$ and $R = \{(x, y): 0 \le x \le 1, 0 \le y \le 1\}$.

a. 2 b. $\frac{7}{3}$ c. 3 d. $\frac{5}{3}$

[a] 215. Determine the volume between the given surface $z = f(x, y)$ and the region R, where $f(x, y) = x + y + 1$ and $R = \{(x, y): 0 \le x \le 1, 0 \le y \le 2\}$.

a. 5 b. $\frac{11}{2}$ c. 6 d. $\frac{13}{2}$

[b] 216. Determine the volume between the given surface $z = f(x,y)$ and the region R, where $f(x, y) = 2 - x^2 - y^2$ and $R = \{(x, y): 0 \le x \le 1, 0 \le y \le 1\}$.

a. 1 b. $\frac{4}{3}$ c. $\frac{5}{3}$ d. 2

[b] 217. Evaluate $\int_0^1 \int_0^x (x + y)dydx$.

a. $\frac{1}{4}$ b. $\frac{1}{2}$ c. 1 d. $\frac{3}{2}$

[b] 218. Evaluate $\int_0^1 \int_y^{\sqrt{y}} (2x + y)dxdy$.

a. $\frac{16}{30}$ b. $\frac{7}{30}$ c. $\frac{8}{15}$ d. $\frac{39}{70}$

[a] 219. Use the double integration to find the volume of the solid bounded above by the surface $Z = f(x, y) = 8 - 2x - 4y$ and below by the rectangle with vertices (0, 0), (0, 2), (1, 0), and (1, 2).

a. 6 b. 4 c. 10 d. 8

[b] 220. Use double integration to find the volume of the solid bounded above by the surface $Z = f(x, y) = y^{-2} \ln x$ and below by the region bounded by $y = 3x$, $y = x$, $x = 1$ and $x = 2$ in the xy-plane.

a. 0.06 b. 0.16 c. 0.26 d. 0.36

SHORT ANSWER 7.7

221. Evaluate the following single integral $\int_{2.5}^{4.7} 12x^2y^5\,dx$.

Answer: $352.792y^5$

222. Evaluate the following single integral $\int_{1}^{y^2} (5x - 3y)\,dx$.

Answer: $\frac{5y^4}{2} - 3y^3 - \frac{5}{2} + 3y$

223. Evaluate the following iterated integral $\int_{0}^{3}\int_{-2}^{0}\left(\frac{1}{2}x^2y - xy\right)dydx$.

Answer: 0

224. Evaluate the following iterated integral $\int_{0}^{2}\int_{-1}^{1} 3ye^{3x}\,dxdy$.

Answer: $2e^3 - \frac{2}{e^3}$

225. Evaluate the following iterated integral $\int_{0}^{3}\int_{0}^{y} 8xy\,dxdy$.

Answer: 81

226. Evaluate the following iterated integral $\int_{0}^{1}\int_{y}^{\sqrt{y}} (2x + y)\,dxdy$.

Answer: $\frac{7}{30}$

227. Use integration to find the volume under the surface $f(x, y) = xe^y$ above the region $R = \{(x, y) \mid 0 \le x \le 4, 0 \le y \le 1\}$

Answer: $8(e - 1)$

228. Use integration to find the volume under the surface $f(x, y) = 2y - x$ for the region R:

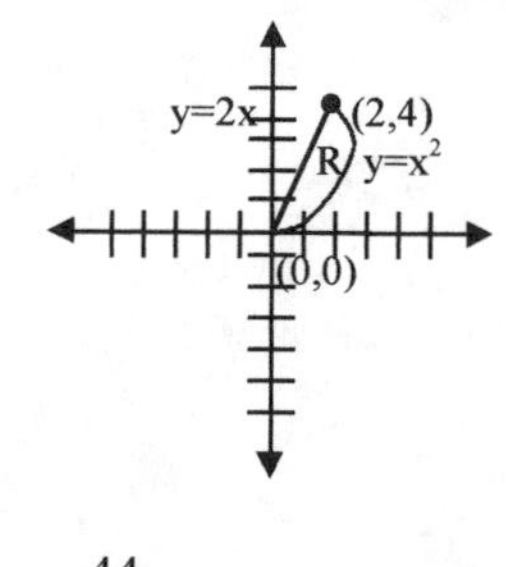

Answer: $\frac{44}{15}$

229. Draw the nonrectangular region over which integration is indicated for $\int_1^2 \int_x^{x^2} f(x, y)dydx$.

Answer:

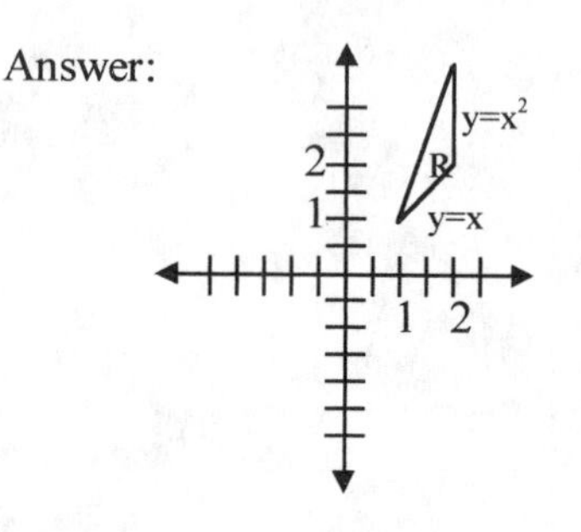

230. The temperature x miles east and y miles north of a weather station is given by the function $f(x,y) = 60 - 4x + 6y$. Find the average temperature over the region shown below.

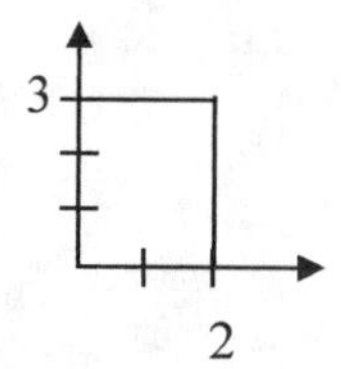

Answer: 65 degrees

231. The air pollution level x miles east and y miles north of a chemical refinery is given by the function $f(x,y) = 40 - 6x^2y$ ppm (parts per million). Find the average pollution level over the region shown below.

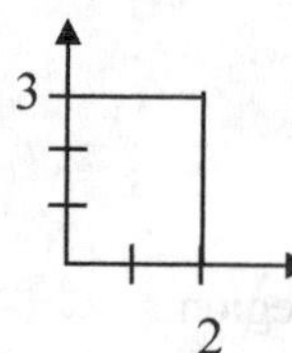

Answer: 28 ppm

Chapter 7 – Graphing Calculator

Calculus of Several Variables

Section 7.1 Functions of Several Variables

1. Use a graphing calculator to evaluate $f(x, y) = 59.9x^{0.25}y^{0.75}$ at f(16, 81).

   Answer: 3234.6

2. Use a graphing calculator to evaluate $f(x, y) = 59.9x^{0.25}y^{0.75}$ at f(32, 162).

   Answer: 6469.2

3. Use a graphing calculator to evaluate $f(x, y) = 59.9x^{0.25}y^{0.75}$ at f(48, 243).

   Answer: 9703.8

4. Use a graphing calculator to evaluate $f(x, y) = 59.9x^{0.25}y^{0.75}$ at f(32, 162), f(16, 81), and f(48, 243). Show that
   a. f(32, 162) = 2f(16, 81)
   b. f(48, 243) = 3f(16, 81)

   Answer: a. both equal 6469.2
   b. both equal 9701.8

Section 7.2 Partial Derivatives

5. Use a graphing calculator to evaluate, given $f(x, y) = 59.9x^{0.25}y^{0.75}$.
   Find $\frac{\partial f}{\partial x}(16,81)$ and compare f(17, 81) with the sum of $f(16, 81) + \frac{\partial f}{\partial x}(16,81)$.

   Answer: $\frac{\partial f}{\partial x} = 50.5406$, f(17, 81) = 3284

   $f(16, 81) + \frac{\partial f}{\partial x}(16,81) = 3285.14$

   The difference is 1.14

6. Use a graphing calculator to evaluate, given $f(x, y) = 59.9x^{0.25}y^{0.75}$.
   Find $\frac{\partial f}{\partial y}(16,81)$ and compare f(17, 82) with the sum of $f(16, 81) + \frac{\partial f}{\partial y}(16,81)$.

   Answer: $\frac{\partial f}{\partial y} = 29.95$, f(16, 82) = 3264.50

   $f(16, 81) + \frac{\partial f}{\partial y}(16,81) = 3264.55$

   The difference is 0.05

Section 7.3 Optimizing Functions of Several Variables

7. Each point P is either a relative maximum point, minimum point, or saddle point. Evaluate the function using a graphing calculator at points near P to determine the nature of the function at P.
   $f(x, y) = 10x^2 - 4xy + 4y^2 - 8x - 8y - 9$ at $P(2/3, 4/3)$

   Answer: relative maximum

8. Each point P is either a relative maximum point, minimum point, or saddle point. Evaluate the function using a graphing calculator at points near P to determine the nature of the function at P.
   $f(x, y) = xy + y^2 - 2x - 2y + 2$ at $P(-2, 2)$

   Answer: saddle point

9. Each point P is either a relative maximum point, minimum point, or saddle point. Evaluate the function using a graphing calculator at points near P to determine the nature of the function at P.
   $f(x, y) = 4x^3 + y^2 - 6xy - 1$ at $P(0, 0)$ and $P(3/2, 9/2)$

   Answer: P(0, 0) is saddle point, P(3/2, 9/2) is relative minimum

10. Each point P is either a relative maximum point, minimum point, or saddle point. Evaluate the function using a graphing calculator at points near P to determine the nature of the function at P.
    $f(x, y) = xy + \ln x + y^2 - 10$ at $P\left(\sqrt{2}, -\frac{1}{\sqrt{2}}\right)$

    Answer: saddle point

11. Each point P is either a relative maximum point, minimum point, or saddle point. Evaluate the function using a graphing calculator at points near P to determine the nature of the function at P.
    $f(x, y) = \sqrt[3]{x^2 + y^2}$ at $P(0, 0)$

    Answer: relative minimum

Section 7.4 Least Squares

12. Use a graphing calculator to find the equation of the least squares line for the data {(0, 10), (5, 22), (10, 31), (15, 46), (20, 51)} Use the equation to estimate y, for $x = 25$.

    Answer: $y = 2.12x + 10.8$
    $y = 63.8$ when $x = 25$

13. Use a graphing calculator to find the equation of the least squares line for the data {(0.5, 25), (2, 22), (3.5, 21), (6.5, 18), (9.5, 12), (11, 11), (12.5, 8), (14, 15), (15.5, 1)}. Use the equation to estimate y, for $x = 8$.

    Answer: $y = -1.53x + 26.67$
    $y = 14.4$ when $x = 8$

Chapter 8

Trigonometric Functions

Section 8.1 Triangles, Angles, and Radian Measure

MULTIPLE CHOICE 8.1

[c] 1. Find the degree measure of the angle.

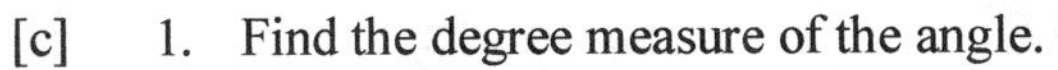

a. 135° b. 315° c. 225° d. 270°

[a] 2. Find the degree measure of the angle.

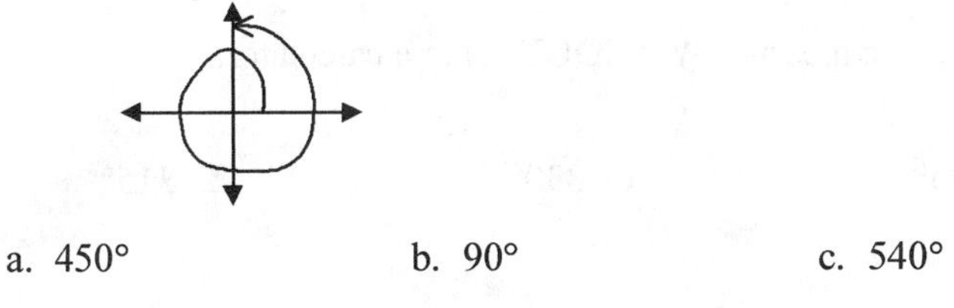

a. 450° b. 90° c. 540° d. 180°

[d] 3. Find the radian measure of the angle.

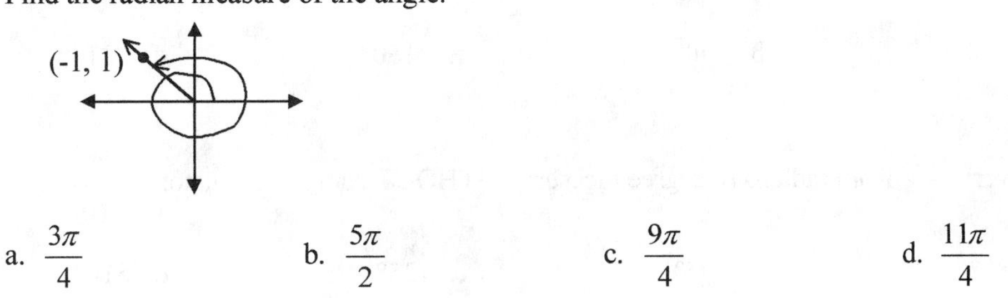

a. $\frac{3\pi}{4}$ b. $\frac{5\pi}{2}$ c. $\frac{9\pi}{4}$ d. $\frac{11\pi}{4}$

[b] 4. Find the radian measure of the angle.

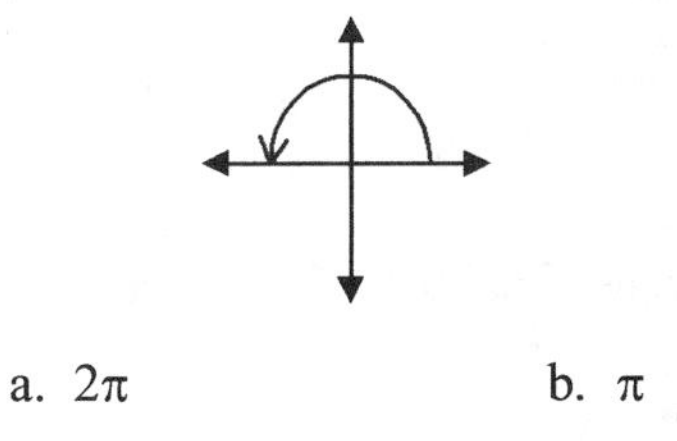

a. 2π b. π c. $\frac{\pi}{2}$ d. 3π

[b] 5. Convert 85° from degrees to radian measure WITHOUT using a calculator.

a. $\frac{\pi}{6}$ b. $\frac{17\pi}{36}$ c. $\frac{15\pi}{36}$ d. $\frac{\pi}{3}$

[b] 6. Convert 480° from degrees to radian measure WITHOUT using a calculator.

a. $\frac{2\pi}{3}$ b. $\frac{8\pi}{3}$ c. $\frac{17\pi}{6}$ d. 3π

[c] 7. Convert –45° from degrees to radian measure WITHOUT using a calculator.

a. $\frac{7\pi}{4}$ b. $\frac{-\pi}{3}$ c. $\frac{-\pi}{4}$ d. $\frac{-\pi}{2}$

[d] 8. Convert 330° from degrees to radian measure WITHOUT using a calculator.

a. $\frac{-\pi}{6}$ b. $\frac{7\pi}{4}$ c. $\frac{5\pi}{3}$ d. $\frac{11\pi}{6}$

[b] 9. Convert $\frac{5\pi}{4}$ from radians to degree measure WITHOUT using a calculator.

a. 270° b. 225° c. 330° d. 315°

[a] 10. Convert $-\frac{2\pi}{3}$ from radians to degree measure WITHOUT using a calculator.

a. –120° b. 240° c. –150° d. –210°

[b] 11. Convert $\frac{11\pi}{4}$ from radians to degree measure WITHOUT using a calculator.

a. 480° b. 495° c. 135° d. 510°

[c] 12. Convert -7π from radians to degree measure WITHOUT using a calculator.

a. –180° b. –2,520° c. –1,260° d. –540°

[c] 13. An angle of 60° cuts off an arc of length 4π inches on a circle of radius r. Find the radius.

a. 0.21 inches b. 37.7 inches c. 12 inches d. 754 inches

SHORT ANSWER 8.1

14. A 36-inch pendulum swings through an angle of $\frac{\pi}{7}$ radians. Find the length of the arc through which it swings. Approximate your answer using $\pi \approx 3.14$.

    Answer: 16.15 inches

15. Find the distance along the surface of the earth between Dallas, Texas and Madison, South Dakota if the two cities determine a central angle of 0.192 radians. Assume that the earth is a sphere of radius 4,000 miles.

    Answer: 768 miles

16. Find the distance along the surface of the earth between Halifax, Nova Scotia and Buenos Aires, Argentina if the two cities determine a central angle of 1.38 radians. Assume that the earth is a sphere of radius 4,000 miles.

    Answer: 5,520 miles

Section 8.2 Sine and Cosine Functions

MULTIPLE CHOICE 8.2

[a] 17. Find sinθ, given θ in the graph below.

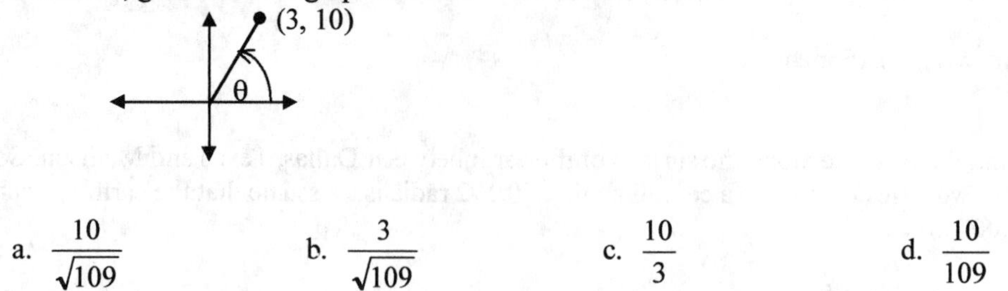

a. $\frac{10}{\sqrt{109}}$ b. $\frac{3}{\sqrt{109}}$ c. $\frac{10}{3}$ d. $\frac{10}{109}$

[c] 18. Find cosθ, given θ in the graph below.

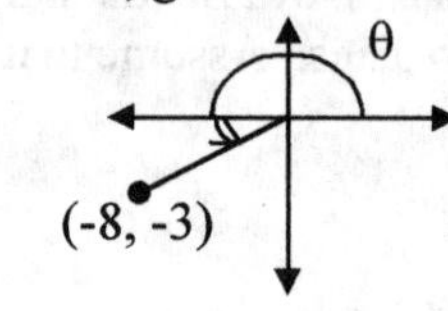

a. $\frac{8}{\sqrt{73}}$ b. $-\frac{3}{\sqrt{73}}$ c. $-\frac{8}{\sqrt{73}}$ d. $-\frac{8}{73}$

[d] 19. Find sinθ, given θ in the graph below.

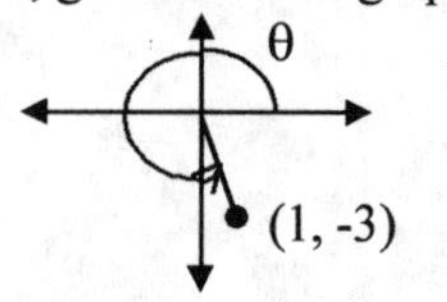

a. $-\frac{3}{10}$ b. $\frac{1}{\sqrt{10}}$ c. $\frac{3}{\sqrt{10}}$ d. $-\frac{3}{\sqrt{10}}$

[b] 20. Find cosθ, given θ in the graph below.

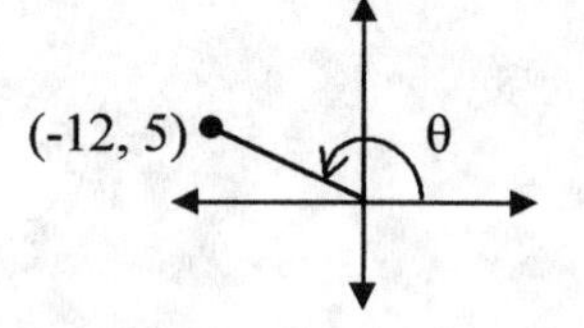

a. $\frac{12}{13}$ b. $-\frac{12}{13}$ c. $\frac{15}{13}$ d. $-\frac{13}{12}$

[a] 21. Evaluate $\dfrac{\cos 67°}{\sin 23°}$, round your answer to four decimal places.

a. 1.0000 b. 0.9657 c. 0.7815 d. 2.5593

[b] 22. Evaluate $(\sin 52.7°)^2 + (\cos 52.7°)^2$, round your answer to four decimal places.

a. 0.6328 b. 1.0000 c. 1.9641 d. 1.5000

[c] 23. Approximate the function value $\sin\dfrac{\pi}{2.5}$ by using a calculator set to radian mode. Round your answer to 3 decimal places.

a. 0.022 b. 0.720 c. 0.951 d. 0.940

[a] 24. Approximate the function value cos8 by using a calculator set to radian mode. Round your answer to 3 decimal places.

a. –0.146 b. 0.989 c. 0.139 d. 0.990

[c] 25. Which of the following represents the equation of the graph?

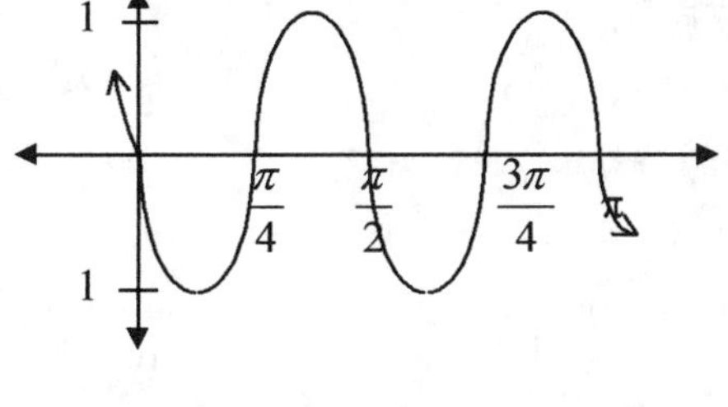

a. y = sin4t b. y = –cos4t c. y = –sin4t d. y = –sin2t

[a] 26. Which of the following represents the equation of this graph?

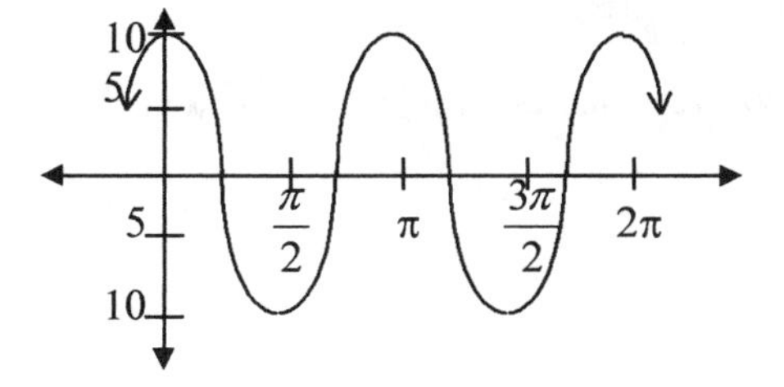

a. y = 10cos2t b. y = 10cost c. y = –10sin2t d. y = –10cost

[c] 27. A ship is sailing due west from a point 100 feet directly north of you until it makes an angle of 32°, as shown below. Find the distance between you and the boat.

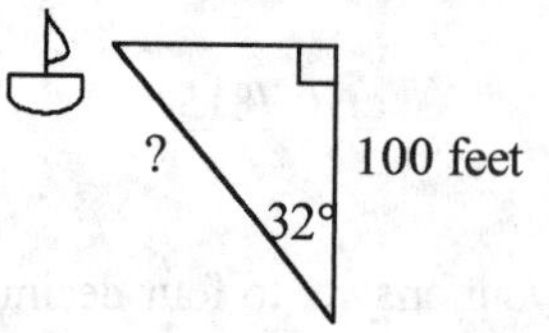

?

100 feet

32°

a. 188.7 feet b. 119.9 feet c. 117.9 feet d. 181.3 feet

[d] 28. A kite string makes an angle of 56° with the ground. How high is the kite if 175 feet of string has been let out?

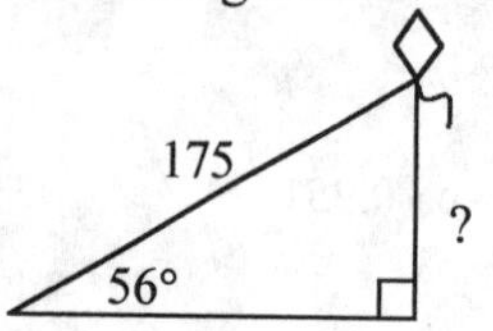

175

?

56°

a. 91.3 feet b. 149.3 feet c. 97.9 feet d. 145.1 feet

A person's blood pressure is tested and the results are given by the formula $P(t) = 100 + 20\cos 5.8t$, where t is time in seconds.

[b] 29. The blood pressure at the beginning of the test was

a. 110 b. 130 c. 90 d. 115

[b] 30. The diastolic (minimum) pressure was

a. 105 b. 90 c. 100 d. 75

[c] 31. The systolic (maximum) pressure was

a. 110 b. 120 c. 130 d. 140

[d] 32. After 4 seconds the blood pressure, rounded to the nearest whole number, was

a. 107 b. 126 c. 99 d. 103

SHORT ANSWER 8.2

33. Evaluate the following items WITHOUT using a calculator, leaving your answer in exact form.

a. $\sin\frac{\pi}{6}$ b. $\cos\frac{7\pi}{6}$

Answer: a. $\frac{1}{2}$ b. $-\frac{\sqrt{3}}{2}$

34. Evaluate the following items WITHOUT using a calculator, leaving your answer in exact form.

a. $\sin\frac{2\pi}{3}$ b. $\cos\frac{4\pi}{3}$

Answer: a. $\frac{\sqrt{3}}{2}$ b. $-\frac{1}{2}$

35. Evaluate the following items WITHOUT using a calculator, leaving your answer in exact form.

a. $\sin\left(-\frac{\pi}{6}\right)$ b. $\cos\left(-\frac{\pi}{6}\right)$

Answer: a. $-\frac{1}{2}$ b. $\frac{\sqrt{3}}{2}$

36. Evaluate the following items WITHOUT using a calculator, leaving your answer in exact form.

a. $\sin\frac{9\pi}{4}$ b. $\cos\frac{11\pi}{4}$

Answer: a. $\frac{1}{\sqrt{2}}$ b. $-\frac{1}{\sqrt{2}}$

37. Given $\sin t = -\frac{4}{5}$ and the point P(t) is in quadrant IV, give an exact value for cos t.

Answer: $\cos t = \frac{3}{5}$

38. Approximate the function value sin 3.36 by using a calculator set to radian mode. Round your answer to 3 decimal places.

Answer: –0.217

39. Approximate the function value $\cos\left(\frac{2\pi}{11}\right)$ by using a calculator set to radian mode. Round your answer to 3 decimal places.

    Answer: 0.841

The amount of air in the lungs of an animal is given by $A(t) = 385 + 350 \sin 0.75t$ cubic inches, where t is the time in seconds.

40. Find the maximum amount of air in the animal's lungs at any time.

    Answer: 735 cubic inches

41. There will always be a small amount of air in the animal's lungs. Find that minimum amount.

    Answer: 35 cubic inches

42. Find the amount of air, rounded to the nearest cubic inch, in the animal's lungs when t = 6 seconds.

    Answer: 43 cubic inches

43. Sketch the graph of the function $y = 3\sin 2t$. Identify the amplitude and period.

    Answer: amplitude = 3, period = π

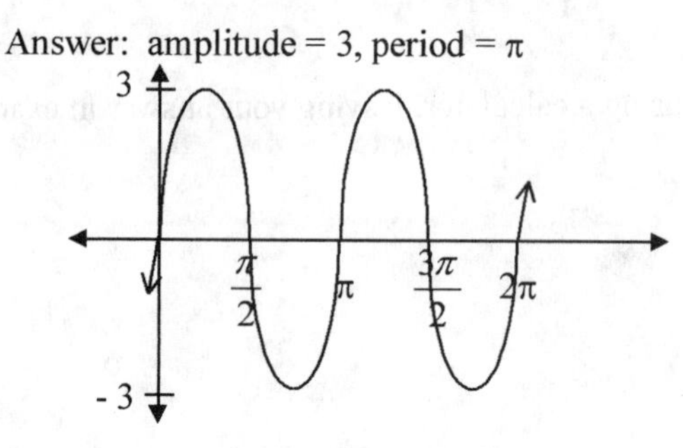

44. Sketch the graph of the function $y = -2\cos 3t$. Identify the amplitude and period.

    Answer: amplitude = 2, period = $\frac{2\pi}{3}$

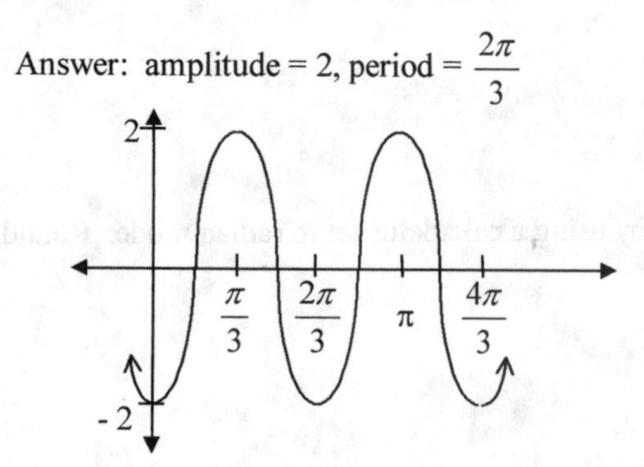

45. A 23-foot ladder is leaning against a wall making a 60° angle with the ground. How high up the wall will the ladder reach?

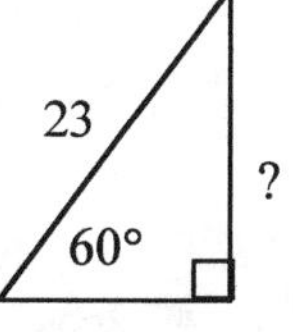

Answer: 19.9 feet

46. A guy wire attached to the top of a tower runs to a point on the ground that is 85 feet from the base of the tower. Find the length of the wire if it makes an angle of 42° with the ground.

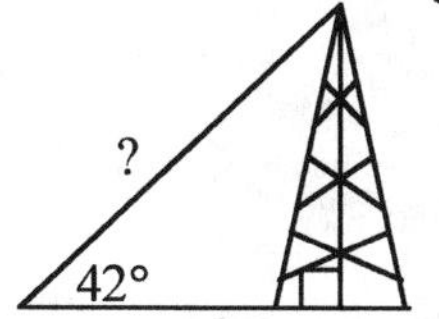

Answer: 114.4 feet

Section 8.3 Derivatives of Sine and Cosine Functions

MULTIPLE CHOICE 8.3

[b] 47. Differentiate the function: sin7.2t.

a. cos7.2t b. 7.2cos7.2t c. –7.2cos7.2t d. –cos7.2t

[a] 48. Differentiate the function: $(1 - 2\cos t)^5$.

a. $5(1 - 2\cos t)^4(2\sin t)$ b. $5(1 - 2\cos t)^4$ c. $5(1 - 2\cos t)^4(-2\sin t)$ d. $5(1 - 2\cos t)^4(-2)$

[c] 49. Differentiate the function: $\dfrac{t}{3\sin t}$.

a. 3sint – 3tcost b. $\dfrac{3\sin t + 3t\cos t}{9\sin^2 t}$ c. $\dfrac{3\sin t - 3t\cos t}{9\sin^2 t}$ d. $\dfrac{3t\cos t - 3\sin t}{9\sin^2 t}$

[d] 50. Differentiate the function: $\cos(2\pi - t)^2$.

a. $-2\cos(2\pi - t)$ b. $2\cos(2\pi - t)$ c. $\sin(2\pi - t)^2(4\pi - 2t)$ d. $-\sin(2\pi - t)^2(-4\pi + 2t)$

[d] 51. Differentiate the function: $\sin^4(2\pi - t)$.

a. $-\cos^4(2\pi - t)$ b. $\cos^4(2\pi - t)$ c. $4\sin^3(2\pi - t)\cos(2\pi - t)$ d. $-4\sin^3(2\pi - t)\cos(2\pi - t)$

[b] 52. Differentiate the function: $\cos\sqrt[4]{1-x}$.

a. $\dfrac{1}{4}(\cos(1-x))^{-\frac{3}{4}}$

b. $\dfrac{\sin\sqrt[4]{1-x}}{4\sqrt[4]{(1-x)^3}}$

c. $-\dfrac{\sin\sqrt[4]{1-x}}{4\sqrt[4]{(1-x)^3}}$

d. $\dfrac{1}{4}(\cos(1-x))^{-\frac{3}{4}}(-\sin(1-x))$

[d] 53. Differentiate the function: $\cos(e^{x-7})$.

a. $-e^{x-7}\cos(e^{x-7})$ b. $-\sin(e^{x-7})$ c. $e^{x-7}\sin(e^{x-7})$ d. $-e^{x-7}\sin(e^{x-7})$

[a] 54. Differentiate the function: $e^{\sin t - t}$.

a. $(\cos t - 1)e^{\sin t - t}$ b. $e^{\sin t - t}$ c. $e^{\cos t - 1}$ d. $(-\cos t - 1)e^{\sin t - t}$

[c] 55. Differentiate the function: ln(cosx).

a. $\frac{\sin x}{\cos x}$ b. $\frac{1}{\cos x}$ c. $-\frac{\sin x}{\cos x}$ d. $-\frac{\cos x}{\sin x}$

[c] 56. Differentiate the function: $x\sin e^{-x}$.

a. $e^{-x}(\sin x - x\cos x)$ b. $-\cos e^{-x}$ c. $-xe^{-x}\cos e^{-x} + \sin e^{-x}$ d. $xe^{-x}\cos e^{-x} + \sin e^{-x}$

[b] 57. Differentiate the function: cos(3x – lnx).

a. $\left(3-\frac{1}{x}\right)\sin(3x - \ln x)$ b. $-\left(3-\frac{1}{x}\right)\sin(3x - \ln x)$

c. $-\sin(3x - \ln x)$ d. $-\sin\left(3-\frac{1}{x}\right)$

[d] 58. Differentiate the function: sin(cos2x).

a. $-2\sin 2x\sin x + \cos 2x\cos x$ b. $2\cos(\cos 2x)$
c. $-\sin 2x\cos(\cos 2x)$ d. $-2\sin 2x\cos(\cos(2x))$

[a] 59. Differentiate the function: $\cos^3(1 - t^2)$.

a. $3\cos^2(1 - t^2)(2t\sin(1 - t^2))$ b. $3\cos^2(1 - t^2)(-2t)$
c. $-2t\sin^3(1 - t^2)$ d. $3\cos^2(1 - t^2)\sin(1 - t^2)$

[c] 60. Differentiate the function: $3\cos x - \frac{1}{x}\sin x$.

a. $-3\sin x - \cos x$ b. $\frac{\sin x - x\cos x}{x^2}$

c. $-3\sin x - \frac{1}{x}\cos x + \frac{\sin x}{x^2}$ d. $3\sin x - \frac{1}{x}\cos x - \frac{\sin x}{x^2}$

[b] 61. Differentiate the function: $\sin\left(\frac{\pi}{90}t\right)$.

a. $-\frac{\pi}{90}\cos\left(\frac{\pi}{90}t\right)$ b. $\frac{\pi}{90}\cos\left(\frac{\pi}{90}t\right)$ c. $\cos\left(\frac{\pi}{90}t\right)$ d. $\pi\cos\left(\frac{\pi}{90}t\right)$

[b] 62. Find the indicated derivative value for $f(t) = 24\sin\frac{t}{6}$; $f'(3\pi)$.

a. 1 b. 0 c. 24 d. –24

[a] 63. Find the indicated derivative value for $f(x) = x^3 - \cos\pi x$; $f'\left(-\frac{1}{2}\right)$.

a. $\frac{3}{4}-\pi$ b. $\frac{3}{4}+\pi$ c. $\frac{3}{4}$ d. $-\frac{3}{4}-\pi$

[b] 64. Find the indicated derivative value for $f(x) = \frac{\cos 3x}{\sin x}$; $f'\left(\frac{\pi}{2}\right)$.

a. 0 b. 3 c. –3 d. undefined

[d] 65. Find the indicated derivative value for $f(x) = \frac{1-\sin x}{\cos x}$; $f'(\pi)$.

a. 1 b. 0 c. undefined d. –1

[d] 66. Find $f'(x)$ for the function $f(x) = e^{1-\sin x}$.

a. $-\cos x e^{1-\sin x}$ b. $e^{1-\sin x}(-\cos^2 x + \sin x)$ c. $e^{1-\sin x}(\cos^2 x - \sin x)$ d. $e^{1-\sin x}(\cos^2 x + \sin x)$

[d] 67. Find $f''(x)$ for the function $f(x) = 2x - 3\cos\frac{1}{2}x$.

a. $3\cos\frac{1}{2}x$ b. $-\frac{3}{4}\cos\frac{1}{2}x$ c. $2-\frac{3}{2}\sin\frac{1}{2}x$ d. $\frac{3}{4}\cos\frac{1}{2}x$

[c] 68. The slope of the line tangent to the curve $y = \sin^2 0.4x$ at $x = 10\pi/3$ is

a. $0.2\frac{\sqrt{3}}{3}$ b. $-\frac{\sqrt{2}}{3}$ c. $0.2\sqrt{3}$ d. $-\frac{0.2\sqrt{3}}{3}$

[c] 69. The slope of the line tangent to the curve $y = \sin 0.25x$ at $x = 8\pi/3$ is

a. 0.2 b. $-\frac{\sqrt{3}}{2}$ c. –0.125 d. –0.2

[d] 70. The equation of the line tangent to $y = \sin x$ at $(\pi/3, \sqrt{3}/2)$ is $y =$

a. $\frac{1}{2}\left(x-\frac{\pi}{3}\right)-\frac{\sqrt{3}}{2}$ b. $\frac{1}{2}\left(x-\frac{\pi}{3}\right)+\sqrt{2}$ c. $2\left(x-\frac{\pi}{3}\right)-\sqrt{2}$ d. $\frac{1}{2}\left(x-\frac{\pi}{3}\right)+\frac{\sqrt{3}}{2}$

[c] 71. The amount of water, in thousands of gallons, in a storage tank is given by $f(t) = 20 + 2\sin\left(\frac{\pi t}{6}\right)$ where t is time measured in hours. At the end of 8 hours, the amount of water in the tank is

a. increasing at the rate of $\frac{\pi}{6}$ thousand gallons per hour

b. increasing at the rate of $\frac{5\pi}{6}$ thousand gallons per hour

c. decreasing at the rate of $\frac{\pi}{6}$ thousand gallons per hour

d. decreasing at the rate of $\frac{5\pi}{6}$ thousand gallons per hour

[d] 72. The sales of personal computers in a computer store is given by $f(t) = 100 + 95\cos\left(\frac{\pi t}{6}\right)$ where f is the number of computers sold in month t (January is month 1). In August, the sales of computers are

a. decreasing at the rate of $\frac{95\sqrt{3}\pi}{6}$ per month

b. decreasing at the rate of $\frac{95\sqrt{3}\pi}{12}$ per month

c. increasing at the rate of $\frac{95\sqrt{3}\pi}{6}$ per month

d. increasing at the rate of $\frac{95\sqrt{3}\pi}{12}$ per month

SHORT ANSWER 8.3

73. Differentiate the function: $\cos 2.5t$.

    Answer: $-2.5 \sin 2.5t$

74. Differentiate the function: $(3\sin t + 2)^8$.

    Answer: $8(3\sin t + 2)^7(3\cos t)$

75. Differentiate the function: $\dfrac{t^2}{5 \cos t}$.

    Answer: $\dfrac{10t \cos t + 5t^2 \sin t}{25 \cos^2 t}$

76. Differentiate the function: $\sin(\pi - 3t)^4$.

    Answer: $-12(\pi - 3t)^3\cos(\pi - 3t)^4$

77. Differentiate the function: $\cos^2(2t - \pi)$.

    Answer: $2\cos(2t - \pi)[-2\sin(2t - \pi)]$

78. Differentiate the function: $\sin \sqrt[3]{x+5}$.

    Answer: $\dfrac{\cos \sqrt[3]{x+5}}{3\sqrt[3]{(x+5)^2}}$

79. Differentiate the function: $\sin\left(e^{3-x^2}\right)$.

    Answer: $-2xe^{3-x^2} \cos\left(e^{3-x^2}\right)$

80. Differentiate the function: $e^{x^3 - \cos x}$.

    Answer: $(3x^2 + \sin x)e^{x^3 - \cos x}$

81. Differentiate the function: $\ln(\sin 1.25x)$.

    Answer: $\dfrac{-1.25 \sin 1.25x}{\cos 1.25x}$

82. Differentiate the function: $x^2\cos e^{2x}$.

Answer: $-2x^2e^{2x}\sin e^{2x} + 2x\cos e^{2x}$

83. Differentiate the function: $\sin(\ln x + 4x^2)$.

Answer: $\left(\frac{1}{x}+8x\right)\cos(\ln x+4x^2)$

84. Differentiate the function: $\cos\left(\sin\frac{x}{3}\right)$.

Answer: $-\frac{1}{3}\cos\frac{x}{3}\sin\left(\sin\frac{x}{3}\right)$

85. Differentiate the function: $\sin^2(3 + t^3)$.

Answer: $6t^2\sin(3 + t^3)\cos(3 + t^3)$

86. Differentiate the function: $\frac{1}{x}\cos 2x - 2\sin x$.

Answer: $-\frac{2\sin 2x}{x}-\frac{\cos 2x}{x^2}-2\cos x$

87. Differentiate the function: $\cos\left(\frac{\pi}{20}t\right)$.

Answer: $-\frac{\pi}{20}\sin\left(\frac{\pi}{20}t\right)$

88. Find the indicated derivative value for $f(t) = t^2\sin\frac{\pi}{2}t$; $f'\left(\frac{1}{2}\right)$.

Answer: $\frac{\pi+8}{8\sqrt{2}}$

89. Find the indicated derivative value for $f(t) = (\cos t - 2)^2$; $f'\left(\frac{2\pi}{3}\right)$.

Answer: $\frac{5\sqrt{3}}{2}$

90. Find the indicated derivative value for $f(x) = \ln(\cos x - x)^2$; $f'\left(\frac{\pi}{2}\right)$

Answer: $\frac{8}{\pi}$

91. Find f″(x) for the function f(x) = ln(sinx).

Answer: $\frac{-\sin^2 x - \cos^2 x}{\sin^2 x} = \frac{-1}{\sin^2 x}$

92. Find f″(x) for the function f(x) = xcos 2.4x.

Answer: –5.76xcos 2.4x – 4.8sin 2.4x

The sales of skis in a sporting goods store is given by $S(t) = 87 + 73\cos(\pi t/6)$, where S is the number of pairs of skis sold in month t. (January is month 1; December is month 12.)

93. Determine the function that describes the rate of change in sales for any month t.

Answer: $S'(t) = -\frac{73\pi}{6}\sin\frac{\pi t}{6}$

94. During which month will sales be a minimum?

Answer: June

95. The number of bacteria f(t) present at time t (t in minutes) is given by $f(t) = 5{,}000 - 3{,}000\sin\left(\frac{\pi(t+5)}{6}\right)$. After 5 minutes, is the number of bacteria increasing or decreasing, and at what rate?

Answer: decreasing at the rate of 250π bacteria per minute

96. The position of an object moving along a straight line is $s(t) = 3\sin\left(\frac{\pi t}{3}\right)$ where s is measured in feet and t in seconds. What is the velocity of the object at the end of 4 seconds?

Answer: $-\frac{\pi}{2}$ feet per second (decreasing)

The equation D(t) = 450 + 225 sin(πt/12) describes the number of predators in a predator-prey relationship at the end of t months.

97. At the end of 3 months, is the number of predators increasing or decreasing, and at what rate?

    Answer: The number is increasing at the rate of $\frac{75\pi\sqrt{2}}{8}$.

98. At the end of 8 months, is the number of predators increasing or decreasing, and at what rate?

    Answer: The number is decreasing at the rate of $\frac{75\pi}{8}$.

The equation Y(t) = 1250 + 675 cos(πt/12) describes the number of prey in a predator-prey relationship at the end of t months.

99. At the end of 4 months, is the number of prey increasing or decreasing, and at what rate?

    Answer: The number is decreasing at the rate of $\frac{225\pi\sqrt{3}}{8}$

100. At then end of 9 months, is the number of prey increasing or decreasing, and at what rate?

    Answer: The number is decreasing at the rate of $\frac{225\pi\sqrt{2}}{8}$.

Section 8.4 Integrals of Sine and Cosine Functions

MULTIPLE CHOICE 8.4

[c] 101. Find the integral: $\int \sin(x-4)dx$.

a. $-4\cos(x-4)+C$ b. $\cos(x-4)+C$ c. $-\cos(x-4)+C$ d. $4\cos(x-4)+C$

[b] 102. Find the integral: $\int 4x^3 \sin x^4 dx$.

a. $\sin\left(\frac{x^5}{5}\right)+C$ b. $-\cos x^4+C$ c. $\cos x^4+C$ d. $-\sin x^4+C$

[a] 103. Find the integral: $\int \cos \pi t dt$.

a. $\frac{1}{\pi}\sin \pi t+C$ b. $\sin\pi t+C$ c. $-\frac{1}{\pi}\sin \pi t+C$ d. $-\sin\pi t+C$

[b] 104. Find the integral: $\int \cos^5 t \sin t dt$.

a. $\frac{\cos^6 t}{6}+C$ b. $-\frac{\cos^6 t}{6}+C$ c. $\frac{\cos^6 t}{6}\cdot\frac{\sin^2 t}{2}+C$ d. $-\cos^6 t+C$

[d] 105. Find the integral: $\int \frac{\cos t}{\sqrt{\sin t}}dt$.

a. $\frac{2}{3}(\sin t)^{\frac{3}{2}}+C$ b. $-2\sqrt{\sin t}+C$ c. $-\frac{2}{3}(\sin t)^{\frac{3}{2}}+C$ d. $2\sqrt{\sin t}+C$

[c] 106. Find the integral: $\int e^{\sin 2x}\cos 2x dx$.

a. $e^{\sin 2x}$ b. $2e^{\sin 2x}+C$ c. $\frac{1}{2}e^{\sin 2x}+C$ d. $-\frac{1}{2}e^{\sin 2x}+C$

[a] 107. Find the integral: $\int \frac{\cos 3t}{2-\sin 3t}dt$.

a. $-\frac{1}{3}\ln|2-\sin 3t|+C$ b. $\ln|2-\sin 3t|+C$ c. $3\ln|2-\sin 3t|+C$ d. $\frac{1}{3}\ln|2-\sin 3t|+C$

[b] 108. Find the integral: $\int \sqrt[3]{1-\cos t}\,\sin t\,dt$.

a. $(1-\cos t)^{\frac{4}{3}}+C$ b. $\frac{3}{4}(1-\cos t)^{\frac{4}{3}}+C$ c. $-\frac{3}{4}(1-\cos t)^{\frac{4}{3}}+C$ d. $\frac{2}{3}(1-\cos t)^{\frac{3}{2}}+C$

[c] 109. Find the integral: $\int \frac{\sin(\ln x)}{x}dx$.

a. $\cos(\ln x)+C$ b. $\sin(\ln x)+C$ c. $-\cos(\ln x)+C$ d. $-\frac{\cos(\ln x)}{x^2}+C$

[a] 110. Find the integral: $\int \frac{\cos x}{\sin^2 x}dx$.

a. $\frac{-1}{\sin x}+C$ b. $-\sin^3 x+C$ c. $\frac{3\cos x}{\sin^3 x}+C$ d. $-\frac{\sin x}{2}+C$

[c] 111. Evaluate the following definite integral by hand leaving answers in "exact" form: $\int_0^{\pi} 4\cos(2x)dx$.

a. 1 b. 2 c. 0 d. $\frac{1}{2}$

[b] 112. Evaluate the following definite integral by hand leaving answers in "exact" form: $\int_0^2 x-\sin\frac{\pi}{2}x\,dx$.

a. $2-\pi$ b. $2-\frac{4}{\pi}$ c. $2+\frac{4}{\pi}$ d. $2+\pi$

[a] 113. Evaluate the following definite integral by hand leaving answers in "exact" form: $\int_0^{\frac{\pi}{4}} \sin\left(t-\frac{\pi}{4}\right)dt$.

a. $-1+\frac{1}{\sqrt{2}}$ b. $1-\frac{1}{\sqrt{2}}$ c. $-1-\frac{1}{\sqrt{2}}$ d. $1+\frac{1}{\sqrt{2}}$

SHORT ANSWER 8.4

114. Find the integral: $\int 3\cos t - \sin 2t dt$.

Answer: $3\sin t + \frac{1}{2}\cos 2t + C$

115. Find the integral: $\int (t-3)\sin(t^2 - 6t + 1) dt$.

Answer: $-\frac{1}{2}\cos(t^2 - 6t + 1) + C$

116. Find the integral: $\int \sin\frac{\pi t}{6} dt$.

Answer: $-\frac{6}{\pi}\cos\frac{\pi t}{6} + C$

117. Find the integral: $\int \sin^{10} t \cos t dt$.

Answer: $\frac{\sin^{11} t}{11} + C$

118. Find the integral: $\int \frac{\sin t}{\sqrt[3]{\cos t}} dt$.

Answer: $-\frac{3}{2}(\cos t)^{\frac{2}{3}} + C$

119. Find the integral: $\int e^{6x} \sin e^{6x} dx$.

Answer: $-\frac{1}{6}\cos e^{6x} + C$

120. Find the integral: $\int \frac{\cos(\ln x)}{x} dx$.

Answer: $\sin(\ln x) + C$

121. Find the integral: $\int \frac{2\sin 5t}{3-\cos 5t}\,dt$.

Answer: $\frac{2}{5}\ln|3-\cos 5t|+C$

122. Find the integral: $\int (\cos^2 x+3)^5 \cos x \sin x\,dx$.

Answer: $\frac{-1}{12}(\cos^2 x+3)^6+C$

123. Find the integral: $\int \frac{1}{x}-e^{3x}+\sin\frac{1}{2}x\,dx$.

Answer: $\ln|x|-\frac{1}{3}e^{3x}-2\cos\frac{1}{2}x+C$

124. Evaluate the following definite integral by hand leaving answers in "exact" form: $\int_0^{\frac{\pi}{4}} e^{\cos 2t}\sin 2t\,dt$.

Answer: $-\frac{1}{2}+\frac{1}{2}e$

125. Evaluate the following definite integral by hand leaving answers in "exact" form: $\int_0^{\frac{\pi}{2}} \frac{\sin x}{1+\cos x}\,dx$.

Answer: ln2

126. Evaluate the following definite integral by hand leaving answers in "exact" form: $\int_0^{\frac{\pi}{3}} (\cos 3t - t^4)\,dt$.

Answer: $-\frac{\pi^5}{1{,}215}$

127. Find the area under the curve $y = \cos(2x)$ and above the x-axis from $x = \frac{\pi}{8}$ to $x = \frac{\pi}{4}$. Leave answer in exact form.

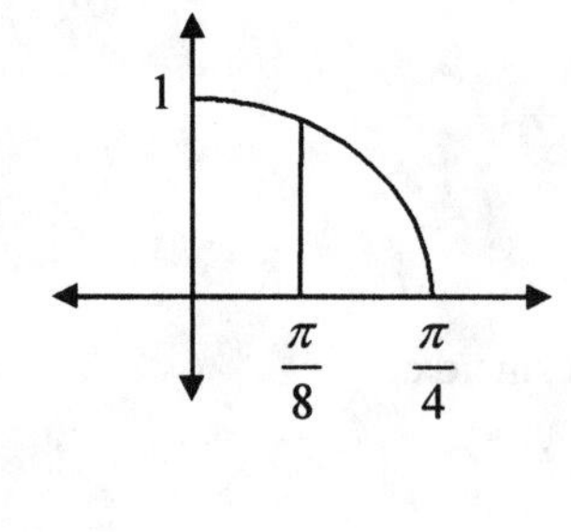

Answer: $\frac{1}{2} - \frac{1}{2\sqrt{2}}$

128. Find the area under the curve $y = \sin x + x$ and above the x-asix from $x = \frac{\pi}{2}$ to $x = \pi$. Leave answer in exact form.

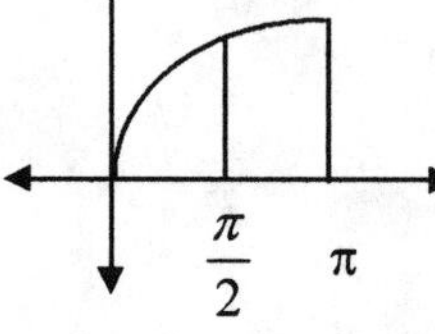

Answer: $1 + \frac{3\pi^2}{8}$

129. A store's inventory at t months is $30 + 20\sin\left(\frac{\pi t}{6}\right)$ units. Find the average inventory for the first 6 months. Round your answer to the nearest unit.

Answer: 43 units

130. The amount of water, in thousands of gallons, is given by $w(t) = 500 + 300\sin\left(\frac{\pi t}{12}\right)$, where t is time measured in hours. Find the average amount of water in the tank during the first 12 hours.

Answer: 691,000 gallons

131. The marginal revenue function for a producer is $R'(x) = 274 + 17\cos(0.1\pi x)$ dollars. Assuming that revenue from the sale of 0 units is 0 dollars, find the revenue function R(x).

Answer: $R(x) = 274x + \frac{170}{\pi}\sin(0.1\pi x)$

132. A manufacturer estimates that the marginal cost for its product is given by $C'(x) = 53 - 20\pi\sin(0.2\pi x)$ dollars. If fixed cost is $150, find the cost function.

Answer: $C(x) = 53x + 100\cos(0.2\pi x) + 150$

133. The rate at which a chain of shoe stores sells outdoor walking shoes is given by the function $n(t) = 537 + 341\sin(\pi t/6)$ pairs per month. The variable t represents months. Let $t = 0$ be the beginning of January, $t = 1$ the end of January, $t = 2$ the end of February, and so on, with $t = 12$ being the end of December. Determine the total number of pairs of outdoor walking shoes (rounded to the nearest pair) sold in the first 3 months of the year.

Answer: 2262 pairs

134. A store's inventory at t months is $15 + 22.5\sin(\pi t/6)$ units. Find the average inventory for the first 6 months. Round your answer to the nearest unit.

Answer: 29 units

Section 8.5 Other Trigonometric Functions

MULTIPLE CHOICE 8.5

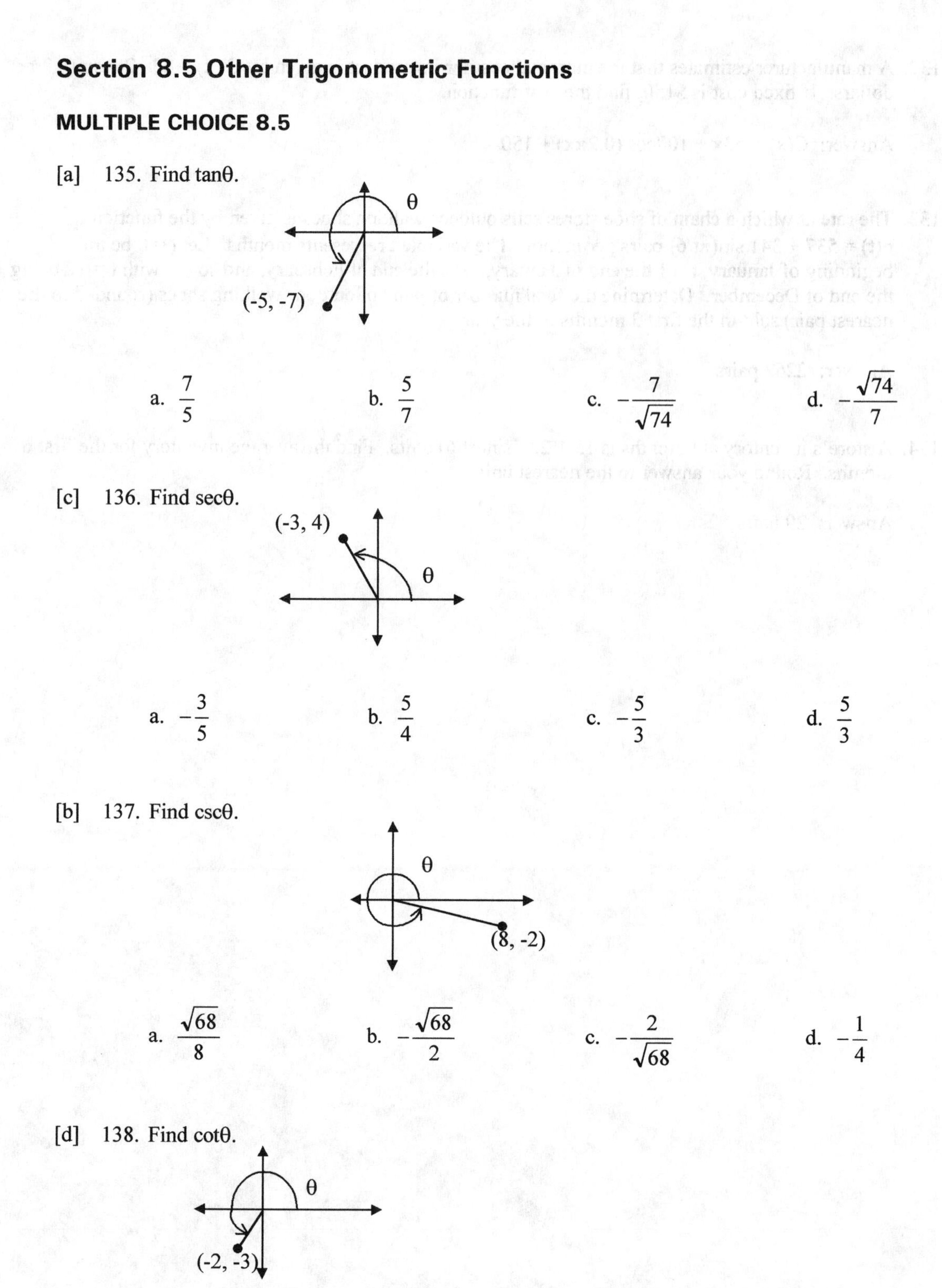

[a] 135. Find tanθ.

a. $\frac{7}{5}$ b. $\frac{5}{7}$ c. $-\frac{7}{\sqrt{74}}$ d. $-\frac{\sqrt{74}}{7}$

[c] 136. Find secθ.

a. $-\frac{3}{5}$ b. $\frac{5}{4}$ c. $-\frac{5}{3}$ d. $\frac{5}{3}$

[b] 137. Find cscθ.

a. $\frac{\sqrt{68}}{8}$ b. $-\frac{\sqrt{68}}{2}$ c. $-\frac{2}{\sqrt{68}}$ d. $-\frac{1}{4}$

[d] 138. Find cotθ.

a. $\frac{3}{2}$ b. $\frac{\sqrt{52}}{4}$ c. $\frac{\sqrt{52}}{6}$ d. $\frac{2}{3}$

[d] 139. Evaluate cot $\pi/3$ – tan $\pi/6$.

a. $\frac{\sqrt{6}}{6}$ b. 3 c. $2\sqrt{3}$ d. 0

[b] 140. Evaluate $(\tan 5\pi/9)^2 - (\sec 5\pi/9)^2$.

a. –2 b. –1 c. $\sqrt{2}$ d. 2

[a] 141. The formula $P(t) = 110 + 25 \cos 5.8t$ gives a person's blood pressure at any time t, in seconds. After 3 seconds, this person's blood pressure will be

a. 113 b. 102 c. 119 d. 108

[c] 142. Evaluate the function $\cot \frac{5\pi}{4}$ without using a calculator.

a. $-\frac{1}{\sqrt{2}}$ b. –1 c. 1 d. $-\sqrt{2}$

[b] 143. Evaluate the function $\sec \frac{2\pi}{3}$ without using a calculator.

a. $\frac{2}{\sqrt{3}}$ b. –2 c. $-\frac{2}{\sqrt{3}}$ d. $\frac{\sqrt{3}}{2}$

[d] 144. Evaluate the function $\csc \pi$ without using a calculator.

a. 0 b. –1 c. 1 d. undefined

[b] 145. Evaluate the function $\tan \frac{5\pi}{6}$ without using a calculator.

a. $-\sqrt{3}$ b. $-\frac{1}{\sqrt{3}}$ c. $\frac{1}{\sqrt{3}}$ d. $\frac{2}{\sqrt{3}}$

[b] 146. Use a calculator to approximate $\cot \frac{2\pi}{5}$.

a. 3.07768 b. 0.32492 c. 45.58722 d. 0.02194

[d] 147. Use a calculator to approximate $\sec \frac{7\pi}{24}$.

a. 0.99987 b. 1.00013 c. 0.60876 d. 1.64268

[b] 148. Use a calculator to approximate $\csc \frac{\pi}{7}$.

a. 0.43388 b. 2.30476 c. 0.00783 d. 127.666

[b] 149. How tall is a utility pole (to the nearest foot) if it casts a 12 foot shadow when the sun shines from an angle of 65° with respect to the ground?

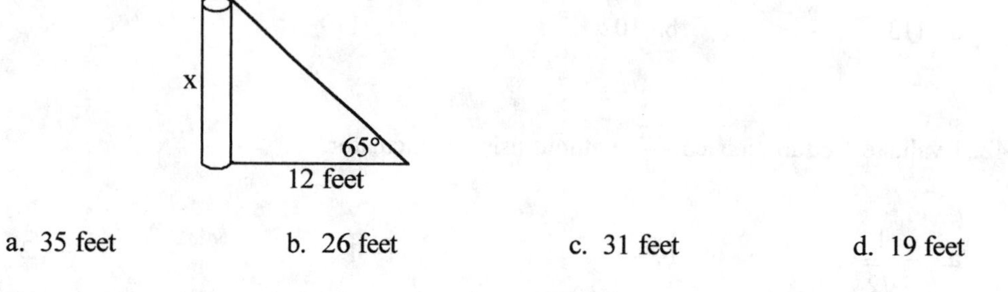

a. 35 feet b. 26 feet c. 31 feet d. 19 feet

[b] 150. The distance from the base of a tree to a point on the ground is 9 feet. At this point, the angle of elevation to the top of the tree is 57.3°. Rounded to the nearest foot, the height of the tree is

a. 13 feet b. 14 feet c. 11 feet d. 17 feet

[b] 151. The figure below shows the position of three large boulders on the shores of a river. The boulders are the vertices of a right triangle. If the distance between the boulders A and B is 16.4 feet and the angle at B is 63.5°, how wide is the river (rounded to the nearest foot)?

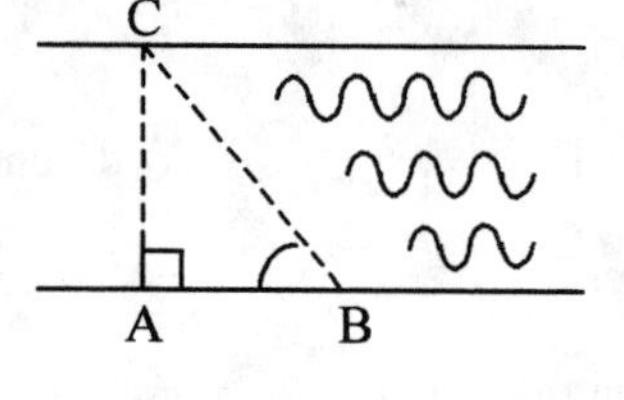

[a] 152. Differentiate the function: $\sec(t^2 - 1)$.

a. $2t\sec(t^2 - 1)\tan(t^2 - 1)$
b. $\sec(t^2 - 1)\tan(t^2 - 1)$
c. $\sec 2t$
d. $\tan^2(t^2 - 1)$

[c] 153. Differentiate the function: $\csc\left(\pi - \frac{x}{4}\right)$.

a. $-\csc\left(\pi - \frac{x}{4}\right)\cot\left(\pi - \frac{x}{4}\right)$

b. $\csc\left(\pi - \frac{x}{4}\right)\cot\left(\pi - \frac{x}{4}\right)$

c. $\frac{1}{4}\csc\left(\pi - \frac{x}{4}\right)\cot\left(\pi - \frac{x}{4}\right)$

d. $-\frac{1}{4}\csc\left(\pi - \frac{x}{4}\right)\cot\left(\pi - \frac{x}{4}\right)$

[c] 154. Find the integral: $\int \sec^2\left(\frac{x}{7}\right)dx$.

a. $2\sec^3\left(\frac{x}{7}\right) + C$

b. $\frac{\sec^3\left(\frac{x}{7}\right)}{7} + C$

c. $7\tan\left(\frac{x}{7}\right) + C$

d. $\frac{\tan\left(\frac{x}{7}\right)}{7} + C$

[d] 155. Find the integral: $\int \sec(2x)\tan(2x)dx$.

a. $\frac{\sec^{2\pi}(2x)\tan^2(2x)}{4} + C$

b. $4\sec^2(2x)\tan^2(2x) + C$

c. $2\sec(2x) + C$

d. $\frac{\sec(2x)}{2} + C$

[c] 156. Find the integral: $\int \sec^2 5x dx$.

a. $5\tan 5x + C$

b. $\frac{\sec^3 5x}{3} + C$

c. $\frac{1}{5}\tan 5x + C$

d. $\tan 5x + C$

[d] 157. Find the integral: $\int t\cot(t^2)\csc(t^2)dt$.

a. $\csc(t^2) + C$

b. $2\csc(t^2) + C$

c. $-\csc(t^2) + C$

d. $-\frac{1}{2}\csc(t^2) + C$

[a] 158. Find the integral: $\int \frac{\csc^2(\ln x)}{x}dx$.

a. $-\cot(\ln x) + C$

b. $\cot(\ln x) + C$

c. $\frac{\csc^3(\ln x)}{3} + C$

d. $-\cot^2(\ln x) + C$

[d] 159. Find the integral: $\int \frac{\tan\sqrt{x}}{\sqrt{x}}dx$.

a. $-\frac{1}{2}\ln\left|\cos\sqrt{x}\right|+C$ b. $-\ln\left|\cos\sqrt{x}\right|+C$ c. $-\frac{1}{2}\sec^2\sqrt{x}+C$ d. $-2\ln\left|\cos\sqrt{x}\right|+C$

[a] 160. Evaluate the definite integral: $\int_{\frac{\pi}{4}}^{\frac{\pi}{2}} e^{\cot x}\csc^2 x dx$.

a. $e-1$ b. $1+e$ c. $1-e$ d. $-1-e$

[c] 161. Find the area under the curve $y=\tan\frac{1}{3}x$ and above the x-axis between $x=0$ and $x=\pi$ without using a graphing calculator.

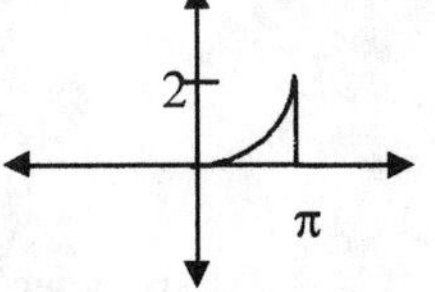

a. $-\ln\left(\frac{\sqrt{3}}{2}\right)$ b. $-3\ln\left(\frac{\sqrt{3}}{2}\right)$ c. $-3\ln\left(\frac{1}{2}\right)$ d. $-\ln\left(\frac{1}{2}\right)$

SHORT ANSWER 8.5

162. How far away is a building that is 250 feet high and whose top makes an angle of 58° with the ground?

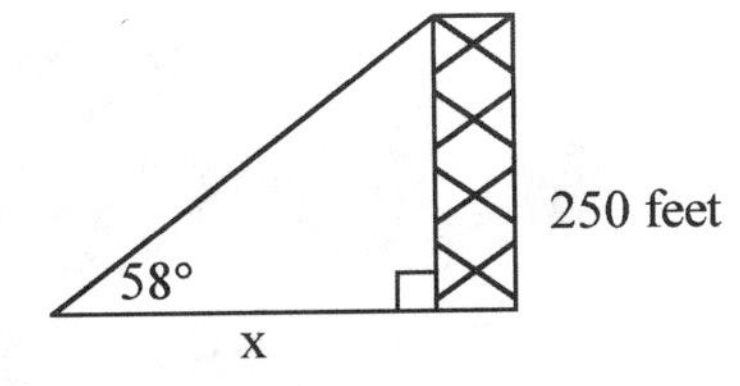

Answer: 156.2 feet

163. A ladder is leaning against a wall making an angle with the ground of 42°. How long is the ladder if the bottom of the ladder is 14 feet from the base of the wall?

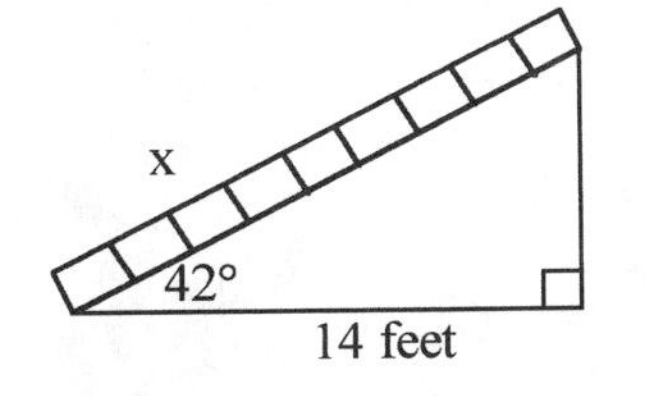

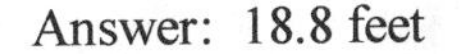

Answer: 18.8 feet

164. A large balloon is used in an advertising promotion. If it is tethered to the ground by a rope that is 300 feet long and the angle between the rope and the ground is 37°, how high is the balloon? Round your answer to the nearest foot.

Answer: 181 feet

165. A ladder leans against a wall, so that the top is 12 feet up the wall and the bottom 3 feet away from the wall. Find the angle the ladder makes with the floor. Round your answer to the nearest degree.

Answer: 76°

166. Differentiate the function: $x^2 \tan x$.

Answer: $x(x\sec^2 x + 2\tan x)$

167. Differentiate the function: $\cot^3 5x$.

Answer: $-15\cot^2 5x\csc^2 5x$

168. Differentiate the function: $t\csc t$.

Answer: $\csc t(-t\cot + 1)$

169. Differentiate the function: tan(ln x).

Answer: $\dfrac{\sec^2(\ln x)}{x}$

170. Differentiate the function: $e^{\sec x}$.

Answer: $\tan x \sec x\, e^{\sec x}$

171. Differentiate the function: $\cot^5 \sqrt{t}$.

Answer: $-5\left(\cot\sqrt{t}\right)^4\left(\dfrac{1}{2\sqrt{t}}\csc^2\sqrt{t}\right)$

172. Find the integral: $\int x^2 \tan(x^3-2)\sec(x^3-2)dx$.

Answer: $\dfrac{1}{3}\sec(x^3-2)+C$

173. Find the integral: $\int \cot\left(\dfrac{\pi}{2}-x\right)dx$

Answer: $-\ln\left|\sin\left(\dfrac{\pi}{2}-x\right)\right|+C$

174. Find the integral: $\int \dfrac{\sec^2 x}{\tan x}dx$.

Answer: $\ln|\tan x| + C$

175. Find the integral: $\int \sqrt{\cot x}\csc^2 x dx$

Answer: $-\dfrac{2}{3}(\cot x)^{\frac{3}{2}}+C$

176. Find the integral: $\int \sec^2(2x)\sqrt{\tan(2x)}dx$.

Answer: $\dfrac{1}{3}\tan(2x)^{\frac{3}{2}}+C$

177. Find the integral: $\int 5x \cdot \sec^2(2.5x^2)dx$.

Answer: $\tan(2.5x^2) + C$

178. Find the integral: $\int \left[\tan\frac{x}{2}\right]\left[\sec^2\frac{x}{2}\right]dx$.

Answer: $\tan^2\left(\frac{x}{2}\right) + C$

179. Evaluate the definite integral: $\int_0^{\frac{\pi}{4}} \sec t\,dt$.

Answer: $\ln\left|\sqrt{2}+1\right|$

180. Find the area under $y = \sec^2(0.1x)$ from $x = 5\pi/2$ to $x = 10\pi/3$.

Answer: $10\left(\sqrt{3}-1\right)$

181. Find the area under the curve $y = \sec 2x \tan 2x$ and above the x-axis between $x = 0$ and $x = \frac{\pi}{8}$ without using a graphing calculator.

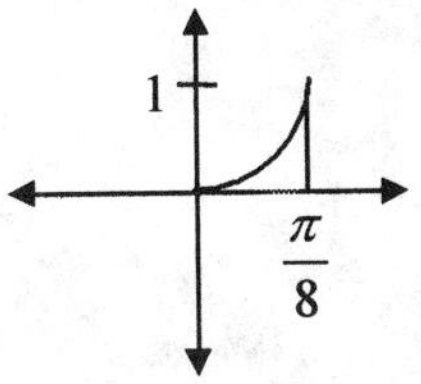

Answer: $\frac{\sqrt{2}-1}{2}$

Chapter 8 – Graphing Calculator

Trigonometric Functions

Section 8.1 Triangles, Angles, and Radian Measure

1. Use your graphing calculator, convert the angle, –45°, given in degrees to radian measure. Use MODE to select radian. Then enter the angle, select MATH menu and choose angle (F3), then ° (F1) for degree mark, then ENTER. Since π is approximated, your calculator will return the angle in decimal radians.

   Answer: –0.785 radians

2. Use your graphing calculator, convert the angle, 270°, given in degrees to radian measure. Use MODE to select radian. Then enter the angle, select MATH menu and choose angle (F3), then ° (F1) for degree mark, then ENTER. Since π is approximated, your calculator will return the angle in decimal radians.

   Answer: 4.712 radians

3. Use your graphing calculator, convert the angle, 580°, given in degrees to radian measure. Use MODE to select radian. Then enter the angle, select MATH menu and choose angle (F3), then ° (F1) for degree mark, then ENTER. Since π is approximated, your calculator will return the angle in decimal radians.

   Answer: 10.123 radians

4. Use your graphing calculator, convert the angle, $\frac{5\pi}{6}$, given in radians to degree measure. Use MODE to select degree. Then enter the angle, select the MATH menu and choose angle (F3), then r (F2) for radian, then ENTER. (Hint: $\frac{\pi}{2}$ must be entered as $\left(\frac{\pi}{2}\right)^{r}$).

   Answer: 150°

5. Use your graphing calculator, convert the angle, $-\frac{13\pi}{6}$, given in radians to degree measure. Use MODE to select degree. Then enter the angle, select the MATH menu and choose angle (F3), then r (F2) for radian, then ENTER. (Hint: $\frac{\pi}{2}$ must be entered as $\left(\frac{\pi}{2}\right)^{r}$).

   Answer: –390°

6. Use your graphing calculator, convert the angle, $\frac{5\pi}{2}$, given in radians to degree measure. Use MODE to select degree. Then enter the angle, select the MATH menu and choose angle (F3), then r (F2) for radian, then ENTER. (Hint: $\frac{\pi}{2}$ must be entered as $\left(\frac{\pi}{2}\right)^r$).

Answer: 450°

7. Graph the functions $y_1 = \sin x$, $y_2 = 3\sin x$, $y_3 = \frac{1}{2}\sin x$ on the window $[-2\pi, 2\pi]$ by $[-5, 5]$.
   a. Do the different coefficients effect the x-intercepts?
   b. How do the different coefficients effect the graph?

Answer: a. no, the x-intercepts remain the same.
b. the larger the coefficient, the larger the amplitude; the smaller the coefficient the smaller the amplitude.

8. Graph the function $y_1 = 2\cos x$ and $y_2 = -2\cos x$ on the window $[-2\pi, 2\pi]$ by $[-3, 3]$. How does the negative coefficient effect the graph?

Answer: it reflects the curve across the x-axis.

9. Graph the functions $y_1 = \sin x$, $y_2 = \sin 2x$, $y_3 = \sin \frac{1}{2}x$ on the window $[-4\pi, 4\pi]$ by $[-2, 2]$.
   a. Do the numbers in front of the x effect the amplitude?
   b. How do the number in front of x effect the graph?
   c. What is the period of this function?

Answer: a. No
b. It changes the <u>period</u> of the function; it makes the graph oscillate faster or slower. A larger number makes the graph oscillate faster while a smaller number makes the graph oscillate slower.
c. $\frac{2\pi}{3}$

Section 8.2 Sine and Cosine Functions

10. Using your graphing calculator, graph the function $f(x) = 4 \sin(4x)$ on $[-\pi, \pi]$ by $[-5, 5]$ with x-scale $\frac{\pi}{4}$, and use the graph to find the period of the curve.

    Answer: $\frac{\pi}{2}$

11. Using your graphing calculator, graph the function $f(x) = -6 \cos(-0.2x)$ on $[-20\pi, 20\pi]$ by $[-8, 8]$ with x-scale 5π, and use the graph to find the period of the curve.

    Answer: 10π

12. Using your graphing calculator, graph the function $f(x) = \sin(2x + 5)$ on $[-2\pi, \pi]$ by $[-6, 0]$ with x-scale $\frac{\pi}{2}$, and use the graph to find the period of the curve.

13. Using your graphing calculator, graph the function $f(x) = 2\cos\left(\frac{\pi}{2}x\right)$ on $[-8, 8]$ by $[-3, 3]$ with x-scale 1, and use the graph to find the period of the curve.

    Answer: 4 radians

14. Using your graphing calculator, graph the function $f(x) = 5 \sin(4\pi x)$ on $[-1, 1]$ by $[-7, 7]$ with x-scale 0.1, and use the graph to find the period of the curve.

    Answer: $\frac{1}{2}$ radian

15. Graph $y_1 = \sin(3x - 2) + \cos(2x)$ on $[-4\pi, 4\pi]$ by $[-3, 3]$ with x-scale π.
    a. Does this function look periodic?
    b. How many periods does the curve complete in this particular window?
    c. Determine the period of the function.

    Answer: a. yes
    b. 4 periods
    c. $8\pi \div 4 = 2\pi$

16. Graph $y_1 = 2 \cos 3x + 3 \sin x$ on $[-4\pi, 4\pi]$ by $[-6, 6]$ with x-scale π.
    a. Does this function look periodic?
    b. How many periods does the curve complete on this window?
    c. Determine the period of this function.
    d. Graph $y_2 = 2 \cos 3x$ and $y_3 = 3 \sin x$ on $[-2\pi, 2\pi]$ by $[-4, 4]$ individually and determine from their graphs the period of each function.
    e. Use the result from part d to explain the answer to part c.

    Answer: a. yes
    b. 4 periods
    c. $8\pi \div 4 = 2\pi$
    d. $2 \cos 3x$ has a period of $\frac{2\pi}{3}$, $3 \sin x$ has a period of 2π.
    e. The combined function repeats when each "part" repeats separately. Although $y = 2 \cos 3x$ repeats every $\frac{2\pi}{3}$, the combined function must "wait" until $y = 3 \sin x$ repeats for it to return to its original value.

17. Suppose the population of a herd of deer is given by $P(t) = 3{,}000 + 500 \sin\left(2\pi t - \frac{\pi}{2}\right)$, where t is measured in years. Graph this function in a window $[0, 1]$ by $[2{,}000, 4{,}000]$.
    a. Find the deer population on April 1 ($t = 0.25$).
    b. Find the deer population on July 1 ($t = 0.5$).
    c. Verify that the deer population is a maximum on July 1 ($t = 0.5$) by using NDERIV to find where this function's derivative is equal to zero.

    Answer: a. 3,000 b. 3,500

Section 8.4 Integrals of Sine and Cosine Functions

18. The integral $\int_{0}^{2.5} \sin x^2 dx$, cannot be evaluated using any of the substitution formulas that we have studied. However, they can be approximated using a Riemann Sum program on your graphing calculator. Approximate the integral to 3 decimal places using a Riemann Sum program.

    Answer: 0.431

19. The integral $\int_{0.2}^{3} \sin\left(\frac{1}{x}\right) dx$, cannot be evaluated using any of the substitution formulas that we have studied. However, they can be approximated using a Riemann Sum program on your graphing calculator. Approximate the integral to 3 decimal places using a Riemann Sum program.

    Answer: 1.532

20. The integral $\int_{0}^{\frac{\pi}{4}} \frac{1}{\cos x} dx$, cannot be evaluated using any of the substitution formulas that we have studied. However, they can be approximated using a Riemann Sum program on your graphing calculator. Approximate the integral to 3 decimal places using a Riemann Sum program.

    Answer: 0.881

21. The integral $\int_{0}^{4} \cos \sqrt{x} dx$, cannot be evaluated using any of the substitution formulas that we have studied. However, they can be approximated using a Riemann Sum program on your graphing calculator. Approximate the integral to 3 decimal places using a Riemann Sum program.

    Answer: 0.805

22. The integral $\int_{0}^{1} \sqrt{1+\cos^2 x} dx$, cannot be evaluated using any of the substitution formulas that we have studied. However, they can be approximated using a Riemann Sum program on your graphing calculator. Approximate the integral to 3 decimal places using a Riemann Sum program.

    Answer: 1.311

23. The number of hours, N, of daylight in Madrid, Spain as a function of date is approximated as $N = 12 + 2.4\sin[0.0172(x - 80)]$ where x is the number of days since the beginning of the year. Use a Riemann sums program to find the average number of hours of daylight in Madrid.
    a. in January ($x = 0$ to $x = 31$)
    b. over the entire year ($x = 0$ to $x = 365$)

    Answer: a. 9.9 hours b. 12.0 hours

Section 8.5 Other Trigonometric Functions

24. Graph the function $f(x) = \frac{1}{2}\csc(2x)$ on the window [–2π, 2π] by [–10, 10], and from the graph determine the period of the function.

    Answer: π

25. Graph the function $f(x) = 3\sec\left(\frac{\pi x}{2}\right)$ on the window [–8π, 8π] by [–10, 10], and from the graph determine the period of the function.

    Answer: 4

26. Graph the function f(x) = 2 cos x – sec x on the window [–2π, 2π] by [–10, 10], and from the graph determine the period of the function.

    Answer: 2π

27. Using a graphing calculator (Riemann Sum program) approximate the area of the bounded region, above $y = \tan(x^2)$, below the x-axis, x = 0 and x = 1, to the nearest hundredth.

    Answer: 0.40

28. Using a graphing calculator (Riemann Sum program) approximate the area of the bounded region, above y = sec x, below the x-axis, $x = \frac{\pi}{4}$, $x = \frac{\pi}{3}$, to the nearest hundredth.

    Answer: 0.44

29. Using a graphing calculator (Riemann Sum program) approximate the area of the bounded region, above $y = 2^x - (\tan x)^{x+1}$, below the x-axis, x = 0, x = 0.75, to the nearest hundredth.

    Answer: 0.74

30. Enter $y_1 = \cot x$ and $y_2 = x$ on $\left[0, \frac{\pi}{2}\right]$ by [0, 4]. Graph both of these curves on the same set of axes. Using ZOOM/TRACE, approximate the intersection point of these two curves to three decimal places.

    Answer: (0.860, 0.860)

Chapter 9

Differential Equations

Section 9.1 Separation of Variables

MULTIPLE CHOICE 9.1

[c] 1. Determine the general solution of $y' = e^{-x} + 1$.

a. $e^{-x} + x + C$ b. $-e^{-x} + C$ c. $-e^{-x} + x + C$ d. $-e^{-2x} + x + C$

[c] 2. Which of the following is the general solution of $xy' = -y$?

a. $y = \frac{1}{x}$ b. $y = \frac{1}{x} + C$ c. $y = \frac{C}{x}$ d. $e^{-x} + C$

[a] 3. Which of the following is the general solution of $y' = 4x^2 + \frac{1}{x}$?

a. $\frac{4}{3}x^3 \ln x + C$ b. $8x - \frac{1}{x^2} + C$ c. $8x + \ln x + C$ d. $\frac{4}{3}x^3 - \frac{1}{x^2} + C$

[d] 4. Which of the following is the particular solution of $y' = 3\sqrt{x}$ and $y(0) = 7$?

a. $\frac{9}{2}x^{\frac{3}{2}} + 7$ b. $3x^{\frac{3}{2}} + 6$ c. $2x^{\frac{3}{2}} + 6$ d. $2x^{\frac{3}{2}} + 7$

[d] 5. Which of the following is the particular solution of $y' = \frac{1}{x} + e^{-x}$ for which $f(1) = 0$?

a. $\ln x + e^{-x} - 1$ b. $\ln x - e^{-x} + \frac{1}{e}$ c. $\ln x - e^{-x} + \frac{1}{e} - 1$ d. $-\frac{1}{x^2} - e^{-x}$

[d] 6. Which of the following is the particular solution of $y' = 5$ and $y(0) = -1$?

a. $y = -1$ b. $y = \frac{5}{x} - 1$ c. $y = 5x - 2$ d. $y = 5x - 1$

[c] 7. Which of the following is a solution to the differential equation $y' = 2y$?

a. $y = x^2$ b. $y = 2x$ c. $y = e^{2x}$ d. $y = x^2 + 2x$

[a] 8. Which of the following is a solution to the differential equation $y' = y + 1$?

a. $y = 3e^x - 1$ b. $y = \ln x + x$ c. $y = 3e^x - x$ d. none of these

[b] 9. Which of the following is the particular solution of $y' = -y$ such that $y(0) = -5$?

a. $y = 5e^{-x}$ b. $y = -5e^{-x}$ c. $y = -5e^{-5x}$ d. $y = x - 5$

[d] 10. Which of the following is the particular solution of $\frac{dy}{dx} = y^2$ that passes through the point $\left(1, -\frac{1}{2}\right)$?

a. $y = x^3 - \frac{1}{2}$ b. $y = -\frac{1}{x}$ c. $y = -\frac{1}{2}e^{x-1}$ d. $y = \frac{-1}{x+1}$

[a] 11. Which of the following is a solution of $y' = \frac{1}{2}\left(3x^3 + x\right)^{-\frac{1}{2}} \cdot (9x^2 + 1)$?

a. $y = \sqrt{3x^2 + x + 17}$ b. $y = \sqrt{3x^2 + x}\,(3x^3 + x)$

c. $y = \sqrt[3]{3x^2 + x}$ d. $y = \left(3x^2 + x\right)^{\frac{1}{2}} + x$

[b] 12. Determine the particular solution of $\frac{dy}{dt} = \frac{20}{t}$ for which $f(1) = -5$.

a. $y = 20 \ln t - 5t$ b. $y = \ln t^{20} - 5$ c. $y = \frac{20}{\ln t} - 5$ d. $y = \frac{-40}{t^2} + 35$

[d] 13. Determine the particular solution of $\frac{dy}{dx} = 5x - e^{2x}$ for which $y(0) = 5$.

a. $y = 5 - 2e^{2x} + 2$ b. $y = 5 - 2e^{2x}$ c. $y = \frac{5}{2}x^2 - \frac{1}{2}e^{2x} + 3$ d. $y = \frac{5}{2}x^2 - \frac{1}{2}e^{2x} + \frac{11}{2}$

[d] 14. Find the general solution of the differential equation $(1 + x^2)\, y' = 2x(y - 1)$ by using separation of variables.

a. $y = x^2e^x + C$ b. $y = Cx^2e^x + 1$ c. $y = (1 + x^2) + Ce^x$ d. $y = 1 + C(1 + x^2)$

[b] 15. Find the general solution of the differential equation $y' = 4x^3y^2$ using separation of variables.

a. $y = \frac{x^4y^3}{3} + C$ b. $y = \frac{1}{C - x^4}$ c. $y = x^4e^{2x} + C$ d. $y = \frac{C}{x^4}$

[d] 16. Find the general solution of the differential equation $\frac{dy}{dx} = 25 - y$.

a. $y = C - e^{-x}$ b. $y = 25x - \frac{y^2}{2}$ c. $y = C - 25e^{-x}$ d. $25 - Ce^{-x}$

[d] 17. Find the general solution of the differential equation $(2 + x^4)\,y' = 4x^3(y - 3)$.

a. $y = 5 + C(2 + x^4)$
b. $y = (2 + x^4)^2 + C$
c. $y = 3 + (2 + x^4)^2 + Cx$
d. $y = 3 + C(2 + x^4)$

[a] 18. Find the particular solution, using separation of variables, for the differential equation $y' = xy + x$ if $y(0) = 2$.

a. $y = 3e^{\frac{x^2}{2}} - 1$ b. $y = e^{\frac{x^2}{2}} + 1$ c. $y^2 = 2ye^{x^2}$ d. $y = \frac{1}{x}\ln(x+1) + 2$

[b] 19. Find the particular solution, using separation of variables, for the differential equation $xyy' = \ln x$ if $y(1) = 1$. State the solution explicitly.

a. $y = \ln(x^2) + 2x - 1$ b. $y = \sqrt{1 + (\ln x)^2}$ c. $y = 2e^{x-1} - x$ d. $y = \frac{1}{x}e^{x-1}$

[c] 20. Find the particular solution, using separation of variables, for the differential equation $y' = (2 - y)^2 e^x$ if $y(0) = \frac{3}{2}$.

a. $y = \frac{3}{2}e^x - 2x^2$ b. $y = (e^x + 1)^{-1} + 1$ c. $y = 2 - \frac{1}{e^x + 1}$ d. $y = \frac{3}{2}e^x + 2x^3$

[a] 21. Find the general solution of $y' = \frac{1+x^2}{1+y^2}$. State the solution implicitly.

a. $y + \frac{1}{3}y^3 = x + \frac{1}{3}x^3 + C$
b. $\frac{y^3}{3} + y^2 = xy + C$
c. $ye^{y^2+1} = e^{x^2+1} + C$
d. $ye^{1+y^2} = x^2 + C$

[b] 22. Use separation of variables to find the particular solution $y' = 0.25y$ and $y(0) = 3.75$. From the particular solution, evaluate $y(4)$.

a. $y(4) = 7.5$ b. $y(4) = 10.2$ c. $y(4) = 11.25$ d. $y(4) = 27.7$

[a] 23. Let $xy' = y^2$ and $y(1) = -1$. Find $y(e)$.

a. $-\frac{1}{2}$ b. $e^2 - 1$ c. -1 d. $1 - e^2$

[a] 24. The annual sales (S) of a company grow over time (t) according to the differential equation $\frac{dS}{dt} = k(5 - S)$, where k is a constant. If the sales are zero initially and $1 million during the fourth year of operation, when will the sales reach $4 million?

a. after 29 years b. after 5 years c. after 19 years d. after 13 years

[c] 25. A rumor spreads through a population of 1000 people at a rate proportional to the product of the number that have heard it and the number that have not. If 5 people start a rumor and 10 people have heard it after 1 day, how many people will have heard it after 7 days?

a. 200 b. 300 c. 400 d. 500

[d] 26. The number N(t) of bacteria in a culture at time t grows according to the differential equation $\frac{dN}{dt} = 100 - 0.5N$. Find the general solution.

a. $N(t) = Ce^{-0.5t} + 200t$

b. $N(t) = -\ln(100 - 0.5N) + C$

c. $N(t) = \frac{C}{\ln(100 - 0.5N)}$

d. $N(t) = 200 - Ce^{-0.5t}$

[b] 27. If the price p(t) of a product satisfies the differential equation $\frac{dp}{dt} = 0.5 - 0.1p$ and $p(0) = \$4.00$, calculate p(2).

a. $1.48 b. $4.18 c. $2.37 d. $4.59

[a] 28. Mothballs evaporate at a rate proportional to their volume, losing half their volume every 5 weeks. If the initial volume is 15 cubic centimeter, when will their volume be 1 cubic centimeter?

a. after 19.5 weeks b. after 1.83 weeks c. after 17.1 weeks d. after 15.9 weeks

[c] 29. A retired couple has life savings of $2,175,000. If inflation stays at a constant 3%, how long will it take for their life savings to erode to a real value of $1,087,500?

a. 22.6 years b. 18.5 years c. 23.1 years d. 27.8 years

SHORT ANSWER 9.1

30. Show that $y = x^{\frac{3}{2}}$ is a solution of the differential equation $2xy' = 3y$.

Answer: $2xy' = 3y$; let $y = x^{\frac{3}{2}}$

$$2xy' = 2x\left(\frac{3}{2}\right)x^{\frac{1}{2}} = 3x^{\frac{3}{2}} = 3y$$

31. Verify that $y = e^{2x} + e^{-x} - x^{-1}$ is a solution of the differential equation $y'' - y' - 2y = 2$.

Answer: Let $y = e^{2x} + e^{-x} - 1$. Then $y' = 2e^{2x} - e^{-x}$ and $y'' = 4e^{2x} + e^{-x}$.
Given: $y'' - y' - 2y = 2$; therefore,
$$4e^{2x} + e^{-x} - (2e^{2x} - e^{-x}) - 2(e^{2x} + e^{-x} - 1) = 4e^{2x} + e^{-x} - 2e^{2x} + e^{-x} - 2e^{2x} - 2e^{-x} + 2 = 2$$

32. Verify that $y = e^{-0.1x} + e^{0.3x}$ is a solution of the differential equation $100y'' - 20y' - 3y = 0$.

Answer: $y = e^{-0.1x} + e^{0.3x}$; $y' = -0.1e^{-0.1x} + 0.3e^{0.3x}$; $y'' = 0.01e^{-0.1x} + 0.09e^{0.3x}$.
Therefore, $100y'' - 20y' - 3y =$
$$= 100(0.01e^{-0.1x} + 0.09e^{0.3x}) - 20(-0.1e^{-0.1x} + 0.3e^{0.3x}) - 3(e^{-0.1x} + e^{0.3x})$$
$$= e^{-0.1x} + 9e^{0.3x} + 2e^{-0.1x} - 6e^{-0.3x} - 3e^{-0.1x} - 3e^{0.3x} = 0$$

33. Show that $y = \sqrt[3]{9x^2 + 1}$ is a solution of the differential equation $y' = \dfrac{6x}{y^2}$.

Answer: $y = (9x^2 + 1)^{\frac{1}{3}}$; $y' = \frac{1}{3}(9x^2 + 1)^{-\frac{2}{3}} \cdot 18x = 6x(9x^2 + 1)^{-\frac{2}{3}} = \dfrac{6x}{(9x^2 + 1)^{\frac{2}{3}}} = \dfrac{6x}{\left(\sqrt[3]{9x^2 + 1}\right)^2} = \dfrac{6x}{y^2}$

34. The general solution of $y' = 6x + \dfrac{3}{2\sqrt{x}}$ is $y =$

Answer: $3x^2 + 3\sqrt{x} + C$

35. Determine the general solution of $f'(x) = e^{-0.1x}$.

Answer: $f(x) = -10e^{-0.1x} + C$

36. Determine the general solution of $y' = \dfrac{6.3}{x}$.

Answer: $\ln x^{6.3} + C$

37. Show that $y = Cx^3 + 5.2$ is the general solution of the differential equation $xy' = 3y - 15.6$.

Answer: $y' = 3Cx^2$; $xy' = 3Cx^3$
$xy' = 3Cx^3 + 15.6 - 15.6 = 3(Cx^3 + 5.2) - 15.6 = 3y - 15.6$

38. The general solution of the differential equation $y' = e^{0.1x} + 22e^{-0.2x}$ is

Answer: $10e^{0.1x} - 10e^{-0.2x} + C$

39. Determine the particular solution of $y' = \frac{4.6}{x}$ and $y(1) = 7.3$.

Answer: $y = 4.6 \ln x + 7.3$

40. Determine the particular solution of $y' = 4.8x^3 - 6.3x^2 + 1.6x$ for which $y(1) = -1$.

Answer: $1.2x^4 - 2.1x^3 + 0.8x^2 - 0.9$

41. Determine the particular solution of $g'(x) = 6\sqrt[3]{x}$ for which $g(1) = 1$.

Answer: $g(x) = \frac{9}{2}x^{\frac{4}{3}} - \frac{7}{2}$

42. Given that $y = Cx^3 + 5.2$ is the general solution of $xy' = 3y - 15.6$, find the particular solution that passes through the point $(-2, 4)$.

Answer: $y = 0.15x^3 + 5.2$

43. Determine the particular solution of $\frac{dy}{dt} = \frac{6.7}{t} + \frac{1}{e}$ such that $y(e) = 10$.

Answer: $y = 6.7 \ln t + \frac{1}{e}t + 2.3$

44. What is the particular solution of $4.6 + e^{-0.2x}$ for which $y(0) = 0$?

Answer: $y = 2.3x^2 - 5e^{-0.2x} + 5$

45. Find the general solution of the differential equation $\frac{dy}{dt} = 7.4t$.

Answer: $y = 3.7t^2 + C$

46. Find the general solution of the differential equation $y' = -0.23y$.

Answer: $y = Ce^{-0.23x}$

47. Find the general solution of the differential equation $x \cdot \frac{dx}{dt} = \frac{5}{7}$ using separation of variables.

Answer: $x^2 = \frac{10t}{7} + C$

48. Find the general solution of the differential equation $y' = y - 5.7$ using separation of variables.

Answer: $y = 5.7 + Ce^x$

49. Find the general solution of the differential equation $\frac{dy}{dx} ye^{-0.1x}$.

Answer: $y = Ce^{-10e^{-0.1x}}$

50. Find the particular solution, using separation of variables, for the differential equation $y' = -0.23y$ if $y(0) = 6.7$.

Answer: $y = 6.7e^{-0.23x}$

51. Find the particular solution, using separation of variables, for the differential equation $x' = \frac{x}{t}$ if $x(1) = 5.4$.

Answer: $x(t) = 5.4t$

52. For the particular solution, using separation of variables, for the differential equation $\frac{dy}{dx} = ye^{-0.1x}$ if $y(0) = 5e^{-10}$.

Answer: $y = 5e^{-10e^{-0.1x}}$

53. Find the particular solution, using separation of variables, for the differential equation $y' = 3.2xy$ if $y(0) = -0.5$.

Answer: $-0.5e^{1.6ex^2}$

54. Let the marginal cost be given by $C'(x) = 100 - 0.1x$ with $C(0) = 57.50$. Find the cost function.

Answer: $C(x) = 100x - 0.05x^2 + 57.50$

55. Let the marginal cost be given by $C'(x) = \frac{32.50}{\sqrt{x}}$ and let C(0) = $9350. Find the cost function.

Answer: $C(x) = 65\sqrt{x} + 9350$

56. Assume that the marginal profit is given by $P'(x) = 165 - 7.5\sqrt{x}$ and $P(0) = -87$. State the profit equation.

Answer: $P(x) = 165x - 5x^{\frac{3}{2}} - 87$

57. If the equation for the marginal revenue is $R'(x) = 13 + 0.62x$ and $R(0) = 0$, what is the revenue equation?

Answer: $R(x) = 13x + 0.31x^2$

58. Write the differential equation that describes this sentence: "The rate of change of y with respect to x is 7.3 less than the product of y^2 and $\sqrt{x}$." You need not solve it.

Answer: $\frac{dy}{dx} = y^2\sqrt{x} - 7.3$

59. Write a differential equation that describes this sentence: "x times the rate of change of y with respect to x is 8.4 more than $\sqrt{y}$." You need not solve it.

Answer: $x \cdot \frac{dy}{dx} = \sqrt{y} + 8.4$

60. Write a differential equation that describes this sentence: "The growth of the amount (A) of money in an account with respect to time (t) is proportional to the amount present." You need not solve it.

Answer: $\frac{dA}{dt} = kA$

61. Write a differential equation that describes this sentence: "The marginal price (P) at x units of demand is proportional to the price." You need not solve it.

Answer: $\frac{dP}{dx} = kP$

62. The annual sales (S) of a company with respect to time (t) in years satisfy the differential equation $\frac{dS}{dt} = \frac{S}{t(t+1)}$. Show that $S(t) = \frac{Ct}{t+1}$ is the general solution.

Answer: $\frac{dS}{dt} = \frac{C(t+1) - Ct}{(t+1)^2} = \frac{C}{(t+1)^2} = \frac{Ct}{t+1} \cdot \frac{1}{t(t+1)} = \frac{S}{t(t+1)}$

63. The annual sales S of a new company are expected to grow at a rate proportional to the difference between the sales and an upper limit of $35 million. State the differential equation that models this situation. You need not solve it.

Answer: $\frac{dS}{dt} = k(35 - S)$

Section 9.2 Further Applications of Differential Equations: Three Models of Growth

MULTIPLE CHOICE 9.2

[c] 64. Determine the type of differential equation $y' = 0.04y(10 - y)$.

a. unlimited growth b. limited growth c. logistical growth d. none of these

[b] 65. Determine the type of differential equation $y' = 200(1 - y)$.

a. unlimited growth b. limited growth c. logistical growth d. none of these

[d] 66. Determine the type of differential equation $y' = y^3(10 - y)$.

a. unlimited growth b. limited growth c. logistical growth d. none of these

[a] 67. Determine the type of differential equation $y' = 0.02y$.

a. unlimited growth b. limited growth c. logistical growth d. none of these

[b] 68. Determine the type of differential equation $y' = 0.09(50 - y)$.

a. unlimited growth b. limited growth c. logistical growth d. none of these

[c] 69. Find the solution y(t) by recognizing the differential equation $y' = -\frac{y}{3}$ with initial condition y(0) = 10 as determining unlimited, limited or logistical growth, and then determining the constants.

a. $y = 10\left[1 - e^{-\frac{1}{3}t}\right]$ b. $y = 10e^{-3t}$ c. $y = 10e^{-\frac{1}{3}t}$ d. $y = -\frac{1}{3}e^{-10t}$

[a] 70. Find the solution y(t) by recognizing the differential equation $y' = 0.05y$ with initial condition y(0) = 15 as determining unlimited, limited or logistical growth, and then determining the constants.

a. $y = 15e^{0.05t}$ b. $y = 15e^{-0.05t}$ c. $y = 15(1 - e^{-0.05t})$ d. $y = 0.05e^{15t}$

[d] 71. Find the solution y(t) by recognizing the differential equation $\frac{y'}{3} = 0.02y$ with initial condition y(0) = 6 as determining unlimited, limited or logistical growth, and then determining the constants.

a. $y = 6(1 - e^{-0.06t})$ b. $y = 6e^{0.02t}$ c. $y = 0.06e^{-6t}$ d. $y = 6e^{0.06t}$

[c] 72. Find the solution y(t) by recognizing the differential equation $y' = 5(20 - y)$ with initial condition $y(0) = 0$ as determining unlimited, limited or logistical growth, and then determining the constants.

a. $y = 5\left(1 - e^{-20t}\right)$ b. $y = 20\left(1 - e^{5t}\right)$ c. $y = 20\left(1 - e^{-5t}\right)$ d. $y = 5\left(1 - e^{20t}\right)$

[a] 73. Find the solution y(t) by recognizing the differential equation $\frac{y'}{0.2} = 5 - y$ with initial condition $y(0) = 0$ as determining unlimited, limited or logistical growth, and then determining the constants.

a. $y = 5\left(1 - e^{-0.2t}\right)$ b. $y = 5\left(1 - e^{0.2t}\right)$ c. $y = 0.2\left(1 - e^{-5t}\right)$ d. $y = 0.2e^{5t}$

[c] 74. Find the solution y(t) by recognizing the differential equation $y' = 36 - 9y$ with initial condition $y(0) = 0$ as determining unlimited, limited or logistical growth, and then determining the constants.

a. $y = 9\left(1 - e^{-4t}\right)$ b. $y = 4\left(1 - e^{9t}\right)$ c. $y = 4\left(1 - e^{-9t}\right)$ d. $y = 9\left(1 - e^{4t}\right)$

[c] 75. Find the solution y(t) by recognizing the differential equation $y' = 2y(50 - y)$ with initial condition $y(0) = 0$ as determining unlimited, limited or logistical growth, and then determining the constants.

a. $y = \frac{50}{1 - 4e^{100t}}$ b. $y = 50\left(1 - e^{-2t}\right)$ c. $y = \frac{50}{1 + 4e^{-100t}}$ d. $y = \frac{50}{1 + 10e^{-100t}}$

[b] 76. Which of the following represents the solution of $\frac{dA}{dt} = rA$ and $A(0) = P$?

a. $A = Pe^{-rt}$ b. $A = Pe^{rt}$ c. $A = \frac{rA^2}{2} + P$ d. $A = \ln(P)\, e^{rt}$

[d] 77. If $1000 is invested at 7% compounded continuously, how much is in the account after 8 years?

a. $2130 b. $1950 c. $1839 d. $1751

[a] 78. What would be the necessary initial investment if $20,000 is needed in an account that has a continuously compounding interest rate of 9.5%? The account has a term of 10 years.

a. $7735 b. $8182 c. $8466 d. $9026

[d] 79. A person opens an account with $4675 and will add $3650 to the account at the end of each year. The account pays 4.5% compounded continuously. How much will be in the account after 15 years?

a. $83,645 b. $54,960 c. $59,425 d. $87,376

[d] 80. A bank account pays 5% compounded continuously; $6000 is initially invested, and $500 is deposited at the end of each year. How much is in the account after 30 years?

a. $49,028 b. $52,905 c. $56,890 d. $61,707

[b] 81. A retirement plan pays 6.5% compounded continuously; $1750 is initially invested, and $1550 is deposited at the end of each year. How much money is in the plan after 25 years?

a. $89,803 b. $106,142 c. $105,766 d. $140,320

[a] 82. A retirement plan pays 6.5% compounded continuously; $1750 is initially invested, and $1550 is deposited at the end of each year. How long will it take for the plan to have a value of $85,000?

a. 22.3 years b. 26.1 years c. 21.1 years d. 18.1 years

[b] 83. Given the logistic growth solution $y = \frac{2000}{1+Ce^{-2000kt}}$, solve for C and k if y(0) = 80 and y(10) = 625.

a. C = 80, k = 0.0019 b. C = 24, k = 0.000119 c. C = 79, k = 0.000119 d. C = 79, k = 0.0019

[a] 84. Eighty frogs are placed in a pond that can support at most 1000 frogs. After 5 months, the frog population is 175. Obtain a formula that gives the frog population y at any time t, according to logistic growth.

a. $y = \frac{1000}{1+11.5e^{-0.178t}}$ b. $y = \frac{1000}{1+79e^{-0.892t}}$ c. $y = \frac{1000}{1+79e^{-0.178t}}$ d. $y = \frac{1000}{1+11.5e^{-0.892t}}$

[c] 85. Eighty frogs are placed in a pond that can support at most 1000 frogs. After 5 months, the frog population is 175. What will the frog population be after 12 months?

a. 312 b. 198 c. 424 d. 290

SHORT ANSWER 9.2

86. Find the solution y(t) by recognizing the differential equation $y' = \frac{1}{2}y(2-y)$ with initial condition $y(0) = 1$ as determining unlimited, limited or logistical growth, and then determining the constants.

Answer: $y = \dfrac{2}{1+e^{-t}}$

87. Find the solution y(t) by recognizing the differential equation $y' = 4y - 12y^2$ with initial condition $y(0) = \frac{1}{9}$ as determining unlimited, limited or logistical growth, and then determining the constants.

Answer: $y = \dfrac{\frac{1}{3}}{1+2e^{-4t}} = \dfrac{1}{3+6e^{-4t}}$

88. The value of an investment increases so that its rate of growth is 7% of its value. The investment is originally worth $5,000.
   a. Write a differential equation that describes this growth.
   b. By identifying the differential equation as unlimited, limited, or logistic, write the solution, obtaining a formula for the value of the investment after t years.
   c. Use your formula to find the value of the investment after 10 years.

Answer: a. $y' = 0.07y$ b. $y = 5000e^{0.07t}$ c. $10,068.76

89. The value of an investment increases so that its rate of growth is 6% of its value. The investment is originally worth $8,000.
   a. Write a differential equation that describes this growth.
   b. By identifying the differential equation as unlimited, limited, or logistic, write the solution, obtaining a formula for the value of the investment after t years.
   c. Use your formula to find the value of the investment after 20 years.

Answer: a. $y' = 0.06y$ b. $y = 8000e^{0.06t}$ c. $25,560.94

90. The value of a home, originally worth $80,000 grows continually by 3% per year.
   a. Write a differential equation that describes this growth.
   b. By identifying the differential equation as unlimited, limited, or logistic, write the solution, obtaining a formula for the value of the home after t years.
   c. Use your formula to find the value of the home after 5 years.

Answer: a. $y' = 0.03y$ b. $y = 80{,}000e^{0.03t}$ c. $92,946.74

91. The value of a card collection initially worth $900 grows continuously by 5% per year.
   a. Write a differential equation with initial condition for this growth.
   b. By identifying the differential equation as one of the 3 growth models, write the solution, obtaining a formula for the value of the collection after t years.
   c. Use your formula to find the value of the collection after 20 years.

Answer: a. $y' = 0.05y$ b. $y = 900e^{0.05t}$ c. $2,446.45

92. Suppose that a person can memorize a maximum of 50 abstract symbols, and that the person can memorize 20 symbols in the first 30 minutes. The rate at which new symbols can be memorized is proportional to the distance below the maximum limit of 50.
   a. Write the differential equation that describes this growth.
   b. By identifying the differential equation as unlimited, limited, or logistic, write the solution, obtaining a formula for the number of symbols that can be memorized in the first t minutes.
   c. Use your formula to estimate the number of symbols that can be memorized in the first 60 minutes.

Answer: a. $y' = a(50 - y)$ b. $y = 50\left(1 - e^{-0.017t}\right)$ c. about 32 symbols

93. A computer manufacturer estimates that he can sell a maximum of 50,000 personal computers in a city. His total sales grow at a rate proportional to the distance below his upper limit. If after 10 months, his sales are 7,000, find a formula for the total sales after t months. Then use your answer to estimate the total sales at the end of 2 years.

Answer: $y' = a(50{,}000 - y)$; $y = 50{,}000\left(1 - e^{-0.015t}\right)$; about 15,116 sales

94. The band club needs to raise $10,000. Fundraisers estimate that the rate of contributions is proportional to the distance from the goal. If $1,500 is raised in the first week, find a formula for the amount raised in t weeks. How many weeks will it take to raise $5,000?

Answer: $y' = a(10{,}000 - y)$; $y = 10{,}000\left(1 - e^{-0.16252t}\right)$; about 4.3 weeks

95. Paul can memorize at most 50 state capitals. If he can memorize 10 state capitals in the first 30 minutes, find a formula for the number that can be memorized in t minutes. Use your answer to estimate how long it will take to memorize 40 state capitals.

Answer: $y = 50\left(1 - e^{-0.00744t}\right)$; about 216 minutes or 3 hours 36 minutes

96. An epidemic of Asian-B flu hits a city of 100,000 people. The epidemic begins with 50 cases, and grows to 1,200 cases in 10 days. The epidemic grows in proportion to the number of people already infected and to the distance below the maximum level of 100,000.
   a. Write the differential equation that describes this growth.
   b. By identifying the differential equation as unlimited, limited, or logistic, write the solution, obtaining a formula for the number of infected people after t days.
   c. Use your formula to estimate the size of the epidemic after 20 days.

Answer: a. $y' = ay(100{,}000 - y)$ b. $y = \dfrac{100{,}000}{1 + 1999e^{-0.319t}}$

c. about 22,773

97. Flu is spreading through a school at a rate proportional to the number of students already infected and the number of students who have not been infected yet. There are a maximum of 1,000 students in the school. If 5 students had the flu at the beginning of the outbreak and after 1 day, 10 students are infected, how many students will be infected after 7 days?

Answer: 400

98. The rate at which a rumor spread through a city is proportional to the product of the number of people who have not heard it and the number of people who have heard it. Suppose 200 people start a rumor and after 5 days, 400 people have heard it. If there are a total of 40,000 people in the city,
a. obtain an equation that will indicate the number of people who have heard the rumor after t days.
b. How long will it take before 5,000 people have heard the rumor?

Answer: a. $y = \dfrac{40{,}000}{1+199e^{-0.14t}}$ b. about 24 days

99. The rate at which a fruit fly colony is growing is proportional to both the population and the remaining room for population growth. The colony began with 4 flies. After 2 days there were 30 flies. The environment can support at most 2,000 flies.
a. Obtain an equation that will indicate the population of flies after t days.
b. How long will it take for the population to reach 1,000?

Answer: a. $y = \dfrac{2{,}000}{1+499e^{-1.014t}}$ b. approximately 6 days

100. Use the technique of separation of variables to show that $A = Pe^{rt}$ is the particular solution of $\dfrac{dA}{dt} = rA$ with $A(0) = P$.

Answer: $\int \dfrac{dA}{A} = \int r\,dt$

$\ln(A) = rt + C$

$A = e^{rt+C} = e^C \cdot e^{rt} = ke^{rt} = (0) = k = P$

$A = Pe^{rt}$

101. A person opens an account with $4675 and will add $3650 to the account at the end of each year. The account pays 4.5% compounded continuously. State the differential equation that models the growth of this investment.

Answer: $\dfrac{dA}{dt} = 0.045A + 3650$

102. A bank account pays 5% compounded continuously; $6000 is initially invested, and $500 is deposited at the end of each year. State the differential equation that models the growth of the account. You need not solve it.

Answer: $\dfrac{dA}{dt} = 0.05A + 500$

103. A retirement plan pays 6.5% compounded continuously; $1750 is initially invested, and $1550 is deposited at the end of each year. State the differential equation that models the growth of this plan.

Answer: $\frac{dA}{dt} = 0.065A + 1550$

104. Complete the following statement: In logistic growth, the rate of growth of a population is proportional to both

Answer: the population size and the remaining room for growth.

105. Eighty frogs are placed in a pond that can support at most 1000 frogs. After 5 months, the frog population is 175. State the differential equation that represents logistic growth, where y = population, t = time, and N = maximum population.

Answer: $\frac{dy}{dt} = ky(N - y)$

Section 9.3 First-Order Linear Differential Equations

MULTIPLE CHOICE 9.3

[c] 106. Solve the first-order linear differential equation: $y' + y = 3x - 5$.

a. $y = 3x - 8 + Ce^{x}$ b. $y = 3x - 4 + Ce^{-x}$ c. $y = 3x - 8 + Ce^{-x}$ d. $y = 3x + 8 + Ce^{-x}$

[a] 107. Solve the first-order linear differential equation: $y' - \frac{6}{x}y = x^4$.

a. $y = -x^5 + Cx^6$ b. $y = x^6 + Cx^5$ c. $y = x^5 + Cx^6$ d. $y = -x^6 + Cx^5$

[d] 108. Solve the first-order linear differential equation: $y' + 2y = 4$.

a. $y = 2 + 2e^{2x}$ b. $y = 2 + e^{-2x}$ c. $y = 4e^{2x}$ d. $y = 2 + 2e^{-2x}$

[d] 109. Solve the first-order linear differential equation: $xy' - 9y = x^5$.

a. $y = \frac{x^9}{4} + Cx^5$ b. $y = \frac{x^5}{4} + Cx^9$ c. $y = -\frac{x^9}{4} + Cx^5$ d. $y = -\frac{x^5}{4} + Cx^9$

[b] 110. Solve the first-order linear differential equation: $y' + 4xy = x^3$.

a. $y = \frac{1}{4}x^2 + \frac{1}{8} + Ce^{-2x^2}$ b. $y = \frac{1}{4}x^2 - \frac{1}{8} + Ce^{-2x^2}$

c. $y = \frac{1}{4}x^2 + Ce^{-2x^2}$ d. $y = \frac{1}{4}x^2 - \frac{1}{8} + Ce^{2x^2}$

[c] 111. Solve the first-order linear differential equation: $y' = \frac{2y}{x} + x + 1$.

a. $y = -x^3 + Cx^2$ b. $y = \frac{x^2 + C}{2 + \ln x^4}$ c. $y = x^2\ln x - x + Cx^2$ d. $y = 6x^2 + C$

[a] 112. Solve the first-order linear differential equation: $y' + 4y = \frac{4}{3}$.

a. $y = \frac{1}{3} + Ce^{-4x}$ b. $y = -\frac{1}{3} + Ce^{-4x}$ c. $y = \frac{1}{3} + Ce^{4x}$ d. $y = -\frac{1}{3} + Ce^{4x}$

[c] 113. Solve the first-order linear differential equation: $y' + 3y = e^{-2x}$.

a. $y = e^{2x} + Ce^{-3x}$ b. $y = Ce^{-2x} + e^{-3x}$ c. $y = e^{-2x} + Ce^{-3x}$ d. $y = Ce^{-3x}$

[b] 114. Solve the first-order linear differential equation: $y' + 2xy = 3x$.

a. $y = \frac{2}{3} + Ce^{-x^2}$ b. $y = \frac{3}{2} + Ce^{-x^2}$ c. $y = -\frac{3}{2} + Ce^{x^2}$ d. $y = \frac{3}{2} + Ce^{x^2}$

[b] 115. Solve the differential equation $y' = x(y + 1)$, with the initial condition $y(0) = 3$.

a. $y = 1 + 4e^{x^2}$ b. $y = -1 + 4e^{x^2}$ c. $y = -4 + e^{x^2}$ d. $y = -1 - 4e^{x^2}$

[d] 116. Solve the differential equation $y' - \frac{1}{x}y = x + 1$, with the initial condition $y(1) = 2$.

a. $y = x + \ln x + 1$ b. $y = -x + x \ln x + 1$ c. $y = x^2 + x \ln x$ d. $y = x(x + \ln x + 1)$

[a] 117. Solve the differential equation $y' + 5y = 20$, with the initial condition $y(0) = 2$.

a. $y = 4 - 2e^{-5x}$ b. $y = 2 - 4e^{-5x}$ c. $y = 4 - e^{-5x}$ d. $y = 4 + 2e^{5x}$

[c] 118. Solve the differential equation $y' + 2xy = 2x^3$, with the initial condition $y(0) = 1$.

a. $y = 2e^{x^2} + x^2 - 1$ b. $y = 2e^{-x^2} + x^2$ c. $y = 2e^{-x^2} + x^2 - 1$ d. $y = e^{-x^2} + x^2 + 1$

[c] 119. Stephanie creates an annuity by placing $165,000 into a bank account that pays 7.5% annual interest compounded continuously. At the end of each year, Stephanie receives $13,500 from the account. How much money is in the annuity after 10 years?

a. $142,561 b. $145,912 c. $148,245 d. $139,908

[b] 120. Stephanie creates an annuity by placing $165,000 into a bank account that pays 7.5% annual interest compounded continuously. At the end of each year, Stephanie receives $13,500 from the account. After how many years will the annuity be worthless?

a. 31.9 years b. 33.1 years c. 35.2 years d. 36.9 years

[a] 121. A retired couple stated an annuity by depositing $350,000 into a bank account that pays 8.5% annual interest compounded continuously. Each year the bank gives them a check for $35,000 from this account. What is the balance in the account at the end of 10 years?

a. $267,257 b. $250,000 c. $272,908 d. $259,208

[d] 122. A retired couple stated an annuity by depositing $350,000 into a bank account that pays 8.5% annual interest compounded continuously. Each year the bank gives them a check for $35,000 from this account. How long will this annuity last unit it becomes worthless?

a. 30 years b. 25.7 years c. 24.1 years d. 22.3 years

SHORT ANSWER 9.3

123. Solve the first-order linear differential equation: $y' + 3y = x + 2$.

Answer: $y = \frac{1}{9}(3x + 5 + Ce^{-3x})$

124. Solve the first-order linear differential equation: $y' + \left(\frac{x}{1+x^2}\right)y = -x$.

Answer: $y = -\frac{1}{3}(1+x^2) + C(1+x^2)^{-\frac{1}{2}}$

125. Solve the first-order linear differential equation: $y' - \frac{3}{x^2}y = \frac{1}{x^2}$.

Answer: $y = Ce^{-\frac{3}{x}} - \frac{1}{3}$

126. Solve the first-order linear differential equation: $y' + x^2y = x^2$.

Answer: $y = Ce^{-\frac{x^3}{3}} + 1$

127. Solve the first-order linear differential equation: $y' + \frac{4}{x}y = x^2 - 1$

Answer: $y = \frac{1}{7}x^3 - \frac{1}{5}x + \frac{C}{x^4}$

128. Solve the differential equation $y' + \frac{1}{x}y = 0$, with the initial condition $y(2) = 2$.

Answer: $y = \frac{4}{x}$

129. Solve the differential equation $y' + \frac{1}{x}y = \frac{1}{x}$, with the initial condition $y(1) = \frac{1}{5}$.

Answer: $y = 1 - \frac{4}{5x}$

130. Solve $y' + (2x - 1)y = 0$ by separation of variables and using an integrating factor.

Answer: $y = Ce^{x-x^2}$

131. Solve $y' + 6xy = 0$ with the initial condition $y(\pi) = 5$ by separation of variables and using an integrating factor.

Answer: $y = 5e^{-3(x^2-\pi^2)}$

132. Solve $y' + 2y \cot x = 0$ by separation of variables and using an integrating factor.

Answer: $y = C\sin^{-2}x$

133. Solve $y' + \left(\frac{e^x}{1+e^x}\right)y = 0$ by separation of variables and using an integrating factor.

Answer: $y = \frac{C}{e^x + 1}$

134. Solve $y' - (\sec x)\, y = 0$ by separation of variables and using an integrating factor.

Answer: $y = C(\sec x + \tan x)$

135. Stephanie creates an annuity by placing $165,000 into a bank account that pays 7.5% annual interest compounded continuously. At the end of each year, Stephanie receives $13,500 from the account. Write the differential equation that describes this situation.

Answer: $\frac{dA}{dt} = 0.075A - 13{,}500$

136. A retired couple stated an annuity by depositing $350,000 into a bank account that pays 8.5% annual interest compounded continuously. Each year the bank gives them a check for $35,000 from this account. Write a differential equation for this account where A is the amount of money in the account at time t, in years.

Answer: $\frac{dA}{dt} = 0.085A - 35{,}000$

Section 9.4 Approximate Solutions of Differential Equations: Euler's Method

MULTIPLE CHOICE 9.4

[c] 137. If the solution to $y' = \frac{2}{x}y + x^2$ passes through the point (–1, 4), what is the slope of the solution at that point?

a. –10 b. $\frac{31}{2}$ c. –7 d. 7

[d] 138. If the solution to $y' = 3x - \frac{1}{y}$ passes through the point (2, –1), what is the slope of the solution at that point?

a. 5 b. –5 c. $\frac{5}{2}$ d. 7

[c] 139. For the initial value problem $y' = \frac{5x}{y}$ with initial condition $y(2) = \frac{3}{2}$, state the initial point (x_0, y_0) and calculate the slope of the solution at this point.

a. $\left(2, \frac{3}{2}\right)$, slope = 15 b. $\left(\frac{3}{2}, 2\right)$, slope $= \frac{20}{3}$ c. $\left(2, \frac{3}{2}\right)$, slope $= \frac{20}{3}$ d. $\left(2, \frac{3}{2}\right)$, slope $= \frac{15}{4}$

[d] 140. Use Euler's method to obtain the approximate solution y(0.3) for $y' = x^2y$ with the initial condition y(0) = 2 on the interval [0, 0.3] using n = 3 segments. Round your approximations to 3 decimal places.

a. 2.089 b. 2.131 c. 2.002 d. 2.010

[a] 141. Use Euler's method to obtain the approximate solution y(0.6) for $y' = 2\sqrt{y} - 8x$ with the initial condition y(0) = 1 on the interval [0, 0.6] using n = 3 segments. Round your approximations to 2 decimal places.

a. 1.41 b. 2.38 c. 0.67 d. 3.16

[c] 142. Use Euler's method to obtain the approximate solution y(1) for y′ = 1 + y with the initial condition y(0) = 0 on the interval [0, 1] using n = 5 segments. Round your approximations to 2 decimal places.

a. 1.23 b. 0.65 c. 1.49 d. 1.08

[b] 143. Use Euler's method to obtain the approximate solution y(1) for y′ = y – 6x with initial condition y(0) = 1 on the interval [0, 1] using n = 5 segments. Round your approximations to 2 decimal places.

a. 0.44 b. –0.44 c. 0.82 d. –0.79

[c] 144. Use Euler's method to obtain the approximate solution y(0.2) for $y' = 2.5xy^2$ and y(0) = 1 on the interval [0, 0.2] using n = 2 segments. Round your approximations to two decimal places.

a. 1.01 b. 1.03 c. 1.025 d. 1.04

[c] 145. Use Euler's method to obtain the approximate solution y(0.2) for $y' = 2.5x^2y$ and y(0) = 1 on the interval [0, 0.2] using n = 2 segments.

a. 1.01 b. 1.003 c. 1.0025 d. 1.04

[a] 146. Use Euler's method to obtain the approximate solution y(0.3) for $y' = 0.2xy^2$ and y(0) = 1 on the interval [0, 0.3] using n = 3 segments.

a. 1.006 b. 1.0531 c. 1.1352 d. 1.1857

[d] 147. Use Euler's method to obtain the approximate solution y(0.3) for $y' = 2x^2y$ and y(0) = 1 on the interval [0, 0.3] using n = 3 segments.

a. 1.002 b. 1.00127 c. 1.00089 d. 1.01

[c] 148. Use Euler's method to obtain the approximate solution y(1) for $y' = 0.5x + y$ and y(0) = 1 on the interval [0, 1] using n = 5 segments. Round your approximations to two decimal places.

a. 2.32 b. 2.48 c. 2.73 d. 2.87

[a] 149. Use Euler's method to obtain the approximate solution y(1) for $y' = 5x - 2\sqrt{y}$ and y(0) = 3 on the interval [0, 1] using n = 5 segments. Round your approximations to two decimal places.

a. 1.82 b. 2.08 c. 2.39 d. 2.67

[b] 150. Use Euler's method to approximate y(1.4) for $y' = 4.3\sqrt{y} - 6.7x$ and y(1) = 2 on the interval [1, 1.4] using n = 2 segments.

a. 2.2993 b. 1.4462 c. 1.9420 d. 1.8762

[a] 151. Use Euler's method to approximate y(2) for $y' = 10x - 9\sqrt{y}$ and y(1) = 3 on the interval [1, 2] using n = 5 segments.

a. 3.35 b. 1.88 c. 4.70 d. 5.34

[d] 152. Approximate the solution y(0.5) to the differential equation $y' = y - 8x + 1$ and y(0) = 1 on the interval [0, 0.5] and n = 5 segments.

a. –0.05 b. 1.97 c. 0.05 d. 1.34

[b] 153. Use Euler's method to approximate y(0.4) for $y' = 0.2y$ and $y(0) = 1$ on the interval [0, 0.4] and $n = 2$ segments.

a. 1.0802 b. 1.0816 c. 1.0616 d. 1.04

[a] 154. Approximate the solution y(2.2) to the differential equation $y' = \frac{0.1}{y}$ and $y(2) = 3$ on the interval [2, 2.2] and $n = 2$ segments.

a. 3.0067 b. 3.0665 c. 3.6653 d. 3.9666

[c] 155. Use Euler's method to approximate y(1) for $y' = -2y$ and $y(0) = 3$ on the interval [0, 1] and $n = 5$ segments. Round your approximation to 2 decimal places.

a. 0.65 b. 3.77 c. 0.23 d. 1.80

[d] 156. Use Euler's method to approximate y(1) for $y' = y - 5x$ and $y(0) = 1$ on the interval [0, 1] and $n = 5$ segments. Round your approximation to 2 decimal places.

a. 0.66 b. 1.61 c. 1.29 d. 0.05

[a] 157. Use Euler's method to approximate y(1) for $y' = -\frac{x}{y}$ and $y(0) = 1$ on the interval [0, 1] and $n = 5$ segments. Round your approximation to 2 decimal places.

a. 0.52 b. 0.96 c. 0.11 d. 1.33

[b] 158. Use Euler's method to approximate y(1) for $y' = x + \sqrt{y}$ and $y(0) = 0$ on the interval [0, 1] and $n = 5$ segments.

a. 0.36 b. 0.64 c. 0.16 d. 0.81

[b] 159. Use Euler's method to approximate y(3) for the differential equation $y' = \frac{1}{y} + \frac{1}{x}$ where $y(1) = 1$ on the interval [1, 3] and $n = 5$ segments.

a. –0.227 b. 3.319 c. 5.955 d. 1.296

[d] 160. Use Euler's method to approximate y(1) for $y' = 2y - 10x + 1$ and $y(0) = 1$ on the interval [0, 1] and $n = 5$ segments. Round your approximation to two decimal places.

a. 0.78 b. 2.39 c. –1.55 d. 1.62

[a] 161. Approximate y(0.5) for the differential equation $y' = 2y - 10x + 1$, where $y(0) = 1$. Use Euler's method on the interval [0, 0.5] and n = 5 segments. Round your approximation to two decimal places.

a. 2.01 b. 1.56 c. 0.81 d. 1.77

[c] 162. The annual sales S (in thousands of dollars) of a company with respect to time t (in years) satisfy $\frac{dS}{dt} = 0.1\sqrt{S}(100 - \sqrt{S})$ and $S(0) = 50$. Use Euler's method on the interval [0, 5] and n = 5 segments to approximate S(5) to the nearest thousand dollars.

a. $197,000 b. $456,000 c. $658,000 d. $908,000

[a] 163. The annual sales S (in thousands of dollars) of a new company are expected to satisfy $\frac{dS}{dt} = S(2.1 - \sqrt{S})$. If $S(1) = 1.95$, use Euler's method on the interval [1, 3] and n = 6 segments to approximate the annual sales when t = 3.

a. $4052 b. $4321 c. $3504 d. $4762

[d] 164. The number of people N (in thousands) who have heard of a new product via radio advertising satisfies $\frac{dN}{dt} = 0.1N(10 - \sqrt{N})$ and $N(0) = 1$. Approximate N(5) using Euler's method on the interval [0, 5] and n = 5 segments.

a. 7620 b. 11,986 c. 14,671 d. 18,649

[b] 165. Assume that the rate at which a rumor spreads through a town satisfies $\frac{dN}{dt} = 0.1\sqrt{N}(10 - \sqrt{N})$, where N (in thousands) is the number of people who have heard the rumor at time t (days). If $N(0) = 1$, use Euler's method on the interval [0, 4] and n = 4 segments to approximate N(4).

a. 3991 b. 6213 c. 7480 d. 8107

[b] 166. A disease spreads through a city at the rate $\frac{dN}{dt} = 0.1N^{\frac{2}{3}}(100 - N^{\frac{1}{3}})$, where N is the number of people with the disease at time t. If $N(0) = 1000$, approximate N(4) with Euler's method on the interval [0, 4] and n = 4 segments.

a. 6617 b. 7567 c. 8571 d. 9073

[c] 167. Assume that the rate of population growth of tsetse flies is given by $\frac{dP}{dt} = P$, where P is the population (in thousands) and t is the time in days. If the population starts at 1000 [P(0) = 1], how many tsetse flies will there be after 2 days? Approximate with Euler's method on the interval [0, 2] and n = 10 segments.

a. 7389 b. 7057 c. 6191 d. 6430

[d] 168. Use Euler's method on the interval [0, 0.4] and n = 4 segments to approximate y(0.4) for $y' = \frac{1}{1+x^2} - 2y^2$ and y(0) = 0.

a. 0.2679 b. 0.1985 c. 0.2571 d. 0.3605

SHORT ANSWER 9.4

169. For the initial value problem $y' = y - x$ with initial condition $y(0) = 2$, calculate the Euler approximation for the solution on the interval [0, 0.5] using n = 5 segments. Draw the graph of your approximation. Carry out the calculations by hand with the aid of a calculator, rounding to 3 decimal places. Your answer may differ slightly due to rounding.

Answer:

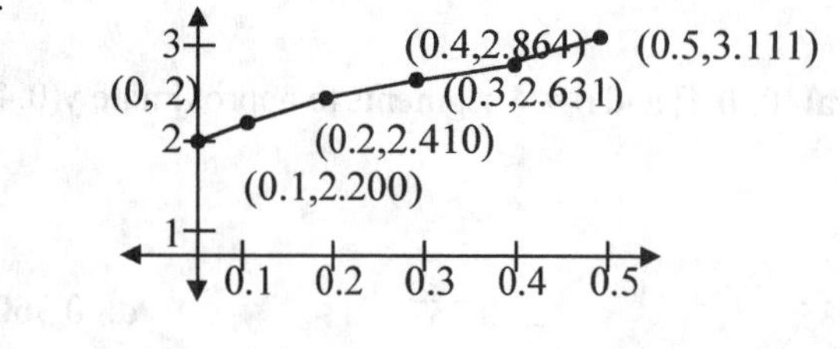

170. For the initial value problem $y' = 1 + y^2$ with initial condition $y(0) = 0$, calculate the Euler approximation for the solution on the interval [0, 0.5] using n = 5 segments. Draw the graph of your approximation. Carry out the calculations by hand with the aid of a calculator, rounding to 3 decimal places. Your answer may differ slightly due to rounding.

Answer:

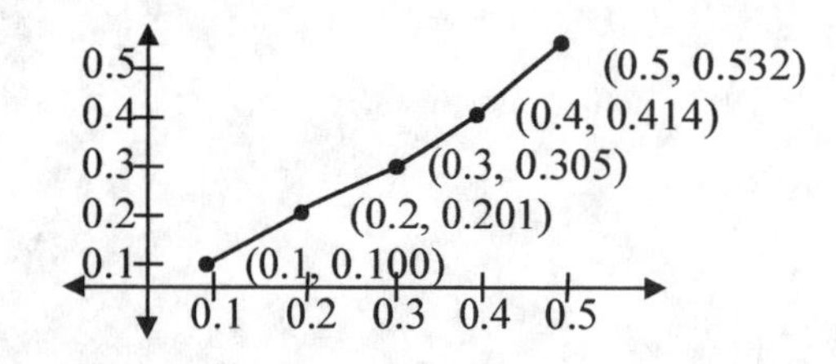

171. For the initial value problem $y' = y$ with initial condition $y(0) = 1$, calculate the Euler approximation for the solution on the interval [0, 0.5] using n = 5 segments. Draw the graph of your approximation. Carry out the calculations by hand with the aid of a calculator, rounding to 3 decimal places. Your answer may differ slightly due to rounding.

Answer:

172. For the initial value problem $y' = e^{-y}$ with initial condition $y(0) = 0$, calculate the Euler approximation for the solution on the interval [0, 0.5] using n = 5 segments. Draw the graph of your approximation. Carry out the calculations by hand with the aid of a calculator, rounding to 3 decimal places. Your answer may differ slightly due to rounding.

Answer:

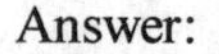

173. For the initial value problem $y' = 4x^3$ with initial condition $y(0) = 0$, calculate the Euler approximation for the solution on the interval [0, 0.5] using n = 5 segments. Draw the graph of your approximation. Carry out the calculations by hand with the aid of a calculator, rounding to 3 decimal places. Your answer may differ slightly due to rounding.

Answer:

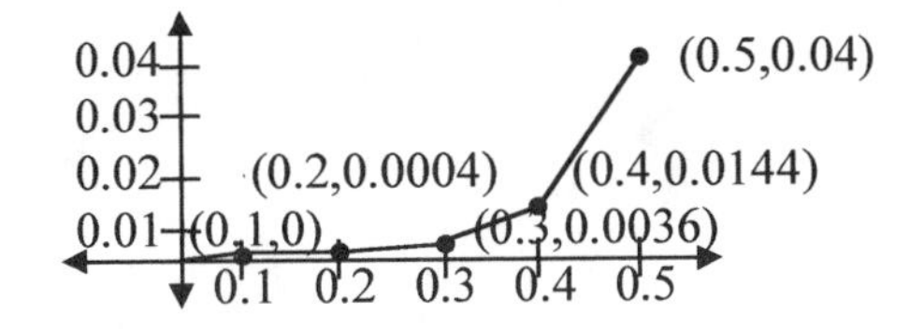

174. Use Euler's method to obtain the approximate solution y(1) for $y' = y - x$ with the initial condition $y(0) = 2$ on the interval [0, 1] using n = 4 segments. Round your approximation to 3 decimal places.

Answer: 4.441

175. Use Euler's method to obtain the approximate solution y(0.4) for $y' = -y + x + 2$ with the initial condition $y(0) = 2$ on the interval [0, 0.4] using n = 4 segments. Round your approximation to 3 decimal places.

Answer: 2.056

176. Use Euler's method to obtain the approximate solution y(0.4) for $y' = -y$ with the initial condition $y(0) = 1$ on the interval [0, 0.4] using n = 4 segments. Round your approximation to 3 decimal places.

Answer: 0.656

Chapter 9 – Graphing Calculator

Differential Equations

Section 9.3 First-Order Linear Differential Equations

1. A bank pays 5% compounded continuously. If $6,000 is initially invested and $500 is deposited at the end of each year,
   a. find the differential equation that models the growth of the savings plan.
   b. solve the equation, use your graphing calculator to graph the solution and use the graph to determine approximately how much is in the account after 30 years.

   Answer: a. $\frac{dy}{dt} = 0.05y + 500$
   b. $61,707

2. Mike creates an annuity by placing $50,000 into a bank account that pays 8% annual interest compounded continuously. At the end of each year, Mike receives $6,000 from the account.
   a. find the differential equation that describes this situation.
   b. solve the equation, use your graphing calculator to graph the solution and use the graph to determine after how many years the annuity will be worthless.

   Answer: a. $\frac{dy}{dt} = 0.08y - 6000$
   b. 13.7 years

3. Forty frogs are placed in a pond that can support at most 1,000 frogs. After 6 months, the grog population is 100. The formula that gives the frog population y at any time t, according to the logistical growth model, is $y = \frac{1000}{1 + 24e^{-0.163t}}$. Using your graphing calculator, graph this function and use the graph to determine the frog population after 12 months.

   Answer: 228

4. If an ice cube tray filled with water at room temperature (70°F) is placed into a freezer at 20°F, the differential equation that applies Newton's Law of cooling for this situation is $\frac{dT}{dt} = k(T - 20)$ where T is the temperature of the water after it has been in the freezer for t minutes. The solution of this differential equation, assuming that after 15 minutes the temperature of the water is 45°F, is $T = 50e^{-0.046t} + 20$. Use your graphing calculator to sketch this solution and use the graph to determine how long it will take for the water to freeze (32°F).

   Answer: 31 minutes approximately

5. The population of a certain city increases at a rate proportional to the number of inhabitants at any time.
   a. state the differential equation that models this situation.
   b. solve this differential equation if the city was originally 10,000 and it doubled in 15 years.
   c. using your graphing calculator, graph this solution and use the graph to determine how long it will take for the city's population to triple.

Answer: a. $\frac{dy}{dt} = ky$

b. $y = 10{,}000e^{0.0462t}$

c. 23.8 years

Section 9.4 Approximate Solutions of Differential Equations: Euler's Method

6. For the initial value problem $y' = y$ with initial condition $y(0) = 1$,
   a. Use a graphing calculator with an Euler approximation program to find the estimate for y(1). Use the interval [0, 1] with n = 100 segments.
   b. Solve the differential equation and initial condition EXACTLY by separating variables or using an integration factor.
   c. Evaluate the solution that you found in part b at x = 1. Compare this ACTUAL value of y(1) with the estimate for y(1) that you found in part a.

   Answer: a. 2.7048 b. $y = e^x$ c. actual y(1) = 2.7183

7. For the initial value problem $y' = -y + x + 2$ with initial condition $y(0) = 2$,
   a. Use a graphing calculator with an Euler approximation program to find the estimate for y(1). Use the interval [0, 1] with n = 100 segments.
   b. Solve the differential equation and initial condition EXACTLY by separating variables or using an integration factor.
   c. Evaluate the solution that you found in part b at x = 1. Compare this ACTUAL value of y(1) with the estimate for y(1) that you found in part a.

   Answer: a. 2.366 b. $y = e^{-x} + x + 1$ c. actual y(1) = 2.3679

8. For the initial value problem $y' = y - x$ with initial condition $y(0) = 2$,
   a. Use a graphing calculator with an Euler approximation program to find the estimate for y(1). Use the interval [0, 1] with n = 100 segments.
   b. Solve the differential equation and initial condition EXACTLY by separating variables or using an integration factor.
   c. Evaluate the solution that you found in part b at x = 1. Compare this ACTUAL value of y(1) with the estimate for y(1) that you found in part a.

   Answer: a. 4.7048 b. $y = e^x + x + 1$ c. actual y(1) = 4.7183

9. For the initial value problem $y' = 4x^3$ with initial condition $y(0) = 0$,
   a. Use a graphing calculator with an Euler approximation program to find the estimate for y(1). Use the interval [0, 1] with n = 100 segments.
   b. Solve the differential equation and initial condition EXACTLY by separating variables or using an integration factor.
   c. Evaluate the solution that you found in part b at x = 1. Compare this ACTUAL value of y(1) with the estimate for y(1) that you found in part a.

   Answer: a. 0.9801 b. $y = x^4$ c. actual y(1) = 1.000

10. For the initial value problem $y' = y^2 + 1$ with initial condition $y(0) = 0$,
    a. Use a graphing calculator with an Euler approximation program to find the estimate for y(1). Use the interval [0, 1] with n = 100 segments.
    b. Solve the differential equation and initial condition EXACTLY by separating variables or using an integration factor.
    c. Evaluate the solution that you found in part b at x = 1. Compare this ACTUAL value of y(1) with the estimate for y(1) that you found in part a.

    Answer: a. 1.537 b. $y = \tan x$ c. actual y(1) = 1.5574

Chapter 10

Sequences and Series

Section 10.1 Geometric Series

MULTIPLE CHOICE 10.1

[c] 1. Find the sum: $\sum_{i=1}^{4} \frac{i+1}{i+2}$.

a. $\frac{131}{6}$ b. $\frac{31}{20}$ c. $\frac{61}{20}$ d. $\frac{133}{60}$

[a] 2. Find the sum $\sum_{i=1}^{5} (-1)^i i^i$.

a. –2,893 b. 3,413 c. –3,413 d. 2,893

[b] 3. Write the infinite series in sigma notation: $\frac{1}{5} - \frac{2}{5} + \frac{3}{5} - \frac{4}{5} + \frac{5}{5} - \ldots$

a. $\sum_{n=1}^{\infty} \frac{(-1)^n n}{5}$ b. $\sum_{n=1}^{\infty} \frac{(-1)^{n+1} n}{5}$ c. $\sum_{n=1}^{\infty} \frac{n}{5}$ d. $\sum_{n=1}^{\infty} \frac{(-n)^n}{5}$

[a] 4. Write the infinite series in sigma notation: $\frac{1}{2} + \frac{2}{3} + \frac{3}{4} + \frac{4}{5} + \ldots$

a. $\sum_{n=1}^{\infty} \frac{n}{n+1}$ b. $\sum_{n=0}^{\infty} \frac{n}{n+1}$ c. $\sum_{n=1}^{\infty} \frac{n}{2n}$ d. $\sum_{n=1}^{\infty} \frac{n+1}{n+2}$

[d] 5. Find the sum of the finite geometric series: $4 + 4 \cdot 2 + 4 \cdot 2^2 + 4 \cdot 2^3 + 4 \cdot 2^4 + \ldots + 4 \cdot 2^8$

a. 1,024 b. 1,020 c. 255 d. 2,044

[b] 6. Find the sum of the finite geometric series: $\frac{1}{3} + \frac{1}{3} \cdot 4 + \frac{1}{3} \cdot 4^2 + \frac{1}{3} \cdot 4^3 + \frac{1}{3} \cdot 4^4 + \ldots + \frac{1}{3} \cdot 4^{10}$

a. $116{,}508\frac{1}{3}$ b. $466{,}033\frac{2}{3}$ c. $466{,}032\frac{2}{3}$ d. $116{,}507\frac{1}{3}$

[d] 7. Determine if the infinite geometric series, $30-\frac{30}{4}+\frac{30}{16}-\frac{30}{64}+\frac{30}{256}-\ldots$, converges or diverges. If it converges, then find the sum.

a. diverges b. converges to 40 c. converges to 37.5 d. converges to 24

[a] 8. Determine if the infinite geometric series, $\frac{1}{10}-\frac{2}{10}+\frac{4}{10}-\frac{8}{10}+\frac{16}{10}-\frac{32}{10}+\ldots$, converges or diverges. If it converges, then find the sum.

a. diverges b. converges to $-\frac{1}{10}$ c. converges to $\frac{1}{5}$ d. converges to -10

[c] 9. Determine if the infinite geometric series, $5-\frac{5}{3}+\frac{5}{9}-\frac{5}{27}+\frac{5}{81}-\ldots$, converges or diverges. If it converges, then find the sum.

a. diverges b. converges to $\frac{15}{2}$ c. converges to $\frac{15}{4}$ d. converges to 15

[b] 10. Determine if the infinite geometric series, $\frac{2}{3}+\frac{2^2}{3^2}+\frac{2^3}{3^3}+\frac{2^4}{3^4}+\frac{2^5}{3^5}+\ldots$, converges or diverges. If it converges, then find the sum.

a. diverges b. converges to 2 c. converges to $\frac{2}{5}$ d. converges to $\frac{25}{4}$

[a] 11. Determine if the infinite geometric series, $\frac{5}{2}+\frac{5^2}{2^3}+\frac{5^3}{2^5}+\frac{5^4}{2^7}+\frac{5^5}{2^9}+\ldots$, converges or diverges. If it converges, then find the sum.

a. diverges b. converges to 100 c. converges to $\frac{199}{100}$ d. converges to $\frac{100}{199}$

[d] 12. Determine if the infinite geometric series, $\sum_{i=0}^{\infty}\left(-\frac{99}{100}\right)^i$, converges or diverges. If it converges, then find the sum.

a. diverges b. converges to 100 c. converges to $\frac{199}{100}$ d. converges to $\frac{100}{199}$

[a] 13. Determine if the infinite geometric series, $\sum_{i=0}^{\infty}\left(\frac{100}{99}\right)^i$, converges or diverges. If it converges, then find the sum.

a. diverges
b. converges to –99
c. converges to $\frac{99}{100}$
d. converges to $\frac{1}{99}$

[b] 14. Determine if the infinite geometric series, $\sum_{i=0}^{\infty} 20(3)^{-i}$, converges or diverges. If it converges, then find the sum.

a. diverges
b. converges to 30
c. converges to $\frac{3}{2}$
d. converges to 15

[b] 15. Find the value of the repeating decimal: $0.232323\ldots = 0.\overline{23}$.

a. $\frac{23}{999}$
b. $\frac{23}{99}$
c. $\frac{23}{9}$
d. $\frac{232}{99}$

[a] 16. Find the value of the repeating decimal: $0.123123123\ldots = 0.\overline{123}$.

a. $\frac{41}{333}$
b. $\frac{123}{99}$
c. $\frac{123}{9{,}999}$
d. $\frac{123}{1{,}000}$

[c] 17. Find the value of the repeating decimal: $0.\overline{4}$.

a. $\frac{4}{11}$
b. $\frac{4}{10}$
c. $\frac{4}{9}$
d. $\frac{9}{4}$

[a] 18. You accept a job with a salary of $30,000 for the first year. Suppose during the next 14 years, you receive a 5% raise each year. What would be your total compensation over the 15-year period?

a. $647,356.91
b. $439,005.87
c. $1,247,356.00
d. $521,419.18

[b] 19. Find the sum of the first seven terms of the following finite geometric series 2 + 1 + ½ + …

a. $4\frac{1}{32}$
b. $\frac{127}{32}$
c. $3\frac{63}{64}$
d. $\frac{125}{32}$

[a] 20. Find the sum of the first six terms of the following finite geometric series 4 + 3 + 9/4 + …

a. $\frac{3367}{256}$
b. $\frac{3375}{256}$
c. $\frac{53{,}968}{4096}$
d. $\frac{53{,}936}{4096}$

[d] 21. Find the sum of the first seven terms of the following finite geometric series 2 – 1 + ½ + ...

a. $\frac{129}{288}$ b. $\frac{127}{96}$ c. $\frac{127}{288}$ d. $\frac{129}{96}$

[a] 22. Find the sum of the first seven terms of the following finite geometric series $1-\frac{1}{3}+\frac{1}{9}-\ldots$

a. $\frac{547}{729}$ b. $\frac{547}{1458}$ c. $\frac{1095}{1458}$ d. $\frac{549}{729}$

[a] 23. Which of the following must be true for the infinite series $2-\frac{3}{2}+\frac{3}{4}-\ldots$?

a. The series is not geometric. b. The series converges.

c. The series diverges. d. The next term is $-\frac{3}{8}$

[a] 24. Determine whether the following series converges or diverges. If it converges, state the number to which it converges. $5-\frac{5}{3}+\frac{5}{9}-\ldots$

a. $\frac{15}{2}$ b. $\frac{15}{4}$ c. $\frac{3}{20}$ d. diverges

[d] 25. Determine whether the following series converges or diverges. If it converge, state the number to which it converges. $\frac{3}{2}-\frac{9}{4}+\frac{27}{8}-\ldots$

a. 1 b. $\frac{2}{3}$ c. $\frac{5}{2}$ d. diverges

[d] 26. A savings account is started with $175, and every month the saver adds $175 to the account. If the annual interest rate if 5.5% compounded monthly, how much is in the account at the end of 4 ½ years?

a. $9821.39 b. $10,193.56 c. $10632.02 d. $10,743.57

[a] 27. A savings account is started with $625, and every 3 months the saver adds $625 to the account. If the annual interest rate is 7.25% compounded quarterly, how much is in the account at the end of 3 years and 3 months?

a. $9234.46 b. $9090.15 c. $9186.16 d. $9302.17

[c] 28. A ball is dropped from 50 feet above the ground, and each time it bounces, it rises to one-half of its preceding height. If it bounces indefinitely, what is the total distance it travels?

a. 92.5 feet b. 87.5 feet c. 100 feet d. 120 feet

[b] 29. A ball is dropped from 50 feet above the ground and bounces 40 feet and then 32 feet. If this continues indefinitely, what is the total distance the ball travels?

a. 225 feet b. 250 feet c. 280 feet d. 320 feet

[a] 30. Assume that $10 billion tax cut is initiated and that people spend 80% of that extra money and save 20%. Use the multiplier effect to calculate the total resulting economic activity.

a. $40 billion b. $25 billion c. $37.5 billion d. $32 billion

[d] 31. Suppose you put one penny in a piggy bank on the first day, three pennies on the second day, and nine pennies on the third day, and continued tripling the amount for a total of 2 weeks. How much money would be in the piggy bank at the end of that time?

a. $993.44 b. $4620.84 c. $13,092.44 d. $23,914.84

SHORT ANSWER 10.1

32. Write out the following series: $\sum_{i=1}^{6} \frac{i}{(1+i)^2}$.

Answer: $\frac{1}{4}+\frac{2}{9}+\frac{3}{16}+\frac{4}{25}+\frac{5}{36}+\frac{6}{49}$

33. Write out the following series: $\sum_{i=1}^{5} (-1)^{i-1}\left(-\frac{1}{2}\right)^{i}$.

Answer: $-\frac{1}{2}-\frac{1}{4}-\frac{1}{8}-\frac{1}{16}-\frac{1}{32}$

34. Write the infinite series in sigma notation: $-1+\frac{1}{8}-\frac{1}{27}+\frac{1}{64}-\ldots$

Answer: $\sum_{n=1}^{\infty} \frac{(-1)^n}{n^3}$

35. Write the infinite series in sigma notation: $\frac{2}{1}+\frac{4}{4}+\frac{6}{9}+\frac{8}{16}+\frac{10}{25}+\frac{12}{36}+\ldots$

Answer: $\sum_{n=1}^{\infty} \frac{2n}{n^2} = \sum_{n=1}^{\infty} \frac{2}{n}$

36. Find the sum of the finite geometric series: $5-5\cdot 3+5\cdot 3^2-5\cdot 3^3+5\cdot 3^4-5\cdot 3^5+\ldots+5\cdot 3^8$

Answer: 24,605

37. Find the sum of the finite geometric series: $2-2\cdot 6+2\cdot 6^2-2\cdot 6^3+2\cdot 6^4-2\cdot 6^5$

Answer: –13,330

38. Determine if the infinite geometric series, $\frac{1}{3}+\frac{5}{3}+\frac{25}{3}+\frac{125}{3}+\frac{625}{3}+\ldots$, converges or diverges. If it converges, then find the sum.

Answer: diverges

39. Determine if the infinite geometric series, $\frac{2}{1}-\frac{2}{6}+\frac{2}{36}-\frac{2}{216}+\ldots$, converges or diverges. If it converges, then find the sum.

    Answer: converges to $\frac{12}{7}$

40. Determine if the infinite geometric series, $\frac{1}{4}+\frac{1}{4^3}+\frac{1}{4^5}+\frac{1}{4^7}+\frac{1}{4^9}+\ldots$, converges or diverges. If it converges, then find the sum.

    Answer: converges to $\frac{4}{15}$

41. Determine if the infinite geometric series, $\frac{2}{3}+\frac{2^3}{3^2}+\frac{2^5}{3^3}+\frac{2^7}{3^4}+\frac{2^9}{3^5}+\ldots$, converges or diverges. If it converges, then find the sum.

    Answer: diverges

42. Determine if the infinite geometric series, $\sum_{n=1}^{\infty} e^n$, converges or diverges. If it converges, then find the sum.

    Answer: diverges

43. Determine if the infinite geometric series, $\sum_{n=0}^{\infty} 15\left(\frac{1}{e}\right)^n$, converges or diverges. If it converges, then find the sum.

    Answer: converges to $\frac{15e}{e-1}$

44. Determine if the infinite geometric series, $\sum_{i=0}^{\infty} \frac{2\cdot 3^i}{5^i}$, converges or diverges. If it converges, then find the sum.

    Answer: converges to 5

45. Determine if the infinite geometric series, $\sum_{i=0}^{\infty} \left(\frac{1}{1.001}\right)^{-i}$, converges or diverges. If it converges, then find the sum.

    Answer: diverges

46. Determine if the infinite geometric series, $\sum_{i=0}^{\infty} \frac{2^i}{3^{i+1}}$, converges or diverges. If it converges, then find the sum.

Answer: converges to 1

47. Find the value of the repeating decimal: $2.\overline{26}$.

Answer: $\frac{224}{99}$

48. Find the value of the repeating decimal: $6.874187418741 = 6.\overline{8741}$.

Answer: $\frac{68{,}735}{9{,}999}$

49. Find the value of the repeating decimal: $0.123451234512345 = 0.\overline{12345}$.

Answer: $\frac{4{,}115}{33{,}333}$

50. Suppose you invested $10,000 at the end of each year for 8 years in an account that paid interest at 5% compounded annually. Use a geometric series to determine how much money you would have in the account at the end of 8 years.

Answer: $95,491.09

51. A force is being applied to a particle, which moves in a straight line in such a way that after each second the particle moves only one-half the distance that it moved in the preceding second. If the particle moved 10 feet in the first second, how far did it move altogether?

Answer: 20 feet

52. A ball is dropped from a height of 24 feet. Each time it drops x feet, it rebounds $\frac{2}{3}x$ feet. Find the total distance traveled by the ball.

Answer: 120 feet

53. Suppose you put one nickel in a piggy bank on the first day, 3 nickels the second day, 9 nickels the third day and continued tripling the number of nickels each day for a total of 1 week. How much money would be in the piggy bank at the end of that time?

Answer: $54.65

54. What is the ratio, r, in the geometric series $5-\frac{9}{2}+\frac{81}{20}-\ldots$? Does the series converge?

Answer: $r=-\frac{9}{10}$; the series converges because $|r|<1$

55. Find the sum of the first six terms of the following finite geometric series $1-\frac{5}{4}+\frac{25}{10}-\ldots$.

Answer: $-\frac{1281}{1024}$

56. Determine r for the geometric series $\frac{3}{2}-\frac{21}{16}+\frac{147}{128}-\ldots$, and determine whether the series converges.

Answer: $r=-\frac{7}{8}$; because $|r|<1$, the series converges.

57. Determine r for the geometric series $\frac{10}{3}-1+\frac{3}{10}-\ldots$. Does the series converge?

Answer: $r=-\frac{3}{10}$; because $|r|<1$, the series converges.

58. Determine r for the geometric series $2-3+\frac{9}{2}-\ldots$. Does the series converge?

Answer: $r=-\frac{3}{2}$; because $|r|>1$, the series diverges.

Section 10.2 Taylor Polynomials

MULTIPLE CHOICE 10.2

[a] 59. Find the fourth non-zero term of the Taylor polynomial at x = 0 for f(x) = ln(1 + x).

a. $-\frac{x^4}{4}$ b. $\frac{x^3}{3}$ c. $\frac{x^4}{4}$ d. $-\frac{x^4}{4!}$

[b] 60. Find the third non-zero term of the Taylor polynomial at x = 0 for $f(x) = \frac{1}{(1+x)^2}$.

a. $-3x^2$ b. $3x^2$ c. $-4x^3$ d. $4x^3$

[c] 61. Find the fifth non-zero term of the Taylor polynomial at x = 0 for $f(x) = e^{3x}$.

a. $\frac{27x^4}{6}$ b. $-\frac{81x^4}{24}$ c. $\frac{81x^4}{4!}$ d. $\frac{81x^3}{3!}$

[a] 62. Find the fourth non-zero term of the Taylor polynomial at x = 0 for f(x) = cos3x.

a. $-\frac{81}{80}x^6$ b. $\frac{81}{32}x^6$ c. $-\frac{81}{32}x^6$ d. $\frac{43}{32}x^6$

[c] 63. Find the first two non-zero terms of the Taylor series at x = 0 for $f(x) = e^{\cos x}$.

a. $1+\left(\frac{e}{4}\right)x^2$ b. $e+\left(\frac{e}{4}\right)x$ c. $e-\left(\frac{e}{2}\right)x^2$ d. $1-\left(\frac{e}{2}\right)x^2$

[a] 64. Find the third degree Taylor polynomial at x = 0 for f(x) = arctanx.

a. $1-\frac{x^3}{3}$ b. $x-\frac{x^2}{2}$ c. $x-\frac{x^3}{3!}$ d. $x-\frac{x^3}{3}$

[a] 65. Find the first four non-zero terms of the Taylor series at x = 0 for f(x) = ln(1 + x) to approximate ln(1.4).

a. 0.3349 b. 0.3389 c. 0.3369 d. 0.3399

[c] 66. Given that $e^x \approx 1+x+\frac{x^2}{2!}+\frac{x^3}{3!}$, use the given Taylor polynomial to approximate $e^{0.4}$.

a. 1.467 b. 1.473 c. 1.491 d. 1.517

[a] 67. Given the Taylor series about zero for the function $f(x) = e^{3x}$. Use the first four nonzero terms only to approximate $e^{0.6}$.

a. 1.816 b. 1.820 c. 1.824 d. 1.828

[c] 68. Given the Taylor series about zero for the function $f(x) = e^{3x}$. Use the first four nonzero terms only to approximate $e^{-0.5}$.

a. 0.602 b. 0.603 c. 0.604 d. 0.605

[a] 69. Given that $\sin x = x - \frac{x^3}{3!} + \frac{x^5}{5!} - \frac{x^7}{7!} + \ldots$, use the given four terms to approximate sin(0.6).

a. 0.5646 b. 0.5636 c. 0.5652 d. 0.5659

[c] 70. Given that $\cos x = 1 - \frac{x^2}{2!} + \frac{x^4}{4!} - \frac{x^6}{6!} + \ldots$, use the given four terms to approximate cos(1.4).

a. 0.1676 b. 0.1686 c. 0.1696 d. 0.1706

[d] 71. Given that $\ln(1+x) = x - \frac{x^2}{2} + \frac{x^3}{3} - \frac{x^4}{4} + \ldots$, use the given four terms to approximate ln(0.8).

a. −0.219 b. −0.220 c. −0.221 d. −0.223

[c] 72. Given the Taylor series about zero for $f(x) = e^{\cos x}$. Obtain the first two nonzero terms.

a. $1 - \frac{e}{2}x^2$ b. $e + \frac{e}{4}x$ c. $e - \frac{e}{2}x^2$ d. $1 + \frac{e}{4}x^2$

SHORT ANSWER 10.2

73. Find the third Taylor polynomial at $x = 0$ for $f(x) = 5 - x + 7x^2$.

Answer: $5 - x + 7x^2$

74. Find the third Taylor polynomial at $x = 0$ for $f(x) = (1+x)^{\frac{2}{3}}$.

Answer: $1+\frac{2}{3}x-\frac{1}{9}x^2+\frac{4}{81}x^3$

75. Find the third Taylor polynomial at $x = 0$ for $f(x) = e^{-2x}$.

Answer: $1-2x+2x^2-\frac{4}{3}x^3$

76. Find the third Taylor polynomial at $x = 0$ for $f(x) = \sqrt[3]{1+x}$.

Answer: $1+\frac{x}{3}-\frac{x^2}{9}+\frac{5x^3}{81}$

77. Find the third Taylor polynomial at $x = 0$ for $f(x) = \frac{1}{1-2x}$.

Answer: $1 + 2x + 4x^2 + 8x^3$

78. Find the third Taylor polynomial at $x = 0$ for $f(x) = \frac{2}{1-5x}$.

Answer: $2 + 10x + 50x^2 + 250x^3$

79. Find the sixth degree Taylor polynomial for $\sin x^2$ by taking the third degree Taylor polynomial for $\sin x$ and replacing x by x^2?

Answer: $\sin x^2 = x^2 - \frac{x^6}{6}$

80. Find the fourth degree Taylor polynomial for $\cos 3x$ by taking the fourth Taylor polynomial for $\cos x$ and replacing x by $3x$.

Answer: $1-\frac{9}{2}x^2+\frac{81}{24}x^4=1-\frac{9}{2}x^2+\frac{27}{8}x^4$

81. Find the fourth Taylor polynomial at x = 2 for f(x) = ln x.

Answer: $\ln 2+\frac{1}{2}(x-2)-\frac{1}{8}(x-2)^2+\frac{1}{24}(x-2)^3-\frac{1}{64}(x-2)^4$

82. Find the third Taylor polynomial at x = 3 for $f(x)=\frac{1}{x}$.

Answer: $\frac{1}{3}-\frac{(x-3)}{9}+\frac{(x-3)^2}{27}-\frac{(x-3)^3}{81}$

83. Find the third Taylor polynomial at $x=\frac{\pi}{3}$ for f(x) = cosx.

Answer: $\frac{1}{2}-\frac{\sqrt{3}}{2}\left(x-\frac{\pi}{3}\right)-\frac{1}{4}\left(x-\frac{\pi}{3}\right)^2+\frac{\sqrt{3}}{12}\left(x-\frac{\pi}{3}\right)^3$

84. Find the third Taylor polynomial at x = 1 for $f(x)=\frac{1}{2+x}$.

Answer: $\frac{1}{3}-\frac{1}{9}(x-1)+\frac{1}{27}(x-1)^2-\frac{1}{81}(x-1)^3$

85. Find the third Taylor polynomial at x = 0 of the function $f(x)=\frac{1}{1-2.5x}$.

Answer: $\frac{1}{1-2.5x}=1+2.5x+6.25x^2+15.625x^3+...$

86. Find the third Taylor polynomial at x = 0 for the function $f(x)=\frac{1}{1-5x^3}$.

Answer: $\frac{1}{1-5x^3}=1+5x^3+25x^6+125x^9+...$

87. Find the third Taylor polynomial at x = 0 for the function $f(x)=\frac{3.7}{1-x}$.

Answer: $\frac{3.7}{1-x}=3.7+3.7x+3.7x^2+3.7x^3+...$

88. Find the third Taylor polynomial at x = 0 for the function $f(x)=\frac{5}{1-5x}$.

Answer: $\frac{5}{1-5x}=5+25x+125x^2+625x^3+\ldots$

89. Find the third Taylor polynomial at x = 0 for the function $f(x)=\frac{-4.3}{1-x}$.

Answer: $-\frac{4.3}{1-x}=-4.3-4.3x-4.3x^2-4.3x^3-\ldots$

90. Find the third Taylor polynomial at x = 0 for the function $f(x)=\frac{6}{x-1}$.

Answer: $\frac{6}{x-1}=-\frac{6}{1-x}=-6-6x-6x^2-6x^3-\ldots$

91. Find the third Taylor polynomial at x = 0 for the function $f(x)=\frac{3}{1-4x}$.

Answer: $\frac{3}{1-4x}=3+12x+48x^2+192x^3+\ldots$

92. Find the third Taylor polynomial at x = 0 for the function $f(x)=-\frac{1}{x-1}$.

Answer: $-\frac{1}{x-1}=\frac{1}{1-x}=1+x+x^2+x^3+\ldots$

93. Find the third Taylor polynomial at x = 0 for the function $f(x)=\frac{1}{2-2x}$.

Answer: $\frac{1}{2-2x}=\frac{1}{2}+\frac{1}{2}x+\frac{1}{2}x^2+\frac{1}{2}x^3+\ldots$

94. Find the third Taylor polynomial at x = 0 for the function $f(x)=\frac{1}{3x-3}$.

Answer: $\frac{1}{3x-3}=-\frac{1}{3}-\frac{1}{3}x-\frac{1}{3}x^2-\frac{1}{3}x^3-\ldots$

95. Find the third Taylor polynomial at $x = 0$ for the function $f(x) = \frac{x}{1-x}$.

Answer: $\frac{x}{1-x} = x + x^2 + x^3 + x^4 + \ldots$

96. Find the third Taylor polynomial at $x = 0$ for the function $f(x) = \frac{2x}{3x-1}$.

Answer: $\frac{2x}{3x-1} = -2x - 6x^2 - 18x^3 - 54x^4 - \ldots$

97. Find the third Taylor polynomial at $x = 0$ for the function $f(x) = \frac{1}{1+3x}$.

Answer: $\frac{1}{1+3x} = \frac{1}{1-(-3x)} = 103x + 9x^2 - 27x^3 + \ldots$

98. Find the third Taylor polynomial at $x = 0$ for the function $f(x) = -\frac{1}{x+1}$.

Answer: $-\frac{1}{x+1} = -1 + x - x^2 + x^3 - \ldots$

99. Find the third Taylor polynomial at $x = 0$ for the function $f(x) = \frac{x}{1+x}$.

Answer: $\frac{x}{1+x} = x - x^2 + x^3 - x^4 + \ldots$

100. Find the third Taylor polynomial at $x = 0$ for the function $f(x) = \frac{1}{2x+1}$.

Answer: $\frac{1}{2x+1} = \frac{1}{1-(-2x)} = 1 - 2x + 4x^2 - 8x^3 + \ldots$

101. Find the third Taylor polynomial at $x = 0$ for the function $f(x) = \frac{1}{3x+3}$.

Answer: $\frac{1}{3x+3} = \frac{1}{3} - \frac{1}{3}x + \frac{1}{3}x^2 - \frac{1}{3}x^3 + \ldots$

102. Given that $\sin x = x - \frac{x^3}{3!} + \frac{x^5}{5!} - \frac{x^7}{7!} + \ldots$, use the given four terms to approximate sin (–0.7).

Answer: $\sin(-0.7) \approx -0.644218$

103. Given that $e^x = 1 + x + \frac{x^2}{2!} + \frac{x^3}{3!} + \ldots$, use the given four terms to approximate $e^{-1.8}$.

Answer: $e^{-1.8} \approx -0.152$ (a poor approximation)

104. Given that $\cos x = 1 - \frac{x^2}{2!} + \frac{x^4}{4!} - \frac{x^6}{6!} + \ldots$, use the given four terms to approximate cos(–0.4).

Answer: $\cos(-0.4) \approx 0.921061$

105. Given the Taylor series about zero for $f(x) = e^{\tan x}$. Obtain the first two nonzero terms.

Answer: $f(x) \approx 1 + x$

106. Given the Taylor series about zero for $f(x) = e^{\tan x}$. Use the first two nonzero terms only to estimate f(0.4).

Answer: $f(0.4) \approx 1.4$

Section 10.3 Taylor Series

MULTIPLE CHOICE 10.3

[b] 107. Find the radius of convergence of the power series: $\sum_{n=i}^{\infty} \frac{(2x)^n}{\sqrt{n}}$.

a. 0 b. ½ c. ∞ d. 2

[a] 108. Find the radius of convergence of the power series: $\sum_{n=1}^{\infty} \frac{(-1)^n x^n}{e^n}$.

a. e b. 0 c. $\frac{1}{e}$ d. ∞

[b] 109. Find the radius of convergence of the power series: $\sum_{n=0}^{\infty} \frac{x^{n+2}}{n!}$.

a. 0 b. ∞ c. 2 d. ½

[d] 110. Find the radius of convergence of the power series: $\sum_{n=0}^{\infty} \frac{x^n}{5^n}$.

a. $\frac{1}{5}$ b. 0 c. ∞ d. 5

[d] 111. Find the radius of convergence of the power series: $\sum_{n=1}^{\infty} \frac{2x^n}{n^2}$.

a. 2 b. 0 c. ∞ d. 1

[a] 112. Find the radius of convergence of the power series: $\sum_{n=0}^{\infty} n!x^n$.

a. 0 b. 2 c. ∞ d. 1

[d] 113. Find the radius of convergence of the power series: $\sum_{n=0}^{\infty} \frac{(3x)^n}{(2n)!}$.

a. 0 b. 2 c. ½ d. ∞

[a] 114. Find the radius of convergence of the power series: $\sum_{n=0}^{\infty} \frac{(-1)^n x^n}{n+1}$.

a. 1 b. 0 c. ∞ d. 2

SHORT ANSWER 10.3

115. Find the Taylor series at $x = 0$ for the function $f(x) = \frac{4}{x+2}$, by calculating four derivatives and using the definition of Taylor series.

Answer: $2 - x + \frac{x^2}{2} - \frac{x^3}{4} + \frac{x^4}{8} - \ldots$

116. Find the Taylor series at $x = 0$ for the function $f(x) = e^{-2x}$, by calculating four derivatives and using the definition of Taylor series.

Answer: $1 - 2x + 2x^2 - \frac{4x^3}{3} + \frac{2x^4}{3} + \ldots$

117. Find the Taylor series at $x = 0$ for the function $f(x) = \ln(x^2 + 1)$, by calculating four derivatives and using the definition of Taylor series.

Answer: $x^2 - \frac{x^4}{2} + \frac{x^6}{3} - \frac{x^8}{4} + \ldots$

118. Find the Taylor series at $x = 0$ for the function $f(x) = \sin 2x$, by calculating four derivatives and using the definition of Taylor series.

Answer: $2x - \frac{4x^3}{3} + \frac{4x^5}{15} - \frac{8x^7}{315} + \ldots$

119. Find the Taylor series at $x = 0$ for the function $f(x) = 10x^2 - 3x + 1$, by calculating four derivatives and using the definition of Taylor series.

Answer: $1 - 3x + 10x^2$

120. Find the Taylor series at $x = 0$ for the function $f(x) = \frac{1}{x+6}$, by calculating four derivatives and using the definition of Taylor series.

Answer: $\frac{1}{6} - \frac{x}{36} + \frac{x^2}{216} - \frac{x^3}{1{,}296} + \frac{x^4}{7{,}776} + \ldots$

121. Find the Taylor series for $f(x) = e^x$ at $x = 1$.

Answer: $e + e(x-1) + \frac{e(x-1)^2}{2!} + \frac{e(x-1)^3}{3!} + \frac{e(x-1)^4}{4!} + \ldots$

122. Find the Taylor series for $f(x) = \cos x$ at $x = \frac{\pi}{4}$.

Answer: $\frac{\sqrt{2}}{2} - \frac{\sqrt{2}}{2}\left(x - \frac{\pi}{4}\right) - \frac{\sqrt{2}}{4}\left(x - \frac{\pi}{4}\right)^2 + \frac{\sqrt{2}}{12}\left(x - \frac{\pi}{4}\right)^3 + \frac{\sqrt{2}}{48}\left(x - \frac{\pi}{4}\right)^4 - \ldots$

123. Find the Taylor series at $x = 0$ for the function $f(x) = e^{\frac{x^2}{2}}$, by modifying one of the Taylor series.

Answer: $1 + \frac{x^2}{2} + \frac{x^4}{2^2 \cdot 2!} + \frac{x^6}{2^3 \cdot 3!} + \frac{x^8}{2^4 \cdot 4!} + \ldots$

124. Find the Taylor series at $x = 0$ for the function $f(x) = x\cos x$, by modifying one of the Taylor series.

Answer: $x - \frac{x^3}{2!} + \frac{x^5}{4!} - \frac{x^7}{6!} + \frac{x^9}{8!} - \ldots$

125. Find the Taylor series at $x = 0$ for the function $f(x) = \frac{\sin x}{x}$, by modifying one of the Taylor series.

Answer: $1 - \frac{x^2}{3!} + \frac{x^4}{5!} - \frac{x^6}{7!} + \frac{x^8}{9!} - \ldots$

126. Find the Taylor series at $x = 0$ for the function $f(x) = \frac{\ln(x+1)}{x}$, by modifying one of the Taylor series.

Answer: $1 - \frac{x}{2} + \frac{x^2}{3} - \frac{x^3}{4} + \frac{x^4}{5} - \ldots$

127. Find the Taylor series at $x = 0$ for the function $f(x) = \frac{x}{1-5x}$, by modifying one of the Taylor series.

Answer: $x + 5x^2 + 25x^3 + 125x^4 + 625x^5 + \ldots$

128. Find the Taylor series at $x = 0$ for the function $f(x) = \frac{x^2}{1+2x}$, by modifying one of the Taylor series.

Answer: $x^2 - 2x^3 + 4x^4 - 8x^5 + 16x^6 - \ldots$

129. Find the Taylor series at $x = 0$ for the function $f(x) = \frac{\cos x - 1}{x}$, by modifying one of the Taylor series.

Answer: $-\frac{x}{2!}+\frac{x^3}{4!}-\frac{x^5}{6!}+\frac{x^7}{8!}-\ldots$

130. Find the power series for $f(x) = \sin^2 x$ by using the Taylor series at $x = 0$ for $f(x) = \cos x$ and using the trig identity $\sin^2 x = \frac{1-\cos 2x}{2}$.

Answer: $\frac{2x^2}{2!}-\frac{2^3x^4}{4!}+\frac{2^5x^6}{6!}-\frac{2^7x^8}{8!}+\ldots$

131. Find the power series for $f(x) = \cos^2 x$ by using the Taylor series at $x = 0$ for $f(x) = \cos x$ and using the trig identity $\cos^2 x = \frac{1+\cos 2x}{2}$.

Answer: $1-\frac{2x^2}{2!}+\frac{2^3x^4}{4!}-\frac{2^5x^6}{6!}+\frac{2^7x^8}{8!}-\ldots$

132. Given the Taylor series about zero for the function $f(x) = e^{3x}$. Obtain the first four nonzero terms.

Answer: $e^{3x} \approx 1+3x+\frac{9x^2}{2!}+\frac{27x^3}{3!}+\ldots \approx 1+3x+\frac{9}{2}x^2+\frac{9}{2}x^3$

133. Find the third Taylor polynomial at $x = 0$ of the function $f(x)=\frac{2.4x^2}{x+1}$.

Answer: $\frac{2.4x^2}{x+1}=2.4x^2-2.4x^3+2.4x^4-2.4x^5+\ldots$

134. Obtain the first four nonzero terms of the Taylor series about zero for the function $f(x) = e^{-x}$. Use these four terms to obtain a series for x^2e^{-x}.

Answer: $x^2e^{-x} \approx x^2\left(1-x+\frac{x^2}{2!}-\frac{x^3}{3!}\right)=x^2-x^3+\frac{x^4}{2!}-\frac{x^5}{3!}$

135. Given that $\sin x = x - \frac{x^3}{3!} + \frac{x^5}{5!} - \frac{x^7}{7!} + \ldots$ and $\cos x = 1 - \frac{x^2}{2!} + \frac{x^4}{4!} - \frac{x^6}{6!} + \ldots$, obtain the first five terms of the Taylor series for $f(x) = \sin x - \cos(-x)$.

Answer: $-1 + x + \frac{x^2}{2!} - \frac{x^3}{3!} - \frac{x^4}{4!} + \ldots$

Section 10.4 Newton's Method

MULTIPLE CHOICE 10.4

[b] 136. Use Newton's Method beginning with the given x_0 to find the THIRD iteration, x_3. Carry out the calculations "by hand" with the aid of a calculator, rounding to 4 decimal places after each iteration.
$x^3 - 2x - 2 = 0$; $x_0 = 1.5$

a. 2.003 b. 1.7693 c. 1.8261 d. 1.9871

[c] 137. Use Newton's Method beginning with the given x_0 to find the THIRD iteration, x_3. Carry out the calculations "by hand" with the aid of a calculator, rounding to 4 decimal places after each iteration.
$-x^3 + x + 1 = 0$, $x_0 = 1$

a. 1.1056 b. 1.5471 c. 1.3252 d. 1.3171

[a] 138. Use Newton's Method beginning with the given x_0 to find the THIRD iteration, x_3. Carry out the calculations "by hand" with the aid of a calculator, rounding to 4 decimal places after each iteration.
$x^3 - x + 1$; $x_0 = -1.5$

a. −1.3247 b. −1.4168 c. −1.2874 d. −1.2650

[b] 139. Use Newton's Method beginning with the given x_0 to find the SECOND iteration x_2. Carry out the calculations "by hand" with the aid of a calculator rounding to 3 decimal places after each iteration.
$f(x) = x^3 - 5x^2 + 2$; $x_0 = 5$

a. 4.983 b. 4.917 c. 4.268 d. 4.019

[c] 140. Use Newton's Method beginning with the given x_0 to find the SECOND iteration x_2. Carry out the calculations "by hand" with the aid of a calculator rounding to 3 decimal places after each iteration.
$f(x) = \ln(3x) - 2.3$; $x_0 = 3$

a. 3.147 b. 3.333 c. 3.325 d. 3.241

[c] 141. Use Newton's Method beginning with the given x_0 to find the SECOND iteration x_2. Carry out the calculations "by hand" with the aid of a calculator rounding to 3 decimal places after each iteration.
$f(x) = e^x + x$; $x_0 = 0$

a. 0.567 b. 1.000 c. −0.567 d. −1.000

[d] 142. Use Newton's Method beginning with the given x_0 to find the SECOND iteration x_2. Carry out the calculations "by hand" with the aid of a calculator rounding to 3 decimal places after each iteration.
$f(x) = x^3 - x^2 - 1$; $x_0 = 1$

a. 1.425 b. 1.525 c. 1.725 d. 1.625

[b] 143. Given $x_0 = 2$ and $f(x) = x^3 - 2x - 3$, use two iterations of Newton's method to determine x_2. Keep three decimal places throughout the calculations.

a. 1.856 b. 1.900 c. 1.957 d. 2.002

[d] 144. Given $x_0 = 2$ and $f(x) = x^2 - 8x + 13$, use two iterations of Newton's method to determine x_2. Keep three decimal places throughout the calculations.

a. 1.989 b. 2.079 c. 2.151 d. 2.268

[a] 145. Given $x_0 = 0$ and $f(x) = x^2 - 7x + 2$, use two iterations of Newton's method to determine x_2. Keep three decimal places throughout the calculations.

a. 0.298 b. 0.256 c. 0.315 d. 0.281

[c] 146. Given $x_0 = 1.5$ and $f(x) = 25 - e^{x^2}$, use two iterations of Newton's method to determine x_2. Keep three decimal places throughout the calculations.

a. 1.566 b. 1.713 c. 1.894 d. 2.045

[d] 147. Given $x_0 = 3$ and $f(x) = \ln(3x) - 2.3$, use two iterations of Newton's method to determine x_2. Keep three decimal places throughout the calculations.

a. 3.338 b. 3.291 c. 3.427 d. 3.325

[b] 148. Given $x_0 = 3$ and $f(x) = x^3 - 9x^2 + 15x + 10$, use two iterations of Newton's method to determine x_2. Keep three decimal places throughout the calculations.

a. 3.075 b. 3.083 c. 3.097 d. 3.111

[a] 149. Given $x_0 = 6$ and $f(x) = x^3 - 9x^2 + 15x + 10$, use two iterations of Newton's method to determine x_2. Keep three decimal places throughout the calculations.

a. 6.427 b. 6.533 c. 6.601 d. 6.551

[c] 150. Let $x_0 = 2$ and $f(x) = \ln x + x^2$. Use four iterations of Newton's method to determine x_4.

a. 1.432 b. 1.016 c. 0.653 d. 0.481

[b] 151. A graphing calculator manufacturer produces x thousand calculators each week. The marginal average cost is given by $M(x) = \dfrac{0.03x^3 + 11.75x^2 - 125.5}{x^2}$. Use Newton's method with three iterations of the numerator and $x_0 = 3$ to find the production level that minimizes the average cost per calculator.

a. 2964 b. 3255 c. 3061 d. 3189

[a] 152. The revenue (in thousands of dollars) from the sale of x thousand units of a commodity is given by $R(x) = 100xe^{0.5x}$. Use Newton's method with four iterations and $x_0 = 10$ to calculate how many units must be sold to generate $600,000. (HINT: Let $f(x) = 600 - 100xe^{0.5x}$.)

a. 4735 b. 4910 c. 5090 d. 5156

[d] 153. The pollution level, in parts per million, in a lake t days after an industrial accident is given by $P(t) = 50te^{-0.1t}$. Use Newton's method with three iterations and $t_0 = 5$ to determine when the pollution level reaches 125 parts per million.

a. 3.774 b. 3.729 c. 3.692 d. 3.574

[b] 154. The pollution level, in parts per million, in a lake t days after an industrial accident is given by $P(t) = 50te^{-0.1t}$. Use Newton's method with three iterations and $t_0 = 20$ to determine when the pollution level drops below 125 parts per million.

a. 19.971 b. 21.533 c. 20.994 d. 19.914

[c] 155. Let $x(t) = t^3 - 6t^2 + 25t$ represent the number of letters a person can memorize in t hours. How many hours (to one decimal place) are needed to memorize 500 letters? Use Newton's method with $t_0 = 9$.

a. 9.0 b. 9.1 c. 9.2 d. 9.3

[a] 156. When x milligrams of a drug are given to a person, the change in body temperature T(x) is given by $T(x) = x^2\left(1 - \frac{x}{9}\right)$. Use Newton's method to find the dosage (correct to two decimal places) that would produce a change of 4°. Let $x_0 = 2$.

a. 2.32 b. 2.21 c. 2.09 d. 1.92

[c] 157. The number of bacteria per milliliter in a swimming pool t hours after a treatment is given by $B(t) = 1750 - 800te^{-0.2t}$. Use Newton's method with $t_0 = 2$ to determine when the bacteria level drops below 600 bacteria per milliliter.

a. 2.1 b. 2.2 c. 2.3 d. 2.4

[d] 158. The number of bacteria per milliliter in a swimming pool t hours after a treatment is given by $B(t) = 1750 - 800te^{-0.2t}$. Use Newton's method with $t_0 = 9$ to determine when the bacteria level returns to 600 bacteria per milliliter.

a. 9.1 b. 9.2 c. 9.3 d. 9.4

SHORT ANSWER 10.4

159. Use Newton's Method to approximate the root $\sqrt{7}$, continuing until two successive iterations agree to three decimal places.

Answer: 2.646

160. Use Newton's Method to approximate the root $\sqrt[4]{6}$, continuing until two successive iterations agree to three decimal places.

Answer: 1.565

161. Use Newton's Method to approximate the root $\sqrt{5}$, continuing until two successive iterations agree to three decimal places.

Answer: 2.236

162. Use Newton's Method to approximate the root $\sqrt[3]{15}$, continuing until two successive iterations agree to three decimal places.

Answer: 2.466

163. Use Newton's Method to estimate the x-coordinate of the intersection of the following graph, using the indicated initial guess, x_0. Continue calculating iterations until two successive iterations differ by less than 0.001.
$f(x) = x^2$, $g(x) = x^3 - 2x + 5$; $x_0 = -2$

Answer: −1.757

164. Use Newton's Method to estimate the x-coordinate of the intersection of the following graph, using the indicated initial guess, x_0. Continue calculating iterations until two successive iterations differ by less than 0.001.
$f(x) = x^2$, $g(x) = \sin x$; $x_0 = 1$

Answer: 0.877

165. Use Newton's Method to estimate the x-coordinate of the intersection of the following graph, using the indicated initial guess, x_0. Continue calculating iterations until two successive iterations differ by less than 0.001.

$f(x) = \sin x$, $g(x) = \frac{1}{3}x$; $x_0 = 2$

Answer: 2.279

166. Use Newton's Method to estimate the x-coordinate of the intersection of the following graph, using the indicated initial guess, x_0. Continue calculating iterations until two successive iterations differ by less than 0.001.

$f(x) = 2x+1$, $g(x) = \sqrt{x+4}$; $x_0 = 1$

Answer: 0.569

167. Use Newton's Method to estimate the x-coordinate of the intersection of the following graph, using the indicated initial guess, x_0. Continue calculating iterations until two successive iterations differ by less than 0.001.
$f(x) = x$, $g(x) = \tan x$; $x_0 = 5$

Answer: 4.493

168. Determine two consecutive positive integers between which there is a zero of $f(x) = 2.5x^3 - 6.7x^2 + 3$.

Answer: 2 and 3

169. Determine two consecutive positive integers between which there is a zero of $g(x) = 23 - 4e^{2x}$.

Answer: 1 and 2

170. Determine two consecutive positive integers between which there is a zero of $f(x) = \ln(2.2x) - 2.25$.

Answer: 4 and 5

Chapter 10 – Graphing Calculator

Sequences and Series

Section 10.2 Taylor Polynomials

1. a. Find the 5th degree Taylor polynomial that best approximates e^{2x} near $x = 0$.
   b. What is the maximum error on $[-0.1, 0.1]$?
   c. Graph $y = e^{2x}$ and the 5th degree approximation on $[-1, 1]$ by $[-1, 1]$ to verify that on $[-0.1, 0.1]$ the difference is less than the number found in b.

   Answer: a. $1+2x+2x^2+\frac{4}{3}x^3+\frac{2}{3}x^4+\frac{4}{15}x^5$
   b. 0.9149×10^{-7}

2. a. Find the 4th degree Taylor polynomial that best approximates $\frac{1}{x+1}$ near $x = 0$.
   b. What is the maximum error on $[-0.5, 0.5]$?
   c. Graph $y=\frac{1}{x+1}$ and the 4th degree approximation on $[-1, 1]$ by $[-1, 1]$ to verify that on $[-0.5, 0.5]$ the difference is less than the number found in b.

   Answer: a. $1-x+x^2-x^3+x^4$
   b. 0.0625

3. a. Find the 5th degree Taylor polynomial that best fits $\ln(1 + x)$ near $x = 0$.
   b. What is the maximum error on $[-0.5, 0.5]$?
   c. Graph $y = \ln(1 + x)$ and the 5th degree approximation on $[-1, 1]$ by $[-1, 1]$ to verify that on $[-0.5, 0.5]$ the difference is less than the number found in b.

   Answer: a. $x-\frac{x^2}{2}+\frac{x^3}{3}-\frac{x^4}{4}+\frac{x^5}{5}$
   b. 0.004606

4. a. Find the 5th degree Taylor polynomial that best fits $\sin x$ near $x = 0$.
   b. Use this polynomial to estimate $\sin 1$ and compare this to the actual value of $\sin 1$.
   c. Using the remainder term, find the maximum error in using the Taylor polynomial to approximate $y = \sin x$ on $[-1, 1]$ and verify that the difference in value in part b is less than this error.

   Answer: a. $x-\frac{1}{6}x^3+\frac{1}{120}x^5$
   b. $1-\frac{1}{6}(1)+\frac{1}{120}(1)=0.8417$, $\sin 1 = 0.8415$
   c. maximum error = 0.00139

5. a. Find the 3rd degree Taylor polynimial that best fits arcsin x near x = 0.
   b. Use this polynomial to estimate acrsin(–0.5) and compare this to the actual value of acrsin(–0.5).
   c. Using the remainder term, find th emaximum error in using the Taylor polynimial to approximate y = arcsin x on [–0.5, 0.5] and verify that the difference in values in part b is less than this error.

Answer: a. $x+\frac{x^3}{6}$

b. $-0.5+\frac{(-0.5)^3}{6}=-0.521$, $\arcsin(-0.5)=-0.524$

c. maximum error = 0.0037

6. a. Find the 3rd degree Taylor polynomial that best fits e^{-x} near x = 0.
   b. Use this polynomial to estimate $e^{-\frac{1}{2}}$ and compare this to the actual value of $e^{-\frac{1}{2}}$.

Answer: a. $1-x+\frac{x^2}{2}-\frac{x^3}{6}$

b. $1-\frac{1}{2}+\frac{\left[\frac{1}{2}\right]^2}{2}-\frac{\left[\frac{1}{2}\right]^3}{6}=0.6042$, $e^{-\frac{1}{2}}=0.6065$

Section 10.3 Taylor Series

7. a. Use your graphing calculator to find sin(0.1) to 4 decimal places.

   b. The Taylor series for sin x evaluated at $x = 0.1$ is $\sin(0.1) = \sum_{n=0}^{\infty} \frac{(-1)^n (0.1)^{2n+1}}{(2n+1)!}$. How many terms are required for the sum (rounded to 4 decimal places) to agree with your answer in part a?

   Answer: a. 0.0998
   b. only 2 terms

8. a. Use your graphing calculator to find cos(10°) to 4 decimal places.

   b. The Taylor series for cos x evaluated at $x = \frac{\pi}{18}$ (radians = 10°) is $\cos\frac{\pi}{18} = \sum_{n=0}^{\infty} \frac{(-1)^n \left[\frac{\pi}{18}\right]^{2x}}{(2n)!}$. How many terms are required for the sum (rounded to 4 decimal places) to agree with your answer in part a?

   Answer: a. 0.0985
   b. only 2 terms

9. a. Use your graphing calculator to find $\tan^{-1}(0.2)$ to 3 decimal places.

   b. The Taylor series for $\tan^{-1} x$ evaluated at $x = 0.2$ is $\tan^{-1}(0.2) = \sum_{n=0}^{\infty} \frac{(-1)^n (0.2)^{2n+1}}{2n+1}$. How many terms are required for the sum (rounded to 3 decimal places) to agree with your answer in part a?

   Answer: a. 0.197
   b. only 2 terms

10. a. Use your graphing calculator to find $\frac{1}{\sqrt{e}}$ to four decimal places.

   b. The Taylor series for e^x evaluated at $x = -\frac{1}{2}$ is $e^{-\frac{1}{2}} = \frac{1}{\sqrt{e}} = \sum_{n=0}^{\infty} \frac{\left[-\frac{1}{2}\right]^n}{n!}$. How many terms are required for the sum (rounded to 4 decimal places) to agree with your answer in part a?

   Answer: a. 0.6065
   b. 6 terms

11. a. Use your graphing calculator to find cosh(0.2) to 4 decimal places.

   b. The Taylor series for cosh(x) evaluated at $x = 0.2$ is $\cosh(x) = \sum_{n=0}^{\infty} \frac{(0.2)^{2n}}{(2n)!}$. How many terms are required for the sum (rounded to 4 decimal places) to agree with your answer in part a?

   Answer: a. 1.0201
   b. 3 terms

Section 10.4 Newton's Method

12. Use Newton's method on a graphing calculator to approximate the root of the equation $x^3 - x - 2 = 0$, beginning with $x_0 = 1.5$ and continuing until 2 successive approximations agree to 7 decimal places.

    Answer: 1.5213797

13. Use Newton's method on a graphing calculator to approximate the root of the equation $x^{35} + 34 = 0$, beginning with $x_0 = -2$ and continuing until 2 successive approximations agree to 7 decimal places.

    Answer: –2.0243975

14. Use Newton's method on a graphing calculator to approximate the root of the equation $x^3 - x^2 - 2x + 1 = 0$, beginning with $x_0 = 1.5$ and continuing until 2 successive approximations agree to 7 decimal places.

    Answer: 1.8019377

15. Use Newton's method on a graphing calculator to approximate the root of the equation $\sin x - \frac{1}{3}x = 0$, beginning with $x_0 = 1.5$ and continuing until 2 successive approximations agree to 7 decimal places.

    Answer: 2.2788627

16. Use Newton's method on a graphing calculator to approximate the root of the equation $x^3 + x^2 - 3x - 3 = 0$, beginning with $x_0 = -1$ and continuing until 2 successive approximations agree to 7 decimal places.

    Answer: –1

17. Use Newton's method on a graphing calculator to approximate the root $\sqrt{11}$, continuing until two successive approximations agree to 7 decimal places.

    Answer: 3.3166248

18. Use Newton's method on a graphing calculator to approximate the root $\sqrt[3]{72}$, continuing until two successive approximations agree to 7 decimal places.

    Answer: 4.160167

19. Use Newton's method on a graphing calculator to approximate the root $\sqrt[4]{36}$, continuing until two successive approximations agree to 7 decimal places.

    Answer: 2.4494897

20. Use Newton's method on a graphing calculator to approximate the root $\sqrt{66}$, continuing until two successive approximations agree to 7 decimal places.

    Answer: 8.1240384

21. Use a graphing calculator to graph $f(x) = x^3$ and $g(x) = 3x - 1$ together on a reasonable window and estimate the x-value where the curves meet with TRACE/ZOOM. Then user Newton's method on your graphing calculator to approximate the root of $f(x) - g(x) = 0$, beginning with the x-coordinate of your estimate. Continue until two successive iterations agree to 7 decimal places.

    Answer: 0.3472964

22. Use a graphing calculator to graph $f(x) = 2\sin x$ and $g(x) = x$, $(x > 0)$ together on a reasonable window and estimate the x-value where the curves meet with TRACE/ZOOM. Then user Newton's method on your graphing calculator to approximate the root of $f(x) - g(x) = 0$, beginning with the x-coordinate of your estimate. Continue until two successive iterations agree to 7 decimal places.

    Answer: 1.8954943

23. Use a graphing calculator to graph $f(x) = \tan x$ and $g(x) = x$, $\left(\frac{\pi}{2} < x < \frac{3\pi}{2}\right)$ together on a reasonable window and estimate the x-value where the curves meet with TRACE/ZOOM. Then user Newton's method on your graphing calculator to approximate the root of $f(x) - g(x) = 0$, beginning with the x-coordinate of your estimate. Continue until two successive iterations agree to 7 decimal places.

    Answer: 4.4934095

24. Use a graphing calculator to graph $f(x) = \sqrt{2x+1}$ and $g(x) = x^2$, $(1 < x < 2)$ together on a reasonable window and estimate the x-value where the curves meet with TRACE/ZOOM. Then user Newton's method on your graphing calculator to approximate the root of $f(x) - g(x) = 0$, beginning with the x-coordinate of your estimate. Continue until two successive iterations agree to 7 decimal places.

    Answer: 1.3953370

25. The revenue (in thousands of dollars) from the sale of x thousand units of a commodity is given by $R(x) = 100xe^{0.05x}$. Use Newton's method on your graphing calculator to find how many units must be sold to generate \$600,000. (Hint: let $f(x) = 100xe^{0.05x} - 600$). Use $x_0 = 10$ as your initial estimate.

    Answer: 4,735 units

Chapter 11

Probability

Section 11.1 Discrete Probability

MULTIPLE CHOICE 11.1

[b] 1. For the event of rolling one die, find p (rolling an even number).

a. $\frac{1}{6}$ b. $\frac{1}{2}$ c. 3 d. $\frac{2}{6}$

[a] 2. For the event of rolling one die, find p (rolling at most a 4).

a. $\frac{4}{6}$ b. $\frac{2}{6}$ c. $\frac{3}{6}$ d. 4

[c] 3. For the event of tossing a coin 3 times, find p (tossing more than 1 head).

a. $\frac{3}{8}$ b. $\frac{5}{8}$ c. $\frac{1}{2}$ d. $\frac{1}{8}$

[c] 4. For the spinner below, the arrow is spun and eventually stops, pointing in one of the numbered sector, with probability proportional to the area of the sector. Let x stand for the number chosen. Find E(x) for each distribution.

a. 4 b. 4.5 c. 3.5 d. 3

[c] 5. For the spinner below, the arrow is spun and eventually stops, pointing in one of the numbered sector, with probability proportional to the area of the sector. Let x stand for the number chosen. Find E(x) for each distribution.

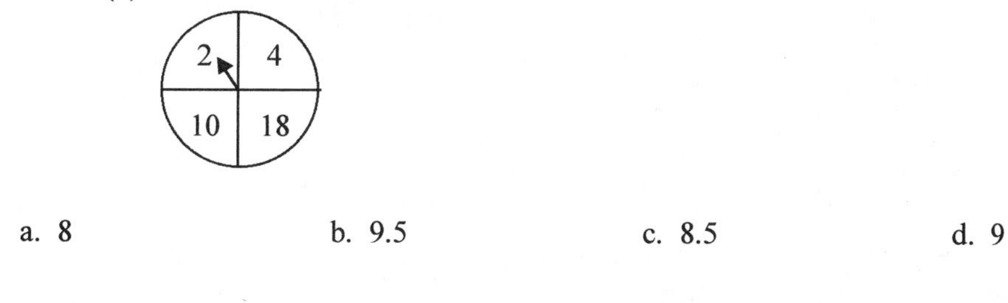

a. 8 b. 9.5 c. 8.5 d. 9

[a] 6. For a Poisson random variable x with mean 3 find P(x = 1).

a. 0.14936 b. 60.25661 c. 0.1527 d. 0.0156

[d] 7. What is the probability that the spinner arrow ends up pointing in the top 20°?

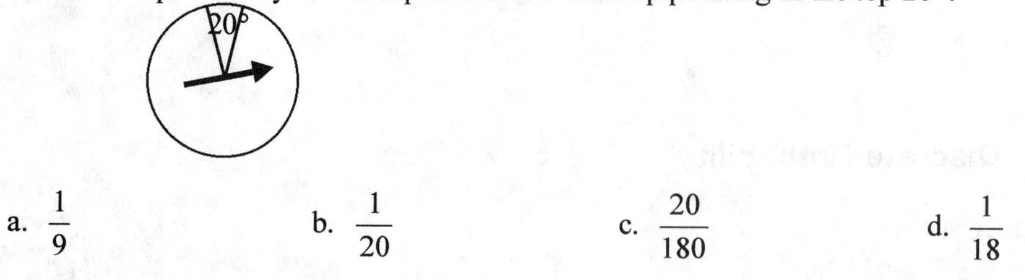

a. $\frac{1}{9}$ b. $\frac{1}{20}$ c. $\frac{20}{180}$ d. $\frac{1}{18}$

[a] 8. In a group of 100 drivers between the ages of 16 and 25, an average of 3.2 received speeding tickets last year. Use the Poisson distribution to find the probability that in a group of 100 drivers, at least one has given a speeding ticket.

a. 96% b. 0.04% c. 4.1% d. 13%

[d] 9. Alfred's Victorian Restaurant has an average of six empty tables during their early bird time of 5 to 6 PM. If eight couples arrive during this time, use the Poisson distribution to find the probability that they all can be accommodated.

a. 96.6% b. 74.4% c. 10.3% d. 25.6%

[b] 10. A pharmaceutical company estimates its new herbal pain relieving product has a probability of 0.25 it will be worth $25,000,000, a probability of 0.67 it will be worth $75,000 and a probability of 0.08 it will be worth less. Find the expected value of the product.

a. $25,750,000 b. $6,752,500 c. $5,747,500 d. $16,937,500

SHORT ANSWER 11.1

11. For the event of tossing a coin twice, find p (tossing 2 heads).

    Answer: $\frac{1}{4}$

12. For the event of tossing a coin 3 times, find p (tossing exactly 3 tails).

    Answer: $\frac{1}{8}$

13. Find the expected value, variance and standard deviation of the random variables: x takes values 14 and 16, each with probability $\frac{1}{2}$.

    Answer: $E(x) = 15$, $\text{var}(x) = 1$, $\sigma(x) = 1$

14. Find the expected value, variance and standard deviation of the random variables: x takes values 10 and 20, each with probability $\frac{1}{2}$.

    Answer: $E(x) = 15$, $\text{var}(x) = 25$, $\sigma(x) = 5$

15. Find the expected value, variance and standard deviation of the random variables: x takes values 5, 10, and 15, each with probability $\frac{1}{3}$.

    Answer: $E(x) = 10$, $\text{var}(x) = \frac{50}{3}$, $\sigma(x) = 4.08248$

16. For the spinner below, the arrow is spun and eventually stops, pointing in one of the numbered sector, with probability proportional to the area of the sector. Let x stand for the number chosen. Find E(x) for each distribution.

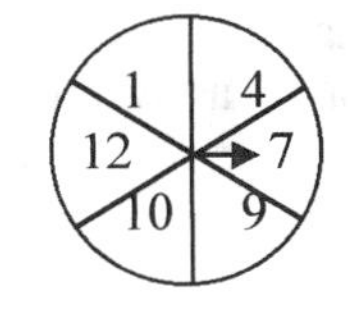

    Answer: $E(x) = 7\frac{1}{6}$

17. What is the probability that the spinner arrow ends up pointing in the top 45°?

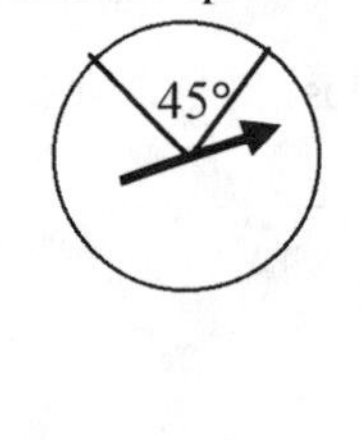

Answer: $\frac{1}{8}$

18. For a Poisson random variable x with mean 2.5 find P(x = 3).

Answer: 0.21376

19. For a Poisson random variable x with mean 5 find P(x = 2).

Answer: 0.8422

20. A raffle claims that there is a 0.001 probability of winning first prize of $500, a 0.15 probability of winning 2nd prize of $250, a 0.3 probability of winning 3rd prize of $100, and 0.549 probability of winning the consolation prize of $1. What is the expected amount of winnings for each person that plays if it costs $50 to play?

Answer: $68.55 or a profit of $18.55

21. You are told that you will win $20 if you roll a die and get an even number, $40 if you roll a die and get a 5 and will win nothing if you roll and get a 1 or 3. If you are offered $15 not to play, should you accept the offer or play, based on expected value?

Answer: You should play. Your expected winnings is $16.67

22. A 20-page research paper has 40 typos, for an average of 2 per page. Use the Poisson distribution to find the probability that a given page has 1 or fewer misprints.

Answer: 0.406

23. A manufacturing company produces 2,000 parts per day and an average of 50 per day fail inspection. Use the Poisson distribution to find the probability that on a given day 25 or fewer parts will fail inspection.

Answer: 0.00007161

Section 11.2 Continuous Probability

MULTIPLE CHOICE 11.2

[b] 24. Find the value of the constant a that makes the function $f(x) = ax(x - 6)$ a probability density function on the interval [0, 1].

a. $-\frac{8}{3}$ b. $-\frac{3}{8}$ c. $\frac{8}{3}$ d. $\frac{3}{8}$

[d] 25. Find the value of the constant a that makes the function $f(x) = ax^3$ a probability density function on the interval [0, 2].

a. 4 b. $-\frac{1}{4}$ c. $\frac{1}{2}$ d. $\frac{1}{4}$

[c] 26. Find the value of the constant a that makes the function $f(x) = a\sin x$ a probability density function on the interval $\left[0, \frac{\pi}{2}\right]$.

a. –1 b. $\frac{1}{2}$ c. 1 d. $-\frac{1}{2}$

[a] 27. Find the value of the constant a that makes the function $f(x) = a\sqrt[3]{x}$ a probability density function on the interval {0, 1].

a. $\frac{4}{3}$ b. $-\frac{4}{3}$ c. $\frac{3}{4}$ d. $\frac{1}{3}$

[c] 28. Given the probability density function $f(x) = 4 - 2x$ for [1, 2], determine E(x).

a. $\frac{7}{8}$ b. $\frac{5}{3}$ c. $\frac{4}{3}$ d. $\frac{3}{5}$

[d] 29. Given the probability density function $f(x) = \frac{1}{2} - \frac{1}{8}x$ for [0, 4], determine E(x).

a. 2 b. 1 c. $\frac{7}{3}$ d. $\frac{4}{3}$

[b] 30. Given the probability density function $f(x) = \frac{10x^3 - x^4}{5{,}000}$ on [0, 10], determine E(x).

a. $\frac{17}{3}$ b. $\frac{20}{3}$ c. $\frac{23}{3}$ d. $\frac{18}{3}$

[c] 31. Given the probability density function $f(x) = \frac{x^2}{9}$ for [0, 3], find $P(1 \le x \le 2)$.

a. $\frac{2}{3}$ b. $\frac{1}{5}$ c. $\frac{7}{27}$ d. $\frac{1}{3}$

[d] 32. Given the probability density function $f(x) = 0.2 - 0.02x$ on [0, 10], find $P(x < 8)$.

a. 0.84 b. 0.73 c. 0.89 d. 0.96

[a] 33. The number of voters (in millions) who vote in a presidential election year in Dallas, TX has the probability density function $f(x) = 1 - \frac{1}{8}x$ on [4, 8]. What is the expected voter turnout?

a. 5,333,333 b. 5,000,000 c. 6,666,667 d. 5,750,000

[c] 34. The number of hours it takes a computer student to learn a new piece of software has the probability density function $f(x) = \frac{4}{9}x^2 - \frac{4}{27}x^3$ for $0 \le x \le 3$ hours. What is the average number of hours required to learn a new piece of software?

a. 2.2 b. 2.0 c. 1.8 d. 1.6

[d] 35. The shelf life, in weeks, of a certain drug has the probability density function $f(x) = \frac{50}{(x+50)^2}$ for $x \ge 0$. The probability that the drug's shelf life is 30 weeks or less is

a. $\frac{11}{16}$ b. $\frac{1}{2}$ c. $\frac{1}{4}$ d. $\frac{3}{8}$

[b] 36. The daily demand for water (in millions of gallons) in New York City has the probability density function $f(x) = 0.4 - 0.08x$ for $0 \le x \le 5$. The probability that the daily demand is greater than 2 million gallons is

a. 0.16 b. 0.36 c. 0.5 d. 0.2

SHORT ANSWER 11.2

37. Find the value of the constant a that makes the function $f(x) = \frac{a}{x^2}$ a probability density function on the interval [1, 2].

    Answer: 2

38. Find the value of the constant a that makes the function $f(x) = \frac{3a}{x}$ a probability density function on the interval [1, e].

    Answer: $\frac{1}{3}$

39. Find the value of the constant a that makes the function $f(x) = ax^2 + 5ax$ a probability density function on the interval [0, 3].

    Answer: $\frac{2}{63}$

40. For the probability density function $f(x) = \frac{2}{9}x(3-x)$ on [0, 3], find E(x), var(x), and σ(x).

    Answer: E(x) = 1.5, var(x) = 0.45, σ(x) = 0.671

41. For the probability density function $f(x) = \frac{9}{4x^3}$ on [1, 3], find E(x), var(x), and σ(x).

    Answer: E(x) = 1.5, var(x) = 0.22188, σ(x) = 0.471

42. If x has the cumulative distribution function $F(x) = x^3$ on [0, 1] find $P(0.5 \leq x \leq 1)$.

    Answer: 0.875

43. If x has the cumulative distribution function $F(x) = \frac{2}{7}x^{\frac{5}{2}}$ on [0, 4], find $P(2 \leq x \leq 4)$.

    Answer: 0.82322

44. If the number of months until a computer game makes a profit (or is removed from the market) is a random variable X with probability density function $f(x) = 0.006x(10 - x)$ on [0, 10], find
 a. The expected number of months.
 b. The variance and standard deviation.
 c. $P(X \geq 7.5)$

 Answer: a. 5 months b. $\sigma^2 = 5$, $\sigma = 2.236$ c. $0.156 \approx 15.6\%$

45. The amount of water (in millions of gallons) used a town is a random variable X with probability density function $f(x) = 0.32x$ on [0, 2.5]. Find
 a. The expected demand E(X).
 b. The supply level that, with probability 0.85 will be sufficient.

 Answer: a. 1.67 million gallons b. 2.3 million gallons

Section 11.3 Uniform and Exponential Random Variables

MULTIPLE CHOICE 11.3

[d] 46. Find the mean of a uniform random variable on the interval [0, 5].

a. 5 b. 1 c. $\frac{1}{5}$ d. 2.5

[c] 47. Find the mean of a uniform random variable on the interval [0, 20].

a. $\frac{1}{20}$ b. 20 c. 10 d. $\frac{1}{10}$

[b] 48. Find the standard deviation of a uniform random variable on the interval [0, 8].

a. $5.3\overline{3}$ b. 2.309 c. 2 d. 4

[d] 49. Find the variance of a uniform random variable on the interval [0, 0.5].

a. 0.1443 b. 0.25 c. 0.0625 d. $0.0208\overline{3}$

[a] 50. State the probability density function for the exponential random variable with mean $\frac{1}{5}$.

a. $f(x) = 5e^{-5x}$ b. $f(x) = \frac{1}{5}e^{\frac{1}{5}x}$ c. $f(x) = \frac{1}{5}e^{-\frac{1}{5}x}$ d. $f(x) = \frac{1}{5}e^{-x}$

[c] 51. State the probability density function for the exponential random variable with mean 4.

a. $f(x) = 4e^{-4x}$ b. $f(x) = 4e^{4x}$ c. $f(x) = \frac{1}{4}e^{-\frac{1}{4}x}$ d. $f(x) = e^{-4x}$

[d] 52. State the probability density function for the exponential random variable with standard deviation 2.

a. $2e^{-2x}$ b. $4e^{-4x}$ c. $\frac{1}{4}e^{-\frac{1}{4}x}$ d. $\frac{1}{2}e^{-\frac{1}{2}x}$

[b] 53. State the probability density function for the exponential random variable with standard deviation $\frac{1}{3}$.

a. $\frac{1}{3}e^{-\frac{1}{3}x}$ b. $3e^{-3x}$ c. $\sqrt{3ex}^{-\sqrt{3}x}$ d. $\frac{1}{9}e^{-\frac{1}{9}x}$

[b] 54. The waiting time at a drive-in bank has an exponential distribution with mean 3 minutes. What is the probability of waiting less than 2 minutes?

a. 0.64 b. 0.49 c. 0.38 d. 0.51

[d] 55. The number (x) of sodas per day at a certain convenience store has an exponential distribution with mean 10 sodas. What is the probability that between 5 and 11 sodas will be sold in a given day?

a. 0.47 b. 0.37 c. 0.57 d. 0.27

[a] 56. The length of time between vacancies for the superintendent of schools in Pittsburgh is exponentially distributed with mean 2.25 years. Find the probability that at least 5 years will elapse between vacancies.

a. 0.108 b. 0.892 c. 0.169 d. 0.396

SHORT ANSWER 11.3

57. A roller coaster ride at Six Flags arrives at the loading station every 2 minutes, so if you arrive at a random time, your wait is uniformly distributed on the interval [0, 2]. Find E(x), var(x), σ(x), and $P(x \le 1)$.

    Answer: E(x) = 1 minute, var(x) = $\frac{1}{3}$ minute, σ(x) = 0.5774 minutes, $P(x \le 1) = \frac{1}{2}$

58. A train arrives at a station every 15 minutes, so if you arrive at a random time, your wait is uniformly distributed on the interval [0, 15]. Find E(x), var(x), σ(x), $P(x \le 5)$.

    Answer: E(x) = 7.5 minutes, var(x) = 18.75 minutes, σ(x) = 4.33 minutes, $P(x \le 5) = \frac{1}{3}$

59. For $f(x) = \frac{1}{3}e^{-\frac{1}{3}x}$, find E(x), var(x), σ(x).

    Answer: E(x) = 3, var(x) = 9, σ(x) = 3

60. For $f(x) = 0.05e^{-0.05x}$, find E(x), var(x), σ(x).

    Answer: E(x) = 20, var(x) = 400, σ(x) = 20

61. For $f(x) = 10e^{-10x}$, find E(x), var(x), σ(x).

    Answer: $E(x) = \frac{1}{10}$, $var(x) = \frac{1}{100}$, $\sigma(x) = \frac{1}{10}$

62. The time (x in seconds) for a rat to find its way through a maze is exponentially distributed with a mean time of 30 seconds. What is the probability that a rat takes less than 20 seconds to complete the maze?

    Answer: 0.4865

63. The length of phone calls (in minutes) at a particular phone booth has the probability density function that is exponential with a mean of 2 minutes. Find the probability that a randomly selected call will last less than 2 minutes.

    Answer: 0.6321

64. Find the median of the random variable with the probability density function f(x) = 0.5x on [0, 2].

    Answer: 1.414

65. Find the median of the random variable with the probability density function $f(x) = 3x^2$ on [0, 1].

Answer: 0.7937

66. Find the median of the random variable with the probability density function $f(x) = 0.08x$ on [0, 5].

Answer: 3.53553

67. The graduate of a business college determines that the average number of weeks until each finds a job is 9 weeks. If the time it takes to find a job is exponentially distributed, what is the probability that a job will be found between 6 and 13 weeks after graduation?

Answer: 28%

68. The number of seconds between placing an order and receiving the order at a fast food drive-through window is exponentially distributed with mean 125 seconds. Find the probability that the next customer will wait no more than 200 seconds.

Answer: 80%

Section 11.4 Normal Random Variables

MULTIPLE CHOICE 11.4

[b] 69. If x is normal with mean 100 and standard deviation 10, find $P(x \geq 80)$.

a. 0.4772 b. 0.9772 c. 0.5228 d. 0.0228

[c] 70. If x is normal with mean 4.5 and standard deviation 0.75, find $P(3 \leq x \leq 5.25)$.

a. 0.8337 b. 0.9161 c. 0.8186 d. 0.7514

[a] 71. If x is normal with mean 50 and standard deviation 15, find $P(40 \leq x \leq 47)$.

a. 0.1682 b. 0.6693 c. 0.2481 d. 0.8307

[c] 72. If x is normal with mean 3 and standard deviation 0.25, find $P(x \geq 2)$.

a. 0.4999 b. 0.5000 c. 0.9999 d. 0.0001

[a] 73. If x is normal with mean 15 and standard deviation 3.2, find $P(8 \leq x \leq 12)$.

a. 0.1599 b. 0.6593 c. 0.8407 d. 0.1671

SHORT ANSWER 11.4

74. For $P(0 \leq z \leq 1.62)$, find the probability for a standard normal variable z.

    Answer: 0.4474

75. For $P(-0.82 \leq z \leq 0)$, find the probability for a standard normal variable z.

    Answer: 0.2939

76. For $P(-0.45 \leq z \leq 2.73)$, find the probability for a standard normal variable z.

    Answer: 0.6705

77. For $P(-2.18 \leq z \leq -0.42)$, find the probability for a standard normal variable z.

    Answer: 0.3226

78. For $P(-1.2 \leq z \leq 2.64)$, find the probability for a standard normal variable z.

    Answer: 0.8808

79. For $P(-0.95 \leq z \leq 0.65)$, find the probability for a standard normal variable z.

    Answer: 0.5711

80. If X is normal with a mean of 4 and standard deviation of 4, find $P(X \leq -1)$.

    Answer: 0.3944

81. If X is normal with mean -1.5 and standard deviation = 1, find $P(-2 \leq X \leq -1)$.

    Answer: 0.3830

82. Weights of Pacific yellowfin tuna follow a normal distribution with mean weight 68 pounds and standard deviation 12 pounds. For a randomly caught Pacific yellowfin tuna, what is the probability that the weight is less than 50 pounds?

    Answer: 0.0668

83. At a ski resort in Colorado, the daytime high temperature is normally distributed during February with mean 22°F and standard deviation of 10°F. What is the probability of skiing there in February and encountering daytime highs between 29°F and 40°F?

    Answer: 0.2060

84. It has been determined that the police response time for a certain city has a normal distribution with mean 8.4 minutes and standard deviation 1.7 minutes. For a randomly received emergency call, what is the probability that the response time will be more than 10 minutes?

Answer: 0.1733

85. A commercial jet uses an average of 718 gallons of jet fuel each hour that it is in cruising position. The standard deviation of fuel consumption is 42 gallons per hour. If the fuel consumption is normally distributed, what is the probability that for a jet in cruising position, the fuel consumption for one hour is
a. between 650 and 815 gallons?
b. less than 600 gallons?

Answer: a. 0.9368 b. 0.0025

86. For a given population of high school seniors, the Scholastic Aptitude Test (SAT) in mathematics has a mean score of 500 with a standard deviation of 100. Assuming SAT scores are normally distributed, what is the probability that a high school senior's score on the mathematics part of the SAT will be
a. more than 675?
b. less than 450?

Answer: a. 0.0401 b. 0.3085

Chapter 11 – Graphing Calculator

Probability

Section 11.1 Discrete Probability

1. For the function $f(x) = \frac{a}{1+x^3}$, find the value of the constant a that makes the function a probability density function, on the interval [1, 2]. Use your Fn Int key on your graphing calculator to approximate the definite integral. Round you r answer to 3 decimal places.

   Answer: $a \approx 3.932$

2. For the function $f(x) = a \sin x^2$, find the value of the constant a that makes the function a probability density function, on the interval $[0, \pi]$. Use your Fn Int key on your graphing calculator to approximate the definite integral. Round you r answer to 3 decimal places.

   Answer: $a \approx 1.294$

3. For the function $f(x) = ae^{-\frac{1}{3}x^3}$, find the value of the constant a that makes the function a probability density function, on the interval [–1, 1]. Use your Fn Int key on your graphing calculator to approximate the definite integral. Round you r answer to 3 decimal places.

   Answer: $a \approx 0.496$

4. Use your calculator's Fn Int key to approximate the man E(x) of the probability density function $f(x) = \frac{3.932}{1+x^3}$ on [1, 2]. Round E(x) to 3 decimal places.

   Answer: $E(x) = 1.377$

5. a. Use your graphing calculator's Fn Int key to approximate the mean E(x) of the probability density function $f(x) = \frac{3.932}{1+x^3}$ on [1, 2].

   b. Using your answer from part a, find var(x) for the function $f(x) = \frac{3.932}{1+x^3}$ on [1, 2] again using your Fn Int key.

   Answer: a. $E(x) = 1.377$ b. $\text{var}(x) = 0.075$

Section 11.2 Continuous Probability

6. Use your graphing calculator's Fn Int key to approximate the mean E(x) of the probability density function $f(x) = 1.294 \sin x^2$ on $[0, \pi]$. Round E(x) to 3 decimal places.

   Answer: $E(x) = 1.231$

7. a. Use your graphing calcultor's Fn Int key to approximate the mean E(x) for the probability density function $f(x) = 1.294 \sin x^2$ on $[0, \pi]$. Round E(x) to 3 decimal places.
   b. Using your answer from part a, find var(x) for the fucntion $f(x) = 1.294 \sin x^2$ on $[0, \pi]$, again using your Fn Int key.

   Answer: a. $E(x) = 1.231$ b. 0.685

8. If x has the probability density function $f(x) = 0.496e^{-\frac{1}{3}x^3}$ on $[-1, 1]$, find $P\left(-\frac{1}{2} \le x \le \frac{1}{2}\right)$ using your graphing calculator and the Fn Int key.

   Answer: 0.496

9. If x has the probability density function $f(x) = 0.5e^{\sqrt{x}}$ on $[0, 1]$, find $P(0 \le x \le 0.5)$ using your graphing calculator and the Fn Int key.

   Answer: 0.406

Section 11.3 Uniform and Exponential Random Variables

10. The average time between innings of a baseball game is found to be 4 minutes. If the time between innings is an exponential random variable, find the probability that the time between innings at a game that you are watching is less than 3 minutes. Use your Fn Int key on your graphing calculator to perform the integration.

    Answer: 0.528

11. The length of time between vacancies on a city council is exponentially distributed with mean 1.245 years. Using your graphing calculator, find the probability that less than 3 years elapses between vacancies.

    Answer: 0.910

12. Using your graphing calculator, find the median of the random variable with the density function $f(x) = 0.5681x^{-0.2}$ on [1, 3] by assigning the cumulative function F(x) to y_1 and the constant $\frac{1}{2}$ to y_2. Then using INTERSECT (or Trace), find the x-coordinate where the two function intersect.

    Answer: 1.95

13. Using your calculator, find the median of the random variable with the density function $f(x) = 0.045x^{1.5}$ on [0, 5] by assigning the cumulative function F(x) to y_1 and the constant $\frac{1}{2}$ to y_2. Then using INTERSECT (or Trace), find the x-coordinate where the 2 functions intersect.

    Answer: 3.78

Section 11.4 Normal Random Variables

14. Use a graphing calculator program to find the probability $P(z \geq -1.5)$ for a standard normal random variable z.

    Answer: 0.9332

15. Using a graphing calculator program to find the probability $P(-2.57 \leq z \leq 1.16)$ for a standard normal random variable z.

    Answer: 0.8719

16. Using a graphing calculator program to find the probability $P(z \leq -2.25)$ for a standard normal random variable z.

    Answer: 0.0122

17. Use a graphing calculator program to find the following probability. If x is a normal distribution with mean 10 and standard deviation 2.5, find $P(6.5 \leq x \leq 7.5)$.

    Answer: 0.0779

18. Use a graphing calculator program to find the following probability. If x is a normal distribution with mean −1.5 and standard deviation 0.3, find $P(-1.5 \leq x \leq -1.02)$.

    Answer: 0.4452

19. The weight of food packed in certain containers is normally distributed with mean 16 ounces and standard deviation 0.1 ounces. Find the probability that a randomly selected container holds between 15.9 ounces and 16.2 ounces.

    Answer: 0.8186

20. The average amount of money spent at a convenience store is found to be $10.32 with standard deviation $2.56. If the amount is normally distributed, find the probability that a randomly-selected customer spends less than $6.48.

    Answer: 0.0668

Chapter 1 Test

Test A

1. Convert $\{x \mid -2 < x \leq 5\}$ to interval notation.

2. Find the equation of the line passing through the points (–1, 2) and (–3, 5).

3. Find the equation of the vertical line that passes through (1, –6).

4. Evaluate $(16)^{-3/4}$.

5. Simplify $\dfrac{(3x^3x)^2}{3(x^2)^3}$.

6. Give the domain and range for $f(x) = \dfrac{1}{x+2}$.

7. Graph $f(x) = 3x - 1$.

8. Graph $f(x) = 2x^2 - 4x - 16$.

9. Solve $3x^2 + 3x - 18 = 0$ by factoring or the quadratic formula.

10. For $f(x) = \dfrac{x+4}{x(x-1)}$, find f(2).

11. For $2x - 5y = 10$, find the slope m and y-intercept.

12. Graph $f(x) = 2^x$.

13. Graph $f(x) = \begin{cases} x - 5 & \text{if } x \geq 4 \\ 7 - 2x & \text{if } x < 4 \end{cases}$

14. For $f(x) = 2x^2 - 1$, find and simplify $\frac{f(x+h) - f(x)}{h}$

15. A company's advertising budget is $A(p) = 3p^{0.25}$, where p is the company's profit and the profit is predicted to be $p(t) = 3t + 10$, t being the number of years from now. (Both A and p are in millions of dollars.) Express the advertising budget A as a function of t and use it to predict the advertising budget 5 years from now.

16. Find the equation of the line that passes through the point (1.5, 7.6) and has a slope of –3.2.

17. A company has a monthly fixed cost of $40,000 and a production cost of $6 for each unit. Each unit sells for $10. Find the monthly profit P as a function of the number of units x.

18. Find the quantity (x units) required to break-even when the cost is $C = 48{,}50x + 15{,}510$, and revenue is $R = 76x$.

19. Evaluate $\left[\frac{1}{1.44}\right]^{-\frac{1}{2}}$.

20. If $f(x) = -6x + 1$ and $g(x) = x^3$, find $f[g(x)]$ and $g[f(x)]$.

Chapter 1 Test

Form B

1. Convert $\{x \mid -3 \le x \le 2\}$ to interval notation and graph on the real number line.

   a. (–3,2) b. [–3, 2) c. [–3, 2] d. (–3, 2]

2. The equation of the line passing through (2, 5) and (3, –1) is

   a. $4x + y = 13$ b. $6x + y = 17$ c. $-6x + y = 12$ d. $-4x + y = 6$

3. The equation of the horizontal line passing through (–3, 4) is

   a. $x = -3$ b. $y = -3$ c. $y = 4$ d. $x = 4$

4. Evaluate $(8)^{-2/3}$

   a. ¼ b. –16/3 c. 1/8 d. 4

5. Simplify $\dfrac{(2y^2y^3)^2}{4(y^3)^3}$

   a. y/2 b. y c. y^4 d. $y^4/2$

6. The domain for $f(x) = \dfrac{1}{3x - 7}$ is

   a. $\{x \mid x \ne 0\}$ b. $\{x \mid x \ne 7/3\}$ c. $\Re$ d. $\{x \mid x \ne -3\}$

7. The equation for this graph is

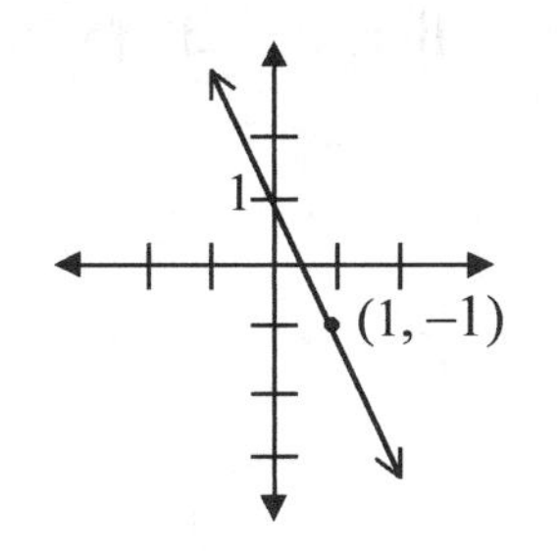

   a. $y = x + 1$ b. $y = 2x + 1$ c. $y = -2x + 1$ d. $y = -2x - 1$

8. The vertex of the parabola $f(x) = -3x^2 + 6x + 24$ is

   a. (1, 27) b. (–1, 27) c. (3, 16) d. (1, –24)

9. Using factoring or the quadratic formula, the solutions to $2x^2 - 2x - 24 = 0$ are

   a. $x = -4, x = 3$ b. $x = 6, x = -2$ c. $x = -4, x = -3$ d. $x = 4, x = -3$

10. Given $f(x) = \frac{x-9}{x(x+5)}$, find $f(-3)$

    a. –2 b. –27/6 c. 2 d. –3

11. The equation of the line that passes through the point (–5, 2) and has slope –1.8 is

    a. $1.8x + y = 0$ b. $1.8x + y - 7 = 0$ c. $1.8x - y = 0$ d. $1.8x + y + 7 = 0$

12. For $f(x) = \begin{cases} 2x - 3 & \text{if } x > 3 \\ 8 - x & \text{if } x \le 3 \end{cases}$ $f(3) =$

    a. 3 b. 5 c. does not exist d. 0

13. For $f(x) = x^2 - 4x + 7$, $\frac{f(x+h) - f(x)}{h}$ simplifies as

    a. $2x + h - 4$ b. $2x + 4h$ c. $2x - 4$ d. $2xh + h - 4$

14. A company's advertising budget is $A(p) = 4p^{0.2}$, where p is the company's profit and the profit is predicted to be $p(t) = 2t + 6$, t being the number of years from now. (Both A and p are in millions of dollars.) Using the advertising budget A as a function of t, the advertising budget 4 years from now will be

    a. \$14 million b. \$1.70 million c. \$6.78 million d. \$5.28 million

15. The x-coordinate of the vertex of the parabola $f(x) = 1.7x^2 + 8.5x + 6.125$ is

a. -2.5 b. -5 c. $-\frac{1}{2}$ d. 8.5

16. Given the two-part function $f(x) = \begin{cases} -3x + 6.7 & x \geq 1 \\ 2 - x^2 & x < 1 \end{cases}$, the largest value that f(x) can assume is

a. undefined b. 6.7 c. 3.7 d. 2

17. If $f(x) = -5x$ and $g(x) = 4x - 1$, then $(f \circ g)(0) =$

a. 0 b. 4 c. 1 d. 5

18. If the cost of producing x sets of vertical blinds is $C(x) = 45.75x + 36.25$ dollars, how many sets of vertical blinds can be produced for $997?

a. 15 b. 21 c. 27 d. 33

19. It costs $C(x) = 0.3x^2 + 40x + 372$ dollars to produce x hand knit dresses. Each dress can be sold for $152. Determine the profit function P(x).

a. $-0.3x^2 + 40x + 220$ b. $-0.3x^2 + 112x - 372$
c. $-0.3x^2 - 112x - 220$ d. $-0.3x^2 - 40x + 524$

20. Find the quantity (x units) required to break-even when $C = 19x + 8750$ and revenue $R = 50.25x$.

a. 280 b. 126 c. 461 d. 174

Chapter 2 Test

Test A

1. Evaluate the limit $\lim_{x \to 2} \frac{x^2 - 2x}{x^2 - 4}$

2. Evaluate the limit $\lim_{h \to 0} \frac{x^2h - 3xh^2}{h}$

3. Determine whether the function is continuous or discontinuous. If it is discontinuous, state where it is discontinuous.
   $f(x) = \begin{cases} 5 - x & \text{if } x \geq 2 \\ x + 2 & \text{if } x < 2 \end{cases}$

4. Define the derivative $f'(x)$ of the function $f(x)$.

5. Use the definition of the derivative to find $f'(x)$ for the function $f(x) = 3.7x^2 - 8.3x + 2.4$.

6. Find the derivative of the function $f(x) = 2\sqrt{x^7} - \frac{6}{\sqrt[3]{x}} + 3$.

7. Find the derivative of the function $f(x) = \frac{3}{x^4}$.

8. Find the derivative of the function $f(x) = (x^2 - 5)(x^3 + 2x)$.

9. Find the derivative of the function $f(x) = \frac{3x - 4}{x + 1}$.

10. Find the derivative of the function $f(x) = \sqrt{x^3 - 2x + 1}$.

11. Find the derivative of the function $f(x) = \frac{1}{(4x^2 - 3x - 5)^2}$.

12. Find the derivative of the function $f(x) = (5x - 1)^4(5x + 1)^3$.

13. Find the derivative of the function $f(x) = \left(\frac{3x-1}{3x+1}\right)^4$.

14. Find $f''(x)$ for the function $f(x) = (x^2 + 1)^5$.

15. Find $f''(x)$ for the function $f(x) = \frac{x}{x+2}$.

16. State where $f'(x)$ does not exist in the following graph:

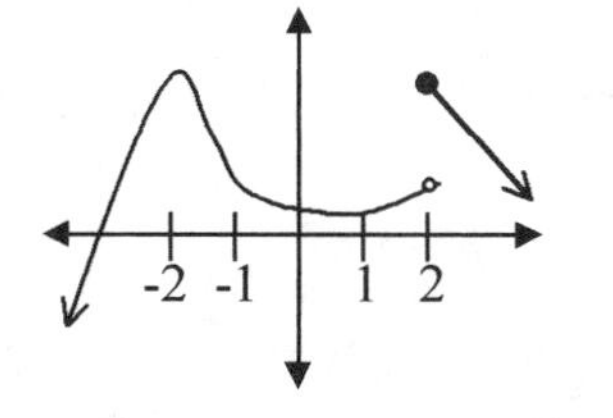

17. A company's cost function is $C(x) = \sqrt{6x^2 + 300}$ dollars.
    a. Find the marginal cost function.
    b. Find the marginal cost at x = 10 and interpret the answer.

18. The number of people newly infected on day t of a flu epidemic is $f(t) = 10t^2 - t^3$ for ($t \leq 10$). Find the instantaneous rate of change of this number on day 7 and interpret the answer.

19. Find the equation of the line tangent to the graph $y = 3x^3 + 2x$ at the point (–2, –20).

20. The profit from the production and sale of x remote controllers is $P(x) = 12x - 0.01x^2 - 7000$ dollars. Use marginal profit to approximate the profit from the production and sale of the 201st controller.

Chapter 2 Test

Test B

1. Evaluate the limit $\lim_{x\to 7}\frac{x^2-2x-35}{x-7}$

a. 7 b. −10 c. 12 d. undefined

2. Evaluate the limit $\lim_{h\to 0}\frac{2x^2h-5xh^2}{h}$

a. undefined b. $2x^2-5x$ c. $2x^2$ d. $4x-5$

3. The function $f(x) = \begin{matrix} 3-x & \text{if } x \geq 2 \\ x+1 & \text{if } x < 2 \end{matrix}$ is

a. continuous
b. discontinuous because f(2) does not exist
c. discontinuous because $\lim_{x\to 2} f(x)$ does not exist
d. discontinuous because it is a piecewise linear function.

4. This function is

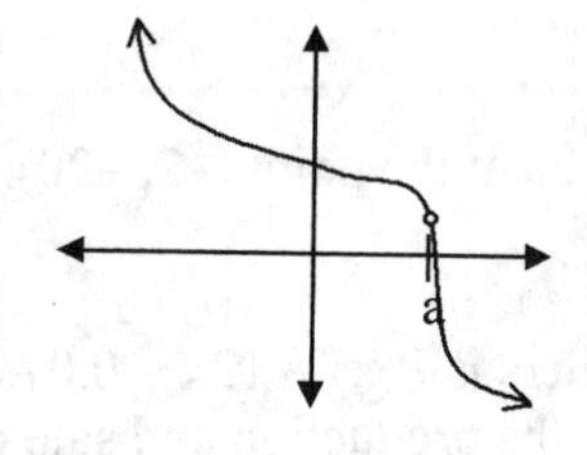

a. continuous
b. discontinuous because f(a) does not exist
c. discontinuous because $\lim_{x\to a} f(x)$ does not exist
d. discontinuous because it is a piecewise linear function.

5. If $f(x) = x-\frac{1}{x}+\frac{1}{x^2}$ then $f'(1) =$

a. 1 b. 1/3 c. ½ d. 0

6. If $f(x) = (2 + x^2)(3 - x^3)$ then $f'(x) =$

a. $5x - 6x^2 + 6x^4$ b. $6x + 5x^2 - 6x^4$ c. $6x - 6x^2 - 5x^4$ d, $5x + 6x^2 + 6x^4$

7. If $f(x) = \dfrac{3x^2}{4x-1}$, then $f'(x) =$

a. $\dfrac{6x}{4}$ b. $\dfrac{6x}{(4x-1)^2}$ c. $\dfrac{6x(6x-1)}{(4x-1)^2}$ d. $\dfrac{6x(2x-1)}{(4x-1)^2}$

8. If $f(x) = \sqrt{4x^2+3}$ then $f'(x) =$

a. $\dfrac{4x}{\sqrt{4x^2+3}}$ b. $\dfrac{1}{\sqrt{4x^2+3}}$ c. $\dfrac{8x}{\sqrt{4x^2+3}}$ d. $\dfrac{8x+3}{\sqrt{4x^2+3}}$

9. If $f(x) = \dfrac{3}{(x^3+3x)^3}$ then $f'(x) =$

a. $\dfrac{3}{(x^3+3x)^4}$ b. $\dfrac{-9x^2}{(x^3+3x)^4}$ c. $\dfrac{-27(x^2+1)}{(x^3+3x)^4}$ d. $\dfrac{18x^2}{(x^3+3x)^4}$

10. If $f(x) = (x^3 + 7)^9(6x - 1)^4$ then $f'(x) =$

a. $36\,(x^3 + 7)^8(6x - 1)^3$
b. $18(x^2 + 2)(x^3 + 7)^8(6x - 1)^3$
c. $18x^2(x^3 + 7)^8(6x - 1)^3$
d. $3(x^3 + 7)^8(6x - 1)^3(62x^3 - 9x^2 + 56)$

11. If $f(x) = \left[\dfrac{x^2-x+1}{2x+5}\right]$ then $f'(x) =$

a. $\dfrac{2x^2+10x-7}{(2x+5)^2}$
b. $\dfrac{(4x-1)(x^2-x+1)}{2x+5}$
c. $\dfrac{2(x^2-x+1)(2x-1)}{(2x+5)^4}$
d. $\dfrac{2x(x-1)(x^2-x+1)}{(2x+5)^2}$

12. If $f(x) = x^{2/3}$ then $f''(x) =$

a. $\dfrac{2}{3x^{2/3}}$ b. $\dfrac{-2}{9x^{4/3}}$ c. $\dfrac{-4}{9x^{5/3}}$ d. $\dfrac{4}{3x^{5/3}}$

13. If $f(x) = (2x+1)^5$ then $f''(1) =$

a. 810 b. 2,160 c. 27 d. 240

14. The graph of f(x) is shown below. Then f′(x)

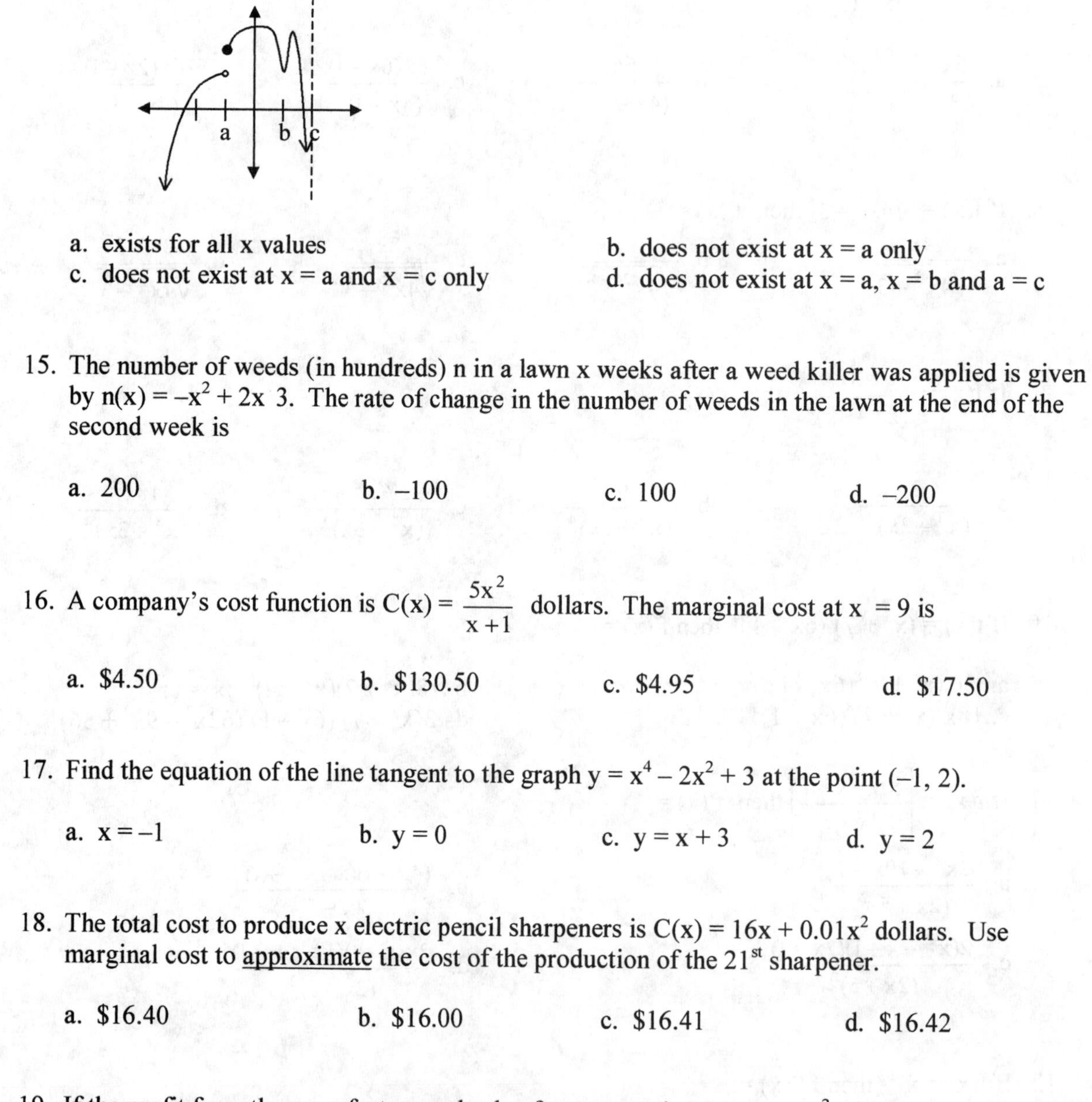

a. exists for all x values
b. does not exist at x = a only
c. does not exist at x = a and x = c only
d. does not exist at x = a, x = b and a = c

15. The number of weeds (in hundreds) n in a lawn x weeks after a weed killer was applied is given by $n(x) = -x^2 + 2x\ 3$. The rate of change in the number of weeds in the lawn at the end of the second week is

a. 200 b. −100 c. 100 d. −200

16. A company's cost function is $C(x) = \dfrac{5x^2}{x+1}$ dollars. The marginal cost at x = 9 is

a. \$4.50 b. \$130.50 c. \$4.95 d. \$17.50

17. Find the equation of the line tangent to the graph $y = x^4 - 2x^2 + 3$ at the point (−1, 2).

a. $x = -1$ b. $y = 0$ c. $y = x + 3$ d. $y = 2$

18. The total cost to produce x electric pencil sharpeners is $C(x) = 16x + 0.01x^2$ dollars. Use marginal cost to approximate the cost of the production of the 21st sharpener.

a. \$16.40 b. \$16.00 c. \$16.41 d. \$16.42

19. If the profit from the manufacture and sale of x cameras is $P(x) = -0.1x^2 + 150x - 2675$ dollars, what production level results in a marginal profit of zero dollars?

a. 750 b. 75 c. 30 d. 300

20. For the following graphed function, state the x-values for which the derivative $f'(x)$ does not exist.

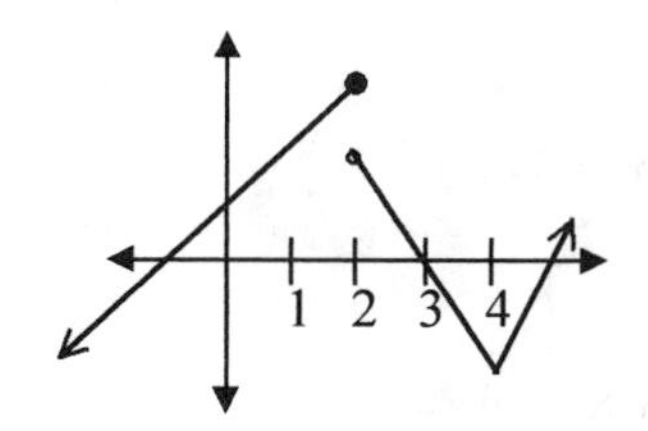

a. $x = 2$ only
b. $f'(x)$ exists for all x
c. $x = 2, x = 4$
d. $x = 4$ only

Chapter 3 Test

Test A

1. Find the critical values for the function $f(x) = x^3 + 3x^2 - 9x - 11$

2. Find the critical values for the function $f(x) = \sqrt{x^2 + x - 20}$

3. For the function, $f(x) = x^3 - 6x^2 + 9x - 1$,
   a. make a sign diagram for $f'(x)$,
   b. make a sign diagram for $f''(x)$,
   c. identify all relative extreme points and inflection points.

4. For the function, $f(x) = x^4 - 8x^3 + 18x^2$,
   a. make a sign diagram for $f'(x)$,
   b. make a sign diagram for $f''(x)$,
   c. identify all relative extreme points and inflection points.

5. Find the absolute extrema for the function $f(x) = x^3 - 3x^2 + 4$ on the interval $[-1, 2.5]$

6. The proportion of the wind's energy that can be obtained from a windmill is given by $E(x) = 4x^3 - 8x^2 + 4x$, where x is the proportion by which wind is slowed as it passes through the windmill. Find the proportion x that maximizes this function on the interval [0, 1].

7. A farmer wants to make four identical rectangular enclosures next to his barn, as shown below. If he has only 200ft of fence and if the side along the barn needs no fence, what is the largest total area that can be enclosed in this way?

   Barn

8. An air conditioner manufacturer will be increasing production at the rate of 70 air conditioners per week. Revenue from the sale of x air conditioners is $R(x) = 100x - 0.001x^2$ dollars. Find the rate of change of revenue with respect to time when the weekly production level is 550 air conditioners.

9. For $x^2 + 4xy + y^2 = 1$, find $\frac{dy}{dx}$ using implicit differentiation.

10. For $\sqrt{x} - \sqrt{y} = -3$, use implicit differentiation to find $\frac{dy}{dx}$ at $x = 1$, $y = 16$.

11. Given the total cost function $C(x) = 2.5x^2 + 1.5x + 40$, find
    a. the average cost function,
    b. the number of units x that will minimize the average cost function,
    c. the minimum average cost.

12. A cable television company currently has 10,000 customers and charges $25 per month. A survey by a marketing firm indicated that each decrease of $1 in monthly charges will result in 1000 new subscribers. Determine the monthly charges that will result in a maximum monthly revenue.

13. A book publisher estimates the demand for a book to be 40,00 copies per year. It costs $10,000 to set up the presses to print the book, plus $12 for each book printed. If it costs $2 to store a book for a year, how many books should be printed at a time and how many productions should there be to minimize costs.

Chapter 3 Test

Test B

1. Find the critical values for the function $f(x) = 3x^5 - 5x^3$.

a. $0, \sqrt{\frac{5}{3}}$ b. $-1, 1, 0$ c. $-1, 1$ d. $0, \sqrt{\frac{5}{3}}, -\sqrt{\frac{5}{3}}$

2. Find the critical values for the function $f(x) = x^4 + 4x^3 + 4x^2 - 1$.

a. 2, 1, 0 b. $-2, -1$ c. $-2, -1, 0$ d. 2, 1

3. Find the critical values for the function $f(x) = (9 - x^2)^{3/5}$.

a. 0 b. 3 c. $-3, 3$ d. $-3, 0, 3$

4. The graph of $f(x) = x^3 - 6x^2 + 9x + 5$ has a relative maximum at x =

a. 5 b. 1 c. 9 d. 0

5. The relative extrema of the function $f(x) = \frac{x^3}{3} - \frac{x^2}{2} - 2x + 5$ occur at x =

a. $-1, -2$ b. $-1, 2$ c. $1, -2$ d. 1, 2

6. The graph of $f(x) = 6(4 - x)^{2/3} + 3$ has

a. a relative maximum at $x = -4$ and no relative minimum
b. a relative maximum at $x = 2$ and no relative minimum
c. a relative minimum at $x = 4$ and no relative maximum
d. a relative minimum at $x = -2$ and no relative maximum

7. The graph of $f(x) = x^3 - 3x^2 - 24x + 1$ is concave up when

a. $x < -2$ b. $x < 4$ c. $x > -6$ d. $x > 1$

8. The point of inflection for the graph of $f(x) = \frac{x^3}{3} - x^2 - 3x + 7$ is

a. $(-1, 10/3)$ b. $(1, 10/3)$ c. $(-1, -8/3)$ d. $(1, -10/3)$

9. The graph below is concave down on the interval

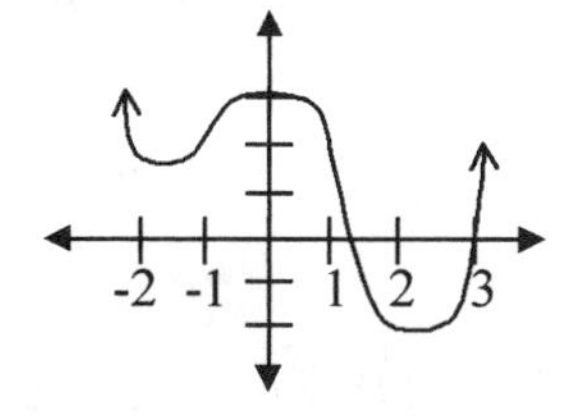

a. $(-3, -1)$ and $(1, \infty)$ b. $(-2, 0)$ and $(2, \infty)$ c. $(-1, 1)$ d. $(-3, -2)$ and $(0, 2)$

10. Given the graph of f(x), on what interval(s) is $f'(x) < 0$?

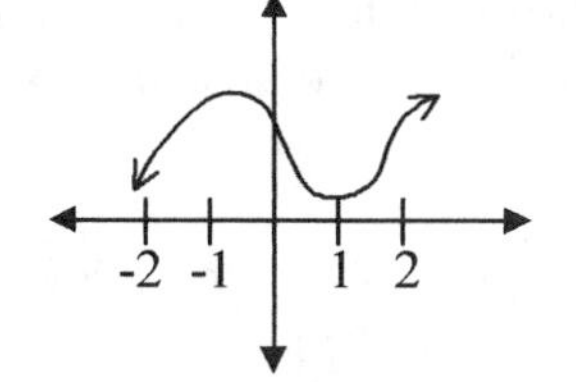

a. $(-\infty,-1)$ and $(1,\infty)$ b. $(-1, 1)$ c. $(0, \infty)$ d. $(-\infty,0)$

11. Given $f(x) = 2x^3 + 3x^2 - 12x - 7$ on the interval $[-3, 0]$ then the absolute maximum of f(x) is

a. 17 and it occurs at $x = -1$ b. 13 and it occurs at $x = -2$
c. 7 and it occurs at $x = 0$ d. 47 and it occurs at $x = -3$

12. The percent of effectiveness of a medicine t hours after it is taken is $P(t) = \frac{75}{16}t^2 - \frac{25}{64}t^3$ $(0 \le t \le 12)$. How many hours will it take for the medicine to achieve maximum effectiveness?

a. 10 b. 8 c. 6 d. 2

13. Find $\frac{dy}{dx}$ using implicit differentiation $y^2 - 3xy + x^2 = 7$

a. $\frac{2x + y}{3x - 2y}$ b. $\frac{3y - 2x}{2y - 3x}$ c. $\frac{2x}{3 - 2y}$ d. $\frac{2x}{y}$

14. For $1 + y^3 = x^2$, find $\frac{dy}{dx}$ at (3, 2) using implicit differentiation.

a. $-1/2$ b. 2 c. ½ d. -2

15. A store expects to sell 500 microwave ovens in a year. Each oven costs the store \$300, and there is a fixed delivery charge of \$200 per order. If it costs \$20 to store an oven for a year, how many ovens should be order at a time in order to minimize costs?

a. 5 b. 100 c. 200 d. 50

16. Given the total cost function $C(x) = 0.1x^2 + 5x + 250$ dollars, find the number of units that will minimize the average cost function.

a. 150 b. 25 c. 35 d. 90

17. A manufacturer can sell x pairs of sneakers for $p = 100 - 0.01x$ dollars per pair. It costs $C(x) = 50x + 9879$ dollars to produce all x pairs. Find the value of x that will maximize the profit.

a. 75 b. 750 c. 197 d. 2500

18. A yo-yo manufacturer will increase production at a rate of 250 yo-yo's per day. The daily revenue from the sale of all x yo-yo's produced is $R = 70x - 0.02x^2$ dollars. What is the rate of change revenue with respect to time, when the daily production level is 1500 yo-yo's per day?

a. \$90,000 b. \$60 c. \$2500 d. \$10

Chapter 4 Test

Test A

1. Find $\frac{dy}{dx}$ for $y = \ln (x^2 + 1)^5$.

2. Find $\frac{dy}{dx}$ for $y = e^{x^2} x^3$.

3. Find $\frac{dy}{dx}$ for $y = \ln (3x + 1) - 4e^{x/3} + \ln e$.

4. Find $\frac{dy}{dx}$ for $y = e^x \sqrt{6 - x^2}$.

5. Find $\frac{dy}{dx}$ for $y = \ln \left[\frac{x^2 - 5x + 3}{(4x + 7)^3} \right]$.

6. Find $\frac{dy}{dx}$ for $y = x^e$.

7. For $f(x) = \frac{x^3}{\ln x}$, find $f'(e)$.

8. The value of a pointing t years after its purchase is estimated to be $V(t) = 25{,}000e^{0.08t}$ dollars. Find the rate of change of its value at
   a. the time of purchase
   b. $t = 5$ years

9. If a country's gross national product (GNP) t years from now is predicted to be $G(t) = 12 + 2e^{0.1t}$ billion dollars, find the country's relative rate of change of the GNP 20 years from now.

10. For the demand equation $D(p) = 45 - 3p^2$, find the elasticity of demand at price $p = 3$. Is the demand elastic or inelastic at this price?

11. The demand function for a magazine is $D(p) = \sqrt{60 - 6p}$ where the price is p dollars. The publisher currently charges \$4. Should she raise or lower her price in order to increase revenues?

12. If a college education costs \$100,000, how large a trust fund must be established at a child's birth, paying 6% compounded continuously to ensure sufficient funds at age 18? (round to the nearest whole number).

13. The cost function is $C(x) = \frac{\ln x}{35 - 3x}$, find the marginal cost (to the nearest cent) when $x = 10$.

14. Find all relative maximum or minimum points for $y = 4x - x \ln x$.

15. At what annual rate of interest (to the nearest tenth percent) compounded continuously should money be invested to double the investment in $4\frac{1}{2}$ years?

16. Find the total amount (to the nearest cent) if interest is compounded continuously for an investment of \$745 at 4.3% for 2 years.

17. Solve for x, $e^{x+1} - 1 = 0$.

18. It is estimated that if x thousand dollars are spend on advertising approximately $S(x) = 50 - 40e^{-0.01x}$ thousand units of a certain commodity will be sold.
    a. How many units will be sold if no money is spent on advertising?
    b. How many units will be sold if \$8000 is spent on advertising?

19. A conglomerate purchased a hotel for \$5.5 million and sold it 6 years later for \$19.1 million. Find the annual rate of return (to the nearest tenth percent). Hint: $A = Pe^{rt}$.

20. Simplify $f(x) = \ln x^5 - \ln x^4 + \ln 1$ using the properties of logarithms.

Chapter 4 Test

Test B

1. An investment grows at a rate of 2.5% each year compounded continuously. Approximately how ling will it take the investment to double?

   a. 51 years b. 73 years c. 34 years d. 28 years

2. After x weeks of practice, a student can type $f(x) = 80(1 - e^{-0.3x})$ words per minute. How soon will the student be able to type 60 words per minute? (Round to the nearest tenth).

   a. 4.6 weeks b. 5.2 weeks c. 10.9 weeks d. 3.8 weeks

3. Find $\frac{dy}{dx}$ for the function $y = \frac{e^x}{x^2}$.

   a. $\frac{e^x}{x^3}$
   b. $\frac{e^x}{x^2} - \frac{2e^x}{x^3}$
   c. $\frac{e^x}{x^3} + \frac{2e^x}{x^2}$
   d. $2e^x - \frac{e^x}{x^3}$

4. Find $\frac{dy}{dx}$ for the function $y = (2x + 1)^4 e^x$.

   a. $4(2x + 1)^3 e^x$
   b. $8e^x(2x + 1)^3(8x + 1)$
   c. $8(2x + 1)^3 e^x$
   d. $e^x (2x + 1)^3(2x + 9)$

5. Find $\frac{dy}{dx}$ for the function $y = \ln(2x^2 - 3x)^4$.

   a. $\frac{16x - 12}{2x^2 - 3x}$
   b. $4(2x^2 - 3x)^3(4x - 3)$
   c. $4\left[\frac{4x - 3}{2x^2 - 3}\right]$
   d. $\frac{4(2x^2 - 3x)^3}{4x - 3}$

6. Find $\frac{dy}{dx}$ for the function $y = x^2 \ln(x^2)$.

   a. $2x[1 + \ln(x^2)]$
   b. $2x + 4\ln(x^2)$
   c. $4x \ln(x^2)$
   d. $2[1 + 4x \ln(x^2)]$

7. Find $\frac{dy}{dx}$ for the function $y = e^{5x^2}$.

a. $e^{5x^2}(2x)$
b. $(10x)x^2$
c. $e^{5x^2}(\ln 5)$
d. $e^{5x^2}(10x)$

8. For $f(x) = 4x - x \ln x$, find $f'(e)$.

a. $3e^2$
b. 2
c. 3
d. 1/3

9. One thousand bacteria are placed in a growth medium. The number of bacteria remaining at the end of x hours is $N(x) = 1{,}000e^{0.35x}$. How fast is the number of bacteria increasing at the end of 6 hours?

a. 1,667 per hour
b. 2,548 per hour
c. 1,993 per hour
d. 2,858 per hour

10. If a country's gross national product (GNP) t years from now is predicted to be $G(t) = 9 + 3e^{0.1t}$ billion dollars, find the relative rate of change of the GNP 20 years from now.

a. 0.5
b. 0.05
c. 0.071
d. 2.21

11. A company's demand equation is given by $D(p) = \sqrt{80 - 2p}$ with a current price of $p = 8$. In order to increase revenue, should the price be

a. raised
b. lowered
c. neither raised nor lowered

12. The demand function for a certain metal is $D(p) = 175 - 3p$, where p is the price per pound and x is the quantity demanded (in millions of pounds). Calculate the elasticity of demand at $p = 35$.

a. 2/3
b. 3/2
c. ½
d. 2

13. If the price at which x units can be sold is given by the equation $p = 15 - 4 \ln x$, approximate the marginal revenue when $x = 7$.

a. $3.22
b. $7.22
c. $14.43
d. $11.22

14. How much money (to the nearest dollar) should be invested now at 5.2% compounded continuously to accrue a total amount of $2150 in 6 years?

a. $1479
b. $2937
c. $787
d. $1574

15. Find all relative extreme points $y = x\,e^{-x}$

a. Min (0, 0) b. Max (1, e) c. Max (1, 1/e) d. Min $(1, e^{-1})$

16. The value of a piece of machinery after t years is given by $V(t) = 35{,}000e^{-0.74t}$, how fast is the machine's value changing at the end of 2 years?

a. \$5896 b. \$7967 c. \$51,800 d. \$5896

17. The solutions of $5xe^{x+1}$ are

a. $x = 0$ b. $x = 0, x = -1$ c. $x = 0, x = 1$ d. $x = -1$

18. Which of the following is the function for the given graph?

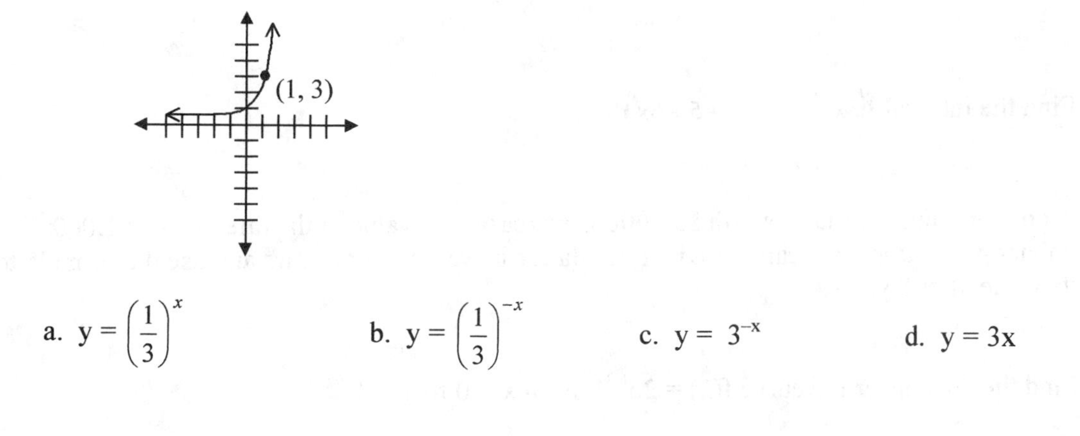

a. $y = \left(\frac{1}{3}\right)^{x}$ b. $y = \left(\frac{1}{3}\right)^{-x}$ c. $y = 3^{-x}$ d. $y = 3x$

19. Simplify $f(x) = \ln \frac{1}{\sqrt{e}} + \ln x^5 + \ln x^2$ using properties of logarithms.

a. $\frac{1}{2} + 7 \ln x$ b. $7 \ln x$ c. $\frac{1}{\sqrt{e}} + x^5 + x^2$ d. $-1/2 + 7 \ln x$

20. After x weeks of practice, a student can type $f(x) = 80(1 - e^{-0.3x})$ words per minute. How soon will the student be able to type 60 words per minute? (Round to the nearest tenth).

a. 4.6 weeks b. 5.2 weeks c. 10.9 weeks d. 3.8 weeks

Chapter 5 Test

Test A

1. Find the integral $\int(8x^3 - 9x^2 + 10x - 11)dx$.

2. Find the integral $\int\left[6\sqrt{x} - \frac{1}{x^4}\right]dx$.

3. Find the integral $\int x(x+12)^2 dx$.

4. Find the integral $\int\left[12e^{4x} + \frac{3}{x}\right]dx$.

5. Find the integral $\int\left(3x^{-2} + 4x^{-1} + 5 + 6x\right)dx$.

6. A condominium, initially worth \$50,000 is increasing in value at the rate of $r(t) = 1{,}000t^{2/3}$ dollars per year after t years. Find a formula for its value after t years and use the formula to find its value after 8 years.

7. Find the area under the curve $f(x) = 2e^{1/3x}$ from $x = 0$ to $x = 3$.

8. Find the area under the curve $f(x) = 8x^3 - 1$ from $x = 1$ to $x = 2$

9. The marginal profit function is $P'(x) = 100 - 2x$, find the profit function $P(x)$ if the profit is 700 when 10 units are produced.

10. Evaluate the definite integral $\int_1^3 (4x + 4x^{-1})dx$.

11. Evaluate the definite integral $\int_0^2 (9x^2 - 9e^{3x})dx$.

12. Find the average value of $f(x) = 5\sqrt[3]{x^2}$ on the interval [0, 8].

13. Find the area bounded by the curves $y = 4x^2 - 5x - 20$ and $y = x^2 + x + 4$.

14. Find the area bounded by the curve $y = x^2 - x - 6$ and the line $y = x + 2$.

15. For the demand function $d(x) = 18 - 0.03x^2$ find the consumers' surplus at the demand level $x = 20$.

16. Find the integral $\int \sqrt{x^4 + 4x}(x^3 + 1)dx$ by using the substitution method.

17. Find the integral $\int \frac{x^4}{x^5 + 1} dx$ by using the substitution method.

18. Find the integral $\int xe^{x^2} dx$ by using the substitution method.

19. Find the integral $\int \frac{x}{\sqrt{x^2 + 9}} dx$ by using the substitution method.

20. The rainfall in a county is predicted to be $R(x) = x^3 e^{x^4}$ inches during week x. Find the total rainfall during the 1st week ($x = 0$ to $x = 1$).

Chapter 5 Test

Form B

1. Find the integral $\int(3x^3 - 2x^2 + 5)dx$.

a. $9x^2 - 4x + C$

b. $\frac{3}{4}x^4 - \frac{2}{3}x^3 + 5x + C$

c. $9x^4 - 8x^3 + 50x + C$

d. $\frac{3}{4}x^4 - \frac{2}{3}x^3 + C$

2. Find the integral $\int\frac{3 + 4x^{3/2}}{\sqrt{x}}dx$.

a. $\frac{3}{2}\sqrt{x} + 2x^2 + C$

b. $\frac{3}{2}x^{\frac{-3}{2}} + 4 + C$

c. $\frac{3}{2}x^{\frac{-3}{2}} + 2x^2 + C$

d. $6\sqrt{x} + 2x^2 + C$

3. Find the integral $\int\frac{x^6 - 3}{x}dx$.

a. $\frac{x^7}{7} - 3x - \ln|x| + C$

b. $\frac{x^5}{5} - 3x + \ln|x| + C$

c. $\frac{x^6}{6} - 3x\ln|x| + C$

d. $\frac{x^6}{6} + 3x\ln|x| + C$

4. Find the integral $\int(x^{-1} + 3x^{-2})dx$

a. $\ln|x| - \frac{3}{x} + C$

b. $\ln|x| - \frac{1}{3x} + C$

c. $\ln|x| - \frac{1}{x^3} + C$

d. $\ln|x| + \frac{3}{x} + C$

5. Find the integral $\int\left(2e^{3x} + \frac{2}{x}\right)dx$.

a. $2e^{3x} + 2\ln|x| + C$

b. $6e^{3x} + 2\ln|x| + C$

c. $6e^{3x} - \frac{1}{x^2} + C$

d. $\frac{2}{3}e^{3x} + 2\ln|x| + C$

6. The marginal cost function for a certain manufacturer is given by $C'(x) = 25 + 20x - 0.03x^2$ and it costs $2,500 to produce 10 units. Find the total production costs for 100 units.

a. $50,000　　b. $92,500　　c. $93,760　　d. $1,725

7. Find the area of the region between the curve $y = x^3 + 2x^2 - 3x$ and the x-axis over the interval from $x = -1$ to $x = 3$.

a. $-\frac{32}{3}$ square units　　b. $\frac{45}{2}$ square units　　c. $\frac{80}{3}$ square units　　d. $\frac{7}{5}$ square units

8. Find the area of the region between the curve $y = \frac{1}{x^2}$ and the x-axis between $x = 1$ and $x = 2$.

a. $\frac{1}{2}$ square units　　b. $-\frac{3}{4}$ square units　　c. $-\frac{3}{2}$ square units　　d. $-\frac{1}{x} + c$ square units

9. Evaluate the definite integral $\int_0^5 e^{0.2t}\,dt$.

a. $5e$　　b. $5e - 1$　　c. $e - 1$　　d. $5e - 5$

10. Evaluate the definite integral $\int_1^e \left(2x + \frac{2}{x}\right)dx$.

a. $2e - 1$　　b. $e^2 + 1$　　c. $e^2 - 2$　　d. $e + 2$

11. The population density x miles from the center of a metropolitan area is given by the rate $P(x) = 350{,}000e^{-0.084x}$ people per square mile. Find the total number of people living between 1 and 2.5 miles from the center of the area.

a. 4,166,667　　b. 3,377,434　　c. 453,529　　d. 38,096

12. The average value of $f(x) = 6x - x^2 + 16$ on the interval [2, 5] is

a. 21　　b. 15　　c. 18　　d. 24

13. The area of the region bounded by the curves $y = x^2$ and $y = -2x^2 + 27$ is

a. 108　　b. 81　　c. 54　　d. 135

14. The area of the region bounded by the curves $y = 6x - x^2$ and $y = x^2 - 2x$ is

a. $\frac{20}{3}$ b. $\frac{64}{3}$ c. $\frac{128}{3}$ d. 32

15. For the demand function $D(x) = 200 - 0.5x$ find the consumers' surplus at the demand level $x = 100$.

a. \$9,000 b. \$7,500 c. \$2,500 d. \$5,500

16. Find the integral $\int x^2 e^{2x^3} dx$ by using the substitution method.

a. $6e^{2x^3} + C$ b. $\frac{1}{6}e^{x^6} + C$

c. $\frac{1}{6}e^{2x^3} + C$ d. cannot be integrated using our substitution formulas

17. Find the integral $\int x\sqrt{8 - 4x^2}\,dx$ by using the substitution method.

a. $-\frac{1}{8}(8 - 4x^2)^{3/2} + C$ b. $-\frac{1}{12}(8 - 4x^2)^{3/2} + C$

c. $-\frac{1}{3}(8 - 4x^2)^{3/2} + C$ d. cannot be integrated using our formulas

18. Find the integral $\int \frac{x}{\sqrt[3]{x^2 + 4x}}dx$ by using the substitution method.

a. $\frac{3}{2}(x^2 + 4x)^{2/3} + C$ b. $\frac{3}{4}(x^2 + 4x)^{2/3} + C$

c. $-\frac{3}{4}(x^2 + 4x)^{2/3} + C$ d. cannot be integrated using our formulas

19. Find the integral $\int \frac{x^2 - 4x}{x^3 - 6x^2}dx$ by using the substitution method.

a. $\ln|x^3 - 6x^2| + C$ b. $\frac{1}{3}\ln|x^3 - 6x^2| + C$

c. $3\ln|x^3 - 6x^2| + C$ d. cannot be integrated using our formulas

20. A student of a foreign language can memorize words and their definitions at the rate of $m(t) = 3t(3t^2 + 1)^{-1/2}$ words per minute, where t is in minutes. Approximately how many words can be memorized between the first and fourth minute?

a. 5 words b. 10 words c. 6 words d. 12 words

Chapter 6 Test

Test A

1. Find the integral $\int xe^{8x}dx$ using integration by parts.

2. Find the integral $\int x^{2/3} \ln x dx$ using integration by parts.

3. Find the integral $\int x\left(\sqrt[3]{x+1}\right)dx$ using integration by parts.

4. Find the integral $\int x(2x+3)^{99} dx$ using integration by parts.

5. Evaluate the definite integral $\int_0^4 x\sqrt{2x+1}dx$ using integration by parts.

6. Find $\int x^3 e^{4x} dx$ using integration by parts with a table.

7. Find the integral $\int \frac{x}{\sqrt{1-x}}dx$ by using the integral table on the inside back cover.

8. Find the integral $\int (\ln x)^3 dx$ by using the integral table on the inside back cover.

9. Find the integral $\int \frac{e^{2x}}{e^x - 1}dx$ by using the integral table on the inside back cover.

10. Find the integral $\int_0^4 \frac{x}{x+1}dx$ by using the integral table on the inside back cover.

11. Evaluate the improper integral $\int_1^\infty \frac{1}{x^4}dx$ or state that the integral is divergent.

12. Evaluate the improper integral $\int_0^\infty 12e^{-3x}dx$ or state that the integral is divergent.

13. Evaluate the improper integral $\int_e^\infty \frac{(\ln x)^{-4}}{x} dx$ or state that the integral is divergent.

14. Find the area between the curve $y = 3e^{-0.2x}$ and the x-axis from $x = 0$ to ∞.

15. Estimate the integral $\int_0^1 \sqrt{1-x^3}dx$ by hand using trapezoidal approximation with $n = 4$ trapezoids. Round all approximations to 3 decimal places.

16. Estimate the integral $\int_1^3 \sqrt{2-\ln x}dx$ by hand using trapezoidal approximation with $n = 4$ trapezoids. Round all approximations to 3 decimal places.

17. Estimate the integral $\int_0^1 \sqrt{1-x^2}dx$ by hand using Simpson's rule with $n = 4$. Round all calculations to 3 decimal places.

18. Estimate the integral $\int_0^1 e^{x^3} dx$ by hand using Simpson's rule with $n = 4$. Round all calculations to 3 decimal places.

19. A company generates a continuous stream of income of 6t million dollars per year, where t is the number of years that the company has been in operation. Find the present value of this income stream for the first 20 years at the continuous rate of 8%.

Chapter 6 Test

Form B

1. Find the integral $\int xe^{2x}dx$.

   a. $x^2e^{x^2}+C$ b. $\frac{e^{2x}}{4}(2x-1)+C$ c. $2e^{2x}(x-2)+C$ d. $\frac{1}{2}x^2e^{2x}+C$

2. Find the integral $\int x^3 \ln x dx$.

   a. $\frac{x^4}{4}-x^4\ln x+C$ b. $\frac{x^4\ln x}{4}-\frac{x^4}{16}+C$ c. $\frac{x^4}{16}-x^4\ln x+C$ d. $\frac{x^4\ln x}{4}-x^4+C$

3. Find the integral $\int x\sqrt{2x+1}dx$.

   a. $\frac{x(2x+1)^{3/2}}{3}-\frac{(2x+1)^{5/2}}{15}+C$ b. $\frac{x(2x+1)^{3/2}}{3}-\frac{2(2x+1)^{5/2}}{15}+C$

   c. $\frac{2x(2x+1)^{3/2}}{3}-\frac{2(2x+1)^{5/2}}{15}+C$ d. $\frac{2x(2x+1)^{3/2}}{3}-\frac{(2x+1)^{5/2}}{15}+C$

4. Find the integral $\int x(x-3)^{50}dx$.

   a. $\frac{x(x-3)^{51}}{51}-\frac{(x-3)^{52}}{52}+C$ b. $\frac{x(x-3)^{51}}{51}-\frac{(x-3)^{52}}{51}+C$

   c. $\frac{x(x-3)^{51}}{51}-\frac{(x-3)^{52}}{2,652}+C$ d. $\frac{x(x-3)^{51}}{51}-\frac{(x-3)^{51}}{2,652}+C$

5. Evaluate $\int_1^3 x\ln x dx$ using integration by parts.

   a. (4.5)ln 3 – 1   b. (4.5)ln 3 – 2   c. 3 ln 2 – 2   d. 3 ln 3 – 1

6. Find $\int x^2e^{3x}dx$ using integration by parts with a table.

   a. $\frac{x^2e^{3x}}{3}-\frac{2xe^{3x}}{9}+\frac{2e^{3x}}{27}+C$ b. $3x^2e^{3x}-18xe^{3x}+54e^{3x}+C$

   c. $\frac{x^2e^{3x}}{3}+\frac{2xe^{3x}}{9}+\frac{2e^{3x}}{27}+C$ d. $\frac{x^2e^{3x}}{3}-\frac{2xe^{3x}}{9}+C$

7. To evaluate the integral $\int \frac{4x}{\sqrt{x^4 - 1}} dx$, which of the following integral formulas would be used?

a. $\int \frac{1}{\sqrt{ax+b}} dx$ b. $\int \frac{x}{\sqrt{ax+b}} dx$ c. $\int \frac{1}{\sqrt{x^2 \pm a^2}} dx$ d. $\int \frac{1}{x\sqrt{x^2 \pm a^2}} dx$

8. To evaluate the integral $\int \frac{2x}{\sqrt{9x - 16}} dx$, which of the following integral formulas would be used?

a. $\int \frac{1}{x\sqrt{ax+b}} dx$ b. $\int \frac{1}{\sqrt{x^2 \pm a^2}} dx$ c. $\int \frac{1}{x\sqrt{x^2 \pm a^2}} dx$ d. $\int \frac{x}{\sqrt{ax+b}} dx$

9. Use the integral table on the inside back cover to find the integral $\int \frac{1}{x^2(9+5x)} dx$.

a. $\frac{1}{9}\left[\frac{1}{9+5x} + \frac{1}{9}\ln\left|\frac{x}{9+5x}\right|\right] + C$ b. $-\frac{1}{9}\left[\frac{1}{x} + \frac{5}{9}\ln\left|\frac{x}{9+5x}\right|\right] + C$

c. $\frac{1}{9}\left[\ln\left|\frac{x}{9+5x}\right|\right] + C$ d. $-\frac{1}{81}\left[\frac{9+10x}{x(9+5x)} + \frac{10}{9}\ln\left|\frac{x}{9+5x}\right|\right] + C$

10. Use the integral table on the inside back cover to find the integral $\int \frac{e^x}{\sqrt{e^{2x}+1}} dx$.

a. $-\ln\left|\frac{1+\sqrt{e^{2x}+1}}{x}\right| + C$ b. $\frac{1}{2}\ln\left|\frac{1+e^x}{1-e^x}\right| + C$ c. $\ln\left|x + \sqrt{e^{2x}+1}\right| + C$ d. $\ln\left|\frac{\sqrt{e^x+1}-1}{\sqrt{e^x+1}+1}\right| + C$

11. Evaluate $\lim_{a \to \infty} 3a^{-2}$

a. 3 b. 0 c. –3 d. ∞

12. Evaluate the improper integral $\int_0^{\infty} e^{-3x} dx$ or state that the integral is divergent.

a. 0 b. divergent c. 3 d. 1/3

13. Evaluate the improper integral $\int_0^{\infty} x^{-1/3}\,dx$ or state that the integral is divergent.

a. 3/2   b. divergent   c. 0   d. 4/3

14. Evaluate the improper integral $\int_e^{\infty} (\ln x)^{-2} \cdot \frac{1}{x}\,dx$ or state that the integral is divergent.

a. 1   b. divergent   c. –1   d. 3

15. Find the area between the curve $y = \frac{1}{(1-x)^2}$ and the x-axis from $-\infty$ to $x = -2$.

a. ½   b. 1/3   c. ¼   d. 1/5

16. Estimate $\int_0^{7} (x^2 - 7x)\,dx$ by hand using trapezoidal approximation with $n = 4$. Round off the approximation to 2 decimal places.

a. –53.59   b. 57.17   c. –57.17   d. 53.59

17. Estimate $\int_2^{6} \frac{1}{x}\,dx$ by hand using trapezoidal approximation with $n = 4$. Round off the approximation to 2 decimal places.

a. 1.76   b. 1.12   c. 1.37   d. 1.09

18. Estimate $\int_{-1}^{1} \sqrt{1 + x^3}\,dx$ by hand using Simpson's rule with $n = 4$. Round off the approximation to 3 decimal places.

a. 1.888   b. 1.852   c. 1.965   d. 1.900

19. Estimate $\int_0^{1} e^{-x^2}\,dx$ by hand using Simpson's rule with $n = 4$. Round off the approximation to 3 decimal places.

a. 0.816   b. 0.717   c. 0.747   d. 0.927

Chapter 7 Test

Test A

1. Find the domain of the function $f(x, y) = \dfrac{\ln y}{y - 2x}$.

2. Evaluate $f(x, y) = \sqrt{1 - x} - e^{x/y}$ at $(-3, 3)$.

3. For $f(x, y) = \dfrac{x^3}{y^4} - \dfrac{y^4}{x}$, find $f_x(x, y)$ and $f_y(x, y)$.

4. For $f(x, y) = \ln(x^5 + y^5) + e^x y^3$, find $f_x(x, y)$ and $f_y(x, y)$.

5. For $g(x, y) = (xy + 1)^6$, find $g_x(0, 2)$ and $g_y(0, 2)$.

6. For $f(x, y) = e^{4x-3y^2}$ find
   a. $f_{xx}(x, y)$
   b. $f_{yy}(x, y)$
   c. $f_{xy}(x, y)$

7. Find the relative extreme values of $f(x, y) = 3x^2 + y^2 + 2xy - 2x + 2y + 12$.

8. Find the least squares line for the following points: (Round to 2 decimal places)

x	1	4	6
y	8	5	2

9. Use least squares to find the exponential curve of the form $y = Be^{Ax}$ for the following points:

x	1	3	4
y	2	3	6

10. Use Lagrange multipliers to find the minimum value of $f(x, y) = 6x^2 + 5y^2 - xy$ subject to $2x + y = 16$.

11. Use Lagrange multipliers to find the maximum value of $f(x, y) = e^{xy}$ subject to $3x + y = 6$.

12. Find the total differential of $f(x, y) = x^3 - x^2y + 3y^2$.

13. Find the total differential of $f(x, y, z) = x^2 \ln(y^2 + z^2)$.

14. The temperature T at the point (x, y, z) in a rectangular coordinate system is given by $T = 8(2x^2 + 4y^2 + 9z^2)^{1/2}$ use differentials to approximate the temperature difference between the points (6, 3, 2) and 6.1, 3.3, 1.98).

15. Evaluate $\int_{-1}^{1}\int_{0}^{3}(x^2 + 2y^2)dydx$.

16. Evaluate $\int_{1}^{2}\int_{e}^{y}(4x + y)dxdy$.

17. Find the volume under the surface $f(x, y) = 3x^2y$ and above the region $R = \{(x, y) | 0 \le x \le 2, 1 \le y \le 3\}$.

18. A manufacturer has profits given by $P(x, y) = -2x^2 + 2xy - y^2 + 10x - 4y + 211$, where x in the number (in millions) of standard units produced and y is the number (in millions) of deluxe units produced and P is the profit (in millions of dollars).
    a. How many units of each should be produced to realize a maximum profit?
    b. What is the maximum profit?

19. The productivity of a company is given by $f(x, y) = 376x^{0.45}y^{0.55}$, where x is the number of units of labor and y is the number of units of capital. If the company is now using 245 units of labor and 120 units of capital, find the marginal productivity of capital.

Chapter 7 Test

Form B

1. Find the domain of $f(x, y) = \dfrac{3x^2 - 2y}{x - y}$.

a. $\{(x, y) | x \neq 1\}$
b. $\{(x, y) | x \neq 1, y \neq 0\}$
c. $\{(x, y) | x \neq y\}$
d. $\{(x, y) | x \in \Re, y \in \Re\}$

2. Evaluate $f(x, y) = x^3 + y^2 - 3xy + 5$ at $(-1, 2)$.

a. 10
b. 14
c. –8
d. 8

3. For $f(x, y) = \ln x + e^{xy}$ find $f_x(x, y)$.

a. $\dfrac{1}{x} + xe^{xy}$
b. $\dfrac{1}{x} + ye^{xy}$
c. $\dfrac{1}{x} + e^{xy}$
d. $\ln x + xe^{xy}$

4. For $f(x, y) = \sqrt{1 - x^2 y}$, find $f_y(x, y)$.

a. $\sqrt{1 - x^2}$
b. $\dfrac{1}{2\sqrt{1 - x^2 y}}$
c. $\dfrac{1 - 2x}{\sqrt{1 - x^2 y}}$
d. $\dfrac{-x^2}{2\sqrt{1 - x^2 y}}$

5. For $f(x, y) = xe^y + \ln(xy)$, find $f_y(e, 3)$.

a. $\dfrac{1}{e} + e$
b. $\dfrac{1}{3e} + e^4$
c. $\dfrac{1}{3} + e^4$
d. $\dfrac{1}{e} + e^3$

6. For $f(x, y) = \dfrac{4x^2}{y} + \dfrac{y^2}{2x}$, find $f_{xy}(2, -1)$.

a. $-\dfrac{63}{4}$
b. 17
c. $-\dfrac{61}{4}$
d. $-\dfrac{65}{4}$

7. For $f(x, y) = x^2 + y^2 + 2x - 6y + 14$, which of the following statements is true?

   a. f has a relative maximum of 14 at $x = 0$, $y = 0$.
   b. f has a relative minimum of 4 at $x = -1$, $y = 3$.
   c. f has a relative maximum of 44 at $x = 1$, $y = 3$.
   d. there are no relative extrema for f

8. A company produces x thousand rugs of type A and y thousand rugs of Type B per year and has a profit equation of $P(x, y) = -4x + 12y - x^2 + 2xy - 2y^2 - 5$. How many of each type of rug should be produced to maximize profit?

   a. 1,000 of type A and 3,000 of type B
   b. 2,000 of type A and 4,000 of type B
   c. 4,000 of type A and 2,000 of type B
   d. 3,000 of type A and 1,000 of type B

9. Determine the least squares line for the following points:

x	10	2	8	6	4
y	1	−2	0	−1	0

   a. $y = 0.3x - 2.2$
   b. $y = 0.3x + 2.2$
   c. $y = 0.7x - 1.9$
   d. $y = 0.7x + 1.9$

10. Use Lagrange multipliers to find the minimum value of $f(x, y) = 2y + x^2$ subject to the constraint $x - 2y - 7 = 0$.

   a. $-\frac{15}{2}$
   b. $-\frac{33}{4}$
   c. $-\frac{23}{4}$
   d. $-\frac{29}{4}$

11. Use Lagrange multipliers to find the maximum value of $f(x, y) = 3xy$ subject to $x + 2y - 7 = 0$.

   a. $\frac{171}{8}$
   b. $\frac{99}{8}$
   c. $\frac{147}{8}$
   d. $\frac{123}{8}$

12. Find the total differential of $f(x, y) = 2x^2y^3$.

   a. $4xy^3\,dx + 6x^2y^2\,dy$
   b. $4xy^3\,dy + 6x^2y^2\,dx$
   c. $4xy^3\,dx + 6xy^2\,dy$
   d. $4xy^2\,dx + 6x^2y^2\,dy$

13. The total differential for $f(x, y, z) = x^2y + y^2z + xz^2$ is

   a. $(2xy + xz^2)\,dx + (2yz + x^2)\,dy + (2xz + y^2)\,dz$
   b. $(2xy + z^2)\,dx + (2y^2z + x^2)\,dy + (2xz + y^2)\,dz$
   c. $(2xy + z^2)\,dx + (2yz + x^2)\,dy + (2y^2z + y^2)\,dz$
   d. $(2xy + z^2)\,dx + (2yz + x^2)\,dy + (2xz + y^2)\,dz$

14. Determine how much $f(x, y, z) = 3xy^2 + 2yz^2$ will change if the point (x, y, z) is moved from $(3, -1, 2)$ to the point $(3.5, -1.2, 2.4)$.

a. −3.7 b. 0.3 c. 3.7 d. −0.3

15. Evaluate $\int_0^1 \int_{-2}^0 (3x^2y^2 - xy)dydx$

a. 5/3 b. 11/3 c. 8/3 d. 7/3

16. Evaluate $\int_0^1 \int_0^x (x + y)dydx$

a. 3/2 b. ½ c. ¾ d. 1

17. Find the volume under the surface $f(x, y) = x^2 + y^2 + 1$ and above the region $R = \{(x, y) \mid 0 \le x \le 1. 0 \le y \le 1\}$.

a. 5/3 b. 3 c. 8/3 d. 2

18. A company has determined that productivity $P(x, y)$ is a result of monthly expenditures of x million dollars in labor and y million dollars in equipment, given by $P(x, y) = -2x^2 - 4xy - 10y^2 + 40x + 80y$. Determine the amount expended for labor which will maximize productivity.

a. $10,000,000 b. $40,000,000 c. $7,500,000 d. $2,500,000

19. The productivity of a company is given by $f(x, y) = 374x^{0.34}y^{0.66}$, where x is the number of units of labor and y is the number of units of capital. The company is using 428 units of labor and 763 units of capital. Determine the marginal productivity of capital.

a. 187 b. 87 c. 203 d. 300

Chapter 8

Form A

1. a. Convert 165° to radian measure.

   b. Convert $\frac{11\pi}{6}$ to degrees.

2. Find the distance along the surface of the earth between New York City, NY and Lima, Peru if the 2 cities determine a central angle of 0.925 radians. Assume that the earth is a sphere of radius 4,000 miles.

3. Find the $\sin\theta$ and $\cos\theta$ for the given θ. Use the Pythagorean theorem to calculate r.

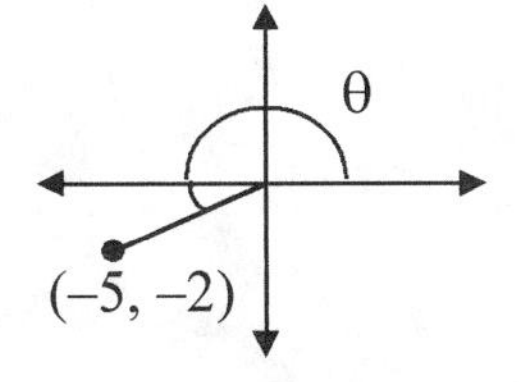

4. Evaluate <u>without</u> using a calculator, leaving your answers in exact form.

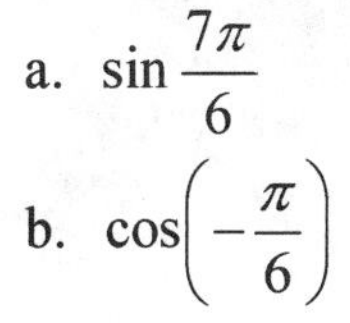

   a. $\sin\frac{7\pi}{6}$

   b. $\cos\left(-\frac{\pi}{6}\right)$

5. Approximate using a calculator in radian mode. Round your answers to 2 decimal places.

   a. $\sin\frac{9\pi}{5}$

   b. $\cos 3$

6. Sketch

   a. $y = -\sin 3t$

   b. $y = 4\cos 2t$

7. A kite string makes an angle of 35° with the ground. If the kite is 50 feet high, how much string has been let out?

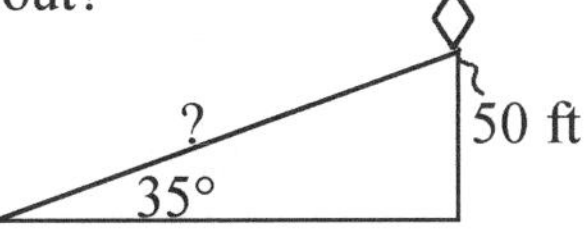

8. Differentiate $2 \sin (t^2 + 4t)$.

9. Differentiate $\cos^2 (t - \pi)$.

10. Differentiate $e^{-x} \cos x^2$.

11. Differentiate $\frac{\sin 2x}{1+\cos x}$.

12. Find $\int \frac{\sin t}{\sqrt[3]{\cos t}} dt$.

13. Find $\int \frac{\sin x}{1-\cos x} dx$.

14. Find $\int \sin x \cos x e^{\sin^2 x} dx$.

15. Find $\int_0^{\frac{1}{2}} (t - \cos \pi t) dt$.

16. Find tan θ, cot θ, sec θ, and csc θ for the given θ. Use Pythagorean theorem to find r.

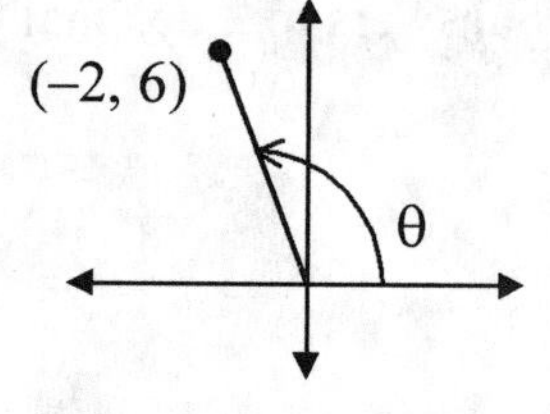

17. Evaluate without using a calculator, leaving answers in exact form.

a. $\tan \frac{5\pi}{6}$

b. $\sec \frac{2\pi}{3}$

18. Estimate the height of a building if the top of the building makes an angle of 55° with the ground when seen from 40 feet away.

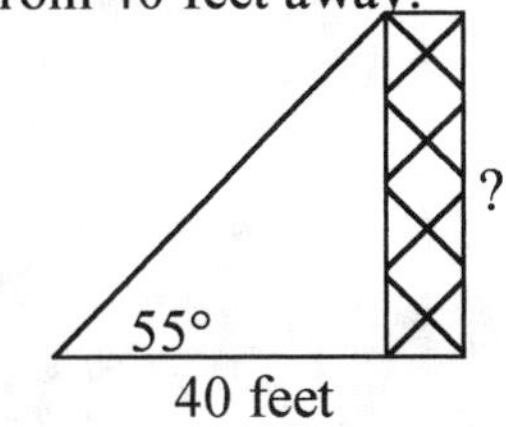

19. Differentiate $t^3 \tan t$.

20. Find the integral $\int \frac{\cot \sqrt{x} \csc \sqrt{x}}{\sqrt{x}} dx$.

Chapter 8

Form B

1. Convert 135° into radian measure.

a. $\frac{2\pi}{3}$ b. $\frac{4}{3}\pi$ c. $\frac{3}{4}\pi$ d. π

2. Convert $\frac{7\pi}{6}$ to degrees.

a. 210° b. 150° c. 240° d. 180°

3. What is the value of cos θ given the figure below?

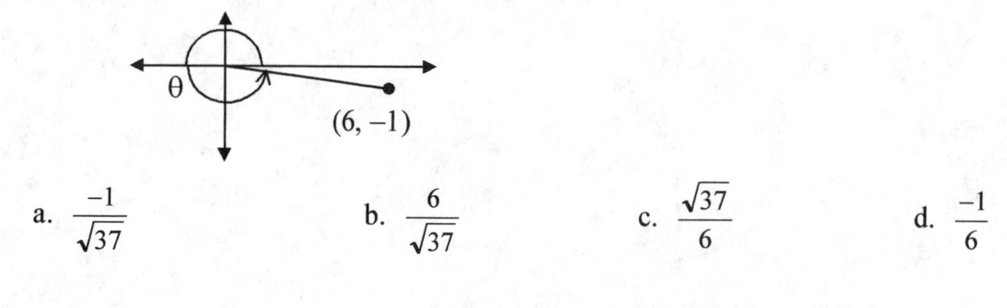

a. $\frac{-1}{\sqrt{37}}$ b. $\frac{6}{\sqrt{37}}$ c. $\frac{\sqrt{37}}{6}$ d. $\frac{-1}{6}$

4. Evaluate $\sin\left[-\frac{\pi}{3}\right]$.

a. $\frac{1}{2}$ b. $-\frac{1}{2}$ c. $-\frac{\sqrt{3}}{2}$ d. $\frac{\sqrt{3}}{2}$

5. Approximate cos 5 to 2 decimal places.

a. 1.00 0.99 c. –0.96 d. 0.28

6. Which of the following is the equation for the graph shown below?

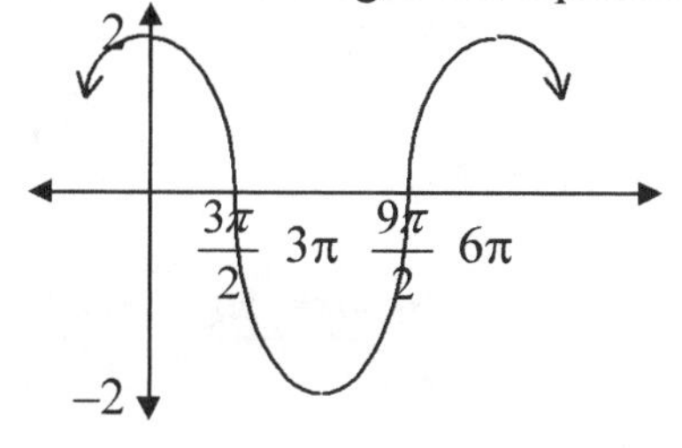

a. $y = 2\sin\frac{1}{3}x$ b. $y = 2\cos\frac{1}{3}x$ c. $y = 2\cos 3x$ d. $y = 2\sin 3x$

7. What is the value of x in the right triangle shown below?

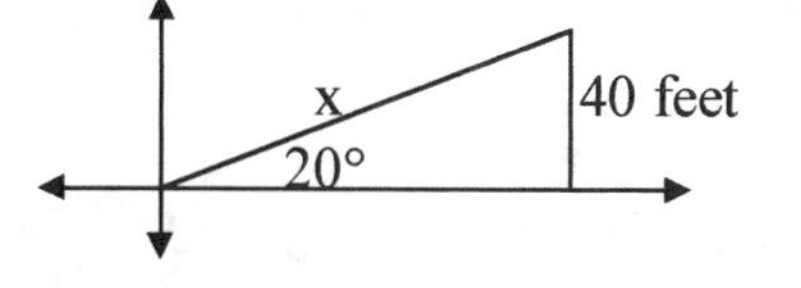

a. 43.8 feet b. 98.0 feet c. 42.6 feet d. 117.0 feet

8. Differentiate $3\cos(3t^2 - 5t)$.

a. $-3\sin(3t^2 - 5t)$ b. $(18t - 15)\sin(3t^2 - 5t)$
c. $-(18t - 15)\sin(3t^2 - 5t)$ d. $-3\sin(6t - 5)$

9. Differentiate $\sin^3(\pi - t)$.

a. $-\cos^3(\pi - t)$ b. $-3\sin^2(\pi - t)\cos(\pi - t)$
c. $-\sin^2(\pi - t)$ d. $3\sin^2(\pi - t)\cos(\pi - t)$

10. Differentiate $(\sin t^2)e^{2t}$.

a. $2e^{2t}(\sin t^2 + t\cos t^2)$ b. $(2t\cos t^2)(2e^{2t})$ c. $e^{2t}(\sin t^2 + \cos t^2)$ d. $(\cos t^2)\,2e^{2t}$

11. Differentiate $\frac{\cos 3x}{1+\sin x}$.

a. $\frac{-3\sin 3x}{\cos x}$ b. $\frac{(\cos 3x)\cos x + 3\sin 3x + 3(\sin x)\sin 3x}{(1+\sin x)^2}$

c. $\frac{-3\sin 3x - 3(\sin x)\sin 3x - (\cos 3x)\cos x}{(1+\sin x)^2}$ d. $\frac{-3\sin 3x - 3\sin 4x - \cos 4x}{(1+\sin x)^2}$

12. Find $\int \sqrt{1-\sin t}\cos t\,dt$.

a. $\frac{2}{3}(1-\sin t)^{\frac{3}{2}}+C$ b. $-(1-\sin t)^{\frac{3}{2}}+C$ c. $(1-\sin t)^{\frac{3}{2}}+C$ d. $-\frac{2}{3}(1-\sin t)^{\frac{3}{2}}+C$

13. Find $\int \frac{\cos 2x}{1-\sin 2x}dx$.

a. $\ln|1-\sin 2x|+C$ b. $\frac{1}{2}\ln|1-\sin 2x|+C$ c. $-\frac{1}{2}\ln|1-\sin 2x|+C$ d. $-\ln|1-\sin 2x|+C$

14. Find $\int e^{\cos^2 t}\sin t\cos t\,dt$.

a. $e^{\cos^2 t}+C$ b. $-e^{\cos^2 t}+C$ c. $\frac{1}{2}e^{\cos^2 t}+C$ d. $-\frac{1}{2}e^{\cos^2 t}+C$

15. Find $\int_0^1 (\sin \pi t - t)dt$.

a. $\frac{2}{\pi}-\frac{1}{2}$ b. $\frac{1}{\pi}-\frac{1}{2}$ c. $-\frac{1}{2}$ d. $-\frac{1}{\pi}-\frac{1}{2}$

16. Given the figure below, find cot θ.

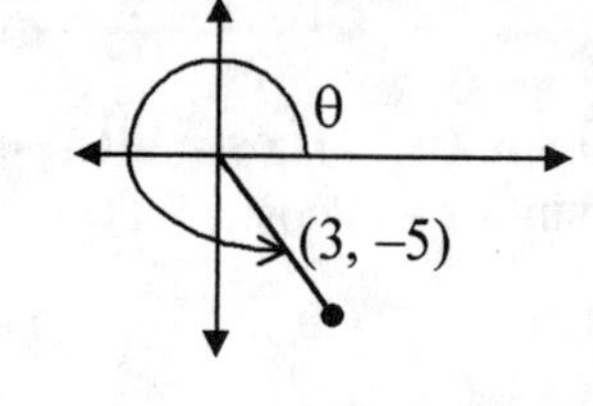

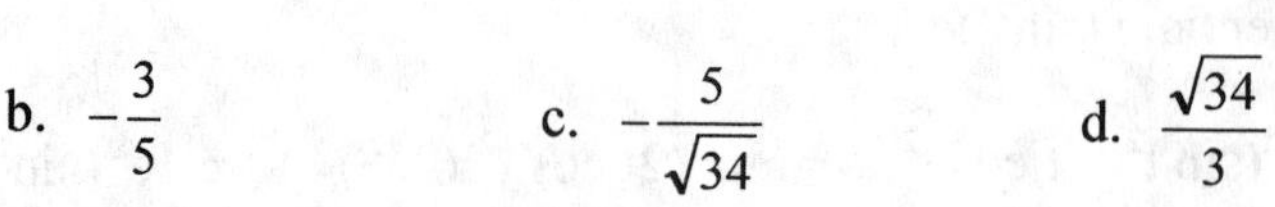

a. $-\frac{5}{3}$ b. $-\frac{3}{5}$ c. $-\frac{5}{\sqrt{34}}$ d. $\frac{\sqrt{34}}{3}$

17. Evaluate $\sec\frac{11\pi}{6}$.

a. -2 b. $\frac{2}{\sqrt{3}}$ c. $-\frac{1}{2}$ d. $\frac{\sqrt{3}}{2}$

18. In the following triangle, what is the value of x?

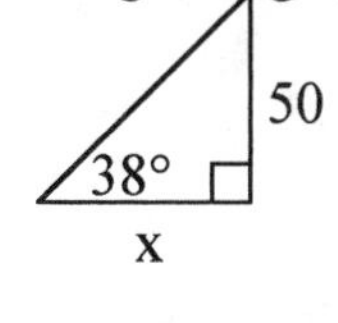

a. 64   b. 161.1   c. 39.1   d. 15.5

19. Differentiate $x^2 \csc x$.

a. $-2x (\cot x) \csc x$
b. $x (\csc x)(2 + x \cot x)$
c. $x (\csc x)(2 - x \cot x)$
d. $-x^2 \cot^2 x + 2x \csc x$

20. Find the integral $\int t \sec^2(2-t^2)dt$.

a. $\tan(2 - t^2) + C$
b. $-2 \tan (2 - t^2) + C$
c. $-\frac{1}{2}\sec(2-t^2)+C$
d. $-\frac{1}{2}\tan(2-t^2)+C$

Chapter 9

Form A

1. Verify that $y = e^{3x} + 10e^{2x}$ satisfies the differential equation $\frac{dy}{dx} - 2y = e^{3x}$.

2. Find the general solution for the differential equation $y' = \frac{x}{2y(x+1)}$ or state that the differential equation is not separable.

3. Find the general solution for the differential equation $xy' = 4y$ or state that the differential equation is not separable.

4. Find the general solution for the differential equation $y' = x + y^2$ or state that the differential equation is not separable.

5. Solve the differential equation $y' = 8y^{\frac{3}{4}}$ with the initial condition $y(1) = 81$.

6. Solve the differential equation $y' = \frac{-2x}{y}$ with the initial condition $y(0) = 1$.

7. Solve the differential equation $y' = 0.02y$ with initial condition $y(0) = 2$, by recognizing as determining unlimited, limited or logistical growth and then determining restraints.

8. Solve the differential equation $y' = 0.08(50 - y)$ with initial condition $y(0) = 0$, by recognizing as determining unlimited, limited or logistical growth and then determining restraints.

9. Solve the differential equation $y' = 2y(15 - y)$ with initial condition $y(0) = 4$, by recognizing as determining unlimited, limited or logistical growth and then determining restraints.

10. A company estimates that it can sell a maximum of 4,000 swimming pools in a city, and the company sells 500 pools in the first two months. The rate at a which new pools can be sold is proportional to the distance below the maximum limit of 4,000.
    a. Write a differential equation that describes this growth.
    b. By identifying the differential equation as unlimited, limited, or logistic, write the solution, obtaining a formula for the number of pools that can be sold in the first t months.
    c. Use your formula to estimate the number of pools that can be sold in the first 6 months.

11. A new lake can support a maximum of 8,000 trout, and it is initially stocked with 1,000 trout. Two years later there are 3,600 trout. The number of trout grows in proportion both to the number of trout already in the lake and to the distance below the maximum level of 8,000.
    a. Write a differential equation that describes this growth.
    b. By identifying the differential equation as unlimited, limited, or logistic, write the solution, obtaining a formula for the number of trout after t years.
    c. Use your formula to estimate the number of trout after 5 years.

12. Solve the first-order linear differential equation $y' - 3y = 0$.

13. Solve the first-order linear differential equation $y' + 2xy = x$.

14. Solve the first-order linear differential equation $y' + 3x^2y = x^2$.

15. Solve $y' + \frac{y}{x} = 2$ with the initial condition $y(1) = 0$.

16. For the initial value problem, $y' = y - 6x$, with the initial condition $y(0) = 1$, state the initial point and calculate the slope of the solution at this point.

17. For the initial value problem, $y' = 3x^2y$, with the initial condition $y(0) = 1$, calculate the Euler approximation for $y(0.2)$ on the interval $[0, 0.2]$ using $n = 2$ segments.

18. The rate of decay of a substance is given by $\frac{dy}{dx} = -0.15y$. Given that $y = ke^{-0.15x}$ is the general solution, find the particular solution through the point $(0, 15)$.

19. Find the particular solution, using separation of variables, for the differential equation $x' = \frac{x}{t}$ if $x(1) = 5.4$.

20. A retirement plan pays 6.5% compounded continuously; $1750 is initially invested, and $1550 is deposited at the end of each year. State the differential equation that models the growth of this plan.

Chapter 9

Form B

1. Which of the following is a solution to the differential equation $\frac{dy}{dx} = 2y$?

a. $y = x^2$ b. $y = x^2 + 2x$ c. $y = 2x$ d. $y = e^{2x}$

2. Find the general solution for the differential equation $\frac{dy}{dx} = \frac{2x(y-1)}{1+x^2}$.

a. $y = Cx^2e^x + 1$ b. $y = 1 + C(1 + x^2)$ c. $y = (1 + x^2) + Ce^x$ d. $y = x^2e^x + C$

3. Find the general solution for the differential equation $\frac{dy}{dx} = 2xy^2$.

a. $y = Ce^{x^2}$ b. $y = \frac{C}{x^2+1}$ c. $y = \frac{-C}{x^2}$ d. $y = \frac{-1}{x^2+C}$

4. Find the general solution for the differential equation $\frac{dy}{dx} - y = x^2$.

a. $y = \frac{x^3}{3} + \frac{y^2}{2} + C$ b. $y = \frac{x^3}{3} + 1 + C$ c. not separable d. $y = \frac{x^3}{3} + C$

5. Solve the differential equation $y' = xy + x$ with the initial condition $y(0) = 2$.

a. $y = 3e^{\frac{x^2}{2}} - 1$ b. $y = 3e^{\frac{x^2}{2}} + 1$ c. $y^2 = 2ye^{x^2}$ d. $y = \frac{1}{x}\ln(x+1) + 2$

6. Solve the differential equation $y' = \frac{\ln x}{xy}$ with the initial condition $y(1) = 1$.

a. $y = 2e^{x-1} - x$ b. $y = \frac{1}{x}e^{x-1}$ c. $y = \sqrt{1 + (\ln x)^2}$ d. $y = \ln(x^2) + 2x - 1$

7. Solve the differential equation $y' = 0.25(100 - y)$ with the initial condition $y(0) = 0$ by recognizing as determining unlimited, limited or logistical growth and then determining constants.

   a. $y = 100(1 - e^{0.25t})$ b. $y = 0.25(1 - e^{100t})$ c. $y = 100(1 + e^{-0.25t})$ d. $y = 100(1 - e^{-0.25t})$

8. Solve the differential equation $y' = 0.75y$ with the initial condition $y(0) = 10$ by recognizing as determining unlimited, limited or logistical growth and then determining constants.

   a. $y = 10e^{0.75t}$ b. $y = 0.75e^{10t}$ c. $y = 10(1 - e^{-0.75t})$ d. $y = 10e^{-0.75t}$

9. Solve the differential equation $y' = 0.25(100 - y)$ with the initial condition $y(0) = 0$ by recognizing as determining unlimited, limited or logistical growth and then determining constants.

   a. $y = 25(1 - e^{-3t})$ b. $y = \frac{25}{1+3e^{-75t}}$ c. $y = \frac{50}{2+23e^{-75t}}$ d. $y = \frac{25}{1+25e^{-3t}}$

10. Suppose that you now have \$10,000 and that you expect to save an additional \$2,000 during each year and all of this is deposited into a bank paying 5% interest compounded continuously. Write a differential equation and boundary condition to model your bank balance after t years.

    a. $y' = 10{,}000 + 0.05y;\ y(0) = 2{,}000$
    b. $y' = 2{,}000 + e^{0.05t};\ y(0) = 10{,}000$
    c. $y' = 2{,}000 + 0.05y;\ y(0) = 10{,}000$
    d. $y' = 2{,}000(1 + 0.05^{y});\ y(0) = 10{,}000$

11. Suppose a person can memorize a maximum of 75 abstract symbols and that the person can memorize 35 symbols in the first 30 minutes. The rate at which new symbols can be memorized is proportional to the distance below the maximum limit of 75. By identifying the differential equation as limited, unlimited, or logistical, write the solution, obtaining a formula for the number of symbols that can be memorized in the first t minutes.

    a. $y = 75(1 - e^{-0.021t})$ b. $y = 75(1 - e^{-35t})$ c. $y = 35e^{0.75t}$ d. $y = 75(1 + e^{-0.021t})$

12. Solve the first-order linear differential equation $y' + 2xy = x$.

    a. $y = \frac{1}{2}e^{x^2} + C$ b. $y = \frac{1}{2} + Ce^{-x^2}$ c. $y = \frac{1}{2}e^{-x^2} + C$ d. $y = \frac{1}{2} + Ce^{x^2}$

13. Solve the first-order linear differential equation $y' + y = e^{3x}$.

    a. $y = \frac{1}{4}e^{3x} + Ce^{x}$ b. $y = e^{3x} + Ce^{-x}$ c. $y = \frac{1}{4}e^{3x} + Ce^{-x}$ d. $y = Ce^{-x}$

14. Solve the first-order linear differential equation $y' + \frac{y}{x} = \frac{1}{x^2}$.

a. $y = x \ln x + \frac{C}{x}$ b. $y = \frac{\ln x}{x} + C$ c. $y = \frac{x}{\ln x} + Cx$ d. $y = \frac{\ln x}{x} + \frac{C}{x}$

15. Solve y′ + 5y = 20 with the initial condition y(0) = 2.

a. $y = 4 - 2e^{-5x}$ b. $y = 2 - e^{-5x}$ c. $y = 4 - 2e^{5x}$ d. $y = 2 - 2e^{-5x}$

16. For the initial value problem $y' = 2y + \frac{x}{y}$, y(1) = 5, calculate the slope of the solution at the initial point.

a. 7 b. $\frac{51}{5}$ c. $\frac{11}{5}$ d. undefined

17. For the initial value problem $y' = 2xy^2$, y(0) = 2, calculate the Euler approximation for y(0.3) on the interval [0, 0.3] using n = 3 segments.

a. 2.0531 b. 2.1857 c. 2.1452 d. 2.2531

18. The number N(t) of bacteria in a culture at time t grows according to the differential equation $\frac{dN}{dt} = 100 - 0.5N$. Find the general solution.

a. $N(t) = Ce^{-0.5t} + 200t$ b. $N(t) = -\ln(100 - 0.5N) + C$

c. $N(t) = \frac{C}{\ln(100 - 0.5N)}$ d. $N(t) = 200 - Ce^{-0.5t} + C$

19. A rumor spreads through a population of 1000 people at a rate proportional to the product of the number that have heard it and the number that have not. If 5 people start a rumor and 10 people have heard it after 1 day, how many people will have heard it after 7 days?

a. 200 b. 300 c. 400 d. 500

20. Use Euler's method to obtain the approximate solution y(0.6) for $y' = 2\sqrt{y} - 8x$ with the initial condition y(0) = 1 on the interval [0, 0.6] with n = 3 segments.

a. 0.67 b. 3.06 c. 2.38 d. 1.41

Chapter 10

Form A

1. Write out the finite series $\sum_{i=2}^{5} \frac{(-1)^i}{i-1}$.

2. Write the infinite series $-\frac{3}{2}+\frac{3}{4}-\frac{3}{8}+\frac{3}{16}-\frac{3}{32}+\ldots$ in sigma notation.

3. Find the sum of the geometric series $5 + 5.2 + 5.2^2 + 5.2^3 + 5.2^4 + 5.2^5 + \ldots + 5.2^9$.

4. For the infinite geometric series, $3-\frac{3}{4}+\frac{3}{16}-\frac{3}{64}+\frac{3}{256}-\ldots$, determine if it converges or diverges. If it converges, find its sum.

5. For the infinite geometric series, $\frac{1}{7}+\frac{5}{7}+\frac{25}{7}+\frac{125}{7}+\frac{625}{7}+\ldots$, determine if it converges or diverges. If it converges, find its sum.

6. For the infinite geometric series, $\sum_{i=1}^{\infty}\left[\frac{3}{4}\right]^{-i}$, determine if it converges or diverges. If it converges, find its sum.

7. For the infinite geometric series, $\sum_{i=0}^{\infty}\frac{2^i}{9\cdot 5^i}$, determine if it converges or diverges. If it converges, find its sum.

8. A rubber ball is dropped from a height of 10 meters. If it rebounds approximately one-half the distance after each fall, use an infinite geometric series to approximate the total distance the ball travels before coming to rest.

9. Find the third Taylor polynomial at x = 0 of the function $f(x) = e^{4x}$.

10. Find the third Taylor polynomial at x = 0 of the function $f(x)=\sqrt[3]{1+x}$.

11. Find the third Taylor polynomial at $x = 0$ of the function $f(x) = \frac{1}{(1+x)^2}$.

12. a. Find the fourth Taylor polynomial at $x = 0$ for $\cos x$.
    b. Use the result of part a to find the eighth Taylor polynomial at $x = 0$ for $\cos x^2$ by replacing x with x^2.

13. For the power series, $\sum_{n=1}^{\infty} \frac{(-1)^n x^n}{n}$, find the radius of convergence.

14. For the power series, $\sum_{n=0}^{\infty} \frac{n! x^n}{2^n}$, find the radius of convergence.

15. Find the Taylor series at $x = 0$ for $f(x) = \frac{1}{x+8}$ by calculating three or four derivatives and using the definition of Taylor series.

16. Find the Taylor series at $x = 0$ for the function $f(x) = \frac{1}{3x-2}$ by modifying one of the Taylor series given.

17. Find the Taylor series at $x = 0$ for the function $f(x) = \frac{x + \cos x}{x^2}$ by modifying one of the Taylor series given.

18. Use Newton's method beginning with $x_0 = 1$ to approximate the root of the equation $x^3 - x^2 - 1 = 0$. Find the first two approximations x_1 and x_2 "by hand" with the aid of a calculator, rounding to three decimal places.

19. The number of bacteria per milliliter in a swimming pool t hours after a treatment is given by $B(t) = 1750 - 800te^{-0.2t}$. Use Newton's method with $t_0 = 9$ to determine when the bacteria level returns to 600 bacteria per milliliter.

20. Represent the following expression $-\frac{4.3}{1-x}$ as a power in x. State at least the first four terms.

Chapter 10

Form B

1. Find the sum $\sum_{i=3}^{6} \frac{3}{i-2}$.

a. $\frac{25}{4}$ b. $\frac{3}{16}$ c. $\frac{1}{2}$ d. $\frac{4}{3}$

2. Use sigma notation to write the sum $\frac{1}{3} - \frac{2}{9} + \frac{3}{27} - \frac{4}{81} + \frac{5}{243} - \ldots$.

a. $\sum_{n=1}^{\infty} \frac{n}{3^n}$ b. $\sum_{n=1}^{\infty} \frac{(-1)^n n}{3^n}$ c. $\sum_{n=1}^{\infty} \frac{(-1)^{n-1} n}{3^n}$ d. $\sum_{n=1}^{\infty} \frac{(-1)^{n-1} n}{3n}$

3. Find the sum of the geometric series $\frac{1}{2} + \frac{1}{2} \cdot 3 + \frac{1}{2} \cdot 3^2 + \frac{1}{2} \cdot 3^3 + \frac{1}{2} \cdot 3^4 + \ldots + \frac{1}{2} \cdot 3^8$.

a. 9,841 b. $\frac{9{,}841}{2}$ c. 19,683 d. $\frac{6{,}561}{2}$

4. For $\frac{1}{3} - \frac{4}{3} + \frac{16}{3} - \frac{64}{3} + \frac{256}{3} - \ldots$, which of the following is true?

a. series diverges
b. series converges to $\frac{1}{15}$
c. series converges to $-\frac{1}{9}$
d. series converges to $\frac{3}{5}$

5. For $7 + \frac{7}{5} + \frac{7}{25} + \frac{7}{125} + \frac{7}{625} + \ldots$, which of the following is true?

a. series diverges
b. series converges to $\frac{7}{5}$
c. series converges to $\frac{28}{5}$
d. series converges to $\frac{35}{4}$

6. For $\sum_{i=0}^{\infty}\left[\frac{2}{5}\right]^{-i}$, which of the following is true?

a. series converges to $\frac{5}{3}$

b. series converges to $\frac{5}{7}$

c. series diverges

d. series converges to $\frac{3}{5}$

7. For $\sum_{i=0}^{\infty}\frac{1}{4\cdot 7^i}$, which of the following is true?

a. series diverges

b. series converges to $\frac{7}{24}$

c. series converges to $\frac{14}{3}$

d. series converges to $\frac{3}{14}$

8. A rubber ball is dropped from a height of 30 feet. If it rebounds three-fourths the distance after each fall, find the infinite geometric series to approximate the total distance the ball travels before coming to rest.

a. $\sum_{i=0}^{\infty}\left[\frac{3}{4}\right]^{i}$

b. $\sum_{i=0}^{\infty}30\left[\frac{3}{4}\right]^{i-1}$

c. $\sum_{i=0}^{\infty}30\left[\frac{3}{4}\right]^{i}$

d. $\sum_{i=0}^{\infty}\left[\frac{3}{4}\right](30)^{i}$

9. Find the 3rd degree term of the Taylor polynomial at $x = 0$ for $f(x) = \sin 2x$.

a. $\frac{2x^3}{3!}$

b. $\frac{-x^3}{3!}$

c. $\frac{x^3}{2^3\cdot 3!}$

d. $-\frac{8x^3}{3!}$

10. Find the 3rd degree term of the Taylor polynomial at $x = 0$ for $f(x) = xe^x$.

a. $\frac{x^3}{2!}$

b. $\frac{x^3}{3!}$

c. $\frac{3x^3}{2!}$

d. no 3rd degree term

11. Find the 3rd degree term of the Taylor polynomial at $x = 0$ for $f(x) = \frac{1}{x+4}$.

a. $\frac{-x^3}{256}$

b. $\frac{-3!}{4^4}x^3$

c. $-\frac{3!}{(x+4)^3}$

d. $\frac{-(x+4)^3}{4^4}$

12. Find the radius of convergence of the series $\sum_{n=0}^{\infty} \frac{(2x)^n}{(3n)!}$.

a. 0 b. 2 c. $\frac{1}{2}$ d. ∞

13. Find the radius of convergence of the series $\sum_{n=0}^{\infty} \frac{x^n}{2^n}$.

a. ∞ b. 2 c. 0 d. $\frac{1}{2}$

14. Find the Taylor series at $x = 0$ for $f(x) = \frac{1}{x+9}$ by calculating three or four derivatives and using the definition of Taylor series.

a. $\sum_{n=0}^{\infty} \frac{(-1)^n (x+9)^n}{9^n}$ b. $\sum_{n=0}^{\infty} \frac{(-1)^n n!}{(x+9)^n}$ c. $\sum_{n=0}^{\infty} \frac{(-1)^n x^n}{9^{n+1}}$ d. $\sum_{n=0}^{\infty} \frac{(-1)^n n! x^n}{9^n}$

15. Find the Taylor series at $x = 0$ for $f(x) = \frac{x^2}{1+2x}$ by modifying one of the Taylor series given.

a. $x^2 + 2x^3 + 4x^4 + 8x^5 + 16x^6 + \ldots$
b. $x^2 - 2x^3 + 4x^4 - 8x^5 + 16x^6 + \ldots$
c. $x^2 - 2x^3 + 4x^4 - 6x^5 + 8x^6 + \ldots$
d. $1 - 2x + 4x^2 - 8x^3 + 16x^4 + \ldots$

16. Find the Taylor series at $x = 0$ for $f(x) = x \cos \sqrt{x}$ by modifying one of the Taylor series given.

a. $x - \frac{x^2}{2!} + \frac{x^3}{3!} - \frac{x^4}{4!} + \frac{x^5}{5!} - \ldots$
b. $x + \frac{x^2}{2!} + \frac{x^3}{4!} + \frac{x^4}{6!} + \frac{x^5}{8!} + \ldots$
c. $x - \frac{x^2}{2!} + \frac{x^4}{4!} - \frac{x^6}{6!} + \frac{x^8}{8!} - \ldots$
d. $x - \frac{x^2}{2!} + \frac{x^3}{4!} - \frac{x^4}{6!} + \frac{x^5}{8!} - \ldots$

17. Use Newton's method beginning with $x_0 = 5$ to find x_2 for the function $f(x) = x^3 - 5x^2 + 2$. Use a calculator and round to three decimal places throughout calculations.

a. 4.197 b. 4.983 c. 4.917 d. 4.031

18. Use Newton's method beginning with $x_0 = 0$ to find x_2 for the function $f(x) = x^2 - 7x + 2$. Use a calculator and round to three decimal places throughout calculations.

a. 0.287 b. 0.351 c. 0.265 d. 0.298

19. A teacher's starting salary is $18,000, and he receives a $700 increase each year starting with the second year. What is his total pay received after k years?

a. $18{,}000 + (k - 1)700$

b. $\sum_{n=1}^{k}(18{,}000 - 700n)$

c. $18{,}000 + \sum_{n=1}^{k} 700n$

d. $\sum_{n=1}^{k}[18{,}000 + (n-1)700]$

20. One dollar is put into a savings account the first week, two dollars the second week, four dollars the third week, and the amount invested continues to double each week. How much is in the account after k weeks?

a. $\sum_{n=1}^{k} 2^n$

b. $\sum_{n=1}^{k} 2^n$

c. $\sum_{n=1}^{k} 2(n-1)$

d. $\sum_{n=1}^{k} 2^{n-1}$

Chapter 11

Form A

1. For the spinner shown below, the arrow is spun and eventually stops, pointing in one of the numbered sectors with probability proportional to the area of the sector. Let x stand for the number chosen and find the
   a. probability distribution of x
   b. E(x)
   c. VAR(x)

2. John is given the opportunity to play a dice game in which he wins \$1.00 if he rolls an odd number, \$5.00 if he rolls a 6, and nothing if he rolls a 2 or 4. Assuming that it costs \$1.50 to play the game, should John play?

3. For a Poisson random variable x with mean 4, find $P(x = 2)$ to 3 decimal places.

4. A fabric company produces bolts of material with an average of 0.3 flaws per square yard. Use the Poisson distribution to find the probability that a given square yard has no flaws.

5. Find the value of a that makes $a\sqrt{x}(x-2)$ on [0, 1] a probability density function.

6. For the probability density function $f(x) = 1.25x^2(3 - x^2)$ on [0, 1], find E(x).

7. For the probability density function $f(x) = \frac{1}{9}x^2$ on [0, 3], find
   a. E(x)
   b. VAR(x)
   c. $\sigma(x)$

8. If x has probability density function $f(x) = \frac{1}{4}x$ on [1, 3], find
   a. the cumulative distribution function F(x)
   b. $P(1 \le x \le 2)$

9. A car dealer's profit per car (in thousands of dollars) has the probability density function $f(x) = \frac{5}{4} - \frac{1}{8}x$ for $6 \le x \le 10$. Find the dealer's average profit per car. (Round to nearest dollar.)

10. The wait for the commuter plane (in minutes) is uniformly distributed on the interval [0, 20], find
    a. $E(x)$
    b. $VAR(x)$
    c. $\sigma(x)$
    d. $P(x < 15)$

11. For the exponential random variable with density $f(x) = \frac{1}{50}e^{-\frac{1}{50}x}$, find
    a. $E(x)$
    b. $VAR(x)$
    c. $\sigma(x)$

12. Find the probability density function for an exponential random variable with standard deviation 2.5.

13. The time until failure of a washing machine is an exponential random variable with mean 15 years. What is the probability that the machine will fail during the 5-year guarantee period?

14. Find the median of the random variable whose probability density function is $f(x) = \frac{3}{64}x^2$ on [0, 4].

15. For a standard normal random variable z, find
    a. $P(-2.37 \leq z \leq 0)$
    b. $P(1.73 \leq z \leq 3.12)$

16. If x is normal with mean 10 and standard deviation 2, find $P(11 \leq x \leq 14)$.

17. If x is normal with mean 100 and standard deviation 15, find $P(x \geq 90)$.

18. A soda machine dispenses soda into a 9.5-ounce cup. The volume dispensed is normally distributed with mean 6.0 ounces and standard deviation 1.0 ounces. What is the probability that the cup will overflow with soda?

Chapter 11

Form B

1. For the spinner shown below, the arrow is spun and eventually stops, pointing in one of the numbered sectors with probability proportional to the area of the sector. Let x stand for the number chosen and find the expected value of x.

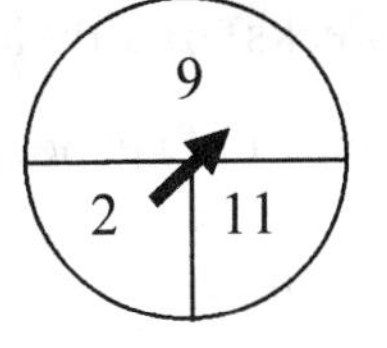

a. E(x) = 8 b. E(x) = 7 c. E(x) = 7.75 d. E(x) = 8.25

2. Paul is given the opportunity to play a dice game in which he wins $2.00 if he rolls an even number, $8.00 if he rolls a 1, $5.00 if he rolls a 3, and nothing if he rolls a 5. Assuming that it costs $3.00 to play the game, what would be his net profit (loss)?

a. profit of $0.16 b. loss of $3.00 c. loss of $0.16 d. profit of $3.16

3. For a Poisson random variable x with mean 3.5, find P(X = 3) to 3 decimal places.

a. 0.017 b. 0.257 c. 0.216 d. 0.315

4. A parts manufacturer produces 800 parts per day and an average of 10 per day fail inspection. Use the Poisson distribution to find the probability that on a given day 6 will fail inspection.

a. 0.0012 b. 0.063 c. 0.129 d. 0.217

5. Find the value of a that makes ax(3 – x) on [0, 1] a probability density function.

a. $\frac{6}{7}$ b. $\frac{7}{6}$ c. $\frac{1}{2}$ d. 2

6. For the probability density function f9x) = $4x(1 - x^2)$ on [0, 1], find E(x).

a. 0.25 b. 0.142 c. 0.158 d. $0.5\overline{3}$

7. For the probability density function $f(x) = \frac{2}{25}x$ on [0, 5], find VAR(x).

a. 1.86 b. 2.415 c. 1.389 d. 3.486

8. If x has probability density function $f(x) = \frac{1}{21}x^2$ on [1, 4], find $P(2 \le x \le 3)$.

a. 0.27141   b. 0.38217   c. 0.561   d. 0.30159

9. The life expectancy (in weeks) of a fly has the probability density function $f(x) = \frac{6x - x^2}{36}$ for the interval [0, 6]. Find the mean life expectancy.

a. 2   b. 3   c. 4.5   d. 4

10. The wait for a school bus (in minutes) is uniformly distributed on the interval [0, 15]. Find the standard deviation of this distribution.

a. 18.75 min   b. 10.25 min   c. $0.0\overline{6}$ min   d. 4.33 min

11. For the exponential random variable with density $f(x) = 2e^{-2x}$, find the variance.

a. $\frac{1}{2}$ b. $\frac{1}{4}$ c. 2   d. 4

12. Find the probability density function for an exponential random variable with standard deviation 20.

a. $0.05e^{0.05x}$ b. $400e^{-400x}$ c. $20e^{-20x}$ d. $\frac{1}{20}e^{-\frac{1}{20}x}$

13. The time until failure of a dishwasher is an exponential random variable with mean 12 years. What is the probability that the machine will fail during the 3-year guarantee period?

a. 0.1941   b. 0.2811   c. 0.2212   d. 0.2017

14. Find the median of the random variable whose probability density function $f(x) = \frac{4}{81}x^3$ on [0, 3].

a. 1.5914   b. 2.52269   c. 2.0164   d. 1.0718

15. For a standard normal random variable z, find $P(-1.78 \le z \le -1.23)$.

a. 0.3192   b. 0.7642   c. 0.0718   d. 0.5718

16. If x is normal with mean 20 standard deviation 1.5, find $P(19 \le x \le 21)$.

    a. 0.2486 b. 0.7486 c. 0.4046 d. 0.4950

17. If x is normal with mean 47 and standard deviation 6.2, fin $P(x \le 60)$.

    a. 0.9820 b. 0.4821 c. 0.5176 d. 0.6179

18. A survey found that the number of hours school children watch TV per week is normally distributed with mean 20 hours and standard deviation 2 hours. If a child is chosen at random, what is the probability that he/she watches TV less than 14 hours per week?

    a. 0.0133 b. 0.0013 c. 0.0113 d. 0.0003

Solutions to Chapter Tests

Chapter 1T Form A

1. $(-2, 5]$
2. $3x + 2y - 1 = 0$
3. $x = 1$
4. 1/8
5. $3x^2$
6. Domain: $\{x \mid x \neq -2\}$, Range: $\{y \mid y \neq 0\}$
7. 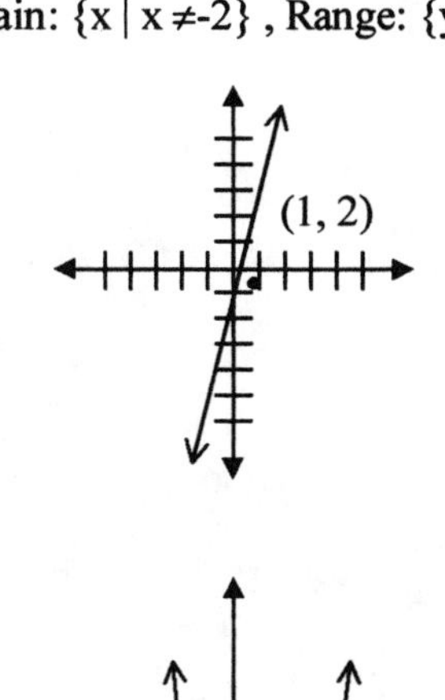

8. 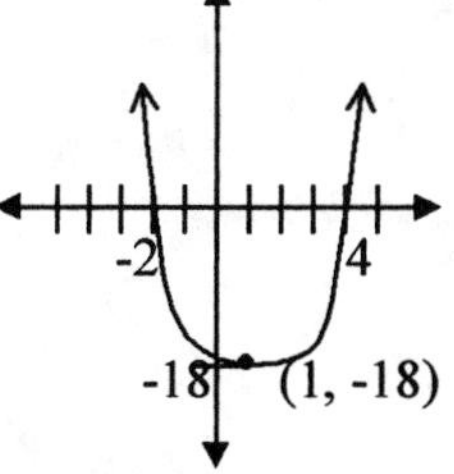

9. $x = 2, x = -3$
10. 3
11. $m = \frac{2}{5}$, y-intercept $= -2$
12. 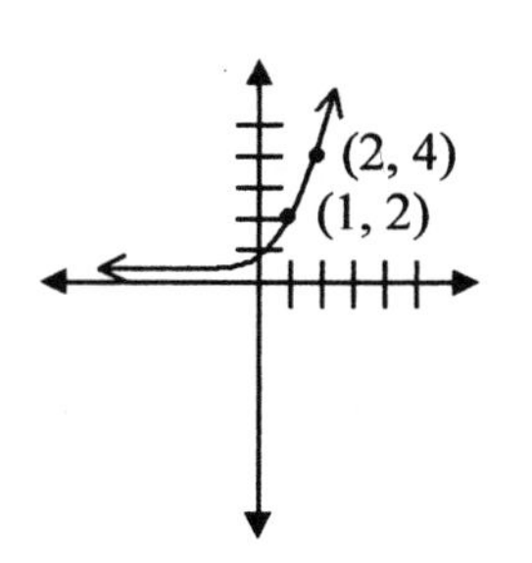

13.

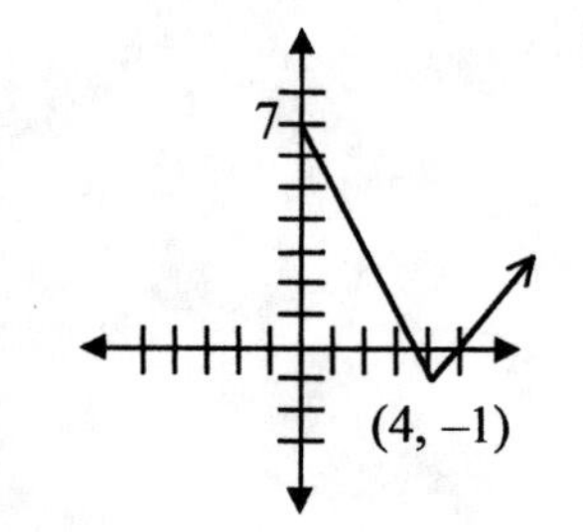

14. $4x + 2h$

15. $A(t) = 3(3t + 10)^{0.25}$, $A(5) = \$6.71$ million

16. $3.2x + y - 12.4 = 0$

17. $P(x) = 2x - 20{,}000$

18. 564 units

19. 1.2

20. $f[g(x)] = -6x^3 + 1$, $g[f(x)] = (-6x + 1)^3$

Chapter 1T Form B

1. b
2. b
3. c
4. a
5. b
6. b
7. c
8. a
9. d
10. c
11. c
12. b
13. a
14. c
15. b
16. a
17. b
18. d
19. b
20. d

Chapter 2T Form A

1. ½

2. x^2

3. discontinuous at $x = 2$

4. $f'(x) = \lim_{h \to 0} \frac{f(x+h) - f(x)}{h}$ if the limit exists

5. $f'(x) = 7.4x - 8.3$

6. $f'(x) = 7x^{5/2} + 2x^{-4/3}$

7. $f'(x) = -12x^{-5}$

8. $f'(x) = 5x^4 - 9x^2 - 10$

9. $f'(x) = \frac{7}{(x+1)^2}$

10. $f'(x) = \frac{3x^2 - 2}{2\sqrt{x^3 - 2x + 1}}$

11. $f'(x) = -2(4x^2 - 3x - 5)^{-3}(8x - 3) = \frac{-16x + 6}{(4x^2 - 3x - 5)^3}$

12. $f'(x) = 20(5x - 1)^3(5x + 1)^3 + 15(5x - 1)^4(5x^2 + 1)^2 = (5x - 1)^3(5x + 1)^2(175x + 5)$

13. $f'(x) = \frac{24(3x - 1)^3}{(3x + 1)^5}$

14. $f'(x) = 10(x^2 + 1)^3(9x^2 + 1)$

15. $f''(x) = \frac{-4}{(x+2)^3}$

16. $f'(x)$ does not exist at $x = -2$ (vertical tangent) and $x = 2$ (point of discontinuity)

17. a. marginal cost $= \frac{6x}{\sqrt{6x^2 + 300}}$
    b. at $x = 10$, marginal cost = \$2. This represents at unit level of 10, cost per unit is \$2.

18. −7; on day 7, the number of people infected by the flu epidemic is <u>decreasing</u> at the rate of 7 per day.

19. $y = 38x + 56$

20. \$8

Chapter 2T Form B

1. c
2. c
3. c
4. b
5. d
6. c
7. d
8. a
9. c
10. d
11. a
12. b
13. b
14. d
15. d
16. c
17. d
18. a
19. a
20. c

Chapter 3T Form A

1. –3 and 1

2. ½, –5, and 4

3. a.

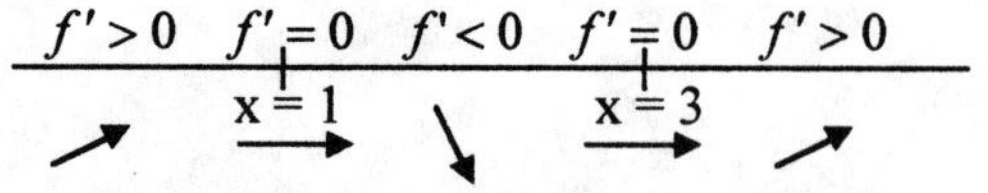

   $f'>0$ $f'=0$ $f'<0$ $f'=0$ $f'>0$
   x = 1 x = 3
   ↗ → ↘ → ↗

   b.

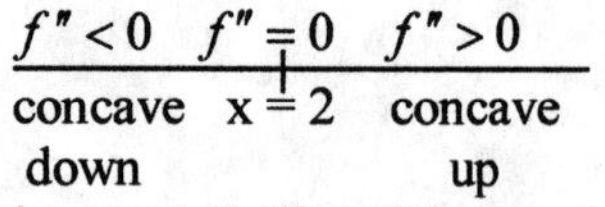

   $f''<0$ $f''=0$ $f''>0$
   concave down x = 2 concave up

   c. maximum at (1, 3), minimum at (3, –1), point of inflection at (2, 1)

4. a.

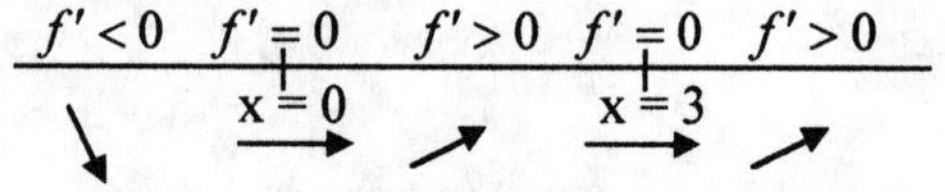

   $f'<0$ $f'=0$ $f'>0$ $f'=0$ $f'>0$
   x = 0 x = 3
   ↘ → ↗ → ↗

   b.

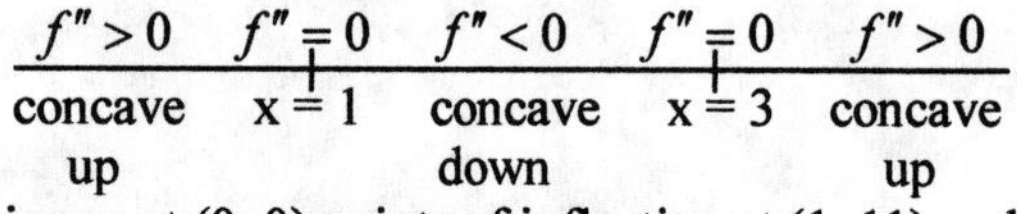

   $f''>0$ $f''=0$ $f''<0$ $f''=0$ $f''>0$
   concave up x = 1 concave down x = 3 concave up

   c. minimum at (0, 0) points of inflection at (1, 11) and (3, 27)

5. Maximum of f is 4 at x = 0
   Minimum of f is 0 at x = –1 and x = 2

6. proportion is 1/3

7. 2000 ft^2

8. $ 6923

9. $\frac{dy}{dx} = \frac{-x-2y}{2x+y}$

10. 4

11. a. 2.5x + 1.5 + 40/x
    b. 4 units
    c. $21.50

12. $ 17.50

13. run size: 20,000; 2 runs per year

Chapter 3T Form B

1. b
2. c
3. d
4. b
5. b
6. c
7. d
8. b
9. c
10. b
11. b
12. b
13. b
14. c
15. b
16. a
17. d
18. c

Chapter 4T Form A

1. $\dfrac{10x}{x^2+1}$

2. $e^{x^2}(3x^2+2x^4)$

3. $\dfrac{3}{3x+1}-\dfrac{4}{3}e^{x/3}$

4. $\dfrac{-xe^x}{\sqrt{6-x^2}}+e^x\sqrt{6-x^2}$

5. $\dfrac{2x-5}{x^2-5x+3}-\dfrac{12}{4x+7}$

6. ex^{e-1}

7. $2e^2$

8. a. increase at \$2,000 / year
   b. decreases at \$2,984 / year

9. 0.055

10. 3: elastic

11. elasticity of demand = 1/3 (inelastic); she should raise the price to increase revenue

12. \$33,960

13. \$ 0.30

14. (e^3, e^3)

15. 15.4%

16. \$811.91

17. $x=-1$

18. a. 10,000
    b. 13,075

19. 20.7%

20. ln x

Chapter 4T Form B

1. d
2. a
3. b
4. d
5. a
6. a
7. d
8. b
9. d
10. c
11. a
12. b
13. a
14. d
15. c
16. d
17. b
18. b
19. d
20. a

Chapter 5T Form A

1. $2x^4 - 3x^3 + 5x^2 - 11x + C$

2. $4x^{3/2} + \frac{1}{3x^3} + C$

3. $\frac{x^4}{4} + 8x^3 + 72x + C$

4. $3e^{4x} + 3 \ln x + C$

5. $-3x^{-1} + 4 \ln x + 5x + 3x^2 + C$

6. $600 t^{5/3} + 50{,}000$; \$69,200

7. $(6e - 6)$ square units

8. 29 square units

9. $P(x) = -x^2 + 100x - 200$

10. $16 + 4 \ln 3$

11. $27 + 3e^6$

12. 12

13. 108 square units

14. 36 square units

15. \$160

16. $\frac{1}{6}(x^4 + 4x)^{3/2} + C$

17. $\frac{1}{5}\ln|x^5 + 1| + C$

18. $\frac{1}{2}e^{x^2} + C$

19. $(x^2 + 9)^{1/2} + C$

20. $\frac{1}{4}e - \frac{1}{4} \approx 0.43$

Chapter 5T Form B

1. b
2. d
3. c
4. a
5. d
6. c
7. c
8. a
9. d
10. b
11. c
12. d
13. a
14. b
15. c
16. c
17. b
18. d
19. b
20. a

Chapter 6T Form A

1. $\frac{1}{8}xe^{8x} - \frac{1}{64}e^{8x} + C$

2. $\frac{3}{5}x^{\frac{5}{3}}\ln x - \frac{9}{25}x^{\frac{5}{3}} + C$

3. $\frac{3}{4}x(x+1)^{\frac{4}{3}} - \frac{9}{28}(x+1)^{\frac{7}{3}} + C$

4. $\frac{1}{40{,}400}(2x+3)^{100}(200x-3)+C$

5. $\frac{298}{15}$

6. $\frac{x^3}{4}e^{4x} - \frac{3}{32}x^2e^{4x} + \frac{3}{32}xe^{4x} - \frac{3}{128}e^{4x} + C$

7. $\frac{-2x-4}{3}\sqrt{1-x} + C$

8. $x(\ln x)^3 - 3x(\ln x)^2 + 6x\ln x - 6x + C$

9. $e^y + \ln|e^y - 1| + C$

10. $4 - \ln 5$

11. 1/3

12. 4

13. 1/3

14. 15

15. 0.797

16. 2.314

17. 0.771

18. 1.346

19. $445.38 million

Chapter 6T Form B

1. b
2. b
3. a
4. c
5. b
6. a
7. c
8. d
9. b
10. c
11. b
12. d
13. b
14. a
15. b
16. a
17. b
18. d
19. c

Chapter 7T Form A

1. $\{(x, y) \mid y \neq 2x, y > 0\}$

2. $2 - 1/e$

3. $f_x(x,y) = \frac{3x^2}{y^4} + \frac{y^4}{x^2}$, $f_y(x,y) = -\frac{4x^3}{y^5} - \frac{4y^3}{x}$

4. $f_x(x,y) = \frac{5x^4}{x^5 + y^5} + e^x y^3$, $f_y(x,y) = \frac{5y^4}{x^5 + y^5} + 3e^x y^2$

5. $g_x(0, 2) = 12$, $g_x(0, 2) = 0$

6. a. $16e^{4x-3y^2}$

   b. $-6e^{4x-3y^2} + 36y^2e^{4x-3y^2}$

   c. $-24ye^{4x-3y^2}$

7. relative minimum value $f = 9$ at $(1, -2)$

8. $y = -1.18x + 9.34$

9. $y = 1.32e^{0.34x}$

10. minimum of f is 272 at (6, 4)

11. maximum of f is e^3 at (1, 3)

12. $(3x^2 - 2xy)dx + (6y - x^2)dy$

13. $2x \ln(y^2 + z^2)dx + \frac{2x^2y}{y^2 + z^2}dy + \frac{2x^2z}{y^2 + z^2}dz$

14. 2.96

15. 38

16. 7

17. 32

18. 3,000,000 standard, 1,000,000 deluxe, P = \$120,000,000

19. 285

Chapter 7T Form B

1. c
2. b
3. b
4. d
5. c
6. a
7. b
8. b
9. a
10. d
11. c
12. a
13. d
14. b
15. b
16. b
17. a
18. d
19. c

Chapter 8T Form A

1. a. $\frac{11}{12}\pi$
   b. 330°

2. 3,700 miles

3. $\sin\theta = \frac{-2}{\sqrt{29}}$, $\cos\theta = \frac{-5}{\sqrt{29}}$

4. a. $-\frac{1}{2}$
   b. $\frac{\sqrt{3}}{2}$

5. a. –0.59
   b. –0.99

6. a.

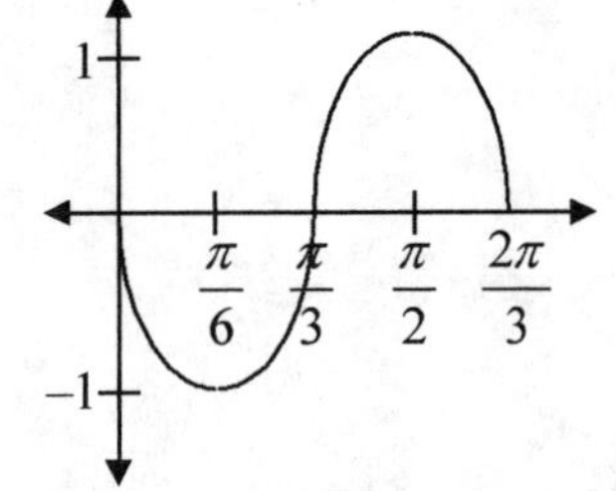

b.

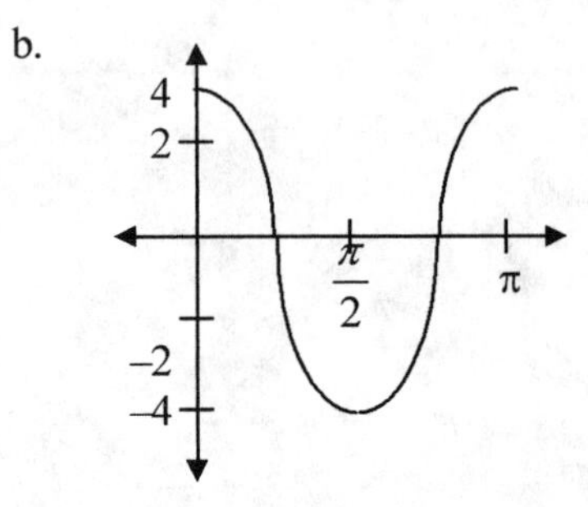

7. 87 feet

8. $(4t + 8)\cos(t^2 + 4t)$

9. $-2\cos(t - \pi)\sin(t - \pi)$

10. $\frac{-2x\sin x^2 - \cos x^2}{e^x}$

11. $\frac{(1+\cos x)(2\cos 2x)+\sin 2x \sin x}{(1+\cos x)^2}$

12. $-\frac{3}{2}(\cos t)^{\frac{2}{3}} + C$

13. $\ln|1 - \cos x| + C$

14. $\frac{1}{2}e^{\sin^2 x} + C$

15. $\frac{1}{8} - \frac{1}{\pi}$

16. $\tan\theta = -3$, $\cot\theta = -\frac{1}{3}$, $\sec\theta = -\sqrt{10}$, $\csc\theta = \frac{\sqrt{10}}{3}$

17. a. $-\frac{1}{\sqrt{3}}$

    b. -2

18. 57.1 feet

19. $t^2(t\sec^2 t + 3\tan t)$

20. $-2\csc\sqrt{x} + C$

Chapter 8T Form B

1. c
2. a
3. b
4. c
5. d
6. b
7. d
8. c
9. b
10. a
11. c
12. d
13. c
14. d
15. a
16. b
17. b
18. a
19. c
20. d

Chapter 9T Form A

1. check that $3e^{3x} + 20e^{2x} - 2(e^{3x} + 10e^{2x}) = e^{3x}$

2. $y = \sqrt{x - \ln|x+1| + C}$

3. $y = Cx^4$

4. not separable

5. $y = (2x + 1)^4$ or $y = (2x - 5)^4$

6. $y = \sqrt{1 - 2x^2}$

7. $y = 2e^{0.02t}$

8. $y = 50(1 - e^{-0.08t})$

9. $y = \dfrac{15}{1 + \frac{11}{4}e^{-30t}} = \dfrac{60}{4 + 11e^{-30t}}$

10. a. $y' = a(4{,}000 - y)$
    b. $y = 4{,}000(1 - e^{-0.067t})$
    c. about 1,324

11. a. $y' = ay(8{,}000 - y)$
    b. $\dfrac{8{,}000}{1 + 7e^{-0.873t}}$
    c. about 7,346

12. $y = Ce^{3x}$

13. $y = \dfrac{1}{2} + Ce^{-x^2}$

14. $y = \dfrac{1}{3} + Ce^{-x^3}$

15. $y = x - \dfrac{1}{x}$

16. initial point: (0, 1), slope = 1

17. 1.003

18. $y = 15e^{-0.15x}$

19. $x(t) = 5.4t$

20. $\frac{dA}{dT} = 0.065A + 1550$

Chapter 9T Form B

1. d
2. b
3. d
4. c
5. a
6. c
7. d
8. a
9. c
10. c
11. a
12. b
13. c
14. d
15. a
16. b
17. d
18. d
19. c
20. d

Chapter 10T Form A

1. $1-\frac{1}{2}+\frac{1}{3}-\frac{1}{4}$

2. $\sum_{n=1}^{\infty}\frac{(-1)^n \cdot 3}{2^n}$

3. 5,115

4. converges to $\frac{12}{5}$

5. diverges

6. diverges

7. converges to $\frac{5}{27}$

8. 20 meters

9. $1+4x+8x^2+\frac{32}{3}x^3$

10. $1+\frac{x}{3}-\frac{x^2}{9}+\frac{5x^3}{81}$

11. $1-2x+3x^2-4x^3$

12. a. $1-\frac{x^2}{2!}+\frac{x^4}{4!}$

    b. $1-\frac{x^4}{2!}+\frac{x^8}{4!}$

13. $R=1$

14. $R=0$

15. $\sum_{n=0}^{\infty}\frac{(-1)^n x^n}{8^{n+1}}$

16. $-\frac{1}{2}-\frac{3x}{4}-\frac{9x^2}{8}-\frac{27x^3}{16}-\ldots$

17. $\frac{1}{x^2}+\frac{1}{x}-\frac{1}{2!}+\frac{x^2}{4!}-\frac{x^4}{6!}+\ldots$

18. $x_1=2, x_2=1.625$

19. 9.4

20. $-\dfrac{4.3}{1-x} = -4.3 - 4.3x - 4.3x^2 - 4.3x^3 - \ldots = -4.3\sum_{k=0}^{\infty} x^k$

Chapter 10T Form B

1. a
2. c
3. b
4. a
5. d
6. c
7. b
8. c
9. d
10. a
11. a
12. d
13. b
14. c
15. b
16. d
17. c
18. d
19. d
20. d

Chapter 11T Form A

1. a. $P(5) = \frac{1}{4}$, $P(10) = \frac{1}{4}$, $P(18) = \frac{1}{2}$
   b. $E(x) = \frac{51}{4} = 12.75$
   c. $VAR(x) = 30.6875$

2. No, the expected value (return) is \$1.33 so in the long run he would lose \$0.17 per game.

3. 0.147

4. 0.7408

5. $a = -\frac{15}{14}$

6. 0.72917

7. a. 2.25
   b. 0.3375
   c. 0.58095

8. a. $F(x) = \frac{1}{8}x^2 - \frac{1}{8}$
   b. $\frac{3}{8}$

9. \$7,333

10. a. 10
    b. $33\frac{1}{3}$
    c. 5.7735
    d. 0.75

11. a. 50
    b. 2,500
    c. 50

12. $f(x) = 0.4e^{-0.4x}$

13. 0.2834

14. 3.1748

15. a. 0.4911
    b. 0.0409

16. 0.2858

17. 0.7486 (table), 0.7475 (calculator)

18. 0.0002

Chapter 11T Form B

1. c
2. a
3. c
4. b
5. a
6. d
7. c
8. d
9. b
10. d
11. b
12. d
13. c
14. b
15. c
16. d
17. a
18. b

JEAN SHUTTERS / CHRISTI VER

TEST ITEM
TO ACCOM

APPLIED CALCULUS, Second Edition and BRIEF APPLIED CALCULUS, Second

BERRESFORD / ROCK